THEOLOGY AND M‹

MW00846069

The new discoveries in physics during the 20th century have stimulated intense debate about their relevance to age-old theological questions. Views range from those holding that modern physics provides a surer road to God than traditional religions, to those who say that physics and theology are incommensurable and so do not relate. At the very least, physics has stimulated renewed theological discussions.

In this critical introduction to the science-theology debate, Peter Hodgson draws on his experience as a physicist to present the results of modern physics and the theological implications. Written for those with little or no scientific background, Hodgson describes connections between physics, philosophy and theology and then explains Newtonian physics and Victorian physics, the theories of relativity, astronomy and quantum mechanics, and distinguishing the actual results of modern physics from speculations. The connections with theology are explored throughout. The concluding section draws discussions together and makes an important new contribution to the debate.

Ashgate Science and Religion Series

Series Editors:

Roger Trigg, *Department of Philosophy, University of Warwick, UK*
J. Wentzel van Huyssteen, *James I. McCord Professor of Theology and Science, Princeton Theological Seminary, USA*

Science and religion have often been thought to be at loggerheads but much contemporary work in this flourishing interdisciplinary field suggests this is far from the case. The *Ashgate Science and Religion Series* presents exciting new work to advance interdisciplinary study, research and debate across key themes in science and religion, exploring the philosophical relations between the physical and social sciences on the one hand and religious belief on the other. Contemporary issues in philosophy and theology are debated, as are prevailing cultural assumptions arising from the 'post-modernist' distaste for many forms of reasoning. The series enables leading international authors from a range of different disciplinary perspectives to apply the insights of the various sciences, theology and philosophy and look at the relations between the different disciplines and the rational connections that can be made between them. These accessible, stimulating new contributions to key topics across science and religion will appeal particularly to individual academics and researchers, graduates, postgraduates and upper-undergraduate students.

Other titles published in this series:

Theology and Psychology
Fraser Watts
0 7546 1672 X (hbk)
0 7546 1673 8 (pbk)

Islam and Science
Muzaffar Iqbal
0 7546 0799 2 (hbk)
0 7546 0800 X (pbk)

Science, Theology, and Ethics
Ted Peters
0 7546 0824 7 (hbk)
0 7546 0825 5 (pbk)

Fifty Years in Science and Religion – Ian G. Barbour and his Legacy
Robert John Russell
0 7546 4117 1 (hbk)
0 7546 4118 X (pbk)

Scientism – Science, Ethics and Religion
Mikael Stenmark
0 7546 0445 4 (hbk)
0 7546 0446 2 (pbk)

Theology and Modern Physics

PETER E. HODGSON
Corpus Christi College, Oxford, UK

ASHGATE

Published by
Ashgate Publishing Limited
Gower House
Croft Road
Aldershot
Hants GU11 3HR
England

Ashgate Publishing Company
Suite 420
101 Cherry Street
Burlington
Vermont, 05401–4405
USA

Ashgate website: http://www.ashgate.com

British Library Cataloguing in Publication Data
Hodgson, P. E. (Peter Edward),
 Theology and Modern Physics. – (Ashgate Science and Religion Series)
 1. Religion and science – History. 2. Physics – Religious aspects. I. Title.
 201.6'53

US Library of Congress Cataloging in Publication Data
Hodgson, P. E. (Peter Edward),
 Theology and Modern Physics / Peter E. Hodgson.
  p. cm. – (Ashgate Science and Religion Series)
 Includes bibliographical references and index.
 1. Physics – Religious aspects. 2. Religion and science. I. Title. II. Series.
 BL265.P4H63 2005
 201'653–dc22

2004025367

ISBN 0 7546 3622 4 (hbk)
ISBN 0 7546 3623 2 (pbk)

This book is printed on acid free paper.

Typeset by Tradespools, Frome, Somerset.

Printed and bound in Great Britain by MPG Books Ltd, Bodmin

Also by P. E. Hodgson

Physics

The Optical Model of Elastic Scattering. Oxford: Clarendon Press, 1963
Nuclear Reactions and Nuclear Structure. Oxford: Clarendon Press, 1971
Nuclear Heavy-Ion Reactions. Oxford University Press, 1978
Growth Points in Nuclear Physics. Vol. 1. Oxford: Pergamon Press, 1980
Growth Points in Nuclear Physics. Vol. 2. Oxford: Pergamon Press, 1980
Growth Points in Nuclear Physics. Vol. 3. Oxford: Pergamon Press, 1981
Nucleon Momentum and Density Distributions in Nuclei (with A. N. Antonov
  and I. Zh. Petkov). Oxford: Clarendon Press, 1988
Spacetime and Electromagnetism (with J. R. Lucas). Oxford: Clarendon Press,
  1990
Pre-Equilibrium Nuclear Reactions (with E. Gadioli). Oxford: Oxford
  University Press, 1991
Nucleon Correlations in Nuclei (with A. N. Antonov and I. Zh. Petkov). Berlin:
  Springer-Verlag, 1993
The Nucleon Optical Potential. Singapore: World Scientific, 1994
Introductory Nuclear Physics (with E. Gadioli and E. Gadioli-Erba). Oxford:
  Oxford University Press, 1996
Nuclear Physics (with S. A. Sofianos). Pretoria: University of South Africa,
  1997

Physics and Society

Nuclear Physics in Peace and War. London: Burns and Oates, 1961
Our Nuclear Future? Belfast: Christian Journals Ltd, 1983
Science and Christianity. Tokyo: Kinseido, 1992
Energy and Environment. Tokyo: Kinseido, 1995
Energy and Environment. London: Bowerdean, 1997
Science, Technology and Society. Tokyo: Kinseido, 1999
Nuclear Power, Energy and the Environment. London: Imperial College Press,
  1999
Christianity and Science. Johannesburg: St Augustine College, 2002
The Roots of Science and its Fruits. London: The Saint Austin Press, 2003
Science and Belief in the Nuclear Era. Naples, FL: Sapientia Press, 2005

Contents

Contents

Preface

The present time has been described as an age of relativism and uncertainty, ideas that inevitably affect religious beliefs. These ideas come from Einstein's relativity theory and from quantum mechanics, and it is therefore interesting to see in what ways they can contribute to theology.

The main purpose of this book is to survey the interactions of theology and science through the centuries, with particular emphasis on the theological problems and pseudo-problems raised by the new physics of the twentieth century. This physics has profoundly altered our conceptions of space and time, matter and energy, causality and chance, and this has affected theological discourse in many ways. Some of the problems raised appear on further examination to be based on misunderstandings, but it is a sufficient reason to discuss these problems if they are thought to be problems. If this task is avoided, believers are defenceless against attacks on their faith made in the name of the new physics.

Theological statements are often based on scientific results that are highly controversial. Thus a proper understanding of current discussions on theology and the new physics requires some knowledge of the development of physics during the preceding centuries. Indeed, Duhem has remarked that in order to speak about the relations of theology to science one must have studied pure science for at least ten or fifteen years (see Jaki, 1984, p. 114). Some of the main lines of this development of physics are briefly sketched here. Such a summary is inevitably inadequate to convey a thorough understanding of all the difficulties, frustrations, false starts and mistaken hypotheses experienced by those who have struggled through the centuries to increase our knowledge of the natural world. In no sense is this book a systematic account of the development of physics. It is possible only to mention some of the main advances, in particular those that have, rightly or wrongly, been connected with theology, and to provide references to more detailed works. Certain topics, such as the wave–particle duality, action at a distance, macroscopic (statistical) and microscopic (deterministic) explanation and the black-body radiation, recur in different forms and serve to unify the discussion.

Theology and science have interacted throughout history, and so it is important to examine to what extent modern science is based on theological beliefs about the natural world. We begin in Chapter 1 by defining and discussing the relationship of theology, philosophy and science; Chapter 2 describes the theological presuppositions of science and offers a historical account of the origin of modern science in the High Middle Ages.

The Muslim civilization inherited the writings of the ancient Greeks and made some notable advances in astronomy, mathematics and medicine. Science flourished in Muslim countries from about the eighth to the fourteenth century, after which it declined, while in Western Europe it forged ahead. The reasons for this, and the implications for today, are discussed in Chapter 3.

Modern science came to maturity in the Renaissance with the dynamical and astronomical researches of Copernicus, Galileo, Kepler and Newton, as described in Chapter 4. Such advances set modern science on a path of continuous and self-sustaining growth during the following centuries, and classical physics reached maturity in the nineteenth century, as described in Chapter 5. All this work was underpinned, inspired and sustained by the theological beliefs of the scientists themselves.

The new physics is usually taken to mean Einstein's theory of relativity and the subsequent development of quantum mechanics and cosmology. The modifications of Newton's ideas of space and time by Einstein's theories are discussed in Chapter 6. New experimental results forced Planck to admit that energy is quantized, and this idea was used by Bohr to construct a new model of atomic structure that was both brilliantly successful and fatally flawed, as described in Chapter 7.

The difficulties inherent in Bohr's atomic model were removed by the development in the 1920s of quantum mechanics, which was very successful in accounting for a wide range of phenomena. However, the interpretation of quantum mechanics that was developed in Copenhagen gave rise to a series of paradoxes that have now been resolved by the statistical interpretation of Einstein. These successes and difficulties of quantum mechanics are described in Chapters 8 and 9.

Einstein's general theory of relativity established the universe as a whole as a subject for scientific investigation. The astronomical observations of Hubble, combined with the results of nuclear and elementary particle physics, enable the evolution of the universe to be described in some detail from very soon after the initial singularity to the present time, as summarized in Chapter 10.

More recently, chaos theory has thrown new light on the behaviour of many natural systems. In addition, detailed studies of the symmetries in nature have deepened our appreciation of the intricate order of matter. This is briefly considered in Chapter 11.

Seen as a whole, the development of science over the last two millennia has been closely linked to prevailing theological beliefs. In particular, modern science was born and developed only in a predominantly Christian culture, and this is attributable to the beliefs about the natural world provided by Catholic theology. This raises the question of whether modern science could develop in a non-Christian culture, and how science already existing in a Christian culture is affected when that culture is replaced by a totalitarian or materialistic regime opposed to Christianity. These questions are considered in the final chapter.

A notable characteristic of modern science is the way it increasingly uses mathematical concepts to define and articulate its ideas. Mathematics has a long history from Babylonian times to its spectacular flowering in ancient Greece. In the Middle Ages, Roger Bacon (1897, pp. 97–8) emphasized that 'mathematics is the door and the key to the sciences'. In optics, 'nothing can be known without the power of geometry'. Furthermore, 'the things of this world cannot be made known without a knowledge of mathematics'. Surveying the contemporary scene, he fulminated: 'The neglect of mathematics for the past thirty or forty years has nearly destroyed the entire learning of Western

Christendom. For he who does not know mathematics does not know any of the other sciences.' Later the Mertonian philosophers enunciated the mean speed theorem verbally, though with great difficulty. One of them, Bradwardine,[1] declared: 'it is mathematics which reveals every genuine truth, for it knows every hidden secret, and bears the key to every subtlety of letters. Whoever, then, has the effrontery to study physics while neglecting mathematics, should know from the start that he will never make his entry through the portals of wisdom.' The fourteenth-century Muslim philosopher Ibn Khaldoun remarked that geometry did for the mind what soap does for the body. Galileo (see Drake, 1957, pp. 237–8) emphasized that the book of nature 'cannot be understood unless one first learns to comprehend the language and interpret the characters in which it is written. It is written in the language of mathematics, circles and other geometrical forms, without which it is humanly impossible to understand a single word of it; without these, one is wandering about in a dark labyrinth.' To express his thoughts, Newton had to invent the mathematical language of the differential and integral calculus. His laws of nature are written in the language of mathematics, and provide the eyes we use to understand phenomena. Newton (see Burtt, 1932, p. 223) knew that 'science is the exact mathematical formulation of the processes of the natural world'. We can express the relations between measurable quantities mathematically and derive new relations in a way that is impossible verbally. It seemed to Dirac (1982, p. 85) 'that the foundation of the work of a mathematical physicist is to get the correct equations, that the interpretation of those equations was only of secondary importance'. Feynman (in Sykes, 1994, pp. 146–9) has remarked that physicists always like to have a physical picture of what is going on in terms of everyday experiences, but this is not always possible. Thus 'we cannot understand superconductivity, but it comes out of the equations – we have the theory but not the picture'. 'At present the only way to understand the ultimate character of the physical world is through a mathematical type of reasoning.' 'I don't think that a person can fully appreciate much of the aspects of the world, the great depth and character of the universality of laws, the relationship of things, without an understanding of mathematics.' Certainly, theoretical physics is not possible without mathematics. It has also been maintained that mathematics is basic to theological reasoning (Davis and Hersh, 1983, pp. 39–40). In his book on relativity, Angel (1980, p. 80) remarks that 'the philosopher who professes to be concerned with the nature of reality but is too indifferent to acquire the appropriate mathematical tools to uncover it is at best a dilettante and at worst a charlatan but, in any case, a prisoner'. This is echoed by Woodhouse (2003, p. v), who emphasizes that 'mathematics frees our minds to explore the world in which we live beyond the limits of our physical intuition'.

Einstein (1976, p. 49) expressed his 'deep conviction of the rationality of the universe' and Wigner (1960) was surprised by 'the unreasonable effectiveness of mathematics'. This pervasive rational structure of the world can be attributed

---

[1] Bradwardine, Thomas, *Tractatus de Coninuo*, MS Erfurt Amplon, Q.385, fol. 31v.

to God's creative power, so that we can expect to find harmony in nature, and that harmony is expressed mathematically. God is not only the transcendent creator, but is immanent in his creation. This 'provides us with an experience of the sacred that transcends the domain of empirical observations' and may be called theological (Zycinski, 2003, p. 18).

Apart from observable facts, all that we can really rely on are the mathematical equations that describe, more or less accurately, certain types of phenomena. I have therefore not hesitated to introduce mathematical expressions and equations where necessary, although this is inevitably harder on some readers than on others. Most of the arguments can be followed by those without mathematics, but I hope that even such readers can appreciate something of its power. Who, for example, can fail to be impressed by the austere beauty of Maxwell's four simple equations that unify and describe all electromagnetic phenomena? Most of the mathematics used here is indeed quite simple, and some readers may be encouraged to explore it in more detail.

The actual development of science is a highly complex story. The work of scientific discovery is full of misconceptions, false starts, errors, misfortunes and blind alleys (Franklin, 1986). It is only by dogged perseverance that an experimentalist finally gets his apparatus to work as he intends and to give sensible results. It is only by months and years of effort that a theoretician finally manages to express his ideas and to work out their consequences. At the end of his struggles a scientist finally writes a paper describing only a smooth path from his starting point to his conclusions (Kragh, 1996). In the next stage the writers of reviews and textbooks read thousands of such papers and once again construct a smooth and simple path, with no hint of the trials and tribulations that made it possible. It is only such smooth paths that are described here, although some references are given to more detailed accounts. No one really understands science, and is qualified to talk about it, unless he knows how science is actually done.

It is hardly necessary to remark that when we consider past struggles to understand the world we inevitably look at them through twenty-first-century eyes. It is very difficult to appreciate the thoughts, presuppositions and mindsets of the pioneers, and many scholars have spent their lives trying to understand the writings of any one of the hundreds of theologians, philosophers and scientists mentioned here.

In all these discussions it is essential to distinguish between what is established, what is very likely and what is still speculative. Future work will force us to modify and extend our scientific theories, and historical research will surely change our views on what has been accomplished in the past. Many areas are the subject of intense discussion, and so a work like this cannot present a final, complete picture; rather it is a preliminary survey of some of the questions that have to be further explored. In addition, I am aware that some of my views are not generally shared, so I put them forward with due reserve, expressing my willingness to change them if this proves necessary, as has indeed happened in the past.

By simply stating my own views, I implicitly express my disagreement with opposing views. I would have preferred to leave it at that, but it was pointed out to me that this might be taken to imply that I was not aware of the opposing views, and so I should mention them and explain why I disagree with them. To some extent I have tried to do this, although it is obviously not possible to consider all opposing views. I am, however, concerned to criticize ideas, and not the people responsible for them, so in many cases I have simply discussed the ideas, without giving references.

It is of course hazardous for a physicist to tackle so vast a theme. I am well aware that armies of specialists fight over questions that I have mentioned in a sentence or two. It is easy to cultivate the reputation of a sound scholar by concentrating one's energies on some small recondite area of knowledge, but if everyone were to do that, knowledge would be splintered into numerous fragments. It is desirable that efforts should be made to see the whole picture, even though this is inevitably from a particular vantage point. Some of the physics mentioned here is based on first-hand knowledge, but most of the book relies on secondary sources. I cannot prove the truth of all I have written, if only because every proof rests on certain assumptions which may be acceptable to one person but not to another. By saying that an assumption is evidently true, we affirm that we see that it is true, but this requires insight into the concepts involved. The very notion of what constitutes a proof is questionable: how can we prove that our concept of proof is correct? What is accepted as a proof in one age is superseded in another, and very often great advances have been made by questioning what was previously accepted as obvious (Franklin, 1986, pp. 70–72). What we can do, however, is first to ensure consistency, and then to test our ideas against experience. In physics this can often be done experimentally to high accuracy, and this makes physics a relatively easy subject. Theological beliefs can also be tested by seeing if we can live our lives in accord with them; this takes rather longer but is no less certain. The beliefs I hold and try to follow have endured for two thousand years, and no one can credibly say that their demise is in sight (Macaulay, 1840, p. 548). I trust that readers will distinguish between what I believe, what seems to me to be reasonable but may be modified by further work, and what is mere speculation.

Many scientists have reflected on their work and on the development of science, and quotations from their writings are included. These frequently contradict the views of other scientists. This serves to show that the views of scientists, however eminent, on matters outside and even within science are not always reliable. Before deciding what to accept, it is therefore necessary to subject them to critical examination. The same applies, of course, to my own views. Everyone writes from a particular viewpoint and has definite motives: mine are to explore the contribution of Christianity to the foundations of modern science and also to defend the integrity of science against attempts to use it to support philosophical and theological tenets to which it has no relevance. My views as expressed here should be seen as a contribution to an ongoing debate, not as a set of polished conclusions. There are certainly many loose ends and questions that require further study, and in such cases references to opposing views are given. The attempt to survey so vast a theme is inevitably superficial, and omits many of the qualifications and further discussion that I would make if space allowed. For the same reason, many interesting subjects have been omitted. My aim is to be clear, even if, in some readers' view, I am clearly wrong. If all I have done is to provide signposts to far better books, I shall be well satisfied.

It remains for me to thank all those who have tried to teach me. I owe much to my physics teachers, from the De La Salle Brothers who taught me at school to my lecturers at Imperial College, and particularly my research supervisor Sir George Thomson, and numerous colleagues during the subsequent years. My friend and colleague Thomas A. Brody transformed my understanding of quantum mechanics, and William Carroll has earned my deep gratitude by reading the whole text and making many valuable suggestions that have deepened and corrected my knowledge of medieval thought. I thank Mehdi Golshami and Munawar Anees for reading Chapter 3 and making useful suggestions. I am also most grateful to John Bell, Alistair Crombie, Fr Stanley L. Jaki, John Lucas, Fr Ernan McMullin and Fr John L. Russell SJ for many valuable conversations and for their books and articles. To all these I add numerous friends and colleagues and the authors of many other books and articles. Needless to say, they have no responsibility for what I have written.

It is a particular pleasure to thank the Templeton Foundation for supporting a course of lectures on 'God and Physics from Aquinas to Quantum Mechanics' given jointly with Prof. William E. Carroll in Oxford in 1997 and in Iowa in 1998. The texts of my contribution to this course form the foundation of this book.

P. E. Hodgson,
Corpus Christi College,
Oxford, OX1 4JF, UK
2005

Note

When referring to scientists and philosophers in general I have for convenience used the pronoun 'he' to include men and women.

CHAPTER 1

Theology, Philosophy and Physics

Introduction

At the end of the nineteenth century it was generally believed that physics was essentially complete. Newton's dynamics enabled the motions of the moon and the planets to be calculated with great accuracy, and Maxwell's electromagnetic theory unified electric and magnetic phenomena. There were a few problems that still remained, but it was confidently expected that they would soon be cleared up. The future truths of physics, an eminent scientist remarked, are to be looked for in the sixth decimal place. The young Planck was undecided whether to devote his life to physics or to philology; he was advised to choose philology because there was nothing much left to discover in physics.

The twentieth century, however, has seen an unprecedented increase in our knowledge of the world. In a few years there came Planck's discovery of the quantum and Einstein's theory of relativity, the discovery of the nucleus and the formulation of quantum mechanics. The structure of matter has been probed to reveal finer and finer detail: first the structure of the atom, then of the nucleus and finally of the nuclear particles themselves. At the other end of the scale, the universe as a whole has become the object of scientific study, and the knowledge of nuclear and elementary particle physics has been used to reconstruct the processes occurring in the first few instants after what is called the big bang. Our knowledge of space and time has been profoundly changed by Einstein's theory of relativity, and experiments have revealed the strange phenomena of the quantum world. Taken together, these advances in understanding that constitute the new physics have changed our view of the world.

This scientific knowledge of the world has led to a vast range of technological developments that have changed our lives beyond all recognition. Communication and transport have brought people throughout the world closer together, and electronic computers enable us to perform with ease complicated tasks quite beyond the resources of previous generations.

More profoundly, science has altered the way we think about ourselves and our world. We know that we live on a relatively small blue ball, poised in space, orbiting the sun. Our resplendent sun is a rather undistinguished star in one of the spiral arms of a vast galaxy of about two hundred thousand million stars, and that galaxy is but one of many billions of such galaxies spread through the unimaginable vastness of space. We understand to some extent how we have arrived here by a long process of cosmic and biological evolution. This is the stage on which the drama of our salvation is enacted. Our ideas of space and time, determinism and causality, have been changed, inevitably affecting the imagery of theology.

People have always, in quiet moments, thought about the meaning of existence, why we are here and what will become of us all. Answers have been proposed by the great religions, using the language and concepts derived from the cosmology of the times. The ancient Hebrews thought of the world as a flat surface with the stars fixed to the underside of an upturned dish. Each day the sun travels from the east to the west, and then returns to its starting point by voyaging through the underworld. The Bible implicitly accepts this world view, speaking about the sun moving around the earth. The heavens above the earth are the abode of the saints, and the wicked are thrust down into the hell below the earth. Not only was the earth at the centre of the universe, but also Jerusalem was at the centre of the world, as indeed is often shown in old maps. The Crucifixion thus had a central place in space as well as in time.

The Greeks also developed a cosmology, and Pythagoras taught that the earth is a sphere in the centre of the universe. Faced with the challenge of Hellenistic philosophy, the theologians of the Alexandrine school maintained that it is the duty of Christians to study the new ideas, and not to fear them.

A serious challenge came with the heliocentric theory of Copernicus and Galileo. This seemed to many theologians to be quite contrary to the evident meaning of Scripture. It deposed the earth from its central position in the universe and with it the centrality of Jerusalem. Eventually it was realized that passages such as that in Joshua simply use the familiar manner of speaking and were not intended to imply any specific cosmological theory.

Over the ages, the cosmologies and the ways of thinking about the world have changed, and with them the ways we express the accompanying theology. The more we learn about the universe, the more we know about our situation in it. At a deeper level, new scientific advances often bring with them new concepts, thus expanding our mental horizons, and this again affects our theology. More subtly, it affects the very words and concepts we use. Modern physics has changed the way we think about nature and about ourselves, and this has raised many questions about human freedom, our responsibility for our actions, miracles and the providence of God. To explore these questions we have to study the relation between theology and science.

Many answers have been proposed. At one extreme it could be said that the new physics has no effect whatever on our theological ideas. We can hold fast to our traditional beliefs and lead our lives just as in the previous centuries. This is indeed possible, but it carries with it the hazard of living in a time capsule, insulated from the new ideas, speaking a language that becomes more and more isolated from contemporary thought, and defenceless against attacks on traditional beliefs made in the name of the new physics.

The opposite extreme is to maintain that 'the knowledge of God and His designs can only be obtained through a knowledge of his works' (Weber, quoted in Basalla, 1968). More recently Davies (1983) has claimed that the new physics provides a surer road to God than the ancient religions. The more we learn about the universe, the more we will know the mind of God. Some believe that age-old problems will be solved by the application of modern physics, and old arguments will be shown to be invalid. Thus it has been suggested that the indeterminism of quantum mechanics and the unpredictability of chaotic systems implies a breakdown of causality, and with it one of the traditional ways to God, and that the Heisenberg uncertainty principle provides a loophole for the exercise of free will. These and similar questions must be critically examined.

The first requirement for such discussions is a knowledge of the physics on which they are based. Physics is first of all an experimental science, and it was a series of key experiments, together with the theories that were developed to account for them, that led to modern physics. Then there are the interpretations of these theories in terms of more general philosophical categories, and finally the theological implications.

Theology, Philosophy and Physics

Before considering the relations between theology and the new physics it is desirable to summarize briefly the relations between theology, philosophy and science that lie behind the above remarks. This is a highly complex and disputed matter, and it might be thought more appropriate to wait until the end of the book to do this. However, to avoid misunderstandings, what follows is an attempt to outline as clearly as possible the presuppositions underlying the discussion. This is not intended to be a definitive statement, but an indication of the meanings that I attach to the words. At the end we may be able to see how useful they are.

Theology

Theology is the result of our rational attempts to understand God and His relations with us and with the natural world. It is based on Divine Revelation and on the teaching of the Church as contained in the Old and New Testaments, the decrees of church councils and other church documents.

Theology is thus unchanging in essence, although it is inevitably expressed in terms of philosophical concepts initially derived from the Hebrews and the Greeks. From time to time the Church, through the medium of councils, defines theological beliefs more precisely in order to remove erroneous ideas. Our understanding of the truths of theology has developed over the centuries (Newman, 1960). Theologians sometimes use terms derived from the sciences and inevitably accept the current scientific world view. This has to change when the science changes, for otherwise the theology will appear outdated. Such accommodation is not easy, and takes time, so that there is often a lag between the establishment of a new world view and its assimilation by theology. A particular difficulty is that often a new scientific idea is generally accepted long before it is definitively established. It is also unwise for theology to move too rapidly because the new scientific idea may not long survive.

Philosophy

Philosophy initially arose from attempts, particularly by the ancient Greeks, to make sense of the whole of life, our origin, our experiences, our hopes and our destiny. Starting from self-evident principles, and applying reason to our experiences, natural philosophers, as they were called, built up a theory of the natural world. Primarily this was the work of Aristotle, and it endured with some developments for two millennia. During the Renaissance several philosophers, in particular Bacon, Galileo and Descartes, realized that such activities are often sterile and that a new approach is needed based on careful measurements that show the interrelationships between various measurable properties. At this point science separated from philosophy and became a distinct activity, although it was still based on philosophical beliefs about the world. This implies a radical distinction between philosophical and scientific knowledge: in principle philosophical knowledge is exact and certain, whereas scientific knowledge is always subject to uncertainties due to the inevitable inaccuracies of measurement. Over the centuries various parts of knowledge become specialized into separate disciplines; thus for example science became natural philosophy and then divided into physics, chemistry and biology.

Historically, there are many philosophical systems that are based on certain fundamental presuppositions. A great philosopher is one who has worked out the consequences of the starting point with thoroughness and consistency to the (often bitter) end. Whether the philosophical system is true is another matter, though that is usually settled by the examination of its fruits. A connected function of philosophy is to examine critically the words and concepts we use, and how they are related to each other. It is concerned always to ask what we mean by what we say, how we know it is true, what criteria we apply, how we justify our criteria and so on. It addresses these questions to the theologian and to the scientist.

There is an important connection between theology and philosophy. Some truths may be obtained with difficulty by purely philosophical reasoning, but can be reached more fully and easily from theological considerations (Gilson, 1955). This is particularly relevant to the origin of the philosophical truths underlying science.

As an example of philosophical reflection, consider a man who writes a book denying realism, purpose, cause and free will. However, the book itself is a real object. It is written with a purpose, namely to cause other people to modify their beliefs, an activity that makes sense only if they have free will. Thus the very means by which the author conveys his message contradicts that message (Jaki, 1999b).

The fundamental philosophical activity is the immediate grasp of external reality by the mind. As Duhem emphasized, we 'grasp reality and its lawfulness in a spontaneous natural way' (see Jaki, 1984, pp. 321–2; all other quotes from this source). Jaki comments that 'objective reality for Duhem is an unquestioned and unquestionable truth which man grasps in the very act of knowing a realm external to him'. 'There is thus no need for any metaphysical elaboration of what reality is meant by words such as body, law, extension, time and motion'. 'These notions appear to our intelligence sufficiently certain, so that we may, without fear of confusion and error, make them operate in the experimental method'. This certainty cannot be found in physical theories because these are interpretations of facts, and there is no one-to-one correspondence of theory with reality, of formalism with facts. Thus physical theories, and their associated formalisms, serve only as convenient summaries of facts, and may not correspond exactly to reality, although as physics advances they approach closer to this ideal. In all these discussions, philosophy carries out its perennial task of critically analysing and assessing the validity of the arguments used.

The ancient Greeks provided many of the beliefs about the material world that are essential for science, in particular that it is worthy of study and also rational and orderly, and open to the human mind. Additional beliefs essential for modern science came from the Hebrews and from Christian theology, as suggested in Chapter 2. To be efficacious in this way, a belief needs to be firmly held by the whole community, to the exclusion of other beliefs. Among the Greeks, many different beliefs were held by different philosophers, whereas the Hebrew and Christian belief in the orderly creation of the world by God was century by century hammered into the European mind to the exclusion of all other beliefs until in the High Middle Ages it provided the fertile ground for the birth of modern science.

It may be asked whether it is possible to argue from the success of science to the philosophical principles on which it is based. Certainly not in a strictly deductive sense, because scientific theories are subject to change and revision. Nevertheless it is possible to find the philosophy behind physics by examining the consequences of the denial of any of these tenets. Furthermore, examination of the way science is actually done shows that scientists, often unconsciously, make certain assumptions about the natural world and, to the extent that science based on them is successful, they are retrospectively justified. This may not be logically conclusive, since it is conceivable that successful science can be carried out within the framework of different philosophies of the natural world. However, in cases where there is a simple choice between two alternatives, such as that between realism and idealism, this retrospective inference is justified (Brody, 1993).

The further question whether, if we admit that science is based on Christian beliefs, the success of science provides evidence for the truth of Christianity must be answered in the negative, because we cannot prove that science could not have arisen in the context and on the foundations provided by other beliefs. However, as a matter of historical fact, it has never done so.

Physics

Science may conveniently be divided into empirical knowledge obtained by observation and experience, and the much more detailed knowledge we have today. The former, which may be called primitive science, describes knowledge about the properties of materials gained by craftsmen working with wood, stone and metals, and that of plants and animals obtained by observation and experiment. It includes also the observational knowledge of the planets and stars. This primitive science is found in all human societies, including past civilizations, and is to be distinguished from the knowledge we have today. As our knowledge of the world increases, it is convenient to divide it into the physical and the biological sciences; it is only the former that are considered here.

Our own civilization is unique in that it has a detailed knowledge of the natural world that goes far beyond primitive science. Science proceeds by observation and experiment, whenever possible under controlled conditions, accompanied by attempts to make sense of the results by speculations, hypotheses, models and theories, expressed mathematically wherever possible. The first observations of a new phenomenon sometimes suggest ideas about the underlying process that may eventually form a theory. This theory may suggest further observations that serve as a test, and the result of the new observations or experiments may suggest some modification of the theory, which may itself be tested in turn. Most physical theories can be expressed mathematically, and predict very precisely what will happen in given circumstances; thus precise measurements enable a very sharp test to be made.

This continuous dialectic between experiment and theory is the life-blood of science. New scientific advances may be stimulated in a variety of ways, and even by extra-scientific ideas that are bizarre or even false. Thus Kepler was practically a sun-worshipper and so believed that the sun was at the centre of the universe. The success of a scientific idea does not validate the beliefs on which it is based.

The difficulty of experiments in physics is often underestimated. Anyone who has ever tried to perform an experiment of even moderate complexity knows very well that if anything can conceivably go wrong, it probably will (Murphy's law). It requires extraordinary skill to perform a reliable experiment. It is often necessary to make a number of corrections to the result to allow for unwanted extraneous disturbing influences, and it requires great skill to identify and evaluate them. There are numerous examples in the history of physics of experiments that have been made with great care, but which are now recognized to have given wrong results. When reading about the history of science it is well to realize that many stories of events in the history of science that are frequently repeated in popular accounts are now known to be false.

Particular care was devoted to the accurate determination of the fundamental constants such as the velocity of light and the charge on the electron. Many of these determinations gave results that are quite outside the uncertainties associated with the values that are now believed to be correct, which shows the difficulty of obtaining accurate results. A connected problem is to know which observations to discard as spurious. Thus Millikan (1911, 1913), in his account of his determination of the charge on the electron, stressed that every single measurement gave essentially the same result. Yet examination of his laboratory notebooks showed that many measurements in fact gave different results, and Millikan discarded these with the comment: 'not an electron'. This was initially regarded as rather sharp practice on Millikan's part, but properly understood it shows the strength of his physical intuition (Holton, 1978, 1996; see also Kohn, 1986, pp. 57–62; Franklin, 1986, pp. 138–64).

Each stage in this process is fraught with difficulties. The history of physics provides many examples of reports of phenomena now regarded as completely without foundation. In this category come Blondlot's N-rays (Klotz, 1986, pp. 39–65, Gratzer, 2000, ch. 1), polywater (Klotz, 1986, pp. 67–75) and the planet Vulcan postulated by Le Verrier in 1859 to explain the shift in the perihelion of the planet Mercury that was subsequently shown to be given by Einstein's general theory of relativity (Peterson, 1993, p. 114; Baum and Sheehan, 1977; Cushing, 1998, p. 154). Such examples, and many others, show that one of the great strengths of physics is that such errors are eventually identified and removed (Kohn, 1986). They also show, however, that new results should be treated with some caution, and that they should be tested most rigorously before being accepted.

The acceptance of an experimental result may depend on current theories: if it is completely outside their scope it is likely to be disregarded, however cogent the evidence. This happened to the experiments made by Cox et al. (1928) and by Chase (1930) that strongly suggested that parity is not conserved in weak interactions. Many years later, when Lee and Yang (1956) had prepared the way by reviewing all the available evidence (except that of the authors just mentioned), the result of Wu et al. (1957) providing experimental evidence for parity non-conservation was immediately accepted.

There have been many reports of experiments, often with results of impressive statistical accuracy, that show the possibility of extra-sensory perception, the effect of prayer on the growth of plants and similar unexpected phenomena. These are not accepted by physicists because there seems to be no mechanism by which such effects can occur. However, non-local quantum interactions are considered seriously despite the lack of a mechanism and even though they appear to be in contradiction to special relativity. Acceptance in such cases is because the effect can be expressed mathematically, even though the mechanism is unknown. A cautious scepticism would seem to be the appropriate reaction here, since it has not been proved that such effects cannot occur.

The next stage is to make sense of the experimental results by theories. The results of observations and measurements have to be interpreted before they can give knowledge of reality. This act of interpretation requires the belief that there is a meaning to be found, and the background knowledge to put it into context. Science does not advance by a series of logical steps, but by leaps of the imagination. Of course what is imagined must afterwards be checked and verified logically, but logic alone would never get there. Scientific theories cannot be deduced or induced from the experimental facts (Duhem, 1954, ch. 6, sections 4 and 5); they are free creations of the human mind, and stand or fall by their internal and external consistency and by the agreement of their consequences with the experiment. The phrase 'scientific method' might be taken to imply that anyone who follows a prescribed set of rules can make scientific discoveries. This is far from the truth. Scientific discovery depends on the creative genius of the individual scientist, and often he himself cannot describe how it happens.

The scientist uses basic notions such as space and time, mass and inertia, and these can in a qualitative way be obtained directly from our experiences. This is, however, insufficient for the precise formulation required for a physical theory. Such formulations can be based on different principles and yet still agree with a wide range of experimental facts, as shown for example by the dynamics of Newton and Einstein. Scientific theories, though they may be suggested by our experiences, are free creations of the mind and require precise experimental tests to validate them. Even then, there always remains the possibility of further changes as new facts become known (Einstein, 1954, p. 270).

When a scientist first studies a problem, it often makes little sense. He gathers together all the results of observations and experiments and thinks about them. Newton was once asked how he made his great discoveries. 'By setting my mind continually unto the problem', he replied. And then, quite suddenly, and often when the scientist is thinking about something entirely different, the light dawns and all become clear. He knows that everything will fall into place and it is then just a matter of putting it all together and tidying up the details. This faculty of seeing the truth directly is sometimes called intuition. Great scientists 'know, without analysis, without reasoning, what is important for them to know'. They 'instinctively take the path leading to a discovery' (Carrell, 1961, pp. 85–6). Nevertheless, intuition can be mistaken, so it always remains essential to test the new insights experimentally.

There are many examples of this process of discovery in the history of science, such as Kekulé's discovery of the structure of benzene, Hamilton's discovery of quaternions and Poincaré's discovery of the Fuchsian functions. In each case there was an extended period of intense work when all the information was collected together, followed by a period of relaxation. Then suddenly and unpredictably the solution comes, Kekulé's in a dream,[1] Hamilton's when he was crossing a bridge and Poincaré's[2] when he was putting his foot on a step (Gill, 1944). It should be remarked that sometimes two quite different theories fit the available facts equally well. This, incidentally, shows how hazardous it is to try to obtain theological consequences from scientific theories.

In physics, theories are expressed mathematically, and this enables them to be tested very accurately by comparing their predictions with the experimental data. Sometimes it happens that experimental results are not accepted until they have a theoretical explanation. This is in opposition to the more familiar statement that a theory is not accepted until it is shown to be in accord with experiment. This is true in general but also requires caution. A theory is always at the mercy of future experiments, and all that is usually established is that the

---

[1] There is now evidence that this story is a fiction invented by Kekulé to avoid giving credit to non-German scientists, who preceded him in using cyclic structures. See Kohn (1986), pp. 214–16.

[2] See Poincaré (nd), ch. 3.

theory is valid for some specified range of phenomena to a certain degree of accuracy, as, for example, Newtonian dynamics is valid only for velocities much less than that of light. Further experiments may limit the scope of a theory without affecting its validity in a certain domain. The possibility that a completely different theory may also account for the same range of experimental data is a reminder that theories can never be established in the same way as facts. This throws serious doubt on the very possibility of drawing philosophical conclusions from physical theories. If the theory is interpreted philosophically, this validates neither the physical theory nor the philosophical ideas that are used. Philosophical systems must be established by the proper methods of philosophy, and the same applies to theological beliefs. It cannot be too strongly emphasized that theories, however well they predict experimental results, must be sharply distinguished from the reality they try to describe. It is always possible that further research will show that they fail for new types of phenomena and are therefore only partial accounts of reality. Many examples of this occur: a most notable one is the distinction between what is called the quantum world described by quantum mechanics and the real world in which we live.

In spite of all these difficulties, it is possible to describe the behaviour of matter in a precise quantitative way by differential equations. Once the initial conditions are specified, solution of the equations gives all the subsequent behaviour of the system. Thus Newton's laws, together with his theory of gravitation, enable the motions of the planets and other celestial bodies to be calculated to high accuracy. Maxwell's equations similarly describe electro-magnetic phenomena and Schrödinger's equation the phenomena of the atomic and nuclear realms. This understanding of nature is the unique achievement of the Western European civilization.

It is not always possible to find out about the results of scientific research just by reading books. One can easily find descriptions of experiments, complete with results, that omit to mention that the experiment exists only in the imagination of the writer, and has never in fact been done. Thought experiments have indeed a valuable place in physics, since they often help to clarify concepts, but they should not be confused with real experiments. Any discussion should therefore be based on an experiment that has indeed been done.

Many popular books fail to distinguish clearly between well-supported theories and speculations that have not been subjected to any serious experimental test. Theories are sometimes expressed using particular philo-sophical terms and ideas, and this can lead to their acquiring a spurious validity if it is believed that they are in some way endorsed by their use in describing physical theories. Critical attention to what has really been established and what has not is essential to any discussion of the relation of theology to modern physics.

Another source of confusion is that the arguments in favour of a particular theory or result may be strong but not compelling. Someone who, perhaps for quite other reasons, is unwilling to accept the theory is then quite justified in emphasizing that it has not been proved beyond doubt. It is almost always possible to formulate quite plausible objections, but ultimately the time comes when it is obvious to all but a few diehards that it is a lost cause. On the other hand, the pioneers of science are quite often convinced of the correctness of their views long before an unassailable proof is forthcoming and so they are naturally exasperated by opponents who do no more than draw attention to the difficulties.

Disagreements can also arise if the theory is such that a complete proof can never be forthcoming. The opponents are then on very strong ground, but they may still be acting in an unscientific way if there is no real scientifically acceptable alternative. The theory of evolution is an example of this, typified by the myth of the Huxley–Wilberforce debate (Lucas, 1979).

As scientists advance into the unknown, they encounter new phenomena. To describe these, scientists sometimes coin new words such as 'electron' and 'gene', but more frequently they continue to use the old words with a new but related meaning. This is a trap for the unwary, who may assume that words such as space and time, energy and force, have the same meanings as in common speech. It requires familiarity with science itself to understand the meanings of familiar words in a new context. As Oppenheimer (1954, p. 3) remarked, 'often the very fact that the words of science are the same as those of our common life and tongue can be more misleading than enlightening, more frustrating to understanding than recognisably technical jargon. For the words of science, – relativity, if you will, or atom or mutation or action – have been given a refinement, a precision and in the end a wholly altered meaning.'

A revealing example is provided by the use of the concept of wave in quantum mechanics. The familiar waves in the ocean are collective phenomena with many molecules acting together in a collective way. However, the so-called interference patterns observed in quantum systems, such as the double slit, are built up by a large number of electrons acting completely independently of each other. It is seldom recognized that quite different phenomena can be described by the same equation, so care is needed when words describing one are used for the other.

This provides a further illustration of the need for a thorough understanding of the science itself before embarking on philosophical reflections or theological speculations. It is fatally easy for those not familiar with science, and even for those who are, to misinterpret the words used to describe a new scientific advance and to use them to promote views that are not supported by the scientific evidence but may well come from some implicitly held philosophical views that have nothing to do with science.

There is thus a hierarchy of knowledge – theological, philosophical and scientific. Knowledge flows easily from theology to philosophy to science, but only partially and with difficulty in the reverse direction. Thus, for example, some knowledge of God can be obtained by purely philosophical means, but the theology of creation immediately implies a really existing world and with it a realistic philosophy. In turn, realism is instinctively accepted by working scientists and its correctness is confirmed by its continuing fruitfulness.

Interactions between Theology and Science

The most important interaction between theology and science is that theology can provide at least some of the essential beliefs about the natural world on which modern science is based. Thus Catholic theology, based on the Old and New Testaments, teaches us that the world is good, rational, contingent and open to the human mind. This all follows from the belief that God created the world and gave each particle the properties which determine its movements and its interactions with other particles until the end of time. Many of these beliefs were also formulated by philosophers from the time of the Greeks onwards. Without these beliefs modern science could not exist.

Theologians live in a particular cultural setting, and they inevitably accept the current world view and use its concepts and terminology in expressing theological truths. Thus they speak of Christ's ascension into heaven and descent into hell. Taken literally, this implies that heaven is up in the sky and hell in the bowels of the earth. Behind this is the geocentric world of Aristotle and Ptolemy, with the central earth surrounded by the spheres of the planets and the stars, surmounted by the empyrean realm. Scripture speaks of the sun standing still, implying that normally it moves around the earth, so that Scripture apparently supports the geocentric theory and not the heliocentric theory. The passage most often quoted is from the book of Joshua (10: 12–13): 'The sun stood still in the middle of the sky and delayed its setting for almost the whole of the day.' When a theologian has expressed the truths of his faith in the context of the current world view, he can easily come to see a threat to that world view as a threat to his theology, and react accordingly.

Science and the Bible

Such problems raise the question of the correct way to interpret the Bible. Those who hold that the surface meaning is true have difficulties when it appears to say something that is contrary to the results of scientific research. This problem has been studied for centuries, and Augustine laid down some principles that have been followed and developed by subsequent authors (see McMullin, 1998). In this view it is accepted that the Bible is literally true, which means that it is true in the sense intended by God, which may or may not be the surface or bare meaning of the words. Augustine emphasized that it simply invites ridicule to interpret the Bible in a way contrary to established scientific knowledge. Indeed, such knowledge can guide us in the interpretation of difficult passages. The Bible is given to us for our salvation, not to teach us things about the world that we can find out by ourselves, and often uses expressions adapted to the minds of its readers. This is obvious when it speaks of God's right hand, or God walking in the garden. It is also true when it adopts modes of common speech, as when it speaks of the rising and setting of the sun. Ultimately, it is the Catholic Church, which was responsible for certifying the definitive text of the Bible at the Council of Trent in 1545, that has the authority to decide on its interpretation.

This problem of biblical interpretation arose in a particularly acute form when Galileo vigorously supported Copernicus' heliocentric theory of the earth and planets going round the sun, which appears to contradict several passages in the Bible. This came to the notice of the leading Catholic theologian of the time, Cardinal Bellarmine, who was head of the Holy Office. Following Augustine, he told Galileo that if a scientific result is established beyond doubt, then any passage in Scripture that it appears to contradict must be re-examined, for truth cannot contradict truth. The Bible may well use phrases from the current world view without making a scientific statement, as indeed we all do when we speak of the sun rising and setting. Thus the use by theologians of the current world view does not imply that they endorse it. Bellarmine also told Galileo that since heliocentrism was not then established beyond doubt it should be taught as a hypothesis (Finocchiaro, 1989, 2001; Sharratt, 1994, p. 114).

All this is not as easy as it at first sounds. At what point can we say that a scientific result is established beyond doubt, and what criteria do we apply to do this? Bellarmine did not specify what he meant by proof, but almost certainly he had in mind the Aristotelian definition as certain knowledge through causes, which is not quite what would be accepted by scientists today. Very often the recognition of truth in science (as in other areas) comes through the interpretation of many different signs that fit together in a convincing way. This is the illative sense of Newman (1947). It is open only to those who have a mastery of all the relevant facts, and so it is virtually impossible for scientists to convince others of the truth that they can clearly see. Thus scientists can achieve practical certainty long before a simple irresistible proof is available; in the case of heliocentrism it came only two hundred years later with the discovery of stellar parallax. It is thus easy for theologians to advise caution in accepting the new results while exasperating scientists, who see things clearly and so regard the theologians as reactionaries fighting a hopeless rearguard action.

Particularly after the Galileo case, there is now no doubt that the Bible should not be treated as a source of scientific knowledge. God is the author of the Bible and of the book of nature, and so we should expect both of them not only to be true but consistent and congruent with each other. We can expect them to cohere into a unified view, without a detailed concordance (Jaki, 1992, 1996, 1999a).

Pope John Paul II (1992, pp. 370–75) admitted that the theologians of the Church erred in their condemnation of heliocentrism and in their censure of Galileo:

> The error of the theologians of the time ... was to think that our understanding of the physical world's structure was in some way imposed by the literal sense of Sacred Scripture ... In fact the Bible does not concern itself with the details of the physical world. There exist two realms of knowledge, one that has its source in revelation and one that reason can discover by its own power ... The methodologies proper to each makes it possible to bring out different aspects of reality.

There are many Christians, particularly in the USA, who hold that the Bible is literally true in the direct verbal sense of the words. In the nineteenth century this led Archbishop Ussher to say that the world was created, essentially in its present form, about six thousand years ago. It was thus created in such a way that scientists would deduce from their observations that it had an immensely longer history. According to the creationists, the fossils of some fishes found in rocks do not indicate that many millions of years ago fishes lived in primeval seas. On the contrary, they believe that the rocks with fossil fishes inside them were directly created by God a few thousand years ago. Creationists who hold such views do indeed recognize the power of the creator, but do so in a way that is both radically unscientific and also insulting to God's integrity. Their secular opponents attack their belief in a creator, and the creationists respond by attacking science. Both have grasped one aspect of the truth but reject the other. It is vital to hold together both truths, namely the creation of all by God, and the scientific discoveries that have shown us how the world has developed over the ages (Kitcher, 1983).

The debates on theology and science often have hidden agendas and hidden motives. People argue strongly for or against a certain position on purely scientific grounds, but their motivation comes from entirely different considerations. Very often scientific theories are opposed, on scientific grounds, by people who are much more concerned with the possible theological implications, real or imagined, of that theory. Obviously, scientific problems must be tackled by scientific methods; it is only when this is done that it is legitimate to discuss implications. Scientific advances may well be initiated or stimulated by theological or philosophical beliefs, but they must be assessed solely by scientific criteria. This has been summed up by Duhem (see Jaki, 1984, pp. 113–14):

> If, therefore, we want to handle with competence and fruitfully the questions which are of the domain common to metaphysics and positive science, let us begin with studying the latter for ten, for fifteen years; let us study it, first of all, in itself and for itself; without seeking to put it in harmony with such and such philosophical assertion; then, as we have mastered its principles, applied it in a thousand ways, we can search for its metaphysical meaning which will not fail to accord with true philosophy. [Therefore] if Catholic theologians and philosophers had not become men with deep scientific knowledge, they must remain silent.

Does Science Lead to Faith?

To what extent can it be said that science implies, teaches or leads us to the acceptance of theological truths? At the simplest level, contemplation of mountains or the starry heavens have led many directly to God. The Psalmist declares that the heavens show forth the glory of the Lord. Similarly the intricate design of the natural world, from the symmetries of plants to the complicated interacting life cycles of plants and animals, can convince us that it all must have had a designer (Jaki, 1990).

The early Christians and the medievals were interested in the natural world as providing symbols of spiritual truths. Thus St Patrick used the shamrock to explain the doctrine of the Trinity, although this could easily be criticized as simplistic and indeed heretical, as it implies the identity of the three persons. St Augustine studied natural phenomena and wrote about their spiritual meaning. He was interested in nature primarily because it reveals God to an attentive observer, but in the process he gathered much useful scientific information. The pelican plucking her breast to draw blood to feed her chicks is a symbol of Christ shedding His blood for us. This was incorporated in a well-known hymn of St Thomas Aquinas to the Eucharist, and also appears in many coats of arms, including that of my own college, Corpus Christi College in Oxford. In this way the natural world was invested with layers of meaning that we should try to discover in order to enhance our spiritual life.

In the Renaissance this interest was continued. In encyclopedias such as Conrad Gesner's *History of Animals*, for example, animals were described together with the meanings of their names in every language, the proverbs associated with them and what they symbolize to Christians. Later writers such as Aldrovandi wove these associations into detailed webs that were described in huge volumes on birds, insects and animals. This emblematic view of nature came to a sudden end around 1650 when the new voyages of discovery brought back a whole range of previously unknown plants and animals that had no emblematic meaning. People became critical of the old stories and began to ask whether they were true, not what was their spiritual meaning. Francis Bacon summed up the new empirical attitude to nature, and rejected the idea that it is a complex of signs revealing God's plan, or a web with hidden meaning. Thereafter the main concern was to describe the natural world as accurately as possible, to seek what is true. This marks the difference between the medieval and the modern world view. Instead of arguing from general principles, scientists established the facts by observation and measurement.

Essential to scientific activity is the distinction between God's absolute and ordained powers. Everything is created by God, so He has absolute power over it. He can change or annihilate it at will; indeed without His conserving power it would immediately cease to be. He is the cause of everything, but sometime He acts directly and sometimes by what is called secondary causality (Davies, 1992). By this we mean that He delegates to material objects the power to cause, so that He now acts through them. In doing so He acts consistently, although He may for some particular purpose act otherwise. He orders everything 'in measure, number and weight' (Wisdom 16: 20) and 'determined His works for all time' (Ecclesiasticus 16: 25). 'The stability of nature is a sign of God's faithfulness' (Jeremiah 31: 35–36; 33: 25–26). This ordered behaviour of matter is the subject of science, so in normal circumstances we may speak of the behaviour of matter as determined by God. In this sense we can accept the uniformity of nature, while leaving open the possibility of miracles. This distinction between God's absolute and ordinary powers, or primary and secondary causality, is due to the medieval theologians Alexander of Hales, Albertus Magnus and Thomas Aquinas; it is to be sharply distinguished from the view of Muslim theologians such as al-Ashari (see Chapter 3) and the occasionalism of the French philosopher Malebranche, who held that God causes everything directly. As Davies (1992) remarks, God is the cause of both bat and ball, but it is still the bat that does the hitting. Apart from miraculous interventions, the physical world is thus a fully determined system, although it is impossible to prove or disprove this on the basis of science alone. These remarks apply to the physical world only, but not to human beings. Each of us is the union of a physical body and a spiritual soul, and God has given us free will. Without this we would be just an assemblage of molecules moving according to deterministic laws, and rational discussion would be impossible. We do not understand this union of body and soul, and discussion of the theories that have been proposed is beyond the scope of this book.

Internal and External Influences on the Development of Science

Does science develop according to internal criteria, unaffected by the beliefs and needs of the surrounding society, or do such external pressures influence or determine the way it develops? Should science be organized and controlled by the state to maximize the likely benefits to society, or should it be left entirely to the scientists themselves to decide what to do next? Many different views have been expressed. Following Marx, the Soviet historian Boris Hessen (1931) believed that the development of pure science is determined by the economic needs of society, and attempted to provide an example of this by a detailed analysis of Newton's *Principia*. The sociological roots of science were also studied by Zilsel (see Basalla, 1968). The Marxist physicist J. D. Bernal (1946) argued that the state should control scientific research. People have to be taxed to obtain the funds needed by scientists, so it seems only fair that the research topics should be chosen to bring the most practical benefits.

These ideas were vigorously opposed by Michael Polanyi (1958), G. P. Thomson, J. Baker (1942, 1945) and others, who founded the Society for the Freedom of Science. Polanyi (1958) pointed out, as an example, that the development of methods of illumination, from candles and electric light to fluorescent tubes and lasers, depends on a number of unconnected discoveries, all made by scientists who were solely interested in finding out about different aspects of the natural world. It would therefore have been quite impossible to plan and organize this development in advance.

There are numerous cases in the history of science of discoveries in pure science having quite unexpected applications. Thus Roentgen was studying electrical discharges in gases and discovered X-rays. He would never have done this if he had been told to improve methods of medical diagnosis. Hertz would never have discovered radio waves if he had been told to improve methods of communication. Madame Curie studied radioactivity and discovered radium: she would never have done this if she had been told to discover a way to treat cancer. Scientists cannot predict what they will find: Rutherford said in 1936 that he expected no more than small-scale applications of nuclear physics. Max Planck (1933, p. 137) emphasized that 'scientific discovery and scientific knowledge have been achieved only by those who have gone in pursuit of it without any practical purpose whatever in view'.

The lesson is clear: pure science must be allowed to develop in accord with its own internal criteria. When possible applications are found, it is then up to society to decide how to develop them. Any attempt to force the development of science to satisfy economic criteria is doomed to failure. Specification of required objectives may produce improvements, whereas pure science left alone produces revolutions. Inevitably, the social, cultural and economic state of society has some effects on the way science develops, but does not determine it.

Theological beliefs can have both internal and external influences on the development of science. The very possibility of science depends on definite philosophical and theological beliefs about the world, as described in Chapter 2. For science to develop, these beliefs must be held, at least implicitly, by society as a whole and by the scientists themselves. They are thus both internal and external. It may also happen that a particular scientific result contradicts some theological belief and then pressure may be put on the scientists concerned to stop their work and recant their conclusions. This again is both an internal and external constraint.

Considering the importance of theological beliefs for the development of science, it is not surprising that Jews and Christians have been prominent among the leading scientists from the Middle Ages onwards. They all share the beliefs necessary for science to develop. Thus, throughout all Planck's 'work and all that he has said or says there is always this golden thread of a living faith in the ultimate purposes of creation' (James Murphy in Planck, 1933, introduction, p. 39). It is not accidental 'that the greatest thinkers were always deeply religious souls ... Science furthers a love of truth' that displays 'itself in the constant endeavour to arrive at a more exact knowledge of the world of will and matter' (ibid.).

The Abbé Lemaître (see Weisskopf, 1991, p. 287) has suggested that

> perhaps the believer has the advantage of knowing that the enigma has a solution, it is in the final analysis the work of an intelligent being; so the problems posed by nature are here to be solved, and the degree of difficulty is without doubt appropriate to the present and future intellectual capacity of humanity. This will perhaps not give him greater resources for his investigations, but it will help to support this feeling of healthy optimism without which a sustained effort cannot be maintained.

Commenting on this, Pope John Paul II declared: 'I wish all of you this healthy optimism of which Abbé Lemaître speaks; it is an optimism that takes its mysterious but very real origin in God in whom you have placed your faith' (quoted by Weisskopf, 1991, p. 287).

The correlations between scientific achievements and Christians holding different theological beliefs are much less definite (Hall, 1975, 1983; Kneller,

1995; Davis and Winship, 2002). On the whole, it seems that there is not a strong correlation between scientific activity and theological beliefs that are not directly related to those underlying science itself. The existence of many non-Christian scientists shows that these beliefs need not be held explicitly.

The Presuppositions of Science

It is essential for the development of science that the beliefs about the material world mentioned above are firmly held, even though it is at a deep psychological level where they are implicit rather than explicit. This explains why it is so difficult to teach science in non-Christian countries. This difficulty is not immediately evident because technology is easy to convey, and this is frequently confused with or considered similar to science. It is easy to teach people in other countries how to set up and run manufacturing industries that provide them with their daily needs. On the contrary, it is exceedingly difficult to convey science, that is, to establish flourishing and fruitful research communities in such countries. It is of course easy to build and equip scientific laboratories, but it is almost impossible to fill them with really innovative indigenous scientists. It is not generally realized that the level of research in most non-Christian countries is very low. The few exceptions are those that have been for many centuries in contact with Western Europe; many generations have been taught in Westernized schools and so have absorbed the Christian presuppositions of science. Since Western education is often politically unacceptable, the situation is likely to worsen. Indeed, the decline in Christian belief in Western countries is likely to result in a slow decline of science. Already the falling numbers of aspiring students of physics is a sign of this decline.

To sum up, the principal interaction between theology and science is that Christian theology provided several of the beliefs on which science is based. On that basis, science can develop in accord with its own internal nature, without any further influences or external constraints. In particular, the detailed progress of science cannot be guided by theologians or by church decrees. Many popes have emphasized the freedom of science to search for the truth, so that

> basic research must be free with regard to political and economic authorities, which must co-operate in its development, without hampering its creativity or having to serve their own purposes. Like any other truth, scientific truth is answerable only to itself and to the supreme truth, God, the creator of man and of all things. (Pope John Paul II, 1979)

There is much discussion today about whether the advance of science, in particular of modern physics, can bring with it new theological truths. Certainly it can enhance our appreciation of the wonders of creation, but that wonder is not different in kind from what we feel when we look around us. It is also possible that science provides new concepts and ways of thought useful to theology, as Aristotle's philosophy made possible the medieval development of theology. This provides no new theological truths. Indeed, the provisional nature of scientific theories makes it impossible to use them as the basis of a new theology.

CHAPTER 2

The Judeo-Christian Contribution to the Development of Modern Science

Science in Ancient Civilizations

Viewed in the widest historical perspective, the explosive development of science in seventeenth-century Europe is one of the most astonishing events in the whole of human history. It makes that civilization unlike any other. For the first time people all over the world are joined together by rapid communications, easy travel and extensive trade. Why did this understanding of the detailed structure of the world that we call science develop and come to maturity just when and where it did? This is a question that can lead us to the heart of the relation between science and the Christian basis of our civilization.

It is usual to discuss the relation of science to religion as if they are two independent activities. We can then compare and contrast their objectives, their modes of procedure and the status of their conclusions. This is not without value, but it presupposes that they are two independent activities that have somehow to be related to each other. This directs attention away from the central point that is essential for the understanding of their relationship, namely that when seen in the perspective of history there is an organic connection between them. Science as we know it is based on certain definite beliefs about the world. Many of them were first formulated by the ancient Greeks but were not sufficient to establish science as a continuing enterprise. Modern science began only when they were reinforced and extended by the religious beliefs of the Hebrews and finally brought to completion by the theology of Christian Europe.

If we look at the great civilizations of the past, in China and India, in Babylon and Egypt, in Greece and Rome, we frequently find well-developed social structures, magnificent artistic and architectural achievements, imperishable drama and philosophy, but nothing remotely equivalent to modern science. We find great skill in the working of wood and metal, ingenious mechanical contrivances and perceptive philosophical speculations about the world, but not the detailed quantitative understanding of matter, from quarks to galaxies, expressed as the solution of a few differential equations, that is the hallmark of the more developed areas of modern science.

Most of the great civilizations of the past were able to provide all the material requirements for the growth of science. There was a leisured class, technical skills and systems of writing and mathematics. Obviously this by itself is not enough. What was lacking was the attitude towards the material world that is the essential precondition of science, and in some cases a social structure that allows new ideas to flourish.

What do we have to believe before we can hope to become scientists? We must believe that the world is in some sense good, so that it is worthy of careful study. We must believe that it is orderly and rational, so that what we find out one day will still be true on the next day. We must believe that this order is open to the human mind, for otherwise there would be no point in trying to find it. We must believe that this order is not a necessary order that could be found out by pure thought like the truths of mathematics, but is rather a contingent or dependent order that can only be found by making experiments.

In addition to these beliefs about the world itself, the development of science depends on moral convictions such as the obligation freely to share any knowledge that is gained. Furthermore, once it becomes clear that scientific understanding can be applied to grow more food and to cure diseases, then its further development is encouraged if we believe that we should do these things to help our fellow men.

These beliefs may seem obvious to us, but in the context of human history they are very special. They are not found in the ancient civilizations, and that is why science in the modern sense never developed among them. In some cases, particularly in ancient Greece, an impressive start was made by a few individuals of genius, but they lacked the support of a coherent set of beliefs shared by the whole community, and science never became a self-sustaining enterprise.

Why were these beliefs found in Christian Europe? Is there any connection between the medieval theology that formed the mind of Europe in the critical centuries before the birth of science? In each case we find that there is indeed such a connection. In order to see that this is so we have to look in more detail at the historical development of science.

The Origin of Science

Our present scientific and technical knowledge has been attained by a long, hard and winding road from the astronomical observations of the Babylonians to the quantum theory and supercomputers of today. Initially, science was not distinguished from philosophy and its roots are to be found in the early struggles to make sense of the world. Before answers can be found, we must ask the right questions. What methods should we use to understand nature? How can we know that our answers are right? Why do things change? Is there an unchangeable reality beneath the changes that surround us? Over the centuries these questions have been answered in different ways under the influence of the surrounding culture.

It was extremely difficult to get started. The early Ionian philosophers made some tentative speculations, but the first really systematic attempt was made by Aristotle. He took all knowledge for his province and proposed a vast rational structure embracing all fields of activity from mathematics, physics and biology to politics, art and music. He was an exceptionally acute observer, and many of his biological descriptions and discoveries were not surpassed until the invention of the microscope about two millennia later.

Aristotle was primarily concerned with the general principles of nature and with the qualitative relations among things, and not with precise quantitative analysis. He recognized that some natural phenomena such as optics and musical harmonies could be described mathematically, but he distinguished this from mathematics on the one hand and natural philosophy on the other.

Aristotle considered the world as an organism acting for a purpose. Every material body has a natural place and always moves towards that place. This may be seen most clearly in his discussion of motion, the most fundamental phenomenon that lies at the basis of physics and hence of all science. He distinguished between two types of natural motion: the circular motion characteristic of the celestial bodies, and linear motion characteristic of bodies on the earth. The celestial realm is changeless and incorruptible, and the planets must move in circular orbits because the circle is the most perfect curve. On the earth, bodies strive to reach their natural place, fire going upwards and heavy bodies downwards. Their rate of fall depends on their weights, as heavy bodies strive more strongly to reach their natural place; a body of a certain weight thus falls twice as fast as one of half its weight. Thus although Aristotle maintained that all knowledge come to us through the senses, he often preferred his deductions to the simplest observations. In this case a thought experiment suffices, as according to him two equal weights joined by a light rod should fall at twice the speed of the unconnected weights.

Aristotle analysed the concepts of space, time and motion, and came to the conclusion that the world is eternal. He also believed that time is cyclic, so that after a long time everything is repeated again and again, without end.

The Aristotelian world picture is a logically coherent structure that served as a framework for thinking for almost two thousand years. By its emphasis on purpose, a concept that has no place in physics, its over-optimistic belief that it is possible to intuit the structure of the world and its lack of understanding of the importance of quantitative measurement it prevented the development of genuine science. Other Greeks, notably Archimedes, Aristarchus and Euclid, made fundamental advances in geometry and the analysis of natural phenomena, but in spite of this heroic beginning Greek science never developed into a self-sustaining enterprise (Jaki, 1986).

To sum up, Aristotle believed in the eternity of the world, in a cyclic universe, and in a world of purpose, even in material things. He also believed that celestial matter, the world of the stars and planets, is incorruptible, unlike terrestrial matter that can undergo change. These beliefs prevented the development of science for two thousand years. Their stranglehold had to be broken before science could develop into its modern form.

A new beginning, a fresh style of scientific thinking, was made possible by the Judeo-Christian vision of the world. The God of the Hebrews is very different from the God of Plato or the Prime Mover of Aristotle. In sharp contrast, the God of the Hebrews freely created a world completely distinct from Himself, and His actions are inscrutable to men unless He freely chooses to reveal His plans.

The book of Genesis bears witness to the Hebrew belief in a transcendent creator from its opening phrases: 'In the beginning God created the heavens and the earth ... And God saw all that He had made, and indeed it was very good' (Genesis 1: 31). The Hebrew word translated as 'good' also means 'beautiful', and beauty is one of the most important characteristics of a scientific theory.[1] In contrast to the confused creation myths of the surrounding nations, the creation story in Genesis has a clear logical structure, expressed in poetic form. It clearly expresses belief in the absolute sovereignty, rationality and benevolence of God, who brings everything into being by His command and communicates His own goodness to them. Although not expressed in modern language, it contains the essential beliefs about the world that must be held if science is to flourish.

The earliest psalms tell us how God made the world and prepared it for man: He sets the heavens, the moon and the stars in their places, obeying a law that is fixed for ever (Psalm 148). He makes man the ruler over his works, ordering everything 'in measure, number and weight' (Wisdom 11: 20). In His reply to Job, Yahweh asks

> Where were you when I laid the earth's foundations?
> Tell me, since you are so well informed!
> Who decided the dimensions of it, do you know?
> Or who stretched the measuring line across it? (Job 38: 4–7)

God is all-powerful, and He alone is to be worshipped. The sun and the moon are not gods but parts of nature. The animist beliefs of the Egyptians and the Babylonians, the gods of the forest grove, the fates and furies, dryads and nereids, the belief in the divine earth-mother – are all totally rejected. In this way the natural world is desacralized, so that it becomes a proper object for scientific study.

Nothing comes into being, nothing remains in being, without being loved and willed by God:

> You made all that exists; you hold nothing
> of what you have made in abhorrence,
> For had you hated anything you would not have formed it.
> And how, had you not willed it, could a thing persist?
> how be conserved if not called forth by you? (Wisdom 11: 24–26).

The heroic mother of the seven martyred brothers in Maccabees (2 Maccabees 7: 22–29) likewise expressed her belief in creation when she exhorted her sons to stand firm, saying to them:

---

[1] The theoretical physicist Dirac remarked in 1963 that he always looked for beautiful mathematical equations. See Pais (2000), p. 69; Chandrasekhar (1979a and 1979b, p. 25). See also Jaki (1980), p. 26.

I do not know how you appeared in my womb; it was not I who endowed you with breath and life. I had not the shaping of your every part. It is the creator of the world, ordaining the process of man's birth and presiding over the origin of things, who in his mercy will most surely give you back both breath and life, seeing that you now despise your own existence for the sake of his laws.

When it came to the last son, Antiochus tried to persuade him to abandon the traditions of his ancestors, and appealed to his mother to advise the young man to save his life. She finally agreed to persuade her son, but she fooled the cruel tyrant with the words:

I implore you, my child, observe heaven and earth, consider all that is in them, and acknowledge that God made them out of what did not exist, and mankind comes to being in the same way. Do not fear this executioner, but prove yourself worthy of your brothers, and make death welcome, so that in the day of mercy I may receive you back in your brothers' company. (2 Maccabees 7: 22–29)

The faithfulness of God to Israel is compared with the reliability of natural phenomena (Jeremiah 31: 35).

Your word, O Lord, for ever
Stands firm in the heaven.
Your truth lasts from age to age
like the earth your creator. (Psalms 118: 89)

The order and stability of natural phenomena are taken for granted with the same quiet certainty as shown by the mother of the seven brothers:

God's laws are permanently valid, and endure for ever:
'When God created His works in the beginning
he allotted them their portions as soon as they were made
he determined his works for all time
from their beginnings to their distant future.
They know neither hunger nor weariness,
and they never desert their duties.
None has jostled ever his neighbour,
they will never disobey his word.' (Ecclesiasticus 16: 24–26).

Matter is entirely passive and it consequently endures, obedient to God's will. It is a perfect model for us.

In all these accounts of creation there is no distinction between the heavens and the earth, between the celestial and the terrestrial realms; both are made by God and are totally subject to His laws.

Thus according to Judeo-Christian beliefs the world is the free creation of God from nothing. The structure of the world cannot therefore be deduced from first principles; we have to look at it, to make observations and experiments to find out how God made it. This reinforces the Aristotelian principle that all knowledge comes through the senses, but requires it to be situated within a wider set of beliefs concerning the nature of the world that is implicit in the doctrine of creation. Aristotle's natural theology is thus transformed into the Christian notion of divine providence: God is not simply the Prime Mover or First Cause; He is the cause of the very existence of the world and its continuance in being.

We know that the world is rational because it was made and is kept in being by a rational God. It is contingent because it depends on the divine fiat: God could have chosen to make the world in a different way. There is here a delicate balance between the rationality and the freedom of God: tip the balance one way or the other and you have a belief in a necessary or in a chaotic world, both inimical to the growth of science. Finally, we are assured that the enterprise is a practicable one, that the world is open to the human mind, because God charged us to have dominion over it, and He does not command the impossible: 'Be fruitful, multiply, fill the earth and conquer it. Be masters of the fishes of the sea, the birds of heaven and all living animals on the earth' (Genesis 1: 28). Whatever wisdom we acquire, we must pass on to others: 'What I have learned without self-interest, I pass on without reserve; I do not intend to hide her riches. For she is an inexhaustible treasure to men, and those who acquire it win God's friendship' (Wisdom 7: 13).

The first study of the effect of the Hebrew theology of creation on Greek philosophy was made in the first century BC by Philo Judaeus of Alexandria. He accepted the Greek idea of unchangeable causality, but not the modes of causality proposed by Plato, Aristotle and the Stoics. Following Scripture, he argued that

> God did not act as Aristotle had maintained as an essentially passive first cause co-eternal with the world emanating by necessity from divine reason, that God did not make the world out of pre-existing matter as Plato proposed in the Timaeus, that God was neither material nor in the world as supposed by the Stoics, and that God is in no way necessitated, but that he had acted with entirely free omnipotence in creating *ex nihilo* a world separate from himself. (Crombie, 1994, p. 294)

He used the word *logos* to denote the rational pattern on which God modelled His creation, the immutable laws governing the world that shows God's power within it. They are often obscure to us, but they lie behind the motions of the stars and all natural phenomena. God is the absolute Lord of the universe; He has laid down its laws but can overrule them at will.

The Early Christian Centuries

The birth of Christ further ennobled the matter of the universe, and his teaching reinforced and enhanced the teaching contained in the Old Testament. The debilitating belief in a cyclic universe, held in all ancient cultures, was decisively broken by the Christian belief in the uniqueness of the Incarnation. Henceforth history was no longer an infinite series of dreary cycles, but a linear story with a beginning and an end. Inherent in Christ's teaching is a set of beliefs about the world that eventually led to the first viable birth of modern science in the High Middle Ages, and to its subsequent flowering in the Renaissance.

In the early Christian centuries several philosophers examined the cosmology of creation in the context of Christian theology. In the third century AD Lactantius rejected the Stoic belief that nature is animate and that God is within the world, and also the Epicurean belief that the world is simply the product of chance, without any providential design. He emphasized that God with infinite power created the world out of nothing, so that He is absolutely separate from His creation. Nature is designed by God ultimately for the benefit of man, and has no power of its own that does not come from God. This implies that nature is an inanimate mechanism operating according to fixed laws. In the fourth century AD Basil of Cappodocia insisted, contrary to Plato, Aristotle and other Greek philosophers, that nature is not animate, nor is it a living thing endowed with senses. When plants and animals grow, they do so following God's command and in accord with His laws.

The Christian beliefs concerning creation emphasize not only that the universe was created by God out of nothing and in time, but that the universe is totally dependent on God and totally distinct from God. The universe at any instant is sustained in being by God, and without this sustaining power it would immediately lapse into nothingness.

At that time there were passionate debates about the nature of Christ, and heresies abounded. To define the true nature of Christ was the task of a series of councils of the Church, and of these the Council of Nicea (325) formulated the creed that is widely held today:

> *Credo in unum Deum. Patrem omnipotentum, factorem coeli et terrae, visibilium omnium et invisibilium. Et in unum Dominum Jesum Christum, Filium Dei unigenitum. Et ex Patre natum ante omnia saecula. Deum de Deo, lumen de luminae, Deum verum de Deum vero. Genitum, non factum, consubstantialem Patri; per quem omnia facta sunt ...*

It is easy to recite these hallowed phrases without fully realizing their impact, and still more their importance for science. The beginning of the Nicene creed asserts the creation of the universe by God: '*Factorem coeli et terrae*'. One of the early heresies was pantheism, which failed to distinguish between God and His creation, holding that it is in some way part of God. In the Greco-Roman world the universe was thought of as an emanation from a divine principle that is not distinguished from the universe. Pantheism is explicitly excluded by the Nicene creed when it says that Christ is the only-begotten Son of God. Christ is begotten, not made. Only Christ was begotten and thus shared in the substance of God; the universe was made, not begotten. ('*Et in unum Dominum Jesum Christum, Filium Dei unigenitum ... Genitum, non factum*'.) Since pantheism was one of the beliefs preventing the rise of science in all ancient cultures, the

Nicene creed prepared the way for the one viable birth of science in human history.

Many ancient cosmologies held that the world is a battleground between the spirits of good and evil. This dualism is inimical to science because it makes the world unpredictable. Dualism is excluded by the Nicene creed when it says that all creation takes place through Christ ('*per quem omnia facta sunt*').

In his Epistle to the Colossians, St Paul says that in Christ all things took their being, and were all created through him and in him (Colossians 1: 15). He stressed Christ as the divine *logos* and the consequence that the creation must be fully logical and orderly. He referred to creation out of nothing when he praises God 'who restores the dead to life and calls into being those things which had not been' (Romans 4: 17) and promises that through Christ they would understand 'the breadth, the height and the depth' (Ephesians 3: 18).

Inherent in the Christian doctrine of creation is the belief that God freely chose to create the universe. He was not in any way constrained either to create or not to create it in the way that He did. It is therefore not a necessary universe in the sense that it had to be created or could not have been created otherwise. There is therefore no possibility of finding out about the universe by pure thought or by *a priori* reasoning. We can only hope to understand it by studying it and by making experiments. Thus the Christian doctrine of creation encouraged the experimental method, essential for the development of science.

The theology of St Augustine of Hippo encouraged the systematic study of the natural world, since he believed that its sacramental nature is symbolic of spiritual truths. He was a compulsive observer of natural phenomena, always on the lookout for anything that gave even a fleeting glimpse of the reason behind all things. The laws of nature are objective and inexorable, unalterable by us but not by God. He encouraged the study of nature and the search for its laws, to read the book of nature: 'Look above and below, note, read. God, whom you want to discover, did not make the letters with ink; he put in front of your eyes the things that he made.' Following Plato, he recognized the importance of mathematics, saying that the laws of nature are the laws of numbers. There is a rational pattern in nature which follows from the unchanging laws that govern its development through time. He was interested in nature primarily because it reveals God to the attentive observer. His philosophical reflections on the nature of time are still quoted as among the most profound ever written.

In the early Church, and subsequently throughout the Middle Ages, the natural world was studied primarily for the spiritual truths that it reveals. Science was seen as the handmaid of theology. Scientific knowledge for its own sake was without value, but it became valuable when it served a higher purpose. As an example, the regular movements of the heavenly bodies are used to show God's constancy and reliability in His relations to us. An additional reason to study nature is provided by its importance in scriptural interpretation. As Augustine emphasized, Scripture must be interpreted in a way that is not contradicted by established scientific conclusions. Thus when interpreting a passage that impinges on a scientific question it is necessary to determine first of all the relevant scientific knowledge, and then go on to interpret the passage. It is therefore incumbent on Christians to be familiar with contemporary science. Concerning scientific knowledge, Augustine remarks that 'it is a disgraceful and dangerous thing for an infidel to hear a Christian talking nonsense on these topics, and we should take all means to prevent such an embarrassing spectacle in which people see vast ignorance in a Christian and laugh it to scorn' (Augustine, 1982; Lindberg, 2002, p. 47).

In the early sixth century John Philoponus, a Christian Platonist who lived in Alexandria, wrote extensively on the material world, showing the influence of Christian beliefs on those of the surrounding pagan world, particularly those derived from ancient Greece (Sorabji, 1987). He commented extensively on Aristotle, whom he greatly admired, but when the teaching of Aristotle was contrary to Christian belief he did not hesitate to differ from it. This was particularly important in his commentary on Aristotle's physics, where he said, contrary to Aristotle, that all bodies would fall in a vacuum at the same speed, irrespective of their weight, and that projectiles move through the air not due to the motion of the air but because they were initially given a certain quantity of motion. This is a remarkable anticipation of ideas normally associated with Galileo, and shows a decisive break with Aristotelian physics. He was not the first writer in antiquity to break with Aristotle, but he did so more clearly and decisively.

The connection between his rejection of Aristotelian ideas and his Christian beliefs is to be found in the doctrine of creation. Addressing the question of motion, he asked 'could not the sun, moon and the stars be not given by God, their Creator, a certain kinetic force, in the same way as heavy and light things were given their trend to move?' He also believed that the stars are not made of the ether but of ordinary matter, thus rejecting Aristotle's distinction between celestial and terrestrial matter.

This shows very clearly that the Christian beliefs about the world are incompatible with the Aristotelian views on the divinity of celestial matter and the eternity of motion. It was thus inevitable that the spread of Christianity should lead eventually to the destruction of Aristotelian physics, thus opening the way to modern science. This is not to say, however, that Christian beliefs give any specific guidelines for the development of science, but the removal of obstacles is by itself no small service.

Philoponus was also the first to say that Genesis was written for spiritual and not for scientific instruction, a wise statement that was too far in advance of its time to be congenial to contemporary theologians. This theological boldness perhaps explains why Philoponus' ideas did not lead to further scientific developments. His ideas on motion are remarkably similar to those of Buridan and Oresme in the High Middle Ages, which did succeed in initiating the scientific enterprise. To be fruitful, ideas have not only to be right; they need to fall on fertile ground, in this case a society sufficiently developed to make full use of them, and this was lacking for Philoponus. There has been some speculation about whether the ideas of Philoponus were known to Buridan, but nothing seems to be established definitely on this question.

In the eighth century the Venerable Bede in Northumbria wrote not only his well-known *Ecclesiastical History of the English People*, but also a treatise 'On the Nature of Things' and two books on timekeeping and the calendar.

We are now on the threshold of the decisive breakthrough that led eventually to the rise of modern science.

The High Middle Ages

The High Middle Ages was a time of intellectual ferment. Schools, generally associated with cathedrals, and universities were being founded all over Europe, and the writings of the ancient Greeks were becoming available in translation. Christian theology was being re-thought using their unfamiliar but powerful concepts. The writings of Augustine and of others such as Philoponus were already forming new attitudes to the natural world.

In the early twelfth century, Adelard of Bath wrote his *Quaestiones Naturales*, which marks the dawn of medieval science. His nephew believed that the spontaneous appearance of life in a dish of dried soil was miraculous. At a time when there was a strong devotion to miracles, it would have been easy for Adelard to agree. Instead he drew a firm distinction between the action of the Creator and the natural workings of His creation: 'It is the will of the Creator that herbs should sprout from the earth. But the same is not without a reason either.' When his nephew persisted and pointed out that a natural explanation from the doctrine of the four elements was inadequate, he stuck to his point: 'Whatever is, is from Him and through Him. But the realm of being is not a confused one, nor is it lacking in disposition which, so far as human knowledge can go, should be consulted.' In other words, we should persist in seeking a natural explanation, and avoid attributing anything that we do not understand to the direct action of God. This advice, which is still worth heeding today, contains the essential attitude to the natural world that lies at the basis of science.

At the same time, Hugh of St Victor saw the study of the natural world as a twofold process, first the ascent of reason to the purely spiritual and then a descent to examine in this light the information provided by the senses. In so doing he expressed the mathematical rationalism of Plato and inspired his contemporaries William of Conches, Thierry of Chartres and Adelard of Bath, for whom reality was autonomous nature to be grasped by reason.

In the twelfth and thirteenth centuries there was a remarkable flowering of creativity in many areas of human activity. At the sociological level, this was largely due to the new concept of treating a group of people as a separate legal entity. This enabled them to act with considerable freedom, but always subject to the law. It came about as a result of what has been called the papal revolution, by which the Church asserted its freedom from the civil authorities (Huff, 1993, p. 125). Previously, it was usual for clerical appointments to be made by the civil authorities, but now the Church insisted that it alone had the authority to do this. This established the Church as a separate legal entity and put constraints on the power of the civil authorities. The most significant result was the creation of a separate legal system with its own area of jurisdiction. Once this idea was established, both Church and State became federations of many corporations, each with a measure of autonomy. Among these were cities, the first universities, the legal and medical professions, banks and business organizations, and later on, the scientific community itself.

In the High Middle Ages, many universities were founded by the Church to provide higher education for those educated in the monastic schools, to train future clerics and to facilitate the spread of learning. It was in these universities that the decisive breakthrough that led to the rise of modern science took place. The works of Aristotle and the other Greek philosophers were translated into Latin and were used by theologians to express the truths of the faith in more precise language, and by philosophers to refine their view of the natural world.

The two characteristics of the Western intellectual tradition that made science possible are the insistence on logical coherence and experimental verification. These were already present in a qualitative way among the Greeks, and the vital contribution of the Middle Ages was to refine these conditions into a more effective union. This was done principally by emphasizing the quantitative precision that can be attained using mathematics in the formulations of theories and then verifying them not by observation alone, but by precise measurements. This transition was achieved in the twelfth century, principally by Robert Grosseteste, who is regarded as the founder of experimental science. His work on experimental science owed much to Plato, who taught that the pure forms behind the appearances of things are mathematical in nature, so that our theories must also be mathematical, and the results of experiments expressed in numbers (Crombie, 1953).

Grosseteste elaborated his theory of the scientific method in some detail, although he did not himself carry out many experiments. He recommended the method of analysis and synthesis; namely that the problem is first resolved into its simplest parts and when these are understood the results can be combined to give the explanation of the whole. The observations and experiments may themselves suggest hypotheses and theories, and these in turn may be verified or disproved by comparison with further observations and measurements.

He first applied his method to the phenomenon of light. He believed that light is the most fundamental form, so that the laws of light must lie at the basis of scientific explanation. God first created light, and from that all things came. Light itself follows geometrical rules, in the way it is propagated, reflected and refracted, and this is the means whereby higher bodies act on lower. He studied the rainbow, and his criticism of Aristotle and Seneca were useful steps along the road to an adequate explanation. Although he emphasized mathematics, he was clear that mathematical entities have no objective reality but are simply abstractions from material bodies. Implicit in his work is insistence on quantitative measurement, and this in turn comes from the biblical insistence on the rationality of the Creator, who disposed everything in measure, number and weight.

Grosseteste's work on optics was continued by the Franciscan friar Roger Bacon, who also wrote extolling the value of science, and in particular predicted that man could make machines to travel on land, sea and in the air.

- So great was the prestige of Aristotle that the philosophers of the medieval schools taught by commenting on his texts. Some of Aristotle's teaching, however, was inconsistent with the Christian faith, and the philosophers did not hesitate to differ from Aristotle when it seemed necessary. In 1215 the Fourth Lateran Council decreed that all creation, spiritual and material, took place out of nothing and in time. This is directly contrary to Aristotle's belief in the eternity of the world. There was intense discussion on a variety of topics, notably concerning the creation of the world and the motion of bodies. In 1277 the bishop of Paris, Etienne Tempier, found it necessary to condemn 219 philosophical propositions as contrary to Christian belief. His main purpose was to defend God's absolute power against any attempt by Aristotelian philosophers to set limits to it. Several of the condemned propositions set limits to God's power, saying for instance that He cannot make more than one world or move the world so as to produce a vacuum. Tempier thus reasserted the belief that God can freely create any world, just as He chooses.

There has been much discussion of the importance of this condemnation for the development of science. Any such action can have many unintended consequences. It was primarily aimed at Greek necessitarianism and the Aristotelianism of Averroës, but its affirmation of the omnipotence of God encouraged the theologians to consider as tenable several scientific and philosophical propositions previously deemed excluded by the very nature of things. In this way Christian theology 'facilitated, even in science, the opening of new perspectives' (Gilson, 1955). Certainly, 'the condemnation of 1277 does indeed signify or symbolise some critical turning point in the history of medieval thinking' (Emery and Speer, 2001, p. 3). Duhem saw it as the beginning of modern science, when the Church effectively condemned Aristotelianism and Neoplatonism, and thus opened the way to the new physics. His work on medieval science was extended by Dijksterhuis and Michalski. It was subsequently criticized by Koyré, Maier and Clagett, who maintained that there was less continuity between medieval science and modern sciences than Duhem supposed; Grant (1977) considered that Duhem's thesis was 'exaggerated and indefensible'. More recently, Duhem's thesis has been supported by the discovery of continuity between the work of the Parisian philosophers and Galileo. Further support was provided by Jaki, Gilson, and Arieu and Barker (see Murdoch, 2000, p. 23). Additional studies were made by Klaaren (1977), Grant (1981, p. 211), Murdoch (1991, p. 253) and Lindberg (1992, 2000, p. 259).

A serious defect of Duhem's work (1956, ch. IV) was his undervaluing the importance of medieval logic, especially as studied in the Mertonian school in Oxford. Many recent studies have shown its key role in the development of natural philosophy (Wilson, 1956). This attitude to the Mertonian school is not unconnected with Duhem's fervent French patriotism and his fulsome praise of French genius compared with the weak minds of the English physicists.

Although some of Aristotle's ideas were rejected as inconsistent with the Christian faith, he still retained immense prestige during medieval times. Following long-standing church tradition, ideas from the Greco-Roman world were welcomed as providing new tools for the understanding of Scripture and the development of theology (Grant, 2002, p. 34).

Aristotle believed that the world is eternal, but it has always been the Christian belief, following the opening phrases of the Old Testament and reiterated by the Fourth Lateran Council, that God created everything from nothing. One of the medieval philosophers, Jean Buridan, was particularly interested in the nature of motion. This is the most fundamental problem of physics, and so if science is to begin at all it must begin here. Impelled by his belief in creation, Buridan (quoted by Jaki, 1974, p. 233) wrote that 'God, when He created the world, moved each of the celestial orbs as he pleased, and in moving them He impressed on them impetuses which moved them without Him having to move them anymore except by the method of general influence whereby He concurs as co-agent in all things which take place'.

An eternal universe also requires God's creative and sustaining power, and Aquinas (see Baldner and Carroll, 1997) considered that we know only by revelation that the universe was created at the beginning of time. We do not know why God chose this way; perhaps it was because it makes it easier for us to deduce His existence. There are also philosophical arguments against an eternal universe, from Bonaventure (Gilson, 1955, p. 338; Baldner, 1989) to Craig and Smith (1993).

Buridan's concept of impetus reinterprets the dictum of Aristotle, who required the continuing action of the mover throughout the motion, by saying that the mover is now located within the body. Buridan also said that the impetus is proportional to the mass of the body and to its velocity, so it is equivalent to the concept of momentum; this insight became Newton's first law of motion. Buridan's works were widely published and his ideas became known throughout Europe, to Leonardo da Vinci and to the scientists of Renaissance times. Buridan's work thus played a key role in the transition from the qualitative and often erroneous speculations of Aristotle to the rigorous quantitative dynamics of Newton. This transition, and especially the degree of continuity between medieval and Renaissance concepts, is the subject of much scholarly study (Maier, 1949 in Damico, 2000, p. 41; Clagett, 1959; Truesdall, 1968; Weisheipl, 1976; Grant, 1981a and b; Barbour, 1989).

The Christian belief in the creation of the world by God also undermined Aristotle's sharp distinction between celestial and terrestrial matter. Since they are both created, why should they be different? Indeed, Buridan illustrated his concept of impetus with reference to the long jump; thus implicitly presupposing that celestial and terrestrial motions are similar. This made it possible for Newton to see that the same force that pulls an apple to the ground also keeps the moon in its orbit.

Belief in the Order of Nature

A vital component in the rise of science is the belief in the order of the world, that is the idea that every event is the precise result of preceding events. This implies that whatever measurements we make should correspond exactly, that is within the uncertainties of measurement, with our theories. A corollary to this is that if we want to test our theories, we should make the most accurate measurements we can. This insistence on precision is essential for the progress of science. An illustration of this is the work of Kepler on the orbit of the planet Mars. Some very accurate measurements had been made of its position by Tycho Brahe, probably the most accurate that could be made before the invention of the telescope. Kepler resolved to find the orbit. He believed, following Aristotle, that the orbit was circular, as befits incorruptible celestial matter. He found that indeed it is very nearly a circle, but however hard he worked, he could not make it fit Tycho's measurements. He could find a circular orbit that agreed with the measurements to about ten minutes of arc, but not to two, which was the accuracy of the measurements. Many people would have said that this was good enough, and gone on to do something else. But it was not good enough for Kepler, who believed that the fit must be exact, within the uncertainties of the measurements. So he toiled on and on for years, until he finally realized that he could never get the circle to fit. Then he tried an ellipse, and now the orbit could be fitted. This was a breakthrough that made possible Newton's work on the planetary orbits, when he showed from his theory of celestial dynamics that they must indeed be ellipses.

This vital stage in the development of science was made possible by the strong belief in the order of nature. This is what led Whitehead to say, in his Lowell lectures in 1925 (Whitehead, 1926, p. 17) that 'the Middle Ages formed one long training of the intellect of Western Europe in the sense of order'. This by itself is not enough, and he went on:

> I do not think that I have even yet brought out the greatest contribution of medievalism to the formation of the scientific movement. I mean the inexpugnable belief that every detailed occurrence can be correlated with its antecedents in a perfectly definite manner, exemplifying general principles. Without this belief the incredible labours of scientists would be without hope. It is this instinctive conviction, vividly poised before the imagination, which is the motive power of research:– that there is a secret, a secret which can be unveiled.

He went on to ask why this conviction was so vividly implanted on the European mind, and concluded: 'My explanation is that the faith in the possibility of science, generated antecedently to the development of modern scientific theory, is an unconscious derivative from medieval theology' (ibid., p. 17). One might indeed query whether unconscious is the right word, for many of the medievals explicitly saw their work as showing forth the works of the Creator.

The change from the medieval Aristotelian view of the world to that of modern science took place gradually over several centuries. Much is attributable to the unpredictable contributions of individuals of genius, but most is understandable as an inevitable historical development. Some changes were due to direct contradictions between Aristotelian physics and Christian revelation. Thus the unique Incarnation of Christ replaced the concept of eternal recurrence or circular time by linear time with a beginning and an end, and the belief that the universe was created in time forced the abandonment of Aristotle's view that the universe was eternal. Other changes were due to observations made by Galileo and other scientists. Some of these, such as the discovery of sunspots, the mountains on the moon and supernovae directly contradicted Aristotle's view of the immutability of the celestial realm. His theories of dynamics, and in particular his belief that objects fall with velocities proportional to their masses, were also disproved by Galileo. Other discoveries, such as that of the satellites of Jupiter and the phases of Venus, provided exceptions to Aristotle's belief that everything revolves around one centre, and supported the dynamical possibility that the planets all move around the sun. The whole process of discrediting Aristotelian physics was facilitated by the increased precision of the experimental apparatus and by the development of mathematics that enabled the new knowledge to be expressed more concisely and more easily related to other knowledge.

The transition from Greek to modern physics has been graphically described by Duhem (1956, pp. 3–4, quoted in Jaki, 1984, pp. 428–9; see also Duhem, 1985):

> From the start of the fourteenth century the grandiose edifice of Peripatetic physics was doomed to destruction. Christian faith had undermined all its essential principles; observational science, or at least the only observational science that was somewhat developed – astronomy – had rejected its consequences. The ancient monument was about to disappear; modern science was about to replace it. The demolition of Aristotelian physics was not a sudden collapse; the construction of modern physics did not take place on a terrain where nothing was left standing. From one to the other the passage took place by a long sequence of partial transformations of which each pretended to retouch or enlarge some piece of the edifice without changing anything of the ensemble. But when all these modifications of detail had been made, the human mind perceived, as it sized up with a single look all that long work, that nothing remained of that ancient palace and that a new palace rose in its place. Those who in the sixteenth century took stock of this substitution of one science by another were seized by a strange illusion. They imagined that this substitution was sudden and that it was their own work. They proclaimed that Peripatetic physics had just collapsed under their blows and that on the ruins of that physics they had built, as if by magic, the clear abode of truth. About the sincere illusion or arrogantly wilful error of these men, the men of subsequent centuries were either the unsuspecting victims or sheer accomplices. The physicists of the sixteenth century were celebrated as creators to whom the world owed the renaissance of science. They were very often but continuers and sometimes plagiarisers.

It was Duhem (see Jaki, 1984, 1991) who was primarily responsible for uncovering the evidence for the birth of modern science in the Middle Ages. He was a theoretical physicist working mainly in the field of thermodynamics, but had always been interested in the history of science. He was asked to write a series of articles on the history of dynamics, and easily wrote the first one on the ideas of the ancient Greeks. Like most historians of science at that time, he expected to pass rapidly over the Middle Ages to the giants of the Renaissance. But he was a careful man, not content to rely on secondary sources. He found obscure references to the work of Jordanus de Nemore and, following them up, primarily in the archives of the Sorbonne in Paris, he discovered the work of Buridan and his pupil Oresme, and of many other medievals who contributed to the origin of science.

Duhem subsequently wrote two volumes on the history of mechanics, three on Leonardo da Vinci, and then began a monumental account of the history of science in ten volumes, the *Système du Monde*. The first volume, devoted to the Greeks, was published in 1913, and was highly praised by the historian of science George Sarton, founder and editor of the journal *Isis*, who said that he looked forward eagerly to the second volume. When, however, he read the second volume, he realized that what Duhem had found was highly uncongenial to his secularist beliefs. Duhem left him in no doubt whatever. Writing on the Doctrine of the Great Year, the belief that history continually repeats itself in a series of unending cycles, he said:

> To the construction of that system all disciples of Hellenistic philosophy – Peripatetics, Stoics, Neo-Platonists – contributed; to that system Abu Masar offered the homage of the Arabs; the most illustrious rabbis, from Philo of Alexandria to Maimonides, have accepted it. To condemn it and to throw it overboard as a monstrous superstition, Christianity had to come. (Duhem, 1915, p. 390, quoted in Jaki, 1984, p. 403)

Sarton did not try to refute Duhem; that would have been impossible. Instead he used the one remaining weapon, that of silence. None of the following volumes were reviewed in *Isis*, and the name Duhem was hardly ever mentioned. In Sarton's own vast volumes on the history of science Duhem received very few mentions, whereas quite minor figures receive extensive discussion. The weapon of silence is still in use today in certain scholarly circles.

Tragically, Duhem died in 1916 when only five volumes of his *Système du Monde* had been published. Duhem left the text of the remaining five volumes in MSS, and the publisher was bound by the terms of the contract to publish them in successive years. The secularist establishment was, however, bitterly opposed to their publication, and succeeded in preventing this for forty years, despite the continuing efforts of his colleagues and of his daughter Hélène (Jaki, 1992). Only the death of his most determined opponent, and the threat of legal action, finally forced the publishers to act, and the remaining volumes were published in 1954–57.

Duhem is now recognized as the pioneer of the history of medieval science, and indeed as the founder of the history of science as a scholarly discipline. Clagett (1979, quoted by Truesdell, 1984, p. 175) has remarked that 'so rich were Duhem's investigations ... that ... the succeeding study of medieval mechanics has been largely devoted to an extension or refutation of Duhem's work'. His work on medieval science has been continued by many scholars, such as Alistair Crombie, J. H. Randall, Marshall Clagett, Anneliese Maier, Edward Grant, E. A. Moody, Charles Haskins and Dana Durand, who have generally confirmed his work, while correcting it in details. It is thus no longer possible to ignore the scientific work carried out in the Middle Ages that laid the foundations of modern science.

While Duhem's achievement in revealing the development of medieval science is beyond dispute, there remains the question of the contribution attributable to Christian theology. The medieval philosophers and theologians were themselves Christians, but it can be asked whether there is a connection between their personal beliefs and their scientific work.

The beliefs about the material world that form the essential basis of science came from the Greeks and the Hebrews, and these were later reinforced by specifically Christian beliefs. Modern science began in the High Middle Ages when for the first time in history there was a society permeated by these beliefs. It is thus plausible to see a connection between these events and, following Duhem, many writers have supported this thesis (for example Caldin, 1949; Foster, 1934–36; Hesse, 1954; Hooykaas, 1972; Jaki, 1974, 1978, 1984, 1988; Smethurst, 1955), while others have rejected it (Gruner, 1975).

Coincidence in time is insufficient to prove a causal relationship, and so many studies have been made of possible causal influences such as the link between the work of Buridan and the doctrine of creation already mentioned.

Account should also be taken of several aspects of Christian teaching that seem to militate against scientific study. Christianity teaches that the purpose of our lives concerns our spiritual destiny, and all else is frivolous distraction, to be avoided as perilous for our salvation. The natural world may be contemplated as the work of God, but not brutally assaulted by scientific experiments. Against this, one may argue that it may be our Christian duty to study the world, and for the scientist contemplation is not only thinking about God, but also thinking about His works in the light of present knowledge. This is the typical activity of theoreticians and leads to theories that can be tested by further experiments. For Aquinas, the active life follows from contemplation, but the active life is also a preparation for the contemplative life. This exactly parallels the interaction between theory and experiment that lies at the heart of scientific research.

Augustine was interested in the natural world mainly because it provided signs to spiritual truths, and he also realized that it is essential for Christians to be familiar with the science of the day so that they can meet attacks on the faith. Scientific studies lead to knowledge of the works of the Creator, and many scientists are motivated by this consideration. To believe that matter is evil would make science psychologically impossible: this is the Manichean heresy condemned by the Church. Scientific study must be undertaken for its own sake for it to be fruitful. Subsequently its results may be found to have practical applications that can be welcomed, but this possibility cannot be the initial motive power of research.

While it has happened historically that Christian beliefs contributed to the rise and development of science, it remains possible that the necessary beliefs could have been obtained in different ways. Neither can it be reasonably said that the Greek, Hebrew and Christian beliefs inevitably led to modern science. Modern science was reached by a rather narrow path that depended on a series of unlikely features of the world and also on the unpredictable genius of its founders.

Science in Eastern Christendom

This explanation of the rise of science in Western Europe during the High Middle Ages as due to the beliefs concerning the material world inherent in Christian theology raises the question why it happened in Western Europe and not in Eastern Europe, where Christianity also flourishes. One might indeed have expected science to arise first in the East, because it was the heir to the wisdom of ancient Greece, preserved and to some extent developed by Arab scholars. Thus from the eighth to the fourteenth centuries mathematics, astronomy, optics, physics and medicine were far more developed in Islamic countries than in Western Europe. In one vital area, for example, Arabic astronomers had so improved the Ptolemaic system that it was mathematically equivalent to the Copernican system, although it was still geocentric. And yet the lead was lost in one area after another as the West surged ahead and Arabic science decayed. This learning came to the West not via Eastern Christendom, but mainly through translations from the Arabic made in Spain. The Byzantine scientific tradition lacked originality, being content with the achievements of the Greeks and the Romans. Byzantine scientists were thus unable to develop technology and to apply their theoretical knowledge for practical purposes.

Could the explanation of the difference between the vitality of science in the West and its virtual absence in the East be due to a difference between Eastern and Western theologies, or are there other explanations, perhaps in terms of sociological factors, which themselves may or may not have their origin in theology?

The theological beliefs of Eastern and Western Christendom are essentially the same, but there are important differences at the conceptual and practical levels. These differences are difficult to describe, because there are many counter-examples to any general statement that can be made. Thus both attach high value to reason and to prayer, but the emphasis is different. In the West, scholarly work is itself considered to be a form of prayer. Orders of friars, such as the Dominicans, were founded to preach, and to teach in schools and in universities, and their times of prayer are regulated to allow time for study. Dominicans such as Thomas Aquinas taught in the universities and used reason to find out what they could about God, thus developing scholastic theology. In the monasteries of the East, the monks spend long hours in contemplative prayer and thus attain a knowledge of God, but as a result they inevitably have less time for study and for writing.

Of great importance for the origin of science is the concept of time. Before the advent of science our activities followed biological time, governed by the natural processes of night and day, the phases of the moon and the progression of the seasons. In contrast, scientific time is a regular sequence, and to each instant there corresponds a number, measurable to high accuracy. Monasteries need to have a way of marking the time to regulate the hours of prayer and work. Initially they followed biological time, supplemented by sand and water clocks. In the Western monasteries, clocks of high sophistication were developed as early as the twelfth century, whereas clocks, imported from the West, were not used on Mount Athos until the eighteenth century. Even now, the East has a more relaxed sense of time.

The use of biological time is associated with primitive technology, whereas more developed technology comes with scientific time. Thus the larger Western monasteries made many technological advances for domestic and industrial purposes, such as watermills and saws. This is of crucial importance for the development of science.

There are also several sociological reasons why science arose in the West and not in the East. It is essential for creative intellectual work that there are places where it can be carried on without external interference, so that the people there are free to think what they like and to follow wherever their reason leads them. Such opportunities are provided by universities, and many were founded in the West from the twelfth century onwards. The crucial steps that led to the birth of modern science took place in the University of Paris.

In the East, there was a spectacular intellectual and artistic revival in the ninth century after the end of the iconoclastic controversy, and the University of Constantinople attracted many distinguished scholars. There was, however, little interest in science or technology.

Byzantine society was rigidly authoritarian, with Church and State closely linked. The emperor was considered the viceregent of God, and as ruler of both Church and State his word was law. There was a highly centralized state organization with a well-developed civil service, so that practically all activities were controlled by the emperor. Trade and commerce were rigidly controlled, not to serve the interests of the merchants, but to subordinate economic life to the interests of the State. There were indeed schools, but they did not encourage independent discussion, and the static conception of life was not conducive to the development of science. In the West, on the other hand, the universities were centres of intellectual discussions, where novel views were expounded and discussed.

People speak and discuss freely when they are personally secure, when they know that they can say what they like without danger of any kind. This security can be provided by belonging to an organization, such as a university, which encourages free discussions, or by a society that respects the right of private property. In the West this is legally established, whereas in the East property was held subject to the will of the ruler, and might at any time be revoked. If one lives in perpetual fear that the ruler will suddenly take away one's house, one is hardly likely to indulge in any activity that may incur his wrath.

In the twelfth century the Crusaders caused consternation in Byzantium as they passed through on their way to the Holy Land, exacerbating the age-old tensions between East and West. These came to a head with the sack of Constantinople in 1204. Byzantium survived another two hundred years, but was fatally weakened and finally fell to the Turks in 1453.

Such sociological factors are sufficient to explain why science did not arise in Eastern Christendom, and it seems that these are more important than any theological differences.

An instructive example of the effect of sociological factors on intellectual activity is provided by the contrast between the English, French and Spanish colonies in North and Central America on the one hand, and the Dutch colony in South Africa on the other. In America, there was from the first a thriving intellectual activity, with printing presses and newspapers, and great colleges and universities were founded within a few decades of the arrival of the colonists. Mexico was conquered in 1521, and by 1553 had a university. In North America, the colonists arrived in 1619, and Harvard was founded in 1636. In South Africa, on the other hand, everything was controlled by the Dutch East India Company, and profit was the only motive. There were no printing presses, newspapers, colleges or universities. The Calvinist Church was also partly to blame for this situation, because it insisted that its ministers be trained in Holland, and was not willing to establish colleges in South Africa.

Conclusions

Modern science is the fruit of many historical developments over several millennia. It was made possible first of all by the revelation to the Jews, God's chosen people, then by the intellectual achievements of the ancient Greeks and also by the gradual formation of organized and civilized societies. The Jews were the first to recognize the one supreme God, creator of an ordered world that is open to the human mind. The Greeks asked the fundamental questions about the natural world and laid the foundation of the mathematical language that must be used to answer them. The growth of civilized societies provided the essential stability and order without which science is impossible. Yet all this, great and impressive though it is, was not enough to establish science as the ongoing self-sufficient activity that we know today. The destruction of the belief in eternal recurrence that prevented the rise of science in all ancient cultures was the unique achievement of Christianity. It was only in the Middle Ages, in a society permeated by Christian beliefs, that modern science was finally born. The Church founded the universities, where free discussion could take place, and fostered a culture that encouraged interest in the natural world. The pioneers of science were inspired to reveal God's world and thereby to give Him glory, and were conscious of the organic connection between their Christian beliefs and their scientific work. Their Christian beliefs furthermore encouraged them to apply the fruits of their work for the benefit of their fellow men. Modern science never developed in pre-Christian cultures, and it is stifled in cultures that have rejected or ignored their Christian heritage.

This brief survey shows that there are many factors of importance for the rise of science: material, sociological and theological. The material conditions are found in many civilizations, but on their own are not decisive. A very special set of beliefs about the material world is necessary before science can begin, and these beliefs are provided by Christian theology. For science to develop, society must encourage the freedom of thought, and this partly depends on sociological factors, which are themselves often determined by theological beliefs. In all these ways, Christian theology has proved decisive for the birth and development of modern science (see Templeton and Herman, 1989, p. 8).

It cannot be proved that modern science could not have developed in the absence of Christian beliefs about the material world. As it is, they played an important role in bringing about the transition from the science of the ancient Greeks to the physics of the modern world.

CHAPTER 3

The Muslim Centuries[1]

Introduction

The Muslim civilization dominated the known world from the eighth to the fourteenth century, and Islam remains a worldwide power. Together with Christianity, it is the only religion that seeks to bring the whole of mankind into its fold. At the height of its temporal power the Muslim civilization controlled a vast territory from the Pyrenees, through Spain and the coastal regions of North Africa, to Baghdad and beyond as far as the Pamirs. Muslim armies crossed the Pyrenees into France as far as Poitiers and in the East captured Constantinople, invaded the Balkans and reached the gates of Vienna. The literary heritage of ancient Greece first passed to the Byzantine Empire. There the Nestorian Church was established in the fifth century. The Nestorians were persecuted by the Byzantines and emigrated to Mesopotamia, where they founded a centre of intellectual activity at their capital Gondisapur (Jundishapur). There they translated many of the Greek works on philosophy, science and medicine into Syriac. This city became the scientific centre of the new Islamic Empire. From there many scholars came to their capital Damascus in the late seventh and early eighth century; they were mainly Jews and Nestorian Christians (O'Leary, 1949; Sabra, 1987). Through them the Muslim scholars inherited the works of the ancient Greeks and extended their knowledge, particularly in medicine, mathematics, astronomy and philosophy. Early in the ninth century, the caliphs Harun al-Rashid and al-Memun founded a school for translation and a library in Baghdad, and this soon surpassed Gondisapur as a scholarly centre. Means were provided for Christian scholars to travel to collect Greek manuscripts and bring them back for translation. The Nestorian Christian Ibn Masawagh headed an institute in Baghdad that translated ancient texts. His pupil Hunayn wrote many medical treatises and translated all the known Greek works into Arabic. Indian, Syriac and Persian texts were also translated (Singer, 1959). This willingness to learn from other civilizations was emphasized by the scientist and philosopher Ibn Ya'qub al-Kindi: 'We ought not to be ashamed of appreciating truth and of acquiring it wherever it comes from, even if it comes from races different from us.' In this way they learned Greek philosophy and science, Persian literature, Indian medicine and mathematics, and some aspects of Egyptian and Babylonian science (Hoodbhoy, 1991, p. 96). The diffusion of new knowledge throughout the Islamic Empire was greatly facilitated from the

[1] I am grateful to Professor Mehdi Golshani for kindly suggesting many corrections and additions to this chapter.

❦

end of the seventh century by the ready availability of paper, made by techniques learned from the Chinese.

As a result of this scholarly activity, the Islamic Empire in its prime was far more advanced than the Western powers. Unified by a well-developed language, extending over most of the civilized world, possessing numerous libraries and astronomical observatories, with a tradition of technical excellence and a respect for learning and many thinkers of high intelligence, it would seem to be well placed to become the cradle of modern science. And yet in the following centuries the lead was lost and the West surged ahead, eventually to reach heights far greater than the Muslims ever achieved. The writings of the Greeks arrived in the West around the end of the thirteenth century; Buridan made the critical breakthrough soon after. Copernicus followed in 150 years and Newton in 350 years and, based on his work, came the enormous technological achievements of the next 300 years. Although they had a start of 500 years, Muslim scholars never developed modern science themselves, and eventually had to learn it from the West. How and why this happened is one of the most momentous historical questions.

Before discussing this, some of the achievements of Islamic scientists will be briefly surveyed. More detailed accounts of this and related questions have been given by Nasr (1987) and by Iqbal (2002). It should be mentioned that our present knowledge of Islamic science is very incomplete as there are very many unpublished manuscripts that have not been analysed.

Medicine

Basing themselves on Greek authors, many branches of medicine were developed in the Muslim world. The Bukht-Yishu, a family of several generations of scholars, translated many Greek medical works and spread medical knowledge through the Islamic world. The learned Nestorian Hunayn Ibn Ishaq translated most of the medical writings of Galen into Arabic and thus assured Galen's pre-eminence in the following centuries. He also translated the Hippocratic writings. This work was carried on by his son, also named Hunayn, who also practised medicine and wrote medical treatises. One of the greatest Arabic writers on medicine was al-Razi, who wrote a treatise on smallpox and measles, many popular works and a vast encyclopedia of medicine that was reprinted many times during the following centuries The Persian Ali Ibn-Sina (better known as Avicenna) was primarily a philosopher, but also wrote a large systematic treatise on medicine, which was extensively used in medieval times. Medicine was practised throughout the Islamic Empire, hospitals were established in many cities, and the care of the sick was given high priority. In Spain, the Jewish court physician Hasdai ben Shaprut translated into Arabic a manuscript of Discorides on medicine and botany. Particular attention was paid to ophthalmology, a subject of great practical importance in dusty countries. In Damascus the Christian physician Ibn al-Quff taught medicine and wrote one of the first treatises on surgery.

Mathematics

The Greeks developed geometry, and the Hindus arithmetic and algebra, and this knowledge passed to the Muslims. The Persian al-Kwarizmi wrote on algebra in Arabic and showed how mathematical methods can be used to solve inheritance problems. The mathematician Tabit Ibn-Korra translated the works of Euclid, Apollonius, Archimedes and Ptolemy, and developed geometrical methods to solve cubic equations. The poet Omar Khayyam classified algebraic equations and explored the connections between algebra and geometry. Other Arab mathematicians include al-Battani and Abu-al-Wafa, who derived trigonometrical formulae. The Arabs applied mathematics to physical and astronomical problems. Many advances were made in arithmetic, algebra, geometry and trigonometry, as we are reminded by Arabic terms such as algebra and logarithm.

Astronomy

Many astronomical observatories were established in Muslim countries, from Cordoba in Spain to Baghdad, Isfahan and Damascus in the East. Ptolemy's *Almagest* was translated into Arabic, together with Sanskrit writings on astronomy. Observations of solar phenomena were made in observatories in Baghdad and Damascus, and astronomical tables were published. The greatest Arab astronomer al-Battani (Albategnius) carefully re-examined the work of Ptolemy, obtained more accurate values for the obliquity of the ecliptic and the precession of the equinoxes, and discovered that the direction of the sun's eccentric is changing. The positions of the planets and stars were measured, and eclipses predicted. Astronomy was also important for navigation, and many instruments were made to fix the positions of ships by observing the stars. Extensive tables of stellar positions were compiled for this purpose. Sundials were made to determine the times of prayer. The astrolabe was known in early times, and was described by the Syrian Nestorian Severus Sabokt in the seventh century and by the Baghdad Jew Messahala a century later. The earliest known astrolabes are Islamic from the tenth century, and were extensively used in medieval times. Much research was devoted to determining the direction of Mecca, so that the mosques could be correctly oriented. Arab astronomers were well advanced in theoretical astronomy, and some of their work anticipated that of Copernicus. Thus in Chinguetti in Mauritania, the seventh holy city of Islam, the Bibliothèque Al Halott in the old quarter contains thousands of ancient manuscripts, including a copy of the Koran brought from Mecca in 1000 and a book dating from the fourteenth century containing a diagram showing the planets of the solar system circling the sun (Palin, 2002, p. 95). In Spain astronomical studies were made in Cordoba and Toledo, where the astronomer Arzachel complied the Toledan Tables of star positions in 1080. In Seville, al-Bitrugi (Alpetragius) wrote a textbook on astronomy that improved on the system of Ptolemy and influenced Grosseteste and Albertus Magnus. Subsequently, al-Kahalili in the fourteenth century compiled a very accurate set of astronomical tables based on the observations of the Maragha school. Astronomical research continued at the Maragha observatory into the thirteenth and fourteenth centuries.

In the twelfth century scientific work was discouraged due to the influence of al-Ghazali, who thought that it would lead to the loss of belief in the Creator. He maintained that one only needs to know what is required for the performance of duties obligatory for Muslims. Medicine is encouraged for its utility, whereas physics is useless. Muhsin Fayd Kashani thought that knowledge that is not useful for the hereafter is not needed, so that, for example, it is sufficient to learn only the simplest astronomy. Thereafter most scientific writers were Jews, of whom the most eminent was the philosopher Maimonides.

Chemistry

The origin of chemistry is to be found in alchemy, which in turn is based on the belief that all matter is constituted by the same elements in varying proportions. It should therefore be possible to transmute one element to another by altering the proportions. The desirable transmutation of base into noble metals is facilitated by a valuable substance called quintessence or elixir. During their fruitless experiments the alchemists developed many chemical manipulations such as distillation, and identified many useful substances such as mercury, sulphur and camphor. The earliest Arabic writer on alchemy was Jabir (Geber), followed by Rhazes, who also wrote extensively on medicine. Jabir classified minerals as spirits, metals and pulverizable substances. Rhazes had a relatively well-equipped laboratory and was the first to suggest the familiar division into animal, vegetable and mineral. He distinguished six types of mineral: spirits, metals, boraxes, salts, stones and vitriols. Alchemy was practised in Spain, and it was through the Spanish alchemists that their knowledge reached the Latin West. Many of the leading Arabic scholars denounced alchemy as a worthless enterprise.

Physics

One of the earliest Arabic writers on physics was al-Kindi in the ninth century, who worked in Basra and Baghdad on optics, meteorology and the tides. He wrote a treatise summarizing the works of Euclid and Ptolemy, and also discussed the rainbow. At that time there was much interest in the various devices used for irrigation, water wheels and water clocks. Mathematics was applied to problems in statics and optics, and in the twelfth century al-Khazini wrote a treatise on mechanics and hydrostatics. Advances in optics were made by Ibn al-Haithan (Alhazen) in the tenth century. He discussed reflection and refraction, the propagation of light, colours, the rainbow and haloes, and experimented with magnifying glasses. The Persian al-Biruni, physician, astronomer, mathematician, physicist, geographer and historian, was one of the best-known among the scholars in what is known as the Islamic Golden Age. There was a notable controversy between supporters of the atomic theory of matter and the Aristotelianism of the Muslim theologians, who ultimately prevailed.

Philosophy

The vast extent of the Muslim Empire, and the absence of a central religious authority, allowed the proliferation of Muslim schools, often dependent on the patronage of the local ruler. This makes it difficult to generalize about Muslim philosophy. Furthermore, there were many different schools, and only a brief introduction is possible here.

The generally accepted world view was the Neoplatonic version of Aristotelianism, affirming that God is the Creator and ultimate cause of the cosmos, but did not concern Himself directly with its activities. Creation is an emanation from God and proceeds from there to celestial intellects, celestial causes and thence to lower entities. This view was widely accepted and spread through the whole community.

There are three main schools of Muslim theology: the Mu'tazilites who relied on rational arguments, the Asharites who attached central importance to a strictly orthodox interpretation of the Qur'an, and the Shi'ites who relied on rational arguments as well as revelation. All schools tackled the perennial problems of faith and reason. They asked to what extent the God of the Qur'an could be known by natural reason alone. The Mu'tazilite school sought a rational interpretation of the Qur'an. If, according to the Qur'an, God creates everything, then He also creates evil and our evil actions, so what becomes of divine justice and man's punishment? Eventually they concluded that only God and human beings can cause things to happen, and so causation as a result of natural properties was rejected as unintelligible.

The Asharites criticized the Mu'tazilites as sceptical rationalists, and restricted causal agency to God alone. Their founder, the mystic al-Ashari, held that the world consists of atomic events in space and time held together by the will of God, so that there is no connection between cause and effect. He was supported by al-Ghazali, who in his book *The Incoherence of the Philosophers* attacked the Mu'tazilites and emphasized that God is the only cause of all events, so that there is no necessary connection between what appears to be the cause and what appears to be the effect. To believe otherwise would be a denial of God's power. Al-Ghazali approved the 'practical' sciences such as arithmetic and medicine, was sceptical about the value of the 'theoretical' sciences and disapproved of metaphysics and some physical sciences. The mathematician and scientist al-Biruni considered that the natural world should be studied for religious purposes, to provide knowledge of the Creator. He defended the study of astronomy and wrote a book on the determination of latitude and longitude, which is important for establishing the direction of Mecca (Dhanani, 2002, p. 73).

Al-Ghazali's views on causation were contested by Ibn Rushd (Averroës), who believed that science and religious beliefs should be kept entirely separate.

He was a thoroughgoing Aristotelian, wrote extensive commentaries on the works of Aristotle and accepted Aristotelian physics as the final truth about the physical world. Aristotle based his philosophy on eternal truths, so no observations could ever disagree with it. There is thus no need ever to make experiments. The world of Averroës is a pantheistic world in which everything behaves according to an intrinsic necessity. He taught that the world is eternal and is renewed continuously by renewed acts of creation by an external Prime Mover. Thus the world depends on an external cause, but that cause is itself without cause. He also wrote a book called *The Incoherence of the Incoherence of the Philosophers*, which gives detailed answers to the Ashari doctrines. In particular, he maintained that the 'denial of cause implies the denial of knowledge, and the denial of knowledge implies that nothing in the world can really be known'.

The Jewish philosopher Maimonides spent most of his life in Cairo writing on medicine, but is best known through his writings on cosmology, which influenced Aquinas and hence the medieval discussions on creation. He also wrote the *Guide for the Perplexed*, a very popular treatise on philosophy. His work, guided by the Bible, steered between the occasionalism of the Asharites and the pantheism of the Mu'tazilites. He summarized it in words that showed the way to modern science:

> We believe that his universe remains perpetually with the same properties with which the Creator has endowed it, and that none of these will ever be changed except by way of a miracle in some individual instances, or to remove any of its properties. The Universe had, however, a beginning and commencement, for when nothing was yet in existence except God, His wisdom decreed that the Universe be brought into existence at a certain time.

In spite of much original work in many centres, Arabic philosophy and science declined from the thirteenth century onwards. In the following centuries, many Muslim countries were invaded by Western powers, and educational systems based on Western values imposed. This was a mixed blessing: Muslims were glad to learn about Western science, but resented the sidelining of Islamic teaching. When subsequently they obtained independence from the colonial powers, secularism was dominant. The advantages of science and technology were greatly admired, and adopted wherever possible. These momentous changes are described in detail by Iqbal (2002).

Science and the Holy Qur'an (Koran)[2]

The teaching contained in the Qur'an forms the basis of Islamic faith and practice. It consists of more than 750 verses on subjects related in some way to natural phenomena. The prophet emphasized that the 'acquisition

---

[2] This section is based on Golshani (1997).

of knowledge is the duty of every Muslim' and the Qur'an teaches that knowledge must be sought from everyone, even from infidels. Muslim scholars know that religion and science tell us about the Creator, and the vital point is made that God created everything exactly (25: 12). There is order and purpose in nature, since God 'created everything and then ordered it for a purpose' (25: 20) (Golshani, 1997, p. 210). The world is thus ordered, subject to definite laws and to the principle of general causality (p. 224). However, 'the cause of any occurrence is God's will, and it is God's way to create what we call "effect" after what we call "cause", without any relations between them that necessitate the effect to follow the cause. They say: it is not fire that causes the cotton to burn; rather it is Allah who makes the cotton to burn and turns it into ashes; and of course if God does not want fire, the fire will not burn the cotton' (p. 226). Thus God destroys and then recreates the world from instant to instant. This denial of the connection between cause and effect was held, as already remarked, by the philosopher al-Ghazali.

The natural order contains signs of God that may be interpreted to give knowledge of Him. The study of the natural world is therefore encouraged, and this indicates that it is a practicable enterprise: 'We have established you in the earth and made in it means of livelihood for you' (7: 10; p. 82). According to Said Nursi, writing in the twentieth century, the Qur'an is completely consistent with modern science, so science supports the Qur'an (Iqbal, 2002, pp. 269–72). He went too far, however, by attempting to find detailed adumbrations of scientific knowledge there. Others maintained that the Qur'an is not a book that contains scientific knowledge, and so we should not seek it there: 'God did not send down the Qur'an to inform mankind of scientific theories and technological techniques. Whatever is mentioned in the Qur'an about the mysteries of creation and natural phenomena is intended to impel mankind to speculation and enquiry into these matters so that thereby their faith is enhanced' (Mahmud Shaktut in Golshani, 1997, p. 38). Furthermore, the Prophet emphasized that knowledge gained must be freely shared: 'the one who hides knowledge, Allah will seal his mouth with a lash of fire on the day of qiyama' (Iqbal, 2002, p. 150).

Knowledge of the natural world is valued not only for what it teaches us about the Creator, but also for the ways it can be used to strengthen Islamic society. Studies of science and technology should be promoted for this purpose: There is no good in knowledge that does not benefit. The Prophet also says: 'My Lord, save me from useless knowledge' (Golshani, 1997, p. 50). This is not meant in a utilitarian sense, so that, for example, it does not exclude abstract mathematics. As already remarked, Muslims made many important contributions to mathematics. Discrimination is possible for applied knowledge, and the ways to distinguish between useless and useful knowledge were specified by Iman al-Sadiq. Activities that are always good are permitted, and also those, such as making knives, that can be used for good and evil purposes. Activities that are totally corrupt and have no useful result are forbidden; he gives as examples the making of strings for musical instruments, flutes and chess (ibid.,

p. 55). Thus 'from the Qur'anic point of view, the cognition of numbers is not a fruitful occupation except when it helps us to understand the wise Creator of the world (ibid., p. 116).

Ibn al-Haytham considered that truth can only be discovered by the formulation of theories, and these are found in the logic, physics and theology of Aristotle. The knowledge the Qur'an encourages is useful knowledge. According to the Prophet: 'The best fields of knowledge are those that bring benefit' (ibid., p. 53).

Some Muslim scholars such as Tantawi and Sir Sayyid Ahmad Kahn (1817–98) maintained that the Qur'an is not a source of scientific knowledge and tried to interpret it and the Islamic traditions in conformity with science (ibid., p. 38). Others took a different view and claimed that all the sciences are contained in the Qur'an, and that many facts that have recently been discovered can be found there. Such claims are aimed at showing the miraculous nature of the Qur'an. This view was emphasized by Abd al-Rahan al Kwakakibi: 'In recent centuries, science has revealed many facts and these have been attributed to their discoverers who are European or American. But those who examine the Qur'an carefully find that most of these facts were stated, explicitly or implicitly, in the Qur'an thirteen centuries ago' (ibid., p. 98). A French surgeon, M. Bucaille, wrote a book on the Bible, *The Qur'an and Science*, that concluded that whereas the Bible is often wrong when describing natural phenomena, the Qur'an is always correct, and indeed anticipated the discoveries of modern science (Hoodbhoy, 1991, p. 67). The belief that Islam and modern science are consistent was opposed by Sayyed Hosein Nasr, who believes on the contrary that modern science is destroying Islamic faith. He distinguishes between ancient science, which is acceptable because it was principally a way to illustrate theological truths, and modern science, which has a corrosive effect on religion. Other Muslim scholars maintain that the Qur'an is not a source of science and technology, but a book of guidance. It is therefore Allah's will that we find the secrets of nature by using our senses and intellect: 'Go around the globe and find out how He started the Creation' (29: 20). There are also some passages in the Qur'an that 'enjoin thought and meditations on all aspects of creation and require human being to apply their reason and human faculties to the discovery of the secrets of nature' (Golshani, 1997, p. 25), although the emphasis is on attaining knowledge of God the Creator rather than knowledge of the world for its own sake.

More recently, a disciple of Sayyid Ahmad Khan, Syed Ameeer Ali (1849–1924), maintained that Aristotelian philosophy and rationalist thinking are entirely in accord with Islam. He supported the Mu'tazilite philosophers al-Kindi, al-Farabi, Ibn al-Haytham and Ibn Rushd and attributed the decline of Islamic science to fundamentalists such as al-Ashari, Ibn Hanbal, al-Ghazali and Ibn Taymiyya (Hoodbhoy, 1991, p. 58).

These debates on the meaning of the Qur'an are similar to those that took place in the West on the relation between the Bible and science, particularly on concordism and the duty to share knowledge (see Chapters 1 and 2). There is, however, a crucial difference: Christianity has a central authority that can whenever necessary define the meaning of a disputed passage, whereas Islam has no such authority. There are thus many conflicting views on the interpretation of the Qur'an.

The Decline

In spite of all these great achievements, the Muslim civilization went into decline from the end of the fifteenth century onwards. The rate of decline varied from country to country; indeed as late as the fifteenth century there was still an active astronomical observatory at Samarkand. Generally speaking, however, from the twelfth century onwards the lead passed to the West, which soon surpassed the greatest achievements of the Islamic Empire. Modern science was born in the High Middle Ages, and came to maturity in the Renaissance. Nothing remotely similar occurred in the Muslim lands. The Muslim leaders were acute and intelligent men and they saw clearly what was happening but they did not know how to prevent it. What can account for this?

There are two connected problems: first to show why science reached unprecedented heights during the Muslim centuries, and second why the Muslims subsequently failed to make the vital steps that led in the West to modern science.

As shown in the previous section, the Qur'an teaches many of the essential presuppositions of science. Everything is created by God and thereafter behaves in an exact way. Matter is ordered and open to the human mind. Muslims are encouraged to learn more about the natural world and to make use of their discoveries. All these beliefs, together with the heritage of Greek learning and enlightened caliphs and imans, are sufficient to explain why Islamic science developed so well from the seventh century onwards. Nevertheless it did not become part of the educational system and so had little impact on the people as a whole.

Many explanations for the subsequent decline have been suggested, from the technological and sociological to the philosophical and theological (Iqbal, 2002, p. 136). It is an inherently complicated question, particularly due to the paucity of relevant data. Furthermore, it is often taken for granted that the standard against which the development of Islamic science must be judged is Western science, and this ignores the possibility of a different Islamic science. Many analyses of these questions suffer from the defect that they impose 'modern western conceptions on a civilisation whose goals and aims, aspirations and models are vastly different from the modern west' (Iqbal, 2002, p. 143). Some of the suggested reasons for the decline are briefly mentioned below, but much further work is required. Concerning the theological reasons, it is inappropriate for a non-Muslim to try to decide between differing interpretations of the Qur'an; that is best left to Muslim scholars.

First of all there are technological considerations. As the initial expansion of the Muslim civilization depended on the force of arms, so the final decline started with military defeats. In some respects the Muslim armies had superior weapons, including petroleum as an explosive. Although Islam had a long tradition of *jihad*, or Holy War, they disdained to use such cowardly weapons as muskets, and relied on the lance and sword of Mohamed. Gunpowder originated in the East and was used mainly for fireworks, whereas the armies of the West used it in firearms. The Muslim ships were built for relatively placid Mediterranean waters and were no match for Western ships built to withstand Atlantic storms. Frequent warfare among Western powers continually stimulated improvements in the design of ships and weapons.

The West was technologically superior in several other respects. It had far more wind- and watermills, and printing was more highly developed than in Muslim countries. Muslim society was resistant to change, and so gradually its power waned. In 1061 the Normans conquered Sicily, and the Iberian peninsula was steadily regained, from the capture of Toledo in 1085 to the final surrender of the last Muslim kingdom of Grenada in 1492. Far to the East, the Muscovites defeated the Tatars at Kulikovo in 1386, and in 1481 Ivan the Great sealed their defeat in 1480. In 1571 the Muslim fleet was defeated by Don John of Austria at the battle of Lepanto, Malta withstood a siege in 1566 and in 1683 Jan Sobieski threw the Muslim armies back from the gates of Vienna (Lewis, 1995).

The organization of society is critical for the development of science. Science does not flourish in an authoritarian society and needs protected enclaves such as the universities of the West, where free discussion can take place without external constraints. These sociological effects on the development of science have been discussed by Huff (1993) and by Iqbal (2002, pp. 140–51).

Some Muslim scholars still held Aristotelian tenets that are inimical to the development of science. Islamic science lacked the relentless urge to understand the physical world at the deepest level that characterized Western science. After about 1350, due to the dominance of the Asharite school of theology, 'the theological schools excluded all natural science from their curriculum, except classical astronomy and mathematics' (Golshani, 1997, p. 37), and this played a major part in the decline of science in the Muslim world. Some Muslim scholars considered that religion and science were opposed, and this led many Muslims to reject religion. By the thirteenth century, most of the physicians in Muslim society were Jews or Christians.

After an extensive discussion, Iqbal concludes that the real causes of decline are to be found in the

> pleasure-seeking high culture of this age … The courts of Delhi, Istanbul and Isfahan, and now captive of their extravagant routines and almost alienated from the realities of the vast empires they controlled, and the concentration of wealth in fewer and fewer hands are the indicators of a civilisation at the brink of disastrous ruin. The Islamic scientific tradition became a caricature of its past glory. (Iqbal, 2002, p. 169)

The causes of the decline must be sought in these three centres, and 'those who have sought "internal causes" in the very foundation of Islam have misled these efforts for too long and with disastrous results' (ibid.).

Nevertheless, it may be worthwhile to recapitulate some of the theological arguments, and then leave them to the judgement of Islamic scholars. First of all, it may be remarked that pleasure-seeking, extravagant and decadent courts were hardly unknown in the West. In spite of this, as described in the previous chapter, modern science was born in the High Middle Ages in Western Europe, and owed its origin to the Catholic beliefs about the material world. These gradually destroyed the physics of Aristotle that had for two thousand years prevented the growth of modern science, and enabled Buridan, with his firm belief in creation in time, to take the vital first step towards a viable theory of motion. Most Muslim theologians also believed in creation in time, and yet this vital step not taken in the Muslim world.

The only Muslim philosopher who considered inertial motion was ibn-Sina (Avicenna). He began his career by studying the Qur'an in Bukhara, and afterwards read the works of Euclid and Ptolemy, and so was well placed to take the vital step. Although he lived several centuries before Buridan, Avicenna's beliefs were such as to exclude the possibility of anticipating him. He believed in Plotinian emanationism, a form of pantheism that is the opposite of creation. Thus God eternally and necessarily produces the world, but is not a creator. This effectively removed the last opportunity for modern science to be born in the Muslim world (Jaki, 1974, 1988, ch. 9).

Further insights into the failure of Muslim science may be found in the tenets of the Muslim theologians already mentioned. The initial motivation for the study of the natural world comes, in Islam as well as in Christianity, from the desire to know more about the Creator and His works. As these studies proceed, it becomes increasingly evident that studies of the natural world have great intrinsic interest. As we acquire new knowledge and make new discoveries, it becomes an exciting quest. As Richard Feynman (1998, p. 9) remarked in a lecture:

> The work is not done for the sake of an application. It is done for the excitement of what is found out. It is almost impossible for me to convey in a lecture this important aspect, this exciting part, the real reason for science. You cannot understand science and its relation to anything else unless you understand and appreciate the great adventure of our time. You do not live in your time unless you understand that this is a tremendous adventure and a wild and exciting thing.

Note his insistence that the work is done, not for any anticipated application, but for its own sake. New technological advances come from fundamental research, not from research directed towards specific technical needs (see Chapter 1). In this way scientific research becomes a self-sustaining enterprise, carried on by scientists who do not necessarily share the motivation of those who started the whole process.

This ongoing process can be hindered or even stopped in three ways. First, by the debilitating belief, found in all ancient civilizations, that time is cyclic. In the Muslim world this belief was held by al-Kindi and the astrologer Abu-Mashar, but it was rejected by al-Biruni. The belief in a cyclic world discourages progress, and it needed the unique incarnation of Christ to replace it by a linear concept of time (see Chapter 2).

The second is the belief that we have already discovered all that there is to know, that we have reached the end of the road. This belief was held by those who regarded Aristotle as the fount of all knowledge, so that to solve any problem it is sufficient to study his works. For example, it was generally believed in the time of Avicenna that medical knowledge was complete. The belief in the omniscience of Aristotle was gradually broken down by Christian beliefs during the High Middle Ages as described in Chapter 2. It was also believed by some Muslims that the Qur'an contains all that there is to know, even on scientific questions. This is the basis of the story, for which there is little or no historical evidence, that when the invading Muslim armies arrived in Alexandria, they burnt the famous library, saying that the books it contained either repeated what is in the Qur'an, in which case they were superfluous, or they contradicted the Qur'an, in which case they were false. This view is rejected by most Muslim scientists who, like Catholics, believe that the Bible contains truth necessary for our salvation, but nothing about science (see Chapter 1 on the creationists and on the Galileo case). A contemporary example of the debilitating effect of the belief that science has reached the end of the road is provided by the Copenhagen interpretation of quantum mechanics (see Chapter 8).

The third debilitating belief is that science should be pursued only for some extrinsic purpose, and not for its own sake. Islam and Christianity both teach that science should be pursued for the glory of God. This is interpreted in various ways. It is not necessary that scientific studies only teach us about God; related motivations are also encouraged. Thus astronomy must be studied for its contribution to time-keeping and to determine the direction of Mecca. A further acceptable motive is the acquisition of any knowledge that may strengthen Islamic society (Golshani, 1997, p. 17). Although the Qur'an explicitly urges the study of natural phenomena, many Muslims emphasize the importance of practical applications to the detriment of fundamental research. Thus the Professor of Geology at the University of Petroleum and Minerals in Daharan, Saudi Arabia, Raghib El Naggar, rejected the notion of science for science's sake, and considered the social function of science to be more important than science itself. The Vice-President of the King Abdullah Aziz University of Jeddah said that 'under Islam, science is subservient to the goals of society' (Sadar, 1979, p. 354). Eventually this weakens the spirit of enquiry.

Although most Muslim scientists pursue science in order to understand nature, 'it is clear that one of the reasons for the decline of Muslim societies in recent centuries is that they left the study of those [scientific and technical] sciences to others which they deserved to study most, and made themselves dependent on others' (Golshani, 1997, pp. 23, 24). Thus Muslims should equip themselves with the essential of scientific advancement and endeavour to make up their lag in scientific and technical fields.

There are other theological beliefs that are important for the development of science. Science can develop only if the world is believed to be contingent, that is, that it is rational but could be otherwise. This in turn depends on the belief that God is both rational and free so that He freely created the world and gave it an inherent rational nature by which it continues to act unless He decides otherwise. All Muslim philosophers believed in strict causality, together with secondary causes. Of the three schools of theology, the Mu'tazilites and the Shi'ites believed in secondary causes, and only the Asharites denied causality and secondary causes. Their theology emphasizes the freedom of Allah more strongly than the inherent rationality of nature; Allah thus decides from instant to instant how everything behaves. Thus, for instance, it is wrong to say that hydrogen and oxygen combine to form water. Instead, we must say that if hydrogen and water are brought together, by the will of Allah water is created (Hoodbhoy, 1991, p. 54). This is a denial of secondary causality. The theologian al-Ghazali denied causality, saying that any apparent connection is due to the prior decree of God, who creates them side by side (Iqbal, 2002, p. 109). Since science is the search for relations between cause and effect, as they reflect the inherent rationality of things, expressed by exact mathematical formulae, it is inevitably weakened by such beliefs.[3]

Following the teachings of the theolgians al-Ashari, al-Ghazali and others, the fundamentalist interpretations of the Qur'an gradually dominated Muslim society, to the detriment of the more rational interpretation of the Mu'tazilites al-Kindi, Ibn al-Haytham and Ibn Rushd. This school of theology was strongly supported by some Muslim rulers during the eleventh and twelfth centuries, so that by the end of the fourteenth century Islamic science had been practically destroyed. Mu'tazilism was a revolutionary movement within Islam but it was finally rejected, mainly because it exalted reason over revelation.

Although the Asharite mentality has not been prevalent for the last two hundred years, the level of science is still not what it should be. At the present time Muslim countries constitute one-fifth of the world population, more than the USA, Western Europe and Japan combined. And yet the absolute size of the Islamic scientific community is 'incredibly small', less than 1 per cent per capita compared with Israel. With one or two exceptions, there are no great university departments or world-calibre research institutes. There are fewer physicists in all nineteen universities in Pakistan than in Imperial College of the University of London alone. It is not surprising that most Arabic countries remain poor and underdeveloped. In 1999 the combined GNP of all Arab countries amounted to less than that of Spain. The science that now exists in the Muslim world is largely imported from the West. There are some excellent

---

[3] This is illustrated by a story told me by a traveller in Persia. During a journey the car stopped, and the Muslim driver got out to find out why. He unscrewed the cap of the petrol tank and peered inside, using a lighted match. My friend tried to dissuade him, but the driver serenely replied: 'If it is the will of Allah that the petrol explodes, it will explode; if it is not, it will not.' It would, I think, be rather difficult to teach physics to that pious man. For science to flourish, belief in the laws of nature must permeate society.

Muslim scientists, but they have been trained in the West and so have imbibed the necessary presuppositions of science along with the science itself. It remains true that there is rather little highly original science in Muslim countries, and the general level of scientific research is disappointingly low; the most famous contemporary Muslim scientist, Abdus Salam (1987; see also Hoodbhoy, 1991, p. 4), described it as 'abysmal'. The fifty-seven nations in the Islamic world, comprising 1.3 billion people, invest less than 0.2 per cent of their combined GNP in research and development (*Physics World*, April 2003, p. 11). The papers written by their scientists and engineers account for just 2 per cent of the world total. Muslims have readily accepted the technology of the West, and have the resources to pay for it, but in the realm of pure science they lag behind, as they have done for centuries (Golshani, 1997, pp. 72–3).

This had led many scholars to conclude that the decline of Islamic science from its ancient glories is due to the dominance of the fundamentalist Asharite interpretation of the Qur'an. Although this interpretation is held by few Muslim scientists today, its legacy remains. Unless the Qur'an is interpreted in ways that stress the beliefs that led to the birth of modern science in Western Europe in the High Middle Ages it is not easy to see how it will ever be possible to stimulate a truly indigenous renaissance of science in Islamic countries and thereby remove their scientific and technological dependence on the West.

CHAPTER 4

The Renaissance

Introduction

The Renaissance is one of the most brilliant periods of artistic and scientific genius in history. The achievements of classical culture were rediscovered, architecture flourished and artists applied the laws of perspective to give a three-dimensional effect to their paintings. In the same period modern science, born in the Middle Ages through the fundamental work of Grosseteste, Buridan and Oresme, came to maturity with the work of Copernicus and Kepler, Galileo and Newton. Leonardo da Vinci was notable among those who gathered together the ideas of his medieval predecessors, often without acknowledgement, and embodied them in his writings.

Until then, the concepts describing motion, though generally sound, were largely qualitative. It was the great achievement of the Renaissance natural philosophers to make them more precise, to express them numerically, and ultimately to describe their temporal variation by means of differential equations. This was done through studies of the motions of the heavens, particularly of the moon and the planets. The first step was made by Copernicus (1473–1543), who boldly put the sun in the centre of the solar system, thus making possible a theory of planetary motion, and eventually stirring up a theological hornet's nest.

It is essential for the establishment of a scientific theory that its consequences agree with experimental measurements, and it was Tycho Brahe (1546–1601) who made the very careful measurements of the motions of the planets that enabled Kepler (1571–1630) to establish the planetary orbits and the laws of planetary motion.

Meanwhile Galileo (1564–1642) was working on the fundamental dynamical concepts of mass, velocity, acceleration and momentum, expressing them in precise mathematical form and seeing how they related to falling bodies and projectiles. Against his wishes, he also became involved in the debate on the relation of the new scientific ideas to the teaching of the Bible.

Finally Newton (1642–1727) put in place the cornerstone by postulating his laws of motion and developing the differential calculus. This, together with his theory of universal gravitation, enabled him to derive Kepler's laws and to calculate precisely the motions of the moon and of the planets. This achievement established modern science and gave it lasting prestige to the extent that it became the paradigm of intellectual accomplishment. It also led to the idea of the world as a vast mechanism that only needed to be set in motion by God and henceforth would go on for ever without any further action by Him.

Copernicus[1]

Since the earliest times man has observed the motions of the heavenly bodies and noted their regularities. The stars have the same uniform circular motion, as if they are fixed to a gigantic sphere that rotates once every day. The planets are exceptions to this: they have more complicated motions relative to the background of the fixed stars, and the comets come and go at intervals. The sun and the moon have yearly and monthly motions that are familiar to us all.

The ancients from the Babylonians onwards were concerned mainly to describe these motions in a way that would permit accurate predictions. This was necessary to enable them to keep track of the seasons so that they would know when to plant their crops. It was natural to take the earth as the centre and to describe all the motions of heavenly bodies as seen from the earth. Following Aristotle, it was believed that the celestial bodies move in circles. To account for the motions of the planets Ptolemy imagined them to be attached to spheres rolling on spheres so that their motions could be described by a complicated series of cycles and epicycles. This gave the motions of the planets quite well, but as the measurements of the motions became more accurate, more and more epicycles had to be introduced to fit them. Furthermore, Ptolemy's system was purely a description, and gave no physical understanding of why the motions take place as they do.

Copernicus was born in Torun in Poland and, his father dying early, was brought up by his uncle, Lucas Wazelrode, who later became bishop of Varnia. He secured a canonry for his nephew at the cathedral of Frambork (Fraunberg), and Copernicus spent most of his life there dealing with ecclesiastical administration. He studied astronomy in Cracow, and later went to Italy to study canon law in Bologna and subsequently medicine in Padua. As a result of his astronomical studies, he realized that it is altogether simpler to put the sun at the centre and to assume that the earth and planets move around it. This immediately simplified the descriptions of the motions and made them much more coherent and logical. He proposed this as a description of the solar system as it really is, and not just as a convenient calculational tool. This theory immediately encounters the difficulty that if the earth is moving, the stars should appear differently with the seasons. The only way out of this, which was later proved to be correct, is to assume that the stars are at such immense distances away that the motion of the earth makes no difference to their apparent relative positions. However, there was at that time no way of proving this, and so it remained a powerful argument against the heliocentric theory. There are other difficulties: if the earth is moving around the sun it must be moving very rapidly, so why do we not feel a strong wind, why does everything not fly off the earth, and why do not falling bodies lag behind? These difficulties were eventually resolved by Galileo.

---

[1] On Copernicus, see Kesten (1945).

Tycho Brahe[2]

It often happens that important scientific advances are made possible only by more accurate measurements. It is interesting to ask why scientists often devote their lives to increasing the precision of measurements. If all we want to do is to understand what we know already, why go to the trouble? If the new results agree with what we know, we have wasted our time, and if they do not, we give ourselves much more trouble trying to understand them. The reason lies in the passion of scientists to know more about the world, and this knowledge can only come from the comparison of our theories with the most accurate experimental data.

Tycho Brahe devoted thirty-five years of his life to the task of making the most accurate measurements of the positions of the stars and the planets that were possible at that time, before the invention of the telescope. He erected huge instruments at his observatory and made a large number of observations. These were inherited by Kepler, who used them to calculate the orbits of the planets more accurately than ever before.

Brahe also proposed an alternative to the Copernican system, in which the earth remained stationary and all the planets revolved around the sun, which itself revolved around the earth. This system had the advantages that it agreed with observations, avoided theological difficulties and kept the earth in the centre, in agreement with Aristotle. However, it never became popular because it seemed rather contrived, an uneasy compromise between the geocentric and heliocentric systems, and also it could not be modelled with solid spheres.

Kepler[3]

The life of Kepler shows clearly the importance of fundamental beliefs for our work. Kepler followed Plato in his appreciation of the value of numbers. He went so far as to say that our knowledge of numbers is of the same kind as God's. He passionately believed in the order in the universe, and his life's work was to bring order, exact numerical order, into our knowledge of the heavens.

He worked with Tycho Brahe and soon realized the value of the immense treasure that he had accumulated by a lifetime of measurements. He saw that he could use them to calculate the orbits of the planets, which, of course, following Aristotle, he believed to be circular, as befits perfect incorruptible celestial matter. He tried to compute the orbit of Mars and indeed found that it is nearly circular but, as mentioned in Chapter 2, however hard he worked he could not find a circle that fitted Brahe's measurements.

Kepler was not concerned only with geometry; he wanted to understand the origin of the planetary motions. He asked himself: 'If the sun is indeed the

---

[2] On Brahe, see Dreyer (1965), Thoren (1990) and Christianson (2000, 2003).

[3] On Kepler, see Caspar, Max ([1962], 1993), Koestler (1959, 1961), Kozhamthadam (1994) and Barker and Goldstein (2001).

origin and source of planetary motions, then how does this fact manifest itself in the motions of the planets themselves?' He found that Mars moves a little faster when it is nearer to the sun and a little slower when it is further from the sun. After five years' work he discovered that a line (the radius vector) from the sun to the planet sweeps out equal areas in equal times. This does not by itself determine the shape of the orbit, but after three more years' work he found that the orbit is an ellipse. This was a watershed in the history of science, as it finally destroyed Aristotelian physics and opened the way to Newton's theory of planetary orbits. This breakthrough was made possible by Kepler's belief in the order of nature, in a mathematically and numerically exact order that followed from his belief in the rationality of the world created by God. He continued his work and also found that the square of the period of a planet is proportional to the cube of its mean distance from the sun.

It took Kepler over twenty years to establish his three laws by a most arduous analysis of Brahe's measurements. In his early work, *Mysterium Cosmographicum* in 1596, he exclaimed: 'Oh that we could see the day when both sets of figures agree with each other!' When he had discovered the third law, twenty-two years later, he was able to say in a reprint of his book: 'We have lived to see this day after twenty-two years and rejoice in it.'

Kepler thought about the dynamics of the solar system and, following Gilbert's ideas on magnetism, he suggested that every material body is attracted to every other material body. However he was unable to specify the form of this attraction, or to use it to obtain his three laws of planetary motion. That was ultimately the achievement of Newton. Before that could be done, dynamics had to be made a quantitative science, and that was the work of Galileo.

Galileo

Despite the pioneering work of Buridan and Oresme, Copernicus and Kepler, the prevailing view of the world in Renaissance times was still that of Aristotle. It was a world of purpose that could be understood by general philosophical reasoning. It is primarily due to Galileo that this was replaced by the more modern view that the world is a mechanism that we can understand through the use of mathematics. He said, in effect, that purpose has no place in physics, and that bodies move following mathematical laws that we must discover by experiment. We must abandon the absurdly optimistic idea that we can somehow intuit the essences of things, and from that intuition deduce their properties. We no longer speculate about the causes of motion; instead we devote ourselves to the humble yet practicable task of describing motion as accurately as possible using the language of mathematics.

During the Middle Ages, Bradwardine, Dumbleton, Heytesbury and Swineshead, who formed the Mertonian school of natural philosophers in Oxford, considered motion in a more quantitative way, and formulated the mean speed theorem. This says that a uniformly accelerated body moves the same distance in a given time as another body that moves for the same time with the average speed of the first body over that distance. At that time it was a great achievement to make such quantitative statements without the benefit of modern mathematical notation; now it is an easy problem for school-children.

Kepler realized the importance of numerical accuracy in describing how the planets move, and established the laws of planetary motion. Galileo did the same for motions on the surface of the earth. He studied how balls roll down an inclined plane, and how projectiles move through the air, and was able to express the results in simple laws connecting positions, velocities and times.

The fundamental ideas of dynamics were established qualitatively by Buridan and his successors, and subsequently there was much discussion about the motions of falling bodies and of projectiles, in particular about the relationships between the distance fallen, the time taken and the velocity acquired: is there some simple relationship such as the velocity being proportional to the time taken or to the distance fallen? What are the trajectories of projectiles? Are they simple geometrical curves? Concepts such as momentum and energy were only refined to their present precision by centuries of effort, and the first step was to answer these fundamental questions about motion.

Although his work had the effect of discrediting Aristotelian physics, Galileo still remained an Aristotelian in many respects. He failed to appreciate the importance of Kepler's work, and continued to believe that the orbits of the planets were circular.

Galileo realized the importance of accurate measurements, but was in a more difficult situation than Kepler. Long times, such as the periods of rotation of the planets, can be measured quite accurately by primitive means, but it is far more difficult to measure accurately the much shorter time taken by a body to fall a measured distance. Galileo used his own pulse to measure the period of swing of a lamp in the cathedral of Pisa, and found that it is independent of the amplitude. For a falling body a more accurate measure is needed, and he used a thin jet of water coming from a large jar, weighing the amount that came out during the fall. He further increased the accuracy by allowing a ball to roll down an inclined plane instead of falling freely, for then the time is much longer and so easier to measure. Some historians of science, such as Koyré (1978), have doubted whether Galileo ever actually performed this experiment, but Settle (1961, p. 19) has shown that it is perfectly practicable with the means at Galileo's disposal. The story that he dropped two different weights from the top of the leaning tower of Pisa in order to disprove Aristotle's belief that the velocity of fall is proportional to their weights is probably apocryphal.

By his measurements Galileo showed that the velocity acquired is proportional to the time taken and that the distance traversed is proportional to the square of the time taken. This was established for balls rolling down planes inclined at various angles, and by extrapolation he deduced that it also applies when the plane is vertical, corresponding to free fall. From his results he obtained a rough estimate of what we now call the acceleration due to gravity. In this work he assumed that the effect of air resistance is negligible. He also studied the motion of projectiles, and found that their trajectories are parabolas, so that the range is a maximum when the angle of elevation of the gun is 45°.

The work of Galileo shows very clearly many of the features of modern scientific investigation. He believed that the relationships between distance, time and velocity are expressible by simple formulae, and made careful experiments to see which possibility was correct. He knew that his measurements were subject to experimental uncertainties, so that the results agreed only approximately with his formulae. Like any good experimentalist he was able to see through his imperfect results to those corresponding to perfectly accurate measurements in a world where there is no friction, air resistance or other disturbing effects.

As we saw with Kepler, the advance of science often depends on the precision of the measurements. Those of Brahe were the most accurate that could be achieved by direct sighting. The next step, the invention of the telescope, was due to Galileo. Lenses had been known for centuries and were used for spectacles and by Leewenhoek to look at very small things. Galileo realized that they could be put together and used to magnify distant objects. He made the first telescope and turned it to the heavens, and soon made a series of critical discoveries that threw increasing doubt on the correctness of Aristotelian physics.

He discovered four of the satellites of Jupiter, and showed that they revolved around it. This was just like a miniature solar system, and gave support to the Copernican idea of the heliocentric solar system. He saw the phases of the planet Venus, showing that it moves in an orbit around the sun. He saw the sunspots, an imperfection unexpected in a perfect Aristotelian sphere, and the mountains on the moon. He realized that if the earth is at rest, all the stars must rotate about it with a high velocity, so that it is much easier to suppose that it is the earth that is rotating.

All these and many other arguments convinced Galileo that the Copernican heliocentric theory was correct, and he vigorously publicized his beliefs. He was not only a great scientist, but also a brilliant writer and popularizer. He wrote not only in Latin, but also in the vernacular, so his popular writings had wide appeal. This inevitably brought him into conflict with the scientists of the time, namely the Aristotelian philosophical establishment. It is not easy for us to appreciate the strength and still more the psychologically compelling power of the Aristotelian system. It was a well-thought-out, carefully integrated system that offered a plausible and detailed account of the whole of knowledge. Its concepts and world view had been used by the scholastic theologians in the construction of their vast and impressive theological systems. The idea that all this could be upset by looking through some pieces of glass was simply preposterous. To the Aristotelian philosophers Galileo seemed to be advocating, on very shaky grounds, a revolution in thought that struck at the heart of a comprehensive world view that had stood for two thousand years. No wonder they were outraged, and refused even to look through his telescope.

It was easy for Galileo to show that the Aristotelian concept of a perfect unchanging celestial realm is incorrect, but it was quite another matter to prove the Copernican heliocentric theory. He convinced himself that it was correct by the way it unified and made sense of many different observations. This is the method used by scientists today, and indeed we use it continually in our everyday lives. However, it can only be understood by someone who has mastered and is totally familiar with all the evidence, and this was not the case for the Aristotelian philosophers who opposed Galileo. Furthermore, at that time people thought in terms of the Aristotelian concept of proof as certain knowledge through causes, and indeed Galileo accepted this himself. Because he was convinced of the truth of heliocentrism, Galileo thought that it would be easy to find a proof that satisfied this definition, but he was mistaken. His argument from the tides, which he considered the strongest, is in fact false (Shea, 1970). There is also a very strong argument against the heliocentric system from the absence of stellar parallax, and to this Galileo could only reply that the stars must be very far away. It was not until 1725 that the discovery of stellar aberration by Bradley provided evidence of the earth's rotation and precise measurements by Bessel and Henderson in 1840 detected stellar parallax. By then the Copernican system had been accepted for centuries, largely as a result of the work of Newton. It was unfortunate for Galileo that he did not invent the Foucault pendulum, which easily shows the rotation of the earth.

Unable to answer his arguments directly, the Aristotelian philosophers realized that they could make trouble for Galileo by saying that the Copernican theory was contrary to the Bible. They drew attention to passages such as that in the book of Joshua, where it is written that the sun stood still during the battle, implying that normally it is moving. Galileo was a devoted Catholic, and did not believe that his work was in any way contrary to the Bible, and he defended himself with his customary vigour. He followed Augustine in believing that if there is any apparent disagreement between science and the Bible, it must mean that we have misunderstood one or the other. Convinced of the truth of the Copernican system, he therefore suggested that when the Bible speaks of the sun standing still it is just adopting our ordinary everyday language, and is not intended to imply anything about the real nature of the motion of the earth in relation to the sun. However, he was unable to prove the correctness of the Copernican theory to the satisfaction of the Aristotelian philosophers, for the reasons mentioned above. This led to the difficulties with the church authorities that were discussed in Chapter 1.

It is worth mentioning that after many years studying Galileo's work and correspondence, Stillman Drake (1980) suddenly realized that the usual picture of Galileo as a defender of Copernican astronomy opposed by an uncomprehending authoritarian Church is completely at variance with what we know of his character and his life. We can make sense of what we know about him when we realize that he was a zealous Catholic concerned for the future of his Church and opposed by uncomprehending Aristotelian philosophers. His principal aim was to show that it is no part of the mission of the Church to pronounce on purely scientific matters, and thus to prevent the Church from opposing a theory that might subsequently be shown to be true. There is an extensive literature on Galileo's life and work (Blackwell,

1991; Carroll and Hodgson, 1998; Coyne et al., 1985; Drake, 1957, 1967, 1978, 1980; de Santillana, 1976; Feldhay, 1995; Finocchiaro, 1989; Geymonat, 1957; Koyré, 1978; Langford, 1971; McMullin, 1967; Redondi, 1998; Reston, 1994; Seeger, 1996; Settle, 1961; Sharratt, 1994; Shea, 1977; Smith, 1995; Wallace, 1981, 1984, 1986, 1995; Westfall, 1989; Zycinski, 1988).

Newton

In any discussion among physicists about the achievements of the great physicists of the past, there is never any question about who was the greatest. Although he modestly remarked that he was standing on the shoulders of giants, and that he was like a boy playing by the seashore, now and then picking up a smoother pebble or a prettier shell than usual, while the great ocean of truth lay undiscovered before him, a better summary of his achievements is to be found inscribed below his bust in Trinity College Cambridge: 'The marble image of a mind supreme, travelling through strange seas of thought alone'.

Newton was an extremely complex character. His early biographers, such as Brewster (1855), concentrated on his mathematical and physical discoveries, but more recent work on the thousands of pages of his unpublished manuscripts has revealed a man of much wider interests, who spent a great deal of time on alchemy and on theology (More, 1934; Manuel, 1968; Dobbs, 1975; Westfall, 1980; Christianson, 1984; Hall, 1992; White, 1997). It has yet to be fully understood just how these diverse aspects of his character are related to each other. In this section, attention is concentrated on Newton's work in physics, and on its relation to his theological beliefs. His pioneer work on mathematics will be mentioned only briefly.

Newton's predecessors, Copernicus, Brahe, Kepler and Galileo, were indeed giants, and they laid the secure foundations of modern physics. They established the laws of planetary motion and of motion on the earth, but there was no vision of the whole, no way of calculating all motions with precision. That was provided by Newton.

The essential nature of modern science, distinguishing it from the achievements of the past, is that it provides the laws governing the behaviour of matter and the way to apply these laws to calculate what will happen in any situation. Newton did all this for dynamics; it was left to others to do the same for electromagnetism and for atoms and nuclei.

The particular genius of Newton is that instinctively he found the middle way between the empiricism of Bacon[4] and the rationalism of Descartes, and in doing so he brought modern science to maturity. Bacon, the herald of the new learning, emphasized the importance of observation, and the collecting and cataloguing of facts about nature. Thence, by induction, one could come to a knowledge of the laws of nature. It was not specified just how this could be

---

[4] On Bacon, see Eiseley (1961), Farrington (1951), Quinton (1988) and Robertson (1905).

done, and it soon became clear that the empirical approach on its own was inadequate. Descartes, philosopher and mathematician, thought that we can know general principles and then deduce from them the laws of nature, but this rationalist programme likewise failed. Newton combined the empirical and the rational approaches and thus founded modern science.

It is not at all obvious that the world can be described by mathematics, but it is found to be the case. The art of the physicist is to know how to connect the ideal world of mathematics with the complicated world of material things. The mathematics is essentially simple, so we have to identify just those aspects of the world that most nearly approximate to that simplicity. It is often very difficult, if not impossible, to make measurements of a system that is so isolated that the extraneous effects are negligible. The physicist has to abstract the simple elements from the complicated reality, and allow for the external disturbances as far as possible.

Newtonian Dynamics

The first step was to formulate the three laws of motion. They were not entirely new, in the sense that some aspects were glimpsed in the work of Newton's predecessors, but he put them all together in concise form. The first, that every body continues in its state of rest or rectilinear motion until acted upon by a force, was already implicit qualitatively in the work of Buridan. The second law says that the acceleration of a body due to a force is proportional to the force divided by the mass of the body, and the third that to every action there is an equal and opposite reaction. To extract the momentous consequences of these apparently simple laws requires mathematical techniques that were not available. Newton provided them by inventing the differential and integral calculus.

The first law is a plausible extrapolation from our own experiences. Things do tend to stay where they are until they are moved, and moving things come to rest because forces slow them down. If we reduce or remove some of these forces, objects move further. If a stone is rolled along the ground, it eventually stops because of friction. If most of the friction is removed by rolling it along smooth ice, it goes much further. We can then conjecture that if all the friction were removed, the stone would go on forever. This is a critical leap that lies at the heart of physics.

The second law introduces the concept of mass. Newton distinguished between mass and weight. Mass is the amount of matter in a body as measured by its resistance to motion; it is often called inertial mass. Weight depends on the presence of a gravitational field. It is a remarkable and very puzzling fact that the inertial and gravitational masses are equal. Newton verified this experimentally by timing the swings of pendulums of different materials. When the string is at an angle $\theta°$ to the vertical, the gravitational force acting on the bob in its direction of motion is $m\,g\,\sin\theta$ and this is equal to $m\,a$, where m is mass, g is gravitational force, and a is the acceleration. Since the resulting motion is experimentally found to be independent of the material, this implies that the inertial and gravitational masses are equal.

The third law is also supported by our experiences of how things move, and by a symmetry argument: if the actions and reactions between things are unequal, they would always be moving around.

To use these laws to calculate the motions of things, we must also know the forces between bodies, expressed mathematically. Newton took the idea of Kepler and others that all masses attract each other, and postulated that the force between two masses (m_1 and m_2) acts along the line joining them and is proportional to the product of their masses and inversely proportional to the square of the distance between them, $F = G\, m_1\, m_2/r^2$, where F is force, G is the gravitational constant and r is radius. The inverse square law follows from Kepler's third law. Thus, considering motion in a circle, the acceleration towards the centre is v^2/R. Now $v = 2\pi r/T$, where v is velocity and T is the period; Kepler's law is $r^3 = kT^2$, where k is a constant. Hence the force is $4\pi^2 km/r^2$. A simple geometrical construction shows that Kepler's second law implies that the force acts along the line joining the two masses. The inverse square law is very plausible, since space is three-dimensional. The intensity of illumination falls off as the square of the distance from the source, so we might well expect the gravitational force to behave in the same way. It is also reasonable that the force is proportional to the masses, as they act independently of each other. When Newton postulated the law of gravitation it had not been experimentally verified; this was first done by Cavendish in 1797 and subsequently to much higher accuracy by Eötvös. Of all the fundamental constants of nature, G is the least well known; the present value is $6.673\ (\pm 0.010) \times 10^{-11} m^3\, kg^{-1}\, s^{-2}$.

Newton provided no explanation for the law of universal gravitation:

> But hitherto I have not been able to discover the cause of those properties of gravity from phenomenon, and I frame no hypotheses: for whatever is not deduced from the phenomena is to be called an hypothesis; and hypotheses, whether metaphysical or physical, whether of occult qualities or mechanical, have no place in experimental philosophy ... And to us it is enough that gravity does really exist, and act according to the laws which we have explained, and abundantly serves to account for all the motions of the celestial bodies, and of our sea. (Newton, 1686, p. 943)

Writing to his friend Richard Bentley, he remarked:

> You sometimes speak of gravity as essential and inherent in matter. Pray do not ascribe that notion to me; for the cause of gravity is what I do not pretend to know. It is inconceivable that inanimate brute matter should, without the mediation of something else, which is not material, operate on, and effect other matter without mutual contact. (Thayer 1953)

His contemporaries wanted to know the cause of gravitation, and accused Newton of invoking mysterious occult forces that act instantaneously over large distances without apparently requiring or affecting in any way the intervening space. Others, influenced by Descartes's vortex theory, thought of an all-pervasive ether that mediated the force. Leibniz criticized Newton's concept of gravitation as 'the rebirth in England of a theology that is more than papist and a philosophy entirely scholastic since Mr Newton and his partisans have revived the occult qualities of the school with the idea of attraction'. Some attempts to explain gravitation in mechanical terms failed. Eventually Newton invoked 'a most subtle spirit which pervades and lies hid in all gross bodies' that may account for many phenomena. However, 'these are things that cannot be explained in a few words, nor are we furnished with that sufficiency of experiments which is required to an accurate determination and demonstration of the laws by which this elastic and electric spirit operates' (ibid., p. 944). This, he hoped, was enough to acquit him of the charge of occultism. The problem of action at a distance is still with us today.

Newton often said that he made no hypotheses, and yet in practice he made them all the time. The type of hypotheses that Newton shunned was those invoking occult powers, which explain nothing. The hypotheses he did make were those like the law of universal gravitation which had many quantitative consequences that can be tested experimentally. Thus it enabled him to describe how an apple falls without providing any explanation why it does so. The first sentence of his book on optics declares: 'My design in this Book is not to explain the Properties of light by Hypotheses, but to propose and prove them by Reason and Experiments.' This is a key distinction between pre-scientific and scientific thinking.

Taken together, Newton's laws of motion, and the theory of gravitation, established the science of dynamics. We are familiar with the story of the apple, which gave him the idea that an object falling to the earth follows the same law as the moon. It seemed natural to Newton to extend the laws of motion from the terrestrial to the celestial realm; he was not inhibited by the Aristotelian view that they are radically different. Why do we say that the moon is falling towards the earth, when it remains at a constant distance? This is because, according to the First Law, it naturally tends to go in a straight line. It is only the gravitational attraction of the earth that pulls it towards the earth so that its orbit is a circle around the earth. It is falling all the time towards the earth.

To check this idea, Newton calculated the rate of fall, but the result was only approximately correct. Since only exact agreement is acceptable, he concluded that his idea was wrong, and put the calculations aside. Later on he read about a new determination of the radius of the earth, and realized that this might be the explanation for his previous result. He put the new number in his calculation, and it fitted perfectly within the uncertainties. There is some doubt about the veracity of this story. Another possibility is that he put his calculations aside until he could prove that the gravitational pull of the earth is the same as if all its mass were concentrated at the centre, and similarly for the moon.

The importance of this result can hardly be overestimated. Newton had shown that his dynamics applies equally to the motions of the celestial and terrestrial bodies. This is quite contrary to Aristotle, who held that they have quite different natures, the one being incorruptible and the other corruptible. It was the Christian doctrine of creation by God that destroyed this distinction, and thus made Newton's work possible.

Newton's First Law is also directly contrary to Aristotle, who required the continuing action of the mover to sustain motion. Newton's Law, however, says that a body continues in its state of motion or rest without the action of a mover. A force is required not to sustain motion, but to change it.

Newton was of a very retiring nature and seldom published his results, knowing very well that this would only involve him in tiresome controversies with stupid people. He was eventually convinced that it would be worth writing up his results. Hooke was convinced that the motions of the planets could be explained as the result of an inverse square law attraction, but could not prove it. Halley visited Cambridge to ask Newton for his opinion, and Newton told him that he had proved that motion following an inverse square would be on an ellipse. This aroused his interest again, and he was persuaded to write up his work, and in eighteen months he wrote his *Principia*, the most influential book in the whole history of science.[5] While many people have praised it, few, even among scientists, have ever read that formidable tome. Quite recently, a very eminent theoretical physicist, Chandrasekhar (1993), has worked carefully through the *Principia*, and he said that it is almost unbelievable that any man could have written so profound a book in so short a time.

Newton used geometrical arguments, and Whewell (1847, p. 175) remarked:

> The ponderous instrument of synthesis, so effective in his hands, has never since been grasped by one who could use it for such purposes; and we gaze on it with admiring curiosity, as on some gigantic implement of war, which stands idle among the memorials of ancient days, and makes us wonder what manner of man he was who could wield as a weapon what we can hardly lift as a burden!

With the work of Newton, modern science came to maturity. The laws of motion were given in the form of differential equations, and the mathematical techniques needed to solve them were established. In any situation, it is in principle simply necessary to specify the initial conditions and then obtain solutions of the equations of motion that satisfy these conditions. This gives the complete subsequent motion of the system for all time. Kepler's laws and Galileo's laws can be obtained in this way from Newton's laws of motion, together with the law of gravitational attraction that specifies the forces. This problem, which exercised the giants of physics for centuries, is now a relatively simple exercise for an undergraduate.

Newton also calculated the motions of the satellites of planets, and of the planets around the sun, and estimated their masses in terms of that of the earth. He obtained a remarkably accurate value for the ellipticity of the earth, and showed that this accounted for the precession of the equinoxes. He established the orbits of the comets, and showed that those moving in elliptical orbits, like

---

[5] See Cook (1998), Inwood (2002), Bennett et al. (2003), Jardine (2004).

that of Halley, return periodically. He also laid the foundations of the theory of the tides.

In the following centuries his work was extended and powerful new methods were developed that made it possible to tackle a wide range of problems. Particularly important is the work of Laplace, who made extensive calculations of planetary motions, and Lagrange, who expressed Newton's laws in a form that is particularly suited to calculate the motions of systems subject to constraints.

An especially impressive achievement was the discovery of the planet Neptune. The astronomer Sir William Herschel discovered the planet Uranus, and it was realized that it had been observed frequently in the past. Its orbit was calculated, but later it was found that its motion differed slightly from the calculated orbit. It was then conjectured that this was due to the perturbing effect of another, unknown, planet. J. C. Adams in England and Le Verrier in France calculated where this planet should be, and it was soon found. The new planet Neptune was thus discovered solely by working out the consequences of the law of gravitation. This triumph of Newtonian dynamics was later proved somewhat fortuitous: both Adams and Le Verrier made assumptions that were later found to be inaccurate, but the errors thereby introduced largely cancelled out (Peterson, 1993, p. 112).

Newtonian Concepts of Space and Time

Newtonian dynamics is a mathematically abstract theory in the sense that it deals with abstract concepts such as space and time, velocity and acceleration. These exist in an ideal world, related to the real world as the geometrical triangle is related to a triangle that we draw. We know, however, that the deductions we make for the ideal triangle also apply, perhaps allowing for uncertainties of measurement, to triangular things. This analogy does not bring out the difference between geometry and physics: we can immediately grasp the essence of a triangle, but we cannot do the same for space and time. We know what they are in a qualitative way from our everyday experiences, but to be useful in physics they must be precisely defined and accurately measurable. The definitions we use cannot be deduced; they can only be postulated, not proved. From the definitions we can build our dynamics, and then we can test it by comparison with experiment. Newtonian dynamics was supremely successful, but eventually it was found wanting, and this forced a re-examination of the concepts of space and time.

Newtonian dynamics can only be expressed mathematically, and the mathematics is much easier to understand than the physics. It must be emphasized that without an understanding of the mathematics, there is little hope of understanding the physics. Reading verbal descriptions of Newtonian dynamics can give only the illusion of understanding, although this is frequently deemed sufficient by popular writers to serve as a basis for their fantasies. The same applies, much more strongly, to relativity and to quantum mechanics.

The most basic problem in physics is that of local motion: how do material particles move? This includes problems on the earth such as that of the trajectory of a projectile launched in a particular direction with a particular velocity, and celestial problems such as the motions of the moon and the planets. To describe such motions requires a coordinate system, and then the motion of each particle is specified by a function of the spatial and temporal variables. Thus in the Cartesian system the motion is described by a function $f(x,y,z,t)$. We can thus think of the three spatial axes and the one temporal axis as enabling us to define the position and time of any event. Newton described this as the sensorium of God, implying that it is unique. Physicists could not imagine any other possibility. This established the stage, so to speak, on which the events of physics take place.

The concepts of absolute space and absolute time, independent of the existence of any physical objects, are basic to Newtonian physics. In formulating his concepts of space and time, Newton was strongly influenced and guided by his theological beliefs and saw them as the sensorium of God:

> Does it not appear from phenomena that there is a Being incorporeal, living, intelligent, omnipresent, who in infinite space, as it were His sensory, sees the things themselves intimately, and thoroughly perceives them, and comprehends them wholly by their immediate presence to Himself: of which things the images only carried through the organs of our sense into our little sensoriums, are there seen and beheld by that which in us perceives and thinks. (Barbour, 1989, p. 628)

God is omnipresent and eternal and so all space and time is equally present to Him:

> He is eternal and infinite; that is, his duration reaches from eternity to eternity; his presence from infinity to infinity ... He is not eternity and infinity, but eternal and infinite; he is not duration or space, but he endures and is present. He endures forever, and is everywhere present; and, by existing always and everywhere, he constitutes duration and space. Since every particle of space is always, and every indivisible moment of duration is everywhere, certainly the Maker and Lord of all things cannot be never and nowhere. (Ibid.)

Newton concluded that motion 'must be referred to some motionless thing such as extension alone or space' (ibid., p. 617). Extension has 'its own manner of existence which fits neither substance nor accident' (ibid., p. 618). In his *De Gravitatione* he describes the properties of space in more detail:

> space extends infinitely in all directions. For we cannot imagine any limit anywhere without at the same time imagining that there is space beyond it ... The parts of space are motionless ... The parts of duration and space are only understood to be the same as they really are because of their mutual order and position; nor do they have any hint of individuality apart from that order and precision, which consequently cannot be altered ... Space is the disposition of being qua being. No being exists or can exist

which is not related to space in some way. God is everywhere, created minds are somewhere, and body is in the space that it occupies; and whatever is neither everywhere nor anywhere does not exist ... The positions, distance and local motions of bodies are to be referred to the parts of space ... Lastly, space is eternal in duration and immutable in nature, and this is because it is the emanent effect of an eternal and immutable being. (See ibid., pp. 623–4)

Within this rationalist perspective, Newton formulated in his *Principia* the following definitions of space and time:

Absolute space, in its own nature, without relation to anything external, remains always similar and immovable. Relative space is some moveable dimension or measure of the absolute space; which our senses determine by its position to bodies; and which is commonly taken for immovable space. (Ibid.)

In his *Optics*, Newton referred to space as the sensorium of God (Query 28). Newton defined time as follows:

Absolute, true and mathematical time, of itself, and from its own nature, flows equably without relation to anything external, and by another name is called duration: relative, apparent, and common time, is some sensible and external (whether accurate or inequable) measure of duration by means of motion, which is commonly used instead of true time; such as an hour, a day, a month, a year ... All motions may be accelerated and retarded, but the flowing of absolute time is not liable to any change ... All things are placed in time as to order of succession; and in space as to order of situation. It is from their essence or nature that they are places; and that the primary places of things should be movable, is absurd. These are therefore the absolute places; and translations out of those places, are the only absolute motions. (Quoted in Barbour, 1989, pp. 623–5)

These definitions are metaphysical, so that it makes sense to speak of doubling the speed of clocks, or enlarging space. Without the concept of metaphysical time as an ultimate reference this would have no meaning, and similarly for space. Such definitions need to be supplemented by more physical definitions if they are to be of practical use. Absolute space can be defined physically as the unique reference frame that, if it exists, can be recognized as such by all observers irrespective of their velocities with respect to that frame. Absolute time can be defined in a similar way.

We can think of absolute space as constituting a three-dimensional coordinate right-angled grid extending uniformly in all directions to infinity. Each event is situated within that frame, and its position is specified by the values of the three coordinates. Space and time exist independently of any material objects. In his *De Gravitatione* Newton considers the nature of space and by implication time:

It is not substance; on the one hand, because it is not absolute in itself, but is as it were an emanent effect of God, or a disposition of all being; on the other hand, because it is not among the proper dispositions that denote substance, namely actions, such as thoughts in the mind or notions in the body. (Hall and Hall, 1978, p. 132)

In this passage Newton makes it clear that space is not absolute in itself, but only as an emanative effect of God. Space and time are in no way part of God, but God's being implies infinite space and time. They 'are uncreated and co-existent with God and yet on to logically dependent on him for their being' (Craig 2000).

However, for practical purposes,

because the parts of space cannot be seen, or distinguished from one another by our senses, therefore in their stead we use sensible measures of them. For from the positions and distances of things from any body considered as immoveable we define all places, and then with respect to such places we define all motions, considering bodies as transferred from some of these places into others. And so, instead of absolute places and motions we use relative ones; and that without any inconvenience in common affairs; but in philosophical disquisitions, we ought to abstract from our senses and consider things themselves, distinct from what are the only sensible measures of them. For it may be that there is no body really at rest, to which these places and motions may be referred. (Barbour, 1989, p. 625)

He also remarked that 'it is necessary that the definition of place and hence of local motion, be referred to some motionless thing such as extension alone or space so far as it is seen to be truly distinct from bodies' (ibid., p. 617).

Newton thus clearly distinguished these absolute notions of space and time from the results of our attempts to measure them, which he called relative. When we make our measurements we do not know whether we are moving relative to absolute space, or whether this has any effect on the results of our measurements. As we improve the accuracy of our measuring apparatus, we may hope to obtain results that approach the values corresponding to absolute space and time, but we cannot be certain of this. Newton's attempt to measure absolute space by using the curvature of the fluid surface in a rotating bucket can determine absolute rotation, but not absolute motion. This absolute rotation is relative to the whole universe. This may be identified as the ultimate reference frame as there is no sense in saying that the whole universe is rotating, since there is no external reference point. His first Law of Motion does, however, require absolute space for it to be meaningful (Jammer, 1954, pp. 99–103).

It may be remarked, in parenthesis, that even Newton, who so clearly defined the impossibility of determining absolute position, nevertheless found it very difficult to absorb all its implications, for in his treatment of the solar system he makes the hypothesis 'that the centre of this system of the world is immoveable' (Barbour, 1989, p. 642).

In establishing his concepts of space and time, Newton took a God's-eye view of the world. He considered space to be God's sensorium, and since God is omnipresent this establishes absolute simultaneity. Even on the physical level, there is nothing contradictory in conceiving of signals being propagated with an arbitrarily large velocity.

The Galilean Transformation

We can thus imagine that all events take place in a four-dimensional space-time continuum. It is useful to establish a few of its properties, and to express them in matrix notation, in order to facilitate the subsequent discussion of relativity. In any calculation, the choice of coordinate axes is arbitrary, and it is a fundamental principle that the result is independent of the choice of axes. This applies not only to axes that have different origins and orientations, but also to axes moving relative to each other with a constant velocity. The definition in the last section shows that Newton distinguished between absolute and relative motion, and thus believed that there is a unique preferred system of spatial coordinates, fixed in absolute space. He recognized the difficulty of identifying absolute space, and this problem will be discussed later on. We thus frequently have to carry out calculations with moving axes, so it is necessary to know how to transform the equations of motion from one set of axes to another. This is known as the Galilean transformation. Thus if we consider a space-time point (x, y, z, t) in the rest frame, it will appear to have coordinates (x', y', z', t') in a frame moving in the x direction with velocity v, where

$$x' = x - vt$$
$$y' = y$$
$$z' = z$$
$$t' = t.$$

In matrix notation, this is

$$\begin{pmatrix} x' \\ y' \\ z' \\ t' \end{pmatrix} = \begin{pmatrix} 1 & 0 & 0 & -v \\ 0 & 1 & 0 & 0 \\ 0 & 0 & 1 & 0 \\ 0 & 0 & 0 & 1 \end{pmatrix} \begin{pmatrix} x \\ y \\ z \\ t \end{pmatrix}$$

which may be written symbolically

$$X' = G(v)X$$

It follows that

$$G(v)G(-v) = 1$$

Furthermore, the product of two Galilean transformations is also a Galilean transformation, so that the transformations form a group. This implies that there is no unique frame of reference.

Physicists use everyday words like space, time, force and mass in a very precise way, although it is usually only the philosophers of science who worry about their precise definition. It is in fact very difficult to define them in a fully satisfactory way. Can we define them according to their essence, and, if so, how do we know what their essence is? What criteria should we apply in order to see if our definition is correct? How do we know that they are the correct criteria? Is it possible to define them by specifying the way we measure them? But what do we do if they can be measured in several different ways? This immediately leads us to the central problems of the philosophy of science.

Newton was aware of the difficulties, and discussed them at some length. He admitted that 'it may be that there is no body really at rest, to which the places and motions of others may be referred', and speculated that

> it is possible, that in the remote regions of the fixed stars, or perhaps far beyond them, there may be some body absolutely at rest: but impossible to know, from the position of bodies to one another in our regions, whether any of these do keep the same position to that remote body, it follows that absolute rest cannot be determined from the positions of bodies in our regions. [Thus] instead of absolute places and motions, we use relative ones.

He defined time as 'flowing equably', although this is unfortunately circular (Newton, quoted Barbour, 1989, pp. 623–5). As Augustine remarked, we all know what time is until someone asks us to tell them. The usual forms of Newton's Laws of Motion are open to similar criticisms.

Rotational motion poses further problems. We might be inclined to say that, as for systems moving relatively to each other with constant velocity, things should be the same in a rotating system. Newton showed that they are not: if the water in a bucket is rotating, the surface becomes curved, so it matters whether it is the bucket that is rotating or the water. It is suggested that the rotation is relative to the fixed stars, though they are not fixed to anything. This again is a fundamental problem that goes to the heart of physics.

Fortunately for physicists, it is possible to do physics without worrying about such difficulties. We use the concepts and methods forged by pioneers such as Newton to solve our problems. This works well until we run into fundamental difficulties. Then we can no longer rely on established knowledge; we have to go back to the foundations and see if they need to be modified. This indeed happened, even for so secure an edifice as Newtonian dynamics.

The difficulties seemed to be very small. When light was found to be a wave motion, presumably in a medium called the ether, it was hoped that it would be possible to measure the motion of the earth through it, but all attempts to do this failed. Astronomers measured the motion of the perihelion of the planet Mercury and found a discrepancy of about 43 seconds of arc per century, a very small amount. This was worrying: similar discrepancies in the past had later been explained, but this one persisted. Eventually, as we shall see, the explanation came, not from within Newtonian dynamics but from a new way of looking at the world. This first emerged from studies of electromagnetism, which we consider in the next chapter.

Newtonian space extends without limit in all directions, and Newtonian time sets no limits on the past or on the future. In a letter to Richard Bentley Newton remarks:

> It seems to me, that if the matter of our Sun and Planets & all ye matter in the universe was evenly scattered throughout all the heavens, & every particle had an innate gravity towards all the rest & the whole space throughout which this matter was scattered was but finite: the matter on ye outside of this space would by its gravity tend towards all ye matter on the inside & by consequence fall down to ye middle of the whole space & there compose one spherical mass. But if the matter was evenly diffused through an infinite space, it would never convene into one mass but some of it convene into one mass & some into another so as to make an infinite number of great masses scattered at great distances from one to another throughout all that infinite space. (Cohen, 1978, p. 281)

The belief that the world is infinite in all directions has interesting implications for cosmology. If the universe is infinite and the stars are uniformly and randomly distributed, then in whatever direction we look, we must eventually see a star. This in turn implies that the night sky must be infinitely bright. We know, however, that it is dark; this is Olbers's paradox. We might try to avoid the paradox by saying that there is enough intervening matter to absorb the light from the very distant stars before it reaches us. If, however, the universe lives long enough, this absorption will eventually raise the intervening matter to incandescence, when it will re-emit as much light as it absorbs. The paradox can only be solved if one or other of these assumptions is incorrect. We thus conclude that either the universe is finite in space, that is, there is a finite number of stars, or that the universe has not existed for ever (Jaki, 1969).

Newton's Optics

Newton was interested in everything he saw, and made many experiments to find out what happens in various circumstances as a prelude to the search for understanding. The nature of light had long been discussed by natural philosophers, and Newton bought a prism to investigate it in more detail. He made a small hole in the shutters of his room and put the prism in the path of the narrow beam of sunlight that entered. He observed the familiar spectrum of colours. He allowed the spectrum to fall on a screen, and made another hole so that only the light of a selected colour could pass through. This light he passed through another prism, and found that it was deflected but unchanged in nature. The blue rays were deflected more than the red rays. In this way he showed that white light is made up of rays of different colours that are refracted differently. He studied the way light is refracted as it passes from one medium to another, and the coloured rings (known as Newton's rings) seen when a lens is placed on a plane glass surface. Aristotelians such as Grimaldi asked whether light is a substance or an accident; Newton investigated its properties.

Newton thought that these observations could be explained if light consists of a stream of particles of different sizes corresponding to the various colours, red being the largest and violet the smallest. This explains why light travels in straight lines. Each type of particle is refracted differently as it passes from one medium to another; this explains the formation of spectra and Newton's rings. This refraction could occur if the particles are attracted when they enter a denser medium and so move more rapidly inside than outside. He measured what we now call the wavelength of the light. He accounted for the phenomenon of double refraction in Iceland spar by endowing the particles with 'sides', thus coming very near to what we now call polarization. Thus in his account of light Newton already came near to the wave theory.

Newton realized that the dispersion of light set a limit on the resolving power of refracting telescopes, and knew that this could be overcome by using reflecting telescopes. He therefore made a small but powerful reflecting telescope that magnified fifty times. To do this he cast the metal block for the mirror, using an alloy of his own devising that is quite similar to what we now call speculum metal. This was an astonishing achievement since the best craftsmen of the times had failed to do it.

Long after Newton, further experiments on the diffraction and interference of light led to the wave theory of Huygens and Young, and this replaced Newton's corpuscular theory. The wave theory encountered a difficulty when Poisson showed that it implies that when light shines on a small smooth sphere, then on the other side of the sphere there is a maximum in the light intensity in the centre of the shadow. This seemed to be obviously absurd, and so the wave theory was discredited. Arago, however, was not disheartened by this; he made the experiment and found the white spot just as predicted (Hoffmann, 1983, p. 53). Subsequent experiments showed that light travels more slowly in a denser medium, contrary to Newton.

Thus the wave theory triumphed, but many years later the discovery of the quantum showed that light is corpuscular after all.

Theology and Newtonian Physics

The new science brought to maturity in the Renaissance is characterized by the attempt to make new and very accurate measurements, and then to compare these with the predictions of natural laws, expressed mathematically. Heisenberg (quoted in Gingerich, 1975, p. 226) asked what was the basis of the confidence that led Copernicus, Galileo and Kepler to undertake their work:

> I think that we have to say that this basis was mainly theological. Galileo argued that nature is written in mathematical letters, and that we have to learn this alphabet if we want to read it. Kepler is even more explicit in his

work about world harmony. He says, God created the world in accordance with his ideas of creation. These ideas are the pure archetypal forms that Plato termed ideas, and they can be understood by man as mathematical constructs. They can be understood by man, because man was created as a spiritual mage of God. Physics is a reflection on the divine ideas of creation; therefore physics is divine service.

Newton's theology had a fundamental role in establishing his concepts of space and time. God is explicitly mentioned in the first edition of the *Principia*, and in a letter to Richard Bentley on 10 December 1692 he wrote: 'When I wrote my treatise about our System, I had an eye upon such principles as might work with considering men for the belief of a Deity & nothing can rejoyce me more than to find it useful for that purpose' (Cohen, 1978, p. 280). He saw the *Principia* as a demonstration of God's existence and unchangeability, and the universe it describes as evidence of His power. The orderly motions of the planets around the sun provide evidence of careful planning: 'And to compare & adjust all these things together in so great a variety of bodies argues that cause not to be blind & fortuitous but very well skilled in Mechanicks & Geometry' (Newton, 1952, p. 400). He also thought that divine governance prevented comets from striking the earth (Hall, 1954, p. 320).

Newton's concept of the nature of matter was expressed in theological terms:

It seems probable to me that God in the beginning form'd matter in solid, massy, hard, impenetrable, moveable particles ... and that these primitive Particles, being Solids, are incomparably harder than any porous bodies compounded of them; ever so very hard as never to wear or break in pieces; no ordinary power being able to divide what God made one in the first Creation.

Theological beliefs underlie Newton's unification of terrestrial and celestial motions by his three laws: 'If there be a universal life and all space be the sensorium of a thinking being who by immediate presence perceives all things in it ... the laws of motion arising from life or will may be of universal extent.' He realized that this does not prevent God from creating other universes where different laws are obeyed.

The concept of strict laws of nature that could be used to predict all future behaviour had a great influence on contemporary thought. It makes the world into a great machine, created in the beginning and set into motion by God, but afterwards going on inexorably in accord with Newton's laws. As Laplace remarked, if we knew the positions and velocities of all the particles in the universe, and had access to sufficient mathematical power, all the past and all the future would lie before our eyes. After He has created the world, God can no longer have any influence on it; He has been rendered redundant. It is as if He wound up a clock and then let it go thereafter on its own accord. This philosophy is known as deism, and gives rise to many theological problems. It effectively denies the possibility of free actions, and therefore of responsibility and free will. We are all machines, automata that behave strictly in accord with Newton's laws. As we shall see, this is an illegitimate extrapolation of Newton's work. Deism is an extreme form of secondary causality: not even God can influence the natural world once it is created, and so miracles are impossible.

Another implication of Newton's equations is that there is no difference between past and future. Newton's equations are second-order differential equations and so are time invariant: time (t) only enters as time squared, so they remain the same when t is replaced by $-t$. There is something wrong here as well. We know from our everyday experience that time has a definite direction. If we film a bottle shattering as it hits the floor, and then run the film backwards, we know at once that it is wrong. This problem is discussed in Chapter 5.

Newton was not himself a deist. Indeed, he worried about the possibility that, over long stretches of time, the gravitational attractions between planets would introduce small perturbations that might eventually throw the solar system into disarray. He thought that gravity depended on the arbitrary will of God (Hall, 1954, p. 326). He therefore postulated that occasionally God has to intervene to prevent this happening, and this was used as an argument for the existence of God.

Subsequently, however, Laplace showed that the solar system is stable against such perturbations. This is the origin of the story that when Laplace presented his Méchanique Celeste to Napoleon he was asked why he did not mention God. 'I have no need of that hypothesis', replied Laplace, a phrase much quoted by secularists. The hypothesis in question was not, however, the Deity, but Newton's suggested interventions. Laplace, incidentally, though a secularist for most of his life, died a Catholic (Kneller, 1995, p. 74). Newton also argued that the amount of motion in the world is steadily decreasing, and this opened up arguments that were clarified in the nineteenth century, with the development of thermodynamics and the concept of entropy. The problem of God's action in a determined mechanistic world is still a live issue today.

Although Newton was a devout, though unorthodox, Christian, and valued his theology more than his science, it is nevertheless the case that his work, together with that of Copernicus and Galileo, tended to discredit religion and led to the scepticism of the eighteenth century. The achievements of the Renaissance scientists resulted in the replacement of the cosy man-centred medieval world by a vast impersonal machine. Events like thunderstorms and rainbows, injuries and diseases that were formerly ascribed to the direct action of God, are increasingly ascribed to natural causes, so that it seems absurd to pray about them. In place of a God who continually cares for us we have a remote creator of the universe billions of years ago who now lets it continue to evolve in obedience to inexorable natural laws. Pascal was terrified by the vastness of space, and cried out 'What is man, that Thou art mindful of him?' No wonder this led to an age of scepticism and unbelief (Stace, 1952).

Further reflection shows that this is all a mistake. Modern science gives us altogether more detailed, impressive and majestic evidence of God's creative power. He is still among us, and without His sustaining power the universe would immediately lapse into nothingness. He controls the laws of nature and can alter or suspend them at will. He guides our lives and continues to give us signs of His continued presence among us.

Miracles

The success of Newtonian dynamics in accounting for the motions of the moon and the planets strongly reinforced the idea that the physical world behaves like a giant machine inexorably following fixed laws given to it on the day of creation. This immediately raises a problem about human free will, and also about the action of God on the world. If indeed we as part of the physical world are simply machines, then what becomes of our humanity? Is it all, in the words of Whitehead, just the hurrying of material, endlessly, meaninglessly? Yet we know that we are free, and so in a way we do not understand we can make decisions and bear responsibility for them. God is also free and the Lord of nature, and can act freely in the world. How can this happen without breaking the laws of nature?

How does it affect our lives? Do we have any evidence that God cares for us? Does He give us any signs of this care? Many people experience the presence of God in their lives, but this is intensely personal. Does God ever give the public signs that are called miracles? The accounts of the life of Christ and of the saints provide many examples of miracles, but these are difficult to confirm by objective criteria. Are miracles still occurring?

A miracle can be defined as an event that is inexplicable scientifically and is a sign of God's continuing presence. Science is based on the assumption of the uniformity of nature, the belief that things happen in a regular and orderly way. The same causes always produce the same effects. Science is the systematic study of these regularities. The uniformity of nature is thus a methodological presupposition and not a scientific conclusion. It cannot be proved. The fact that a causal sequence has happened a million times is no proof that it will always happen or that it is an unalterable fact of nature; it just makes it extremely probable. The sun has been observed to rise every morning for thousands of years and this makes is extremely likely that it will rise again tomorrow. But this is not a certainty, even in the natural order. We can imagine events such as the impact of an asteroid that would prevent it happening. In addition, God has supreme power over nature and can suspend its laws at will, or override them by more powerful forces (Grisez, 1975).

The condition 'inexplicable scientifically' means that it cannot be explained by contemporary science. How then do we know that it will not eventually be perfectly explicable according to new laws found by scientists in the future? Certainly if the inexplicable event happens regularly it is a suitable subject for scientific investigation. Such events usually occur in situations that are just being opened up to scientific study. This differs from cases where a familiar process is suddenly accelerated, as when, for example, a medical condition that usually takes months to heal is cured almost instantaneously.

It often happens in our experience or in the course of research that some inexplicable event occurs. We assume that it has some obscure natural explanation and try the experiment again. Eventually we may succeed, and then we forget about the glitch. As anyone who has ever made a laboratory experiment knows all too well, all sorts of things mysteriously go wrong and it requires great persistence finally to get the apparatus to work as planned. We certainly do not call such difficulties miracles. For an event to be declared a miracle it has to be identified as a sign from God. By its nature a sign has to be recognized, and it can only be recognized by a prepared mind, that is by a believer in God's creative power. It is no criticism of a particular person if he does not recognize a miracle. Thus an X-ray film is a sign that conveys information about our state of health, but it can only be interpreted by a trained radiographer with years of experience.

As an example, Alexis Carrell was an agnostic medical doctor. He was open-minded enough to go to Lourdes to investigate the cures alleged to take place there. While at Lourdes he observed the almost instantaneous cure of a girl who was dying of acute peritonitis. He did not call it a miracle; as a scientist he simply recorded the event and concluded that such cures can take place in response to prayer. He wrote that they are 'stubborn, irreducible facts, which must be taken into account' (Carrell, [1935], 1994, p. 61). As a result he was no longer welcome in the agnostic and anti-clerical medical establishment at Lyons, and was forced to leave France. He joined the Rockefeller Institute for Medical Research in the United States, where his work on heart surgery led to the award of the Nobel Prize and, incidentally, saved my own life many decades later. A few years before he died Carrell returned to the Catholic faith of his childhood; remarkably, this happened soon after the death from natural causes of the girl he had seen cured (Carrell, [1935], 1994, pp. 144–5).

The Church has established extremely strict criteria that must be satisfied before a miracle is confirmed. Cases considered must be for medical conditions that are physical and not psychological. The Medical Bureau at Lourdes keeps detailed records, and doctors of all faiths and none are welcome to examine the patients. Most cases are rejected at an early stage because the evidence is not sufficient. It is only when the medical doctors have certified that there is no natural explanation that the Church will set up a committee to consider the possibility that it is a miracle. Nearly all modern miracles are cures of diseases and other medical conditions. An exception is provided by the phenomenon of the sun at Fatima, which is particularly interesting to physicists, although it has not been declared a miracle. This has recently been subjected to detailed study and analysis by a physicist (Jaki, 1999). Although this phenomenon was unprecedented, and seen by a large crowd of witnesses, it cannot be proved that it was not an extremely rare meteorological phenomenon. The argument that it was indeed a miracle rests on its being predicted many months in advance to take place on that particular day. As a result, many tens of thousands of people came to see what would happen, many expecting or hoping that nothing would happen. Furthermore, it was not just a pointless display of divine power; it had a critical effect on the political situation in Portugal and hence on the subsequent history of Europe.

Most people nowadays reject miracles out of hand and refuse to consider the evidence. They see anyone who even admits the possibility of miracles as credulous and naïve. However, it is they who are credulous by accepting that the uniformity of nature is an established truth that always holds without exception. They laugh at the Aristotelian philosophers who refused to look through Galileo's telescope, and yet they are behaving in just the same way by refusing even to examine the evidence for miracles. In both cases the underlying thought is the same: even to look at the evidence implies recognition of the possibility that it might force them to change their minds – and they are afraid that this might happen.

CHAPTER 5

Classical Physics

Introduction

In the last chapter we saw how Newton established the laws and methods of classical physics, and so founded modern science. There was still much debate about the philosophical justification of what he had done, but the agreement of his calculations with observations was so impressive that all opposition was silenced. The Newtonian method was generally seen as the paradigm of scientific endeavour, and scientists in other areas applied it in their own work, often with indifferent success. Attempts were even made to use it in such areas as economics, sociology and psychology. Henceforth physics was set on its road of continual progress, and the physicists knew that now they could go on with their work without bothering any more about what the philosophers said. For the most part this attitude was well justified, but in times of crisis the philosophical issues inevitably come again to the fore.

During the eighteenth century important advances were made, particularly in celestial mechanics by Laplace and in dynamics by Lagrange. Ever more accurate calculations were made, almost all of them agreeing with the observations to high accuracy. Chemistry was further developed by Lavoisier and many of the chemical elements were identified. Here we are principally concerned with the state of physics at the end of the nineteenth century, on the threshold of the new physics of the twentieth century.

It was during the nineteenth century that science ceased to be the preserve of a few university professors and some enthusiastic amateurs and entered the mainstream of public life. The ever-increasing momentum of the Industrial Revolution brought together the traditional skills and empirical knowledge of the craftsmen and the knowledge of the scientists, and the result of that marriage was a plethora of inventions and new industrial processes. Thousands of factories poured out a wide range of products, textiles, ironware, pottery and china that altered the lifestyles of the whole population in an unprecedented way. The Great Exhibition of 1851 publicized a vast range of new products, and showed the world what could now be done. Chemistry, and later on physics, were recognized as legitimate subjects for university education, and produced professional scientists in ever-increasing numbers.

It was an era brimming over with confidence and looking hopefully to the future. With the aid of science and technology, it was confidently believed that all problems could be solved and all obstacles to human development overcome. Inevitably this mood spread beyond science itself and many embraced scientism as the new religion. The events of the twentieth century have somewhat dampened that enthusiasm.

In the nineteenth century classical physics came to maturity. Our understanding of the physical world developed apace, and much previous knowledge was unified and given mathematical expression. The different forms of energy were identified and related to each other, and electricity and magnetism were unified by Maxwell's equations of the electromagnetic field. The chemists established the atomic theory and the physicists showed how spectra can be measured to give information on atomic structure. Classical thermodynamics gave a macroscopic description of thermal phenomena and this was related to a microscopic description by statistical mechanics.

Taken as a whole, classical physics provided a detailed description of a vast range of phenomena, and many thought that it was essentially complete. At the end of the century, there remained a few puzzling phenomena and some philosophical difficulties, but this was not enough to dampen the prevailing optimism. In the space of a few years, however, the discovery of the quantum opened the way to a new world, and classical physics was seen as a limited account of some realms of phenomena. Some old puzzles were solved and replaced by new ones, and most of the philosophical difficulties are still with us, though often in different forms. Some of the main achievements of nineteenth-century physics are summarized in the following sections (Basalla et al., 1970; Knight, 1986).

The Conservation of Energy

Energy exists in many forms, and one of the achievements of nineteenth-century physics was to show how they are related in a quantitative way. We are familiar with kinetic energy, or the energy of motion, and this is directly related to heat energy. All matter is made up of tiny particles in incessant motion. The more rapid the motion, the hotter is the matter. It is then easy to connect the average speed of the particles with the temperature.

We are also familiar with potential energy: we have to do work to raise a mass from one level to a higher one. Conversely, if a mass falls, its potential energy is converted into kinetic energy, as happens when we drop something, or when a ball runs down a slope. Potential energy can also be converted into heat: the water at the bottom of a waterfall is hotter than at the top. This was verified in the Alps by Joule (on his honeymoon!), and he determined the conversion factor. Kinetic energy can also be converted into heat by agitating water with paddles and measuring the resulting rise in temperature. These experiments were very difficult, as the temperature rises were only a few hundredths of a degree. Many scientists did not believe that such accurate measurements could be made, but the agreement between the values of the mechanical equivalent of heat obtained in different ways eventually convinced them that Joule's new experimental techniques were sufficiently reliable (Steffens, 1979).

The increasing knowledge of electricity made it possible to study a new source of heat. When an electric current passes through a wire it is heated by an amount that is proportional to the square of the current multiplied by the resistance of the wire. If the wire is thin, the resistance is high, and it can be raised to incandescence, as we see in a light bulb. We also know that the bulb gets very hot. Another familiar source of heat is in chemical reactions. Thus the chemical reactions in a battery produce an electric current, and this in turn can heat a wire (Elkana, 1974).

A whole series of increasingly accurate measurements related all these forms of energy to each other, and it was found that whatever form it takes, energy is always conserved. This is one of the most important conservation laws. Joule's confidence in the conservation of energy was rooted in his theological beliefs. Concerning his experiment he wrote: 'I shall lose no time in repeating and extending these experiments, being satisfied that the grand agents of nature are, by the Creator's fiat, indestructible and that whenever mechanical force is applied, an exact equivalence of heat is *always* obtained' (Steffens, 1979, p. 48). He thus believed that the world was created by God and set into activity, and that no further action was needed because the agents of nature are indestructible.

Following James Watt's realization of the power of steam, the first steam-driven railway engine was made by Stephenson, and huge steam-driven pumps were used to pump water from the mines. Continuing efforts to improve their efficiency stimulated the development of thermodynamics, and this was put into mathematical form by Sadi Carnot, Rudolph Clausius, William Thomson (later Lord Kelvin) and others. To the first law of thermodynamics, that energy is conserved, was added the second, that entropy, a measure of disorder, always increases. This implies that everything is inexorably running down, so that the days of activity in the universe are numbered. Eventually it will reach a state known as heat death, when everything is at the same temperature, and nothing can happen.

This raises a serious problem. The second law of thermodynamics implies a direction of time. Most of our everyday activities are irreversible. If we break a glass, or stir milk into our coffee, we cannot reverse our actions. How can this be understood on the basis of the laws of classical physics, since these are second-order differential equations that are unchanged if we reverse the direction of time? This was studied by Ludwig Boltzmann, who showed that indeed all processes are reversible but most of the reversed states are highly improbable. For any given system, of a gas for example, for each initial state there is an immense number of subsequent states so that the probability of the process reversing is so improbable that we can say that it will never happen (Cereignani, 1998).

As usual in science, the laws of thermodynamics were enthusiastically applied to realms of phenomena far removed from the limited area where they were first established. They were applied to living organisms and to the whole universe, and this raised theological problems. How can the mind act on the body without violating the principle of the conservation of energy? If the mind cannot act on the body, then what becomes of free will? If the universe is running down, does this provide a scientific basis for the doctrine of creation and for the belief in the end of the world? Such questions became a battleground for theologians and philosophers in the nineteenth century.

Neo-Thomists of Mercier's Louvain school pointed out that to go from some experiments in physics to such general statements is an unjustified leap from positive science to very speculative metaphysics. The physicist Duhem, a devout Catholic who made important contributions to thermodynamics, firmly opposed those who drew such far-reaching conclusions from physical laws. Their first assumption is that the laws of thermodynamics apply to an infinite universe. Furthermore, it is unjustified to conclude from the second law that there is a beginning and an end to the universe because it is equally possible for the entropy to change from minus infinity to plus infinity over an unlimited time. Finally, it would be easy to construct a thermodynamics that agrees with all our observations and yet gives quite different predictions for events in the distant past and future. Thus, 'by its very essence, experimental science is incapable of predicting the end of the world as well as of asserting its perpetual activity. Only a gross misconception of its scope could have claimed for it the proof of a dogma affirmed by our faith.' According to Duhem, 'The metaphysician should know physical theory in order not to make illegitimate use of it in his speculations.'

The Ages of the Earth and the Sun

The application of physics to geology made possible the first crude estimates of the age of the earth. By measuring the salinity of rivers and oceans Joly (Windle, 1926, p. 261) estimated in 1899 and 1908 that it would take about one hundred million years to build up the concentration of salts in the oceans today. Subsequently he raised the estimate to 400 million years, and now radioactive methods give 4600 million years. In a similar way one can estimate how long it would take for a river to carve out a valley, and this gave times of the order of billions of years. This timescale was supported by estimates of the time it would take for species of plants and animals to evolve from primitive forms to the great diversity we see today.

Estimates of the age of the sun gave much shorter times. Kelvin estimated that even if it were made of coal it would only last for a few tens of millions of years (Burchfield, 1980, p. 180). It was suggested that the heat of the sun could be continually replenished by meteorites falling into it, but this proved quite inadequate. Its gravitational energy was also insufficient.

This conflict between the times required by the geologists and biologists on the one hand and those estimated by the physicists on the other was eventually solved by the discovery of radioactivity, which provides an additional source of heat that can prolong the life of the sun to times similar to those required by the geologists and biologists. Subsequently in 1935 Bethe identified the cycles of nuclear reactions that provide the energy of the sun by building up helium from its constituent nucleons.

These processes require times much greater than the six thousand years indicated by a superficial reading of the Bible. This once again raised the problem of biblical interpretation, which is particularly acute for those who accept it as the sole rule of faith. They are inevitably faced with the unpalatable choice between rejecting science or finding a different way to interpret the Bible. Those who recognize that the Church has authority to interpret the Bible, since it was the Church who gave us the Bible in the first place, have no such problems.

Electricity and Magnetism

From the earliest times people had been familiar with the properties of lodestone, and with thunder and lightning. In the eighteenth century Volta discovered how to produce an electric current, and in the nineteenth Faraday made extensive researches into a wide range of electric and magnetic phenomena. Ohm and Ampère formulated laws governing electric currents and finally Maxwell united them by his equations of the electromagnetic field, thus doing for electromagnetism what Newton did for dynamics.

Once again this advance was accompanied by a conceptual shift. Following the success of Newtonian dynamics, the world was thought of as a mechanism. Every phenomenon was considered to be a manifestation of mechanical principles following Newton's laws. Indeed, the concept of scientific explanation simply meant identifying phenomena as such. Accordingly Faraday, unwilling to accept action at a distance, thought of electricity as a fluid flowing along the lines of force, and Maxwell used complicated mechanical models to try to understand what was going on. When, however, he finally found his equations, he realized that the mechanical models he used were just scaffolding that were no longer needed and could be discarded. It was sufficient to have the electric and magnetic fields, represented by the vectors that gave their strengths and directions. The electromagnetic field is a real entity in its own right and is the second of the four fundamental forces of nature. It is real and not just a mathematical abstraction because it is able to carry energy and momentum (Berkson, 1974).

Maxwell's equations contain the laws of the electric and magnetic fields that were established experimentally, but are much more general. They can be written in the following simple form:

div $\mathbf{E} = \rho$	Gauss's Law
curl $\mathbf{E} = -\partial \mathbf{B}/\partial t$	Faraday–Lenz Law
div $\mathbf{B} = 0$	No magnetic monopoles
curl $\mathbf{B} = \mathbf{j} + \partial \mathbf{E}/\partial t$	Modified Ampère's Law

These simple equations for the electric and magnetic fields represented by the vectors $\mathbf{E}$ and $\mathbf{B}$ enable all electric and magnetic phenomena to be calculated to a high degree of accuracy (May, 1964). In their book *The Evolution of Physics* (n.d.) Einstein and Infeld remark that 'the formulation of these equations is the most important event in physics since Newton's time, not only because of their wealth of content but also because they form a pattern for a new type of law'.

Maxwell's equations have many interesting consequences. Thus if we consider empty space where the charge ρ and the current $\mathbf{j}$ are both zero and take the curl of the Faraday–Lenz Law and use the other equations, we find that

$$\nabla^2 \mathbf{E} = \partial^2 \mathbf{E}/\partial t^2$$

and a similar equation for $\mathbf{B}$. These are wave equations and thus suggest that electromagnetic waves can propagate through empty space. Maxwell calculated the velocity of these waves and found that it is the same as the velocity of light, thus showing that light is electromagnetic radiation. Maxwell thus not only unified electricity and magnetism but also provided the theory of light.

This identification of light with electromagnetic radiation in turn suggested that there may be electromagnetic waves having frequencies outside the visible region. Such waves were found by Herz, and are radio waves. In another series of experiments Roentgen discovered X-rays. Thus the whole of the electromagnetic spectrum is now known, from radio waves at one end to the high-energy photons of cosmic radiation at the other.

Further studies of electromagnetic radiation gave rise to a serious difficulty. If light is a wave, then it must be a wave in something, and this was called the aether. This is supported by the observation that the equations for heat flow and for electrostatic forces in space are identical. It is possible to deduce the properties of the aether, and they turned out to be rather strange. To account for the high frequency of electromagnetic waves, it had to be extremely rigid, and yet it offers no resistance to bodies moving through it. Nevertheless, Maxwell (1870, p. 568) declared that the aether was the one substance in the whole of physics that we can describe with the greatest precision: 'There can be no doubt that the interplanetary and interstellar spaces are not empty but are occupied by a material substance or body, which is certainly the largest, and probably the most uniform, body of which we have any knowledge.' In view of subsequent events, this confident statement of Maxwell about the aether is a reminder that even scientific statements by the most eminent scientists are subject to subsequent revision.

Maxwell's belief about the aether implies that it pervades all space and provides an inertial system to which all velocities can be related. This suggested that it is important to try to measure the velocity of the earth through the aether, which must change periodically as the earth moves around the sun. The experiment was made by Michelson and Morley (1887). It is well known that the apparent frequency of any wave motion changes with the relative velocity between source and observer. This is known as the Doppler effect, and is experienced as a drop in the frequency of the sound of the whistle of an approaching train as it passes us. Michelson and Morley used a delicate interferometric technique to measure the frequency of light from a laboratory source at six-monthly intervals. Since the earth is moving through the aether, they expected the frequency to change according to the relation implied by the Doppler effect. In spite of sustained efforts, however, they failed to detect any effect at all. This was another flaw in the imposing structure of classical physics. This failure, apparently so small, eventually required a radical change in our notions of space and time. It did not come from attempts to solve the problem directly, which even if successful would inevitably have an *ad hoc* character. It came from the efforts of another physicist, of almost the stature of Newton, to understand the structure of the world from a fundamental standpoint. This work of Einstein which led to the special theory of relativity is described in the next chapter.

In their book *The Unseen Universe*, Tait and Stewart ([1875], 1889) used the aether as the basis of theological speculations. Realizing that there is no room in Newton's fully predictable universe for free will or even for a God who speaks to us, they appealed to the aether as 'the great unseen element of the universe, in which God's thought could ricochet and echo around, affecting the material world we inhabit, and in the aether too, perhaps our own thoughts could be preserved, giving us a aetherial afterlife'. These speculations were enthusiastically received by the general public and the book was many times reprinted. As a devout Christian, Maxwell also rejected the mechanistic universe, but he was strongly against such attempts to support the arguments for an afterlife by invoking the aether (Hiebert, 1967).

Atomism and the Electron

The ancient Greeks recognized that matter is either continuous or discrete. If we take a piece of matter and cut it again and again, can we go on for ever or will we eventually come to a piece that 'cannot be cut' (called atom from the Greek *a tomos*, meaning 'cannot be cut')? They had no way of answering this question, but in the nineteenth century Dalton used the atomic hypothesis to bring order into chemical laws, although it was not for some decades that the existence of atoms was definitely proved by Perrin's studies of the Brownian motion (Nye, 1972).

Towards the end of the nineteenth century there was much interest in the phenomena associated with the discharge of electricity through gases at low pressure. J. J. Thomson (1906) found that the cathode rays were beams of particles, and by seeing how they were deflected by electric and magnetic fields (using apparatus that is the ancestor of the television set) was able to show that they had a mass much smaller than the lightest atom, that of hydrogen. These particles were called electrons. This showed that the atom has a structure, and Thomson thought that the negatively charged electrons might be spread uniformly through positively charged material (like plums in a pudding), so that the atom as a whole is neutral. When any material is heated to a high temperature, electrons are emitted, and these formed the cathode rays studied by Thomson (1906). This of course meant that the atom is no longer uncuttable, but nevertheless the word has been retained to describe the smallest particles of the chemical elements.

The charge on the electron was measured by Millikan (see Chapter 1) by observing the motion of charged oil drops supported by an electrostatic field.

These oil drops are acted on by the gravitational field pulling them downwards and the electrostatic field pulling them upwards. Since the electrostatic force is proportional to the charge on the electron, measurement of their rate of fall enables their charge to be calculated. By measuring the statistical fluctuations in the rate of fall it is also possible to calculate Avogadro's constant, and hence the weights of atoms.

Many years later, in the 1930s, Thomson's son G. P. Thomson showed that electrons are diffracted in the same way as light, which was known to consist of waves. So are electrons waves or particles? This problem will be posed in acute form when we come to consider the interpretations of quantum mechanics.

A vitally important discovery was made in 1896 by Henri Becquerel. He was studying the phenomenon of florescence by exposing certain minerals to sunlight, and then recording on a photographic plate the light subsequently emitted. One day the sun was not shining, so he put the mineral and the photographic plate in a drawer. The next day he prepared to continue his experiments, and by one of those strange impulses he decided to develop the unexposed plate. To his astonishment it showed fogging in the regions in close proximity to the mineral. He realized that a new type of ray was being continuously emitted from the mineral, and that it could penetrate the black wrapping paper surrounding the photographic plate and act on the emulsion in the same way as light.

The rays emitted by radioactive substances were studied by Rutherford, who showed that they are of three types, called alpha, beta and gamma. The alpha rays are heavily ionizing and are stopped by a sheet of paper. They were later shown to be helium nuclei. The beta rays are lightly ionizing and were soon shown to be electrons. The gamma rays are very penetrating and were found to be electromagnetic radiation.

Atomic Spectra

Newton discovered the composition of white light by studying the spectrum produced when a beam of sunlight is refracted by a prism. Subsequent studies used a narrow slit instead of a small hole to define the beam, and Wollaston noticed that the solar spectrum has a large number of dark lines. Since the prism separates the light into its constituent colours, each corresponding to a range of frequencies, this means that some frequencies are absent from the solar spectrum. The dark lines were studied by Fraunhofer, who found that there are two dark lines in the yellow region of the solar spectrum and that they have the same frequencies as a pair of bright yellow lines in the spectrum of an ordinary flame. Bunsen and Kirchoff showed that this can be explained if different substances emit, when heated, light of characteristic frequencies and can also absorb light of the same frequencies. By putting various substances in flames and observing the spectra, the characteristic frequencies of many substances were found. The two lines in the solar spectrum are due to sodium, and they are very familiar to us as responsible for the yellow colour of some street lighting. Other street lamps are bluish-green, and this is characteristic of the spectrum of mercury.

This discovery has far-reaching consequences: as soon as we know the characteristic spectrum of each chemical element we can analyse spectra to find the proportions of the various elements in the sample. This applies not only to material on the earth, but also to sunlight and starlight. In this way the astronomer can determine their chemical composition, and even discover new elements. An example of this is provided by some lines in the solar spectrum that could not be assigned to any known chemical element. Eventually they were shown to be the same as those of a gas in some rare minerals, and the element was appropriately called helium. Spectroscopic analysis can detect very small amounts of elements, and so enables analyses to be made of very small samples.

All this is possible if we just treat the spectra as characteristic fingerprints of each element. Thus, each spectrum is the sign of a particular element and therefore contains information about its structure. If we could find a way to interpret that spectra we would have a powerful tool to study atomic structure.

To make further progress it is necessary to measure the wavelength of the light corresponding to each line in the spectra, and this can be done using an interferometer. In this instrument, a beam of light is split into two beams, and each is reflected back into an eyepiece by mirrors. The observer sees dark and light bands of fringes as the two beams interfere destructively and constructively. As one mirror is moved the fringes move, and the distance corresponding to a movement of one fringe gives the wavelength of the light. In this way the wavelengths of thousands of lines in the spectra of the elements have been measured and tabulated. This is a vast amount of data, even greater than that amassed by Tycho Brahe, and awaited a new Kepler to find the underlying order. This is the road that led to the understanding of atomic structure.

There is another aspect of spectral analysis that has momentous consequences. Some analyses of stellar spectra showed familiar lines, but shifted to a different frequency. This can be interpreted as due to the motion of the star relative to the earth: if it is moving towards us the frequency is increased, while if it is moving away the frequency is reduced, just as in the Doppler effect with sound waves. By measuring the frequency shift we can therefore find the relative velocity of the star and the earth. This technique was used by Hubble to measure the velocities of galaxies and the results showed that the universe is expanding, as described in Chapter 10.

Statistical Physics

Classical thermodynamics relates the pressure, volume and temperature of gases, and makes possible a vast range of calculations from the most efficient design of a steam engine to the interior constitution of stars. These are what are called macroscopic variables as they treat the gas as a continuum without reference to its internal structure.

The English botanist Brown was examining a suspension of very fine lycopodium powder in water, and noticed that the tiny particles executed a random jiggling motion. This cannot be explained if matter is continuous, so it was suggested that the motion was due to the random impacts of thousands of even smaller particles that constituted the liquid. Detailed studies by Perrin confirmed this view, and showed that matter is composed of atoms.

Gases therefore consist of a swarm of tiny particles moving rapidly in all directions, colliding with each other and with the walls of their container. It is obviously not possible to keep track of each one of the particles and to calculate the course of its collisions. Instead, we must make a statistical analysis in terms of the velocity distribution of the particles. If we know this distribution we can calculate the temperature of the gas, since this is related to the sum of the kinetic and potential energies of all the particles. We can also calculate the pressure exerted by the gas on the containing walls, as this is due to the change in momenta of the particles as they bounce back after hitting them. Thus we can connect the macroscopic variables of classical thermodynamics with the microscopic variables of what is called the kinetic theory of gases.

The gas particles, atoms or molecules, as the case may be, do not all have the same energy, but a statistical distribution of energies. This is the Maxwellian distribution, after Maxwell to whom the theory is due. He showed that the probability that a particle has energy between E and $E + dE$ is given by $E^{1/2}$ exp $(-E/kT)\ dE$, where T is the temperature of the gas and k is Boltzmann's constant. As the temperature increases, the distribution shifts to higher energies.

Maxwell proved from his theory that the viscosity of a gas should be independent of the pressure, a somewhat surprising result. He therefore made some measurements, and found that this is indeed so.

This is the time to mention the intriguing story of Maxwell's demon. Consider a container of gas divided into two halves by a partition. There is a small hole in the partition, with a frictionless shutter that enables the hole to be opened or shut. Stationed by the hole is Maxwell's demon. When he sees a fast particle coming towards the hole from the first half of the container he opens the shutter, and when he sees a slow particle coming he closes it. He does the opposite for particles coming from the second half of the container. The result of these activities is that the gas in the first half gets colder and colder, while that in the second half gets hotter and hotter. This contradicts the second law of thermodynamics. What is wrong with this argument?

Even if there were no Maxwell demon present, the above situation could come about by chance, if all the fast particles moved one way and all the slow ones the other. The second law of thermodynamics is therefore essentially statistical.

Conclusion

The nineteenth century saw the extension of quantitative physics to a very wide range of terrestrial phenomena. Apparently different phenomena were shown to be linked together or to be manifestations of a simpler underlying structure. Thus all the forms of energy were united, and their behaviour specified by the laws of thermodynamics. Likewise electricity and magnetism were united by Maxwell's equations. Matter was shown to be made up of atoms and their spectra shown to be characteristic of their structure. Thermodynamics was generalized and related to statistical mechanics. There were just a few problems remaining, such as the failure to detect the motion of the earth through the aether, the nature of radioactivity and the structure of atoms. Although it did not seem so at the time, classical physics had been found inadequate and drastic changes would soon be imperative. These eventually led to the physics of the twentieth century.

CHAPTER 6

Space, Time and Relativity

Einstein's Special Theory of Relativity

It might well be asked what relativity has to do with theology. For our purpose it is sufficient that many people think, rightly or wrongly, that there is a connection. It is certainly the case that arguments about the timelessness of God invoke relativistic considerations. More generally, relativity provides a more sophisticated and indeed a more correct way of talking about space and time, so if theology involves spatio-temporal concepts it is desirable to consider them relativistically.

This theory, according to a perceptive writer, has

> overturned the concepts of absolute space and time which formed the framework within which the laws governing the behaviour of matter were described in Newtonian physics. By disproving the existence of temporal simultaneity, demonstrating the variability of the lengths and masses of bodies moving at high velocity, establishing the equivalence of mass and energy, and tying together space and time in a four-dimensional manifold of varying curvature, Einstein created a world picture that differed radically from that of Newton in its theoretical principles. (Graham, 1981, p. 35)

To this list may be added time dilation, namely that moving clocks appear to run slow. Many of these implications of the theory, well confirmed by experiment, seemed contrary to common sense, and engendered the feeling that familiar and traditional landmarks had melted away, that physics had become strange and mysterious. It is not surprising that in the early years it encountered much opposition (Goldberg, 1984). It is essential to realize that relativity theory is the fruit of a rigorous quest for objective knowledge, and if anyone says that it does not make sense, that means that he derives his views from superficial appearances and lacks the mathematical tools that are essential for understanding reality (Angel, 1980, p. 80).

The word 'relativity' was taken by many to mean the denial of any absolutes, and the equivalence of mass and energy seemed to mark the end of nineteenth-century materialism. Many writers drew out the implications of such beliefs for moral and sociological questions.

Properly understood, relativity is a much simpler and more natural way of dealing with space and time. To see this simplicity we have first to remove some ingrained prejudices, and this is why it may at first seem difficult. Additional and quite unnecessary difficulties are often introduced by failing to define relativistic quantities in a consistent way. It is then seen that relativity is principally concerned with establishing the objective and invariant features of

the world, that its apparently paradoxical aspects are readily understandable
and that absolute space and time remain at the basis of physics.

The fundamental principle underlying the theory of relativity is that the laws
of nature always have the same form for all observers. This follows from our
belief that there are laws that describe, precisely and mathematically, the
connections between causes and effects. This invariance of the laws of nature is
sometimes called the principle of covariance, or the principle of relativity. It
says that the laws of nature are completely objective, and do not depend on
who is looking at the phenomena or from what vantage point. This principle is
also implicit in classical physics, but its radical implications were not
sufficiently appreciated.

This is yet another example of a very profound truth, that apparently simple
and obvious statements have the most far-reaching and detailed consequences.
Our systems of thought are locked together far more tightly than we usually
suppose. As we shall see, the relativistic transformations can be derived in
many ways, starting from many different beliefs. If one wants to deny their
truth, this implies that one must also deny a whole range of other beliefs that
one never thought to question. It is thus not surprising that the most profound
results in science are often reached by asking the simplest questions.

As he recalls in his autobiographical notes, Einstein began by asking himself
a very simple question: what would a light wave look like to someone who is
travelling alongside it? It was known that a light wave is an electromagnetic
wave that is described by Maxwell's equations, so Einstein looked for a
solution of these equations that describes a stationary light wave, and found
that there is none. However we describe a light wave, it is always moving with
the speed of light.

This led him to study very carefully the transformation equations that relate
the spatio-temporal coordinates of events in one frame of reference to those in
another frame moving with constant velocity with respect to the first. It had
always been assumed to be obvious that these transformation equations are
those due originally to Galileo. Furthermore, it was also considered obvious,
according to the principle of relativity, that our description of phenomena
should give the same result whichever reference frame we use. Einstein realized
that Maxwell's equations do not satisfy this condition; they are not invariant
under the Galilean transformation.

So he asked himself what the transformation would have to be to ensure that
the light wave looks the same to all observers, whatever their relative velocities.
This was already known as the Lorentz transformation. He then asked what
the consequences would be of assuming that the Lorentz transformation
applied to all phenomena, not just to light waves, and found that this enabled
him to explain many apparently anomalous results, such as the failure of
Michelson and Morley to detect the motion of the earth through the aether.
Similar studies were made by Poincaré.[1]

---

[1] See Whittaker (1951), Truesdell (1984), p. 432, Galison (2003), Ginzburg (2001), p. 217.

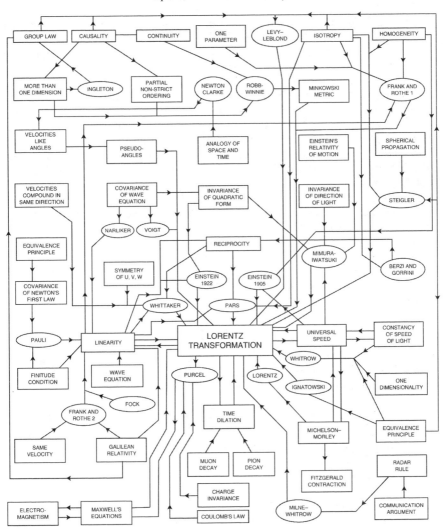

Figure 6.1 Ways to the Lorentz transformation. This diagram shows schematically the interrelationships of some of the arguments leading to the Lorentz transformation. It is intended only as a broad overview. The concepts invoked are in boxes, but note that they are defined and used differently in different approaches. Because only two dimensions are available on the diagram, the Equivalence Principle is given a multiple location. The names in balloons indicate the authors of the particular arguments (Lucas and Hodgson, 1990).

Closer examination shows that the Lorentz transformation may be derived in many different ways from apparently quite simple assumptions, as shown in Figure 6.1 (Lucas and Hodgson, 1990). It is, fundamentally, simpler and more elegant than the Galilean transformation. It is not a consequence of any observations, although it is able to explain several observations that are inconsistent with classical physics. It is sometimes said that Einstein developed his theory in order to explain the result of the Michelson–Morley experiment, but this is not the case. As Lindemann has remarked, 'if only scientists had had their wits about them, they ought to have been able to reach the relativity theory by pure logic soon after Isaac Newton, and not to have to wait for the stimulus given to them by certain empirical observations that were inconsistent with the classical theory' (Harrod, 1971, p. 57).

Einstein made a similar remark, stressing the continuity of physics: 'With respect to the theory of relativity it is not at all a question of a revolutionary act, but of the natural development of a line which can be pursued through centuries' (Seelig, 1956). Writing to Conrad Habicht in 1905, Einstein described his forthcoming paper as 'making use of a modification of the theory of space and time' (Holton, 1974, p. 362). It is therefore possible to maintain that Einstein's special theory of relativity is the last flowering of classical physics, and that modern physics came only with the discovery of the quantum.

The Lorentz transformation connects the space-time coordinates of a point in one reference frame to those in another frame moving with constant velocity with respect to the first frame. It may be derived in many ways, but one will suffice here. This derivation is based on one experimental result and two symmetry conditions:

1   The speed of light is the same in all coordinate systems. That is, whether we measure it in a stationary or a moving frame, we always obtain the same result. This was treated as an axiom by Einstein, and is the experimental result of Michelson and Morley.
2   The transformation depends only on the relative velocity between the two frames of reference, and is symmetric with respect to them.
3   The transformation is a linear function of the space and time coordinates. If it were not, the transformation would not be unique.

We now consider the transformation between two frames, one moving with respect to the other along the x-axis with a velocity v. Since the y and z coordinates are unchanged, they are omitted for convenience. We therefore write the Lorentz transformation

$$L(v) = \begin{pmatrix} A & B \\ C & D \end{pmatrix}$$

where A, B, C and D are functions of v to be determined. The coordinates in the two frames are therefore related by

$$\begin{pmatrix} x' \\ t' \end{pmatrix} = \begin{pmatrix} A & B \\ C & D \end{pmatrix}\begin{pmatrix} x \\ t \end{pmatrix}$$

The coefficients B and C interrelate x and t, so they must change sign with v. Thus

$$L(-v) = \begin{pmatrix} A & -B \\ -C & D \end{pmatrix}$$

Since, by the second postulate,

$$L(v)L(-v) = 1$$

so that $A = D$ and $A^2 - BC = 1$.

Since the origin of one frame of reference is moving with velocity v in the other frame of reference, if $x' = 0$, then $x = vt$, and hence

$$Avt + Bt = 0$$

so that

$$B = -Av$$

The invariance of the velocity of light in the two frames requires that

$$\frac{x}{t} = c = \frac{x'}{t'}$$

A little algebra then gives $A = D = \gamma$, $B = -\gamma v$ and $C = -\gamma v/c^2$, where

$$\gamma = \frac{1}{\sqrt{1 - v^2/c^2}}$$

so that the Lorentz transformation is

$$L(v) = \begin{pmatrix} \gamma & -\gamma v \\ -\gamma v/c^2 & \gamma \end{pmatrix}$$

We now replace t by ict, thus giving the two components of the space-time vector the same dimensions. The factor i, the square root of -1, reminds us that time is not the same as space. The Lorentz transformation then has the more symmetric form

$$\mathscr{L}(\mathbf{v}) = \begin{pmatrix} \gamma & i\beta\gamma \\ -i\beta\gamma & \gamma \end{pmatrix}$$

where $\beta = \mathbf{v}/c$.

This has a symmetry absent from the Galilean transformation, and is equivalent to a rotation of the space-time vector in the complex plane. Such rotations preserve the length of the vector, which is the space-time interval

$$x^2 + y^2 + z^2 - c^2 t^2$$

The theory of relativity thus shows what remains *invariant* when we transform from one coordinate system to another.

The law of addition of velocities may be obtained from the product of two Lorentz transformations, which gives

$$v = \frac{v_1 + v_2}{1 + v_1 v_2 / c^2}$$

This is of course contrary to the simple additivity of velocities in Newtonian dynamics although it reduces to it for velocities much less than that of light. It seems perfectly obvious that velocities add, as indeed they do in Newtonian dynamics. Newton himself says so explicitly in Scholium IV of the *Principia* (Barbour, 1989, p. 624). Thus if I throw a ball from a moving train in the direction of the train, the velocity of the ball as seen by a stationary observer is simply the sum of the velocity of the train and that of the ball relative to the train. This expectation, however, is based on a simple fallacy. We are used to assigning numbers to things and to properties of things. In the case of things, the corresponding numbers obey the laws of arithmetic: two apples plus three apples gives five apples. We may then expect this to be true also for properties of things, but this is not necessarily the case. It is not true for gradients: a gradient of one in four added to a gradient of one in four does not give a gradient of one in two. Gradients are tangents, and $\tan A + \tan B$ is not $\tan (A + B)$. It is the same for velocities. Gradients and tangents are additive only in the limit of very small gradients and velocities. The relativistic formula for the addition of velocities reduces to simple additivity for velocities small compared with that of light. Thus for most practical purposes the Newtonian addition law is still valid. The relativistic form must be used at high velocities when precise results are needed, such as the calculation of satellite orbits and the design of nuclear accelerators. It has been verified experimentally to high precision. A particularly dramatic example is provided by the decay of relativistic neutral pions into two photons. The pions can have 99 per cent of the velocity of light, and so according to Newtonian dynamics the photons emitted in the forward direction should have almost twice the velocity of light. Experimentally, of course, they have just the velocity of light. The relativistic addition law shows that adding any velocity to the velocity of light just gives the velocity of light. Thus when we measure the velocity of light from a moving source, or in a moving frame, we always obtain the same result, independently of the velocity of the source or the frame, as indeed was found by Michelson and Morley.

It is also necessary to know how to transform other physical quantities such as velocity, time, energy, momentum and mass. Here we are faced by a choice. Do we retain the Newtonian definitions, or do we choose new relativistic definitions? We are free to choose new definitions, provided they become the same as the Newtonian definitions in the limit of low velocities. We find that if we keep to the Newtonian definitions, we obtain transformation equations that are complicated (Leighton, 1959) and entail unpleasant consequences such as the variation of mass with velocity. The key is to use relativistic time, called proper time, in place of Newtonian time. If we do this and adopt the appropriate relativistic definitions of momentum and energy, we find that they also transform according to the Lorentz transformation, and that the mass remains constant. This is not only more convenient mathematically, but aids philosophical clarity. It should however be remarked that if an alternative choice is made consistently, the final results of any calculation are the same.

To obtain the proper time we start with the space-time interval for two infinitesimally close points and equate it to $c^2 d\tau^2$, where τ is the proper time. This gives

$$c^2 d\tau^2 = c^2 dt^2 - dx^2 - dy^2 - dz^2$$

and hence

$$\frac{dt}{d\tau} = \gamma$$

Thus the relativistic velocity in the x-direction is

$$\frac{1}{c} \frac{dx}{d\tau} = \beta_x \gamma$$

To obtain the transformation relations for velocities we start from the Lorentz transformation

$$\begin{pmatrix} \gamma_v & i\beta_v\gamma_v \\ -i\beta_v\gamma_v & \gamma_v \end{pmatrix} \begin{pmatrix} x \\ ict \end{pmatrix} = \begin{pmatrix} x' \\ ict' \end{pmatrix}$$

where the subscript v refers to the relative velocity of the two frames of reference.

Differentiating the space-time vectors with respect to time and dividing by c we obtain

$$\begin{pmatrix} \gamma_v & i\beta_v\gamma_v \\ -i\beta_v\gamma_v & \gamma_v \end{pmatrix} \begin{pmatrix} \gamma\beta_x \\ i\gamma \end{pmatrix} = \begin{pmatrix} \gamma'\beta x' \\ i\gamma' \end{pmatrix}$$

which is the transformation equation for velocities along the x-axis.

In Newtonian mechanics the momentum is defined as the product of the mass and the velocity. In relativistic mechanics we retain this definition, but instead of the Newtonian velocity dx/dt we use the relativistic velocity $dx/d\tau$. Thus the transformation equation for momentum is simply that for velocity multiplied by the mass m:

$$\begin{pmatrix} \gamma_v & i\beta_v\gamma_v \\ -i\beta_v\gamma_v & \gamma_v \end{pmatrix} \begin{pmatrix} m\beta_x\gamma \\ im\gamma \end{pmatrix} = \begin{pmatrix} m\beta'_x\gamma' \\ im\gamma' \end{pmatrix}$$

What is the meaning of the component $m\gamma$? Expressing it in terms of $\beta = v/c$, this gives in the limit of small velocities

$$m\gamma = m + \frac{1}{2}mv^2/c^2$$

If we measure mass in units of c^2, this becomes

$$mc^2 + \frac{1}{2}mv^2$$

Now $\frac{1}{2}mv^2$ is the kinetic energy, so $m\gamma$ has the dimensions of energy. We can therefore define $m\gamma$ as the relativistic energy, with $E = mc^2$ as the rest energy and $\frac{1}{2}mv^2$ as the kinetic energy. This shows that every material particle of mass m has an energy equivalent mc^2. Thus if in a nuclear reaction the sum of the masses of the products is less than that of the particles before the reaction, then energy is released. This has been verified experimentally to high precision.

It is very often said (e.g. Planck, 1933) that experiments with beams of electrons show that their mass increases with their velocity according to the relation $m = m_0\gamma$, where now m_0 is invariant. The mass thus tends to infinity as the velocity approaches that of light. This seems very strange, as we are used to thinking of mass as corresponding to quantity of matter, and this should be invariant. The apparent increase of mass with velocity is a consequence of retaining the Newtonian definition of velocity in a relativistic context. This may been seen by recalling that the relativistic momentum is $mv\gamma$. We then have to choose between defining the mass as m and the velocity as $v\gamma$, or the mass as $m\gamma$ and the velocity as v. Since we know that relativistic velocities behave in a non-Newtonian way, it is very natural to make the former choice, and this ensures that velocities transform according to the Lorentz transformation. Thus by defining velocity as $v\gamma$ corresponding to a derivative with respect to the proper time, mass remains an invariant quantity. The apparent variation of mass with velocity is thus not a new and profound property of matter, but simply the result of a failure to use relativistic dynamics in a consistent way (Leighton, 1959, pp. 35, 36).

We have thus, on the basis of one experimental result, namely the constancy of the velocity of light, and a few symmetry conditions, derived the Lorentz transformation and from it a series of results that are contrary to Newtonian dynamics and are verified to high precision by numerous measurements. As shown in Figure 6.1, there are many other ways of deriving the Lorentz transformation, showing that it is rationally coherent with very general features of space, time and causality.

There are two other consequences of the Lorentz transformation that should be mentioned, namely length contraction and time dilation.

One of the early explanations of the null result of the Michelson–Morley experiment was that a moving body contracts in the direction of its motion by a factor just sufficient to cancel the effect expected from the motion through the ether. This is called the Fitzgerald contraction. Attempts were made to understand this in terms of the electronic structure of matter. We can now see that the contraction is only apparent, and that it follows from the Lorentz transformation. It was disproved experimentally in 1932 by Kennedy and Thorndike,[2] who repeated the Michelson–Morley experiment with different lengths for the arms of the interferometer.

Another consequence is that a moving clock appears to a stationary observer to run slow, again by the factor γ. This is called time dilation, and has been verified by experiments made on artificial satellites. A more spectacular demonstration is provided by the absorption and decay of cosmic ray muons as they come down the earth's atmosphere. It is found that they penetrate far into the earth, much further than would be expected from their half-life of about 10^{-6} seconds when at rest. Detailed calculations agreed with the relativistic time dilation. A similar experiment has been repeated in the laboratory using a beam of relativistic pions. Such an experiment gave 62.4 ns (nanoseconds) for the moving pions and 26.03 ns for stopped pions, just as would be expected from the value $\gamma = 2.4$ corresponding to the velocity of the pions. At such velocities, time dilation is not a small effect.

It may be remarked, in parenthesis, that in 1921 Miller repeated the Michelson–Morley experiment, and found a non-zero result. Miller was a highly respected physicist who had worked with Morley and was to become President of the American Physical Society. When Einstein was told of Miller's result, he remarked: 'Raffiniert ist Herr Gott, aber boshaft ist er nicht' (God is refined, but not malicious). He did not for a moment take it seriously; by that time relativity had become so thoroughly integrated into the structure of physics that the aether had gone for ever. In 1958, Miller's results were shown to be invalid because of temperature fluctuations (Powers, 1982, pp. 82–5).

---

[2] See Kennedy and Thorndike (1932), and Taylor and Wheeler (1966), pp. 14, 78.

Causality and Light Cones

One of the consequences of the Lorentz transformation is that events that are simultaneous in one frame of reference are no longer always so in another; it depends on the relative velocity between the observer and the events. We cannot send or receive a signal that travels with infinite velocity, so we have lost the God's-eye view of events implicit in Newtonian space-time, and this has implications for causality.

We may mention at this point that there has recently been much discussion of the possibility of what are called non-local interactions, which seem to imply the possibility of a signal travelling instantly from one point to another, contrary to relativity. This will be discussed in a subsequent chapter.

Since the greatest possible velocity is that of light, we cannot influence events immediately. We have to wait until our light signal gets there. This is conveniently represented by a light cone. Each space-time event is represented by a point in four-dimensional hyperspace and if we omit one of the spatial dimensions we can represent it by a cone.

This cone shows the past and future events that can influence or be influenced by an observer at the origin O. The surface of the cone is the locus of all possible light rays that pass through O. Thus any event such as A within the backward light cone can influence O, and O can influence any event such as B within the forward light cone. Events such as C and D, outside the light cone, can neither influence O nor be influenced by O. Whenever there is a causal relation between two events, their time ordering is absolute.

The theory of relativity, and the concept of space-time, have sometimes given the impression that space and time have somehow been merged together. This is reinforced by the remark by Minkowski (1923) that henceforward space and time have been banished into the shadows and replaced by space-time. There nevertheless remains a fundamental difference between the two, namely that it is possible to travel in any direction in space at a speed we can choose (provided that it is less than the velocity of light), whereas we can travel in only one direction in time, and at a rate that we cannot change. We cannot travel into the past to see what went on, and we cannot travel into the future any faster or slower than we do.

Einstein's Concept of Space and Time

In the years following Newton there were many discussions of space and time. The nineteenth-century French physicist Henri Poincaré was undecided between relativism and absolutism (Holton, 1973, p. 188). He considered defining time with reference to the sensorium of Newton's 'intelligence infinie', 'une sorte de grande conscience qui verrait tout, et qui classerait tout dans son temps', but could not accept this because the infinite intelligence, 'si même elle existerait, serait impénétrable pour nous'. Poincaré was a physicist who used his great abilities to develop and improve existing theories, but failed to make the creative leap that enabled the whole problem to be seen in a new light. That was finally achieved by Einstein (Stachel, 1990).

Einstein always looked for the most general principles underlying phenomena. In his early years he was strongly influenced by the philosopher Ernst Mach, and so he developed his concept of space and time from the point of view of an observer, considering how space and time are actually measured. At that time, he was a pure empiricist (Reiser, 1930, pp. 51–2) and identified reality with what is given by sensations. He learnt about the current theories of electromagnetic phenomena by studying the works of Helmholtz, Maxwell, Kirchhoff, Hertz and Boltzmann, and especially the textbook of Foppl. It is notable that the last work retains the aether and absolute motion, and draws attention to precisely the same problem, namely that of the relative motion of a magnet and an electrical circuit, that Einstein considers at the beginning of his pioneering paper of 1905. In his major work, *The Science of Mechanics*, Mach (1907) criticized 'the conceptual monstrosity of absolute space' because it is 'purely a thought-thing which cannot be pointed to in experience' (Holton, 1973, p. 221). It is thus notable that this paper of Einstein contained two very general hypotheses that are certainly not empirical, namely the constancy of the velocity of light and the extension of the principle of relativity to all branches of physics (Holton, 1973, p. 232). This principle maintains that the behaviour of phenomena, and the laws governing them, is independent of the reference frame used to describe them. Contrary to the usual accounts of the genesis of the special theory of relativity, Einstein was not greatly influenced by the result of the Michelson–Morley experiment, although he was aware of it (Holton, 1973, pp. 261–352). The essential difference between him and Newton is that Einstein's approach is more attuned to the necessity of defining concepts in such a way that they can be measured, and contained 'features of rationalism and extreme empiricism that were both essential to Einstein's achievement'. This does not affect the validity of Newton's absolute space and time.

The reactions to Einstein's paper ranged from the enthusiastic welcome of the positivists to the guarded scepticism of Max Planck. Thus the positivist Josef Petzoldt hailed the theory as 'the victory over the metaphysics of absolutes in the conception of space and time'. Although Planck (1960) defended Einstein's work, he opposed Mach's view that 'nothing is real except the perceptions', and maintained that the basic aim of science is 'the finding of a fixed world picture independent of the variation of time and people' (Holton, 1973, p. 227). In the years following 1905, more physicists came to accept relativity, partly because it explained the result of the Michelson–Morley experiment in a convincing way (unlike the *ad hoc* Fitzgerald contraction) and partly because of its inner consistency (Wien, 1909, p. 32).

Lorentz's Concept of Space and Time

Following Newton, Lorentz retained the concepts of absolute space and time, while admitting that there seems to be no way that they can be established or detected. This does not, however, imply there are no practical differences between his interpretation of the relativistic formalism and that of Einstein. Newton and Lorentz both accepted the possibility of instantaneous action at a distance, without having any physical explanation of how this can occur. It is, however, incompatible with Einstein's interpretation because it implies the affirmation of the absolute simultaneity of two distant events (Popper, 1956, p. 20). Thus experiments like that of Aspect et al. (1983) designed to test the Bell inequalities could provide a proof of the correctness of the Lorentz interpretation.

The acceptance of absolute space means a return to the concept of the aether, and indeed this has already been reappearing in elementary particle theory where what is called the vacuum is teeming with virtual particles. Lorentz's interpretation also allows time dilation to be derived in a physical way by considering a light clock (Craig, 2000).

Once we accept absolute space, absolute time is implied by the success of our continuing efforts to construct more and more accurate clocks. These ever-closer approximations give the time in our reference frame, and this can be related to the absolute time in the absolute spatial system. This raises the question whether time has an absolute beginning. It has been suggested that to ask what happened before the beginning of time is like asking what happens north of the North Pole. Another suggestion is that the infinite past can be transformed into the zero of time by a logarithmic transformation, but this is incompatible with known physical laws.

Thus there is nothing in the formalism of special relativity to exclude the concepts of absolute space and time (Earman, 1970, pp. 288, 371). Although it was not possible to measure or detect them in Newton's or Einstein's days, this can now be done in principle by reference to the unique singularity of the Big Bang. Absolute time can be measured from that event, and an absolute spatial system is provided by the cosmic microwave background radiation. The expanding universe provides an inertial system, and anisotropy measurements can detect motion with respect to that frame (Rosen, 1968). The times taken for the return of two light rays travelling equal distances parallel and perpendicular to the earth's motion will differ by a very small amount that depends on the rate of expansion of the universe. This is far below the level of detectability in a Michelson–Morley experiment, but would be easily measurable if the experiment could be done over cosmic distances. Thus for a distance like that to 'the nearest quasar (about three billion parsecs) it amounts to some two hours' (Ne'eman, 1974). Such an experiment is impracticable, but more recently Conklin (1972) has determined the absolute velocity of the earth by measuring the anisotropy of the cosmic microwave background, and finds it to be 140 km/s in a known specified direction. Such measurements can be made by any observer, and so this satisfies the conditions for absolute space. Such a preferred reference frame is required by realist interpretations of quantum mechanics (Hardy, 1992). If the universe is finite, its centre of gravity also provides an absolute point in space, but this cannot be determined. Of course such considerations do not provide measures of space and time with anything like the accuracy required for practical purposes, but this does not affect their value in defining absolute space and time. Thus, according to Prokhovnik (1992, p. 388),

> astronomical observation and cosmological theory have revealed a unique, observable reference frame, associated with the distribution of matter and the propagation of light in the universe. The existence of such a frame provides a complete physical interpretation of special relativity along the lines of Lorentz' programme as completed by G. Boulder. This approach is considered by John Bell to be entirely valid and pedagogically superior to the usual presentation of the special theory.

Einstein's General Theory of Relativity

Newton, when he postulated his law of gravitation, declined to speculate about the origin of the gravitational force. He was criticized for introducing an occult quality, a force that acts instantaneously from one particle to another without apparently affecting or involving the intervening space. This discussion is still alive today in connection with non-locality in quantum mechanics. Attempts by Le Sage and others to find a mechanism for gravitation were not successful. This problem was solved by Einstein's General Theory of Relativity, which was a generalization of the Special Theory. The Special Theory considers the transformations between reference frames moving relative to each other with a constant velocity. Einstein also considered what happens when one is accelerated with respect to the other, and this led to his General Theory.

Einstein realized that to be in an accelerated frame is just the same as to be in a gravitational field. When, for example, we are sitting on a chair, we feel our body pressed to the chair by the force of gravity. If we were in a rocket in space, far from any gravitational field, we would feel just the same force when the rocket was accelerating. This can be expressed by saying that gravitational mass is equivalent to inertial mass. If then we were to shine a light beam, we would observe that it is deflected from a straight line in both cases, relative to our own reference frame. In one case the deflection is because of the accelerated motion and in the other because of the gravitational field. However, we know that light always takes the shortest distance between two points; usually this is a straight line but in this case it is a curve, and this can only be because space itself is curved.

There are three tests of general relativity: the gravitational red shift, the gravitational deflection of light and the precession of the perihelion of the planet Mercury (Dicke, 1965–68, p. 25). Measurement of the first shows agreement with the theory to about 5 per cent. The second can be tested by seeing if the path of a light ray is indeed bent when it passes through a gravitational field. This is a very difficult measurement, but it can be done by observing the light from a star when it passes very close to the sun. If it is deflected, then the position of the star relative to nearby stars will be changed. The difficulty is that we cannot see the light of a star when it passes near the

Table 6.1 Comparison between measured and precessions of several planets and an asteroid in
seconds of arc per century and the values
calculated by general relativity

Planet	Measured precession	Calculated precession
Mercury	43.1 ± 0.5	43.0″
Icarus	9.8 ± 0.8	10.5″
Venus	8.4 ± 0.5	8.3″
Earth	5.0 ± 1.2	3.8″

Source: Sandin (1989).

sun because of the sun's brilliance. If, however, the sun's light could somehow
be shielded we might be able to see the star, and this indeed happens during a
total eclipse of the sun. This happens very rarely, but fortunately there was a
suitable occasion in 1918, soon after Einstein published his theory (Stanley,
2003). An expedition was organized to the place where the eclipse was
expected, and the necessary observations were made. Newtonian theory
predicted a deflection of 0.87° and Einstein's theory 1.74°: the measurements
gave 1.98 ± 0.96 and 1.61 ± 0.40 for two sets of observations in agreement
with Einstein's theory. Far more accurate results are now obtainable using
radio signals. Thus Robertson and Carter (1984; see also Will, 1987) found the
ratio of the calculated to the observed deflection to be 1.008 ± 0.005 (see
Bernstein, 1996, p. 40).

The General Theory also accounts for the precession of the perihelion of
Mercury. According to Newtonian physics, the orbit of a planet should remain
fixed in space, but because of the perturbations due to the other planets it
gradually rotates. This was measured for the planet Mercury and found to be
1° 33′ 20″ per century. Calculations using Newtonian mechanics gave 1° 32′
37″, a difference of 43″. This is a very small effect, and indicates the precision
of the measurements and of Newtonian dynamics. The difference, however, is
quite outside the experimental uncertainties. Einstein repeated the calculations
according to his general relativity theory, and found 43″. He was so excited
that he nearly had a heart attack. Some comparisons between measured and
calculated precessions are given in Table 6.1.

Other confirmations of general relativity come from measurements of the red
shift (that is, the decrease in frequency) of the light emitted from very massive
stars, the red shift of radar echoes and the emission of gravitational radiation
from radio pulsars.

These comparisons between Newtonian dynamics and Einstein's general
relativity show once again that agreement of a theory with experiment to very
high accuracy does not guarantee that it is correct. There may be more than
one theory that fits the data, and later measurements of higher accuracy may
show some differences.

Popular Reactions to Relativity

The strangeness of relativity took hold of the public imagination. Einstein, with his wayward hair and absent-minded manner, probing the mysteries of the universe by pure thought, was just what they expected a scientist to be. Journalists waxed lyrical and soon people were saying that Einstein had shown that everything is relative. This is clearly unacceptable to a wide range of believers, from Christians to communists, and so the theory was attacked from many directions.

In political and religious circles, the theory of relativity was seen as a threat to be condemned. According to the *New York Times* in 1922, 'The Russian Communist Party condemned the Einstein theory as being "reactionary in character, furnishing support of counter-revolutionary ideas", and also "the product of the bourgeois class in decomposition".' Sakharov (1990, p. 46) has recalled the 'slanderous, ugly and destructive campaigns that had shaken scientific and academic institutions from one end of the country to another in the late 1930s ... The particular offence of Mandelshtam and his associates was their attachment to the "anti-materialist" theory of relativity.' He relates that the theoretical physicist Igor Tamm once remarked of a badly phrased question that it 'was as meaningless as asking whether a meridian is red or green'. At this, Professor Mitskevich jumped up and declared: 'I don't know about Professor Tamm, but for a true Soviet citizen a meridian is always red.' We may be inclined to laugh, but one of Mandelshtam's best students, Alexander Vitt, was arrested and died in detention in 1937, and several more physicists were imprisoned.

In a speech in 1947 Zhadanov called for a fight against 'countless philosophical weeds', against 'the whole arsenal of the philosophical lackeys of imperialism' and even against 'smuggling God into science'. He strongly condemned Einstein's theory of relativity. In 1952, I. V. Kuznetsov, a Party theoretician, wrote on the relation of science to dialectical materialism, and claimed that 'Soviet physics is the standard bearer for the most modern and progressive ideas of contemporary natural science'. He declared that the development of science can only be secured by the 'total renunciation of Einstein's conception, without compromise or half-measure'. In 1953, Yuri Zhandov, a member of the Communist Party Central Committee, was reported in *Pravda*:

> Mr Zhandov denounced as prime examples of bourgeois reactionary tendencies in science the physicists Albert Einstein and Niels Bohr and the British astronomer Sir Arthur Eddington. He said that Soviet scientists who had accepted their views and circulated them within Russia were guilty of allowing virulent enemies of Marxism to circulate their opinions in Soviet society.

Einstein's theory was also reviled in Nazi Germany, largely because Einstein was a Jew. The physicist Lenard declared that relativity is a Jewish fraud, which one could have suspected from the first with more radical knowledge than was then disseminated, since its originator, Einstein, was a Jew ... The most important example of the dangerous influence of Jewish circles on the study of nature has been provided by Herr Einstein with his mathematically botched-up theories consisting of some ancient ideas and a few arbitrary additions. This theory now gradually falls to pieces. (Klotz, 1986, p. 85)

He added that the Jew 'conspicuously lacks any understanding of truth beyond a merely superficial agreement with reality, which is independent of human thought'. He and Stark dismissed relativity theory as nonsense. Scientists such as Heisenberg, who supported and used the theory of relativity, were regarded as 'white Jews' and were also persecuted.

Curiously enough, religious authorities also opposed the theory of relativity, though not for the same reasons. In Boston, an eminent cleric described relativity as 'befogged speculations producing universal doubt about God and His Creation' and 'cloaking the ghastly apparition of atheism'.

The then Archbishop of Canterbury, Randall Davidson, was told by Lord Haldane that 'relativity was going to have a great effect on theology, and that it was his duty as head of the English Church to make himself acquainted with it' (Bell, 1935, p. 1052). The Archbishop took this advice seriously, obtained several books on the subject, and tried to read them. He did not have much success in his attempts to understand relativity, and indeed was driven to a state of intellectual desperation. He therefore asked Einstein what effect relativity would have on religion, and was told: 'None. Relativity is a purely scientific matter and has nothing to do with religion.' So that was that.

The Archbishop comes out of this story rather well. In the first place he actually listened to what he was told, and went to the trouble of getting some books on relativity and trying to understand what it was all about. He made the usual assumption that any highly educated arts man can in a few hours master any scientific subject, but soon realized his mistake. Then instead of forgetting about the whole matter, he asked a scientist for his advice, and chose a scientist who really knew about the subject. If only his example were followed today, we would be spared the acutely embarrassing spectacle of churchmen and churchwomen moralizing on scientific and technical matters without having understood the first thing about them.

In spite of the Archbishop's example, the popularity of the theory of relativity among the general public, reinforced by the image of Einstein as the typical scientist, gave impetus to the idea that physics is relative, and thence that everything is relative. If Einstein had called his work the theory of invariance we would perhaps have been spared this nonsense. Max Planck (1933, p. 142) regarded attempts to show that relativity supports the positivist attitude as entirely mistaken.

A recent example of the way phrases from relativity can be used in a theological context is contained in a book derived from some television programmes on the effects of our new knowledge on theology. Here we read:

It is rare now to find pastoral counsellors referring people to an absolute morality or an absolute set of principles. Spirituality has come to be about exploring one's own frame of reference in order to discover why you see things as you do. How individuals construct reality is more important than how reality is ... in the context of prayer, rigid notions about the present and the past have to loosen up ... where time is flexible relative to each person, the past can be revisited and healed.

Needless to say, this dangerous subjectivism is connected to Einstein's theory only by the name. The author is simply using ill-digested scientific jargon to bolster dubious theological views. Einstein was concerned in this theory to establish the invariant quantities in systems of particles in motion. Furthermore, while the past can be healed, it is false to say that it can be revisited.

Einstein's Religion[3]

Einstein was born into a non-practising Jewish family that had not renounced their Jewish heritage but did not follow traditional rites or attend services in the synagogue. At the age of six Einstein entered a Catholic primary school and at the same time his parents arranged for a relative to give him instruction in the principles of Judaism. This latter teaching filled him with religious enthusiasm, and he fervently followed religious prescriptions. His love for music appeared at an early age and 'Music, Nature and God became intermingled in him in a complex of feeling'. His schooling led him to respect both the Catholic and the Jewish religions, and an attitude of toleration towards all sincerely held religious beliefs remained throughout his life, although he rejected any affiliation with organized religious bodies.

His religious phase came to an end at the age of about twelve as a result of reading some popular science books. These convinced him that many of the biblical stories cannot be true. As he recalls in his autobiography, 'the consequence was a positive orgy of freethinking coupled with the impression that youth is intentionally being deceived by the state through lies. Suspicion against every kind of authority grew out of this experience', and as a result he refused to be bar-mitzvahed.

Later in his life, Einstein wryly remarked that 'to punish me for my contempt of authority, Fate made me an authority myself'. It has been suggested that this 'enabled him to develop the powerful independence of mind that gave him the courage to challenge established scientific beliefs and thereby revolutionize physics'. However, in spite of this attitude to authority, Einstein always regarded science and religion as complementary to each other. In 1930 he declared emphatically that 'I am of the opinion that all the finer speculations in the field of science spring from a deep religious feeling, and without such feeling they would not be fruitful'. The contradiction between such remarks

---

[3] The Einstein quotes in this section are taken from Jammer (1999).

and his aversion to institutional religion is only apparent, and can be understood by recognizing that Einstein used the word 'religion' in two senses: the recognition of a mind behind nature on the one hand, and institutional religion on the other.

Einstein maintained 'that cosmic religious feeling is the strongest and noblest incitement to scientific research'. His closest friend Max von Laue said of him:

> The deepest element in his outlook was his religiosity. For him the world was the work of a creative spirit who – in spite of supreme superiority – remains comprehensible, though this comprehension reveals itself to mortals only gradually, by great effort, step by step, and is never granted in its completeness. This is why the system of a science which searches into nature must be a unified whole. (Rosenthal-Schneider, 1980, p. 105).

When Einstein was asked whether he was deeply religious, he replied: 'Yes, you can call it that. Try and penetrate without limited means the secrets of nature and you will find that, behind all the discernible concatenations, there remains something subtle, intangible and inexplicable. Veneration for this force beyond anything we can comprehend is my religion. To that extent I am, in point of fact, religious.' Speaking of mathematics, he said: 'It seems to me a revelation of the highest Author, and I will never forget it' (Pais, 1994, p. 205). Concerned by accusations that Einstein was an atheist, Rabbi Goldstein asked him whether he believed in God. Einstein replied: 'I believe in Spinoza's God who reveals himself in the orderly harmony of what exists, not in a God who concerns himself with fates and actions of human beings.' When a secularist said that this was indistinguishable from atheism, Einstein replied that 'we followers of Spinoza see our God in the wonderful order and lawfulness of all that exists and in its soul as it reveals itself in man and animal'. On another occasion he remarked: 'I want to know how God created this world. I'm not interested in this or that phenomena, in the spectrum of this or that element. I want to know His thoughts, the rest are details.'

This belief in the lawfulness of nature is the basis of Einstein's epistemological realism: he regarded 'physics as an attempt to grasp reality as it is thought, independently of its being observed'. He believed in the mysterious comprehensibility of the world, that our equations accurately describe an objectively existing reality, and yet he was astonished that this is so. No longer are facts alone the final court of appeal. Thus he was unmoved when the results of the experiments of Kaufmann (1906) disagreed with the predictions of his theory. He was confident that the experiment was faulty, as indeed eventually proved to be the case. It was the same for his theory of gravitation. In a letter to Mach (25 June 1913) he remarks that the next solar eclipse will show whether it is correct or not (Holton, 1973, p. 228). However, as recorded by Rosenthal-Schneider (1980), when he received Eddington's cable confirming that the deflection of light by a gravitational field agreed with relativity and she congratulated him warmly, he was quite unmoved and simply said: 'I knew that the theory is correct.' When she asked him what he would have done if the result had been different, he replied, 'Then I would have been sorry for the dear Lord – the theory is correct.' This story is somewhat puzzling because Einstein knew very well that theories that do not agree with experiment just have to be abandoned, yet it serves to emphasize his strong belief in the order of nature and its openness to the human mind. Holton (1973, p. 389) has suggested a possible explanation for Einstein's remark. Since he knew that the theory is correct,

> the only way in which the expedition could have noticed a different result was if nature had arranged circumstances in a very unusual and painful way for this particular experimental test not to work. Sooner or later it would have worked out, and Einstein would have been sorry for the dear Lord to have gone to so much trouble in order to produce a different result in this case.

Spinoza believed that all natural events follow immutable laws of cause and effect, and this led Einstein to reject a theistic concept of God. This belief implies that the universe is like a giant machine following mathematical laws and so there is no place for purpose or morality. This denies human freedom and is quite contrary to the Judeo-Christian concept of a personal God. And yet Einstein was horrified by the brutalities of Nazi Germany and never forgave the Germans for voting for Hitler. He justified this apparent inconsistency by maintaining that although we are bound by determinism, we must conduct our moral lives as if we are free.

It is widely believed that the theory of relativity is a radical break with the past and that it implies that all beliefs, including religious beliefs, are not absolute but relative. Einstein rejected this view and saw his theory as a natural development of classical physics, remarking that 'the men who have laid the foundations of physics on which I have been able to construct my theory are Galileo, Newton, Maxwell and Lorentz'. The theory of relativity shows that the laws of nature are independent of the viewpoint of the observer, and so it would have been preferable to call it the theory of invariants.

Einstein's religion certainly affected his attitude to his scientific work. He maintained that 'ultimately the belief in the existence of fundamental all-embracing laws also rests on a sort of faith', so that religion provides psychological motivation for the scientists: 'What a deep conviction of the rationality of the universe ... Kepler and Newton must have had to enable them to spend years of solitary labour in disentangling the principles of classical mechanics!' As Whitehead has remarked, it is the conviction that there is a rational order in nature and that it can be found that provides the strength to carry on in spite of the difficulties encountered, and this is essentially a religious conviction. It provided Einstein with the motivation to spend years on an ultimately unsuccessful effort to formulate a unified theory of matter. He wanted to know 'whether God could have created the world in a different way; in other words, whether the requirement of logical simplicity admits a margin of freedom'. In a discussion with the Indian philosopher Rabindranath Tagore, Einstein insisted that the world exists independently of man: 'We attribute to Truth a superhuman objectivity: it is indispensable for us, this reality which is independent of our existence and our experience and our mind.' Tagore disagreed, maintaining that truth is what appears to be true (Pais, 1994, p. 104).

Einstein's belief that the universe is ruled by strict deterministic laws lay behind his opposition to those who maintained that the new quantum mechanics is the final complete theory. This is expressed by the remark that 'quantum mechanics is very worthy of regard, but an inner voice tells me that it is not the true Jacob. The theory yields much, but it hardly brings us close to the secrets of the Old One. In any case, I am convinced that He does not play dice.' He preferred a statistical interpretation whereby the wave function describes the average behaviour of an ensemble of similar systems since this allows one to accept all the results of quantum mechanics as governed by a fully deterministic substratum.

In a contribution to a theological conference in 1939, Einstein began by emphasizing that science on its own cannot tell us the ultimate reason and purpose of our lives. Science cannot teach men to be moral, and 'every attempt to reduce ethics to scientific formulas must fail'. The reason for this is that science tells us what is, whereas morality is concerned with what ought to be.

Einstein's work involved him in two great debates: the first with Lorentz on space and time, and the second with Bohr on quantum mechanics. In the first, it was Lorentz the realist who maintained the existence of absolute space and time, while Einstein the positivist said that we can only consider space and time from the viewpoint of the observer, and thus admit only measurable quantities. In the second, it was Einstein the realist who held an objective deterministic view of the world, whereas Bohr the positivist held that we must consider only measurable quantities. In both cases the positivist theory is generally preferred by the majority of physicists. This may be due partly to the physicists' dislike of being drawn into metaphysical discussions and partly because of the prestige of Einstein as the sole originator of the theory in the case of relativity and the prestige of Bohr, in his position as the leader of the main school of theoretical physics at the time, in the case of quantum mechanics.

When he developed the theory of relativity Einstein was much influenced by Machian sensationalism and took the view that the aim of science is to correlate measurable quantities. Subsequently, his deeply held Judeo-Christian beliefs reasserted themselves and he came to believe that the aim of science is to find out about an objective external world. His experience of scientific creativity taught him that it is not possible to construct science just by ordering sensations (Holton, 1973, pp. 197–271; Jaki, 1978, pp. 183–93). In his autobiographical notes, he remarks that 'in my younger years, Mach's epistemological position influenced me very greatly, a position which today appears essentially untenable' (Schilpp, 1949, p. 21). Einstein knew that his science and his philosophy were closely interrelated and, when writing to Lanczos, recalled:

> I began with a sceptical empiricism rather like that of Mach. But the problem of gravitation converted me into a believing rationalist, that is, into someone who searches for the only reliable source of Truth in mathematical simplicity ... The mind can proceed so far upon what it

knows and can prove. There comes a point where the mind takes a higher plane of knowledge, but it can never prove how it got there. All great discoveries have involved such a leap. (Clark, 1979).

He was well aware that 'there is, of course, no logical way leading to the establishment of a theory but only groping constructive efforts by careful considerations of factual knowledge'. According to Einstein, 'scientific concepts are freely created inventions of the human mind and no logical connection exists between our sense experience and our theoretical concepts of the universe'. In constructing his theories Einstein always found it more fruitful to take a God's-eye view of the world. He adopted a realist stance on the interpretation of quantum mechanics and did not hesitate to speak of unobservables. When Heisenberg asked him why he did not still adhere to the positivist approach underlying the theory of relativity, he replied: 'Maybe I did believe that, but it is nonsense just the same' (Heisenberg, 1971, p. 63).

Modern science is rooted in Christian beliefs about the rationality and contingency of the natural world, and our concepts of space and time derive from the theological beliefs of Newton and Einstein. However, as Einstein remarked, 'an important non-reciprocal relation holds between religion and science: science is greatly dependent upon religion, but not vice-versa'.

CHAPTER 7

Quantum Theory

The Discovery of the Quantum

By the nineteenth century classical physics was well established. Newtonian dynamics provided the way to calculate the behaviour of bodies in motion, and Maxwell's electromagnetic theory accounted for electric and magnetic phenomena. Yet in a few years around the turn of the century several experimental discoveries were made that opened up a whole new world. Becquerel discovered radioactivity, and Planck's explanation of the spectra of black-body radiation required the introduction of the quantum. These and other discoveries could not be explained by existing classical concepts, and it was only after two decades of intensive work that the foundations of a new understanding were laid.

The advent of the quantum was totally unexpected. Unlike the Special Theory of Relativity, it was in no sense a logical extension of what had been known before. It was forced on reluctant physicists by the results of measurements of the spectrum of black-body radiation, and subsequently confirmed by the photoelectric effect and by Compton scattering. Later on, it proved to be the key to understanding the structure of the atom and the nucleus.

Max Planck came from a distinguished family of scholars, lawyers and doctors. He was a rather severe and upright Prussian, in contrast to the more Bohemian Einstein. He was said to personify the German Protestant ideal of an 'excellent, incorruptible, idealistic man, devoted to the service of Church and State' (Heilbron, 1986, p. 168). His early work was on thermodynamics, and he realized that the spectrum of black-body radiation is a universal and fundamental characteristic of matter, and therefore worthy of serious study. Black-body radiation is emitted from a small hole in the side of a furnace. The interior walls of the furnace are rough, and the hole is small, to ensure that the radiation reaches statistical equilibrium before emission. The spectrum of the black-body radiation was measured accurately, and it was a challenging problem to try to understand it.

Rayleigh and Jeans used classical physics to derive the frequency distribution of the radiation at a temperature T and found it to be

$$\rho(v, T) = \frac{8\pi v^2}{c^3} kT$$

where v is the frequency and k is Boltzmann's constant. This agrees quite well with measurements at low frequencies, but tends to infinity for high frequencies, which is obviously wrong. This is the 'ultraviolet catastrophe'.

More generally, Wien (1909) proved his displacement law

$$\rho(v, T) = v^2 f(v/T)$$

He also calculated the spectral distribution, and he found

$$\rho(v, T) = \alpha v^3 \exp(-hv/T)$$

where α and h are constants. This is correct for high frequencies but not for low frequencies. The frequency at the maximum of the spectral distribution is proportional to the temperature, and the total amount of radiation is proportional to the fourth power of the temperature; this is Stefan's law.

To find a formula for the spectral distribution that is correct for all frequencies, and reduces to those of Rayleigh and Jeans for low frequencies and to that of Wien for high frequencies, Planck used the expression for the energy distribution of oscillators that is related to the frequency distribution by

$$\rho(v, T) = \frac{8\pi v^2}{c^3} u(v, T)$$

and then evaluated the second derivative of the entropy S with respect to u, making use of the relation $dS/du = 1/T$. For the Rayleigh–Jeans distribution this gives

$$\frac{d^2 S}{du^2} = \frac{k}{u^2} \qquad \text{for low } v$$

and for the Wien distribution, taking $\alpha = 8\pi/c^3$

$$\frac{d^2 S}{du^2} = -\frac{1}{hv} \cdot \frac{k}{\mu} \qquad \text{for high } v$$

Planck then surmised that the general formula, valid for all frequencies, is

$$\frac{d^2 S}{du^2} = -\frac{k}{\mu(hv + u)}$$

which reduces to the above formulae for low and high v. This gives

$$\rho(v, T) = \frac{8\pi h v^3}{c^3} \cdot \frac{1}{\exp(hv/kT) - 1}$$

This reduces to the Rayleigh–Jeans distribution for low frequencies and for high frequencies gives the Wien distribution in the form

$$\rho(v, T) = \frac{8\pi h v^3}{c^3} \exp(-hv/kT)$$

It also satisfies the other two conditions, and is in excellent agreement with experiment for all frequencies.

The next problem was to see how it might be obtained theoretically. To do this Planck considered a system of radiating oscillators and to facilitate the calculations he assumed that they emit radiation in discrete amounts, or quanta, with energies proportional to the frequency. Thus each quantum has energy hv, where h is a constant (later to be known as Planck's constant). From statistical mechanics, the number of oscillators of energy nhv is proportional to the exponential of $-nhv/kT$. The average energy is thus

$$E = \frac{\sum_{n=0}^{\infty} nhv \exp\ (-nhv/kT)}{\sum_{n=0}^{\infty} \exp\ (-nhv/kT)} = \frac{hv}{\exp\ (+hv/kT) - 1}$$

Multiplying by the number of oscillators per unit volume gives Planck's formula.

Planck intended to obtain the final formula by allowing the discrete elements to become infinitesimally small. To his astonishment, he found that the formula using discrete amounts of energy is correct, whereas that obtained in the infinitesimal limit is not. His conservative nature rebelled against the idea of a discrete quantum of energy, and he tried for a very long time to disprove his result. He failed to do so, and in the meantime there came many other results that confirmed the quantum hypothesis.

The story of the discovery of the quantum is one more illustration of the objectivity of the material world. It shows clearly that physicists do not impose their ideas on nature; on the contrary we have to mould our ideas to agree with the objective results of observations and measurements.

Einstein showed that Planck's distribution can also be derived by considering radiation in a container at temperature T. The number of atoms in a particular quantum state is proportional to $\exp(-E/kT)$, so the ratio N_2/N_1 of the numbers in two states of energies E_1 and E_2 is $\exp(-(E_2-E_1)/kT)$, which is $\exp(-hv/kT)$, where hv is the energy of the radiation emitted in a transition from state 2 to state 1. Now let A_{nm} be the probability per unit time that an atom in state n will make a spontaneous transition to state m. The total number of such transitions is thus $N_n A_{nm}$ per second. In addition, there are transitions induced by the radiation of density $\rho(v)$. The probability per second of an induced transition from state 1 to state 2 is $N_1 B_{12}\rho(v)$ and that from state 2 to state 1 is $N_2 B_{21}\rho(v)$. When the system is in equilibrium, by the principle of detailed balance,

$$N_2 A_{21} + N_2 B_{21}\rho(v) = N_1 B_{12}\rho(v)$$

Making use of the above value of the ratio N_2/N_1 and applying the condition that in the limit of low frequency the expression for $\rho(v)$ must reduce to the Rayleigh–Jeans formula immediately gives the Planck distribution.

There are several other experiments that provided strong evidence for the existence of the quantum, particularly the photoelectric effect and Compton scattering.

When metals are irradiated by light, electrons are emitted, and Lenard found that the energies of these electrons are proportional to the frequency of the light but are unaffected by its intensity, contrary to classical expectations. Einstein realized that these observations can easily be explained if light is propagated in quanta of discrete energy, called photons, and that each photon ejects one electron. The energy of the electron is thus given by the energy of the photon less the energy it loses when it escapes from the metal,

$$E = h\nu - W$$

This simple relation agrees with the measurements and gave the same value for Planck's constant as that found from the black-body radiation. Einstein received a Nobel Prize for this work, not for the theory of relativity, which at that time was considered too controversial.

Compton studied the scattering of light by free electrons, and found that the changes in the frequencies of the photons scattered through various angles are just what would be expected from relativistic kinematics for the collision of a photon with an electron, assuming that they are both particles. This confirmed that light is made of photons of energy, $h\nu$.

The Old Quantum Theory

The idea of the quantum was used by Niels Bohr to make the first successful theory of the structure of the atom. It had long been known that heated bodies emit light of certain definite frequencies that are characteristic of the substance. Each chemical element emits a definite spectrum of frequencies, and these enable it to be identified. We are all familiar with the yellow sodium and the green mercury light from street lamps. Careful studies of spectra showed thousands of frequencies, or lines, as they are called, and they obviously contain information about the emitting atom. It was a challenging problem to try to decipher the spectra. Most spectra are extremely complicated, but that of hydrogen is particularly simple, and shows striking regularities. This had been known for many years, and Balmer found that they can be represented quite accurately by a simple formula

$$\lambda = b \frac{n^2}{n^2 - 4}$$

for the wavelength of a line, where n is an integer greater than two. Expressed in terms of the frequency, this can be rewritten

$$\nu = a \left(\frac{1}{2^2} - \frac{1}{n^2} \right)$$

where a is a constant that is known experimentally to high accuracy.

Bohr knew from the work of Rutherford that the atom consists of a small central nucleus surrounded by a cloud of electrons. He postulated that the electrons revolve around the nucleus in circular orbits, and that they radiate only when they jump from one orbit to a lower one. The frequency of the emitted radiation is given by the Einstein relation

$$v = (E_2 - E_1)/h$$

where E_1 and E_2 are the energies of the electrons in the two orbits and h is Planck's constant.

For an electron in a circular orbit the electrostatic attraction to the nucleus is balanced by the centrifugal force, so that

$$Ze^2/r^2 = mv^2/r$$

where e and Ze are the charges on the electron and on the nucleus, m and v the mass and velocity of the electron and r the radius of the orbit. Bohr now imposed the quantum condition that the angular momentum of the electron is an integral multiple of $h/2\pi$, so that

$$mvr = nh/2\pi$$

This gives for the total energy of a state of an electron

$$E = 1/2\,mv^2 - \frac{Ze^2}{r} = \frac{-2\pi^2 mZ^2 e^4}{h^2 n^2}$$

The frequency of emission corresponding to a transition from a state 2 to a state 1 is therefore given by

$$v = \frac{2\pi^2 mZ^2 e^4}{h^3} \left(\frac{1}{n_1^2} - \frac{1}{n_2^2} \right)$$

which is Balmer's formula with $n_1 = 2$. Inserting the known values of the fundamental constants gives the value of the constant in Balmer's formula, and it was found to be correct within the uncertainties of measurement.

This was an astonishing achievement, and opened the door to our understanding of the structure of the atom. It immediately attracted widespread attention. There are, however, very serious objections to Bohr's atomic theory. In the first place, an electron in an orbit is continually accelerated towards the centre and by the laws of electromagnetism it must continually radiate energy and thus rapidly spiral into the nucleus in about a million millionth of a second. Furthermore, what actually happens when an electron jumps from one orbit to another? How does it know when and where to jump and at what frequency to radiate before it reaches the other orbit? There is no answer to these questions in the context of classical theory. Such objections would have normally been fatal, but it was undeniable that Bohr's theory gave for the first time a way to calculate the frequencies of light emitted from atoms.

Bohr's theory predicted several other series of lines in the hydrogen spectrum. Comparison with Balmer's formula shows that the latter applies to transitions from states with $n = 2$. Obviously there are other series with $n = 1, 3$ and 4, and these have indeed been found; they are the Lyman, Paschen and Brackett series. The theory also applies to singly ionized helium, which is similar to hydrogen but has $Z = 2$. The frequencies of the lines in the ionized helium spectrum should therefore be the same as those of hydrogen, but multiplied by four. This was found to be very nearly the case, apart from a small but significant discrepancy that was resolved as soon as it was realized that one has to take account of the motion of the centre of mass by using the reduced mass of the electron. Full agreement was then restored, and so accurate are spectroscopic measurements that it was possible to deduce an accurate value for the ratio of the mass of the electron to that of the proton.

Many attempts were made to apply Bohr's theory to heavier atoms, but with indifferent success. The old quantum theory led to the discovery of the principal, angular momentum and magnetic quantum numbers, their selection rules, the theory of the Stark effect, the structure of the ground states of complex atoms, the Pauli exclusion principle, electron spin and the Fermi–Dirac and Bose–Einstein statistics. Yet in spite of these successes, it was obviously incorrect (Pais, 1994, p. 34).

This was the situation around 1920. Physicists were reduced to a state of despair. The only theory that even began to make sense of atomic structure was totally unacceptable classically. The distress was poignantly expressed by H. A. Lorentz, one of the greatest of the classical physicists, who wrote in 1924: 'I lost the certitude that my scientific work was bringing me closer to objective truth and I no longer know why I continue to live. I am only sorry not to have died five years ago when everything appeared clear.' Pauli, one of the most brilliant of the younger physicists, remarked in a letter to Kronig (21 May 1925) that 'physics is very muddled again at the moment; it is much too hard for me anyway, and I wish I were a movie comedian instead of a physicist' (Fierz and Weisskopf, 1960, p. 22).

In a very few years the clouds were lifted by the discovery of quantum mechanics, which is the subject of the next chapter. We now describe some other experiments that were important for its development.

Diffraction by a Single Slit

The diffraction of light by a single slit is familiar from optics. The form of the diffraction pattern may be calculated from Huygens's wave theory, and is in excellent agreement with the observations. In the corresponding experiment for electrons, a beam of electrons is incident on a narrow slit, and after passing through it they are detected on a screen. It is found that the beam fans out, and the intensity of the electrons hitting the screen follows a typical diffraction curve. This measurement is very difficult, and it was first made by Jonsson in

1961. The results are identical, and it is very natural to say that therefore electrons are waves. Certainly we can say that the observations are well accounted for by a wave theory, but this does not mean that the electrons are waves. The diffraction pattern is still obtained when the electrons pass through the apparatus one by one; this is quite different physically from a water wave, where all the water molecules act together. Whittaker has remarked (1942, p. 17) that the vibrations of an elliptic membrane and the gyrations of a variety artiste are both governed by Mathieu's equation but that this does not imply that the phenomena are the same.

An important feature of diffraction by a single slit is the reciprocal relation between the width of the slit (Δx) and the width of the diffraction pattern (Δp): if one is increased the other is reduced, and vice versa. More exactly, the product of the two widths is always greater than Planck's constant h. This is the Heisenberg uncertainty principle.

Diffraction by a single slit has been analysed by Beck and Nussenzweig (1958).

Diffraction by a Double Slit

The diffraction of light by two parallel slits is also familiar from optics. In the outer regions the diffraction is similar to that from a single slit, but in the central region there is according to the wave theory interference between the waves passing through one slit and those passing through the other slit. The corresponding experiment for electrons featured as an imaginary experiment for many years, until it was finally done by Jonsson (1961; see also Jonsson, 1974). In this experiment the slit width was 0.5 micron, and the slits were spaced 2 microns (2×10^{-4} cm) apart. This may be compared with the wavelength of the 50 KeV electrons that were used, which is 0.05 angstroms (Å), or 5×10^{-8} cm. More accurate results may be obtained using neutrons, and compared with calculations using the Fresnel–Kirchhoff theory (Zeilinger, 1986, 1988). It is notable that the comparison is with a classical wave theory, not with the result of solving Schrödinger's equation. This is justified because the range of the nuclear forces is much smaller than the dimensions of the slit. So far as I know, the diffraction by a double slit has not yet been solved quantum mechanically. This might indicate that it is hardly justified to make any deductions about quantum mechanics from the results of this experiment. Indeed, all this comparison really shows is that photons and electrons behave in the same way in diffraction experiments.

Experiments on electron scattering show that electrons behave as point particles down to distances of the order of 10^{-15} cm (Jackson, 1975) or 10^{-16} cm (Bender, 1984 p. 515; see also Hestenes and Weingartshofer, 1991, pp. 32, 171) and perhaps down to 10^{-20} cm (Zee, 1999, p. 303). The particle nature of electrons is also shown by the tracks of electrons in nuclear emulsions (Powell et al., 1959). It is thus very natural to suppose that an electron goes through one slit or the other, so if the particle theory is correct we would expect to see just the superposition of two single-slit diffraction patterns, and not the interference pattern that is observed. There is no possibility that electrons going through one slit interfere with electrons going through the other slit, because the electron intensity can be adjusted so that only one electron goes through the apparatus at a time (Merli et al., 1976; Tonamura, 1989). The interference pattern thus builds up gradually, electron by electron.

The presence of both particle and wave behaviour in the experiment has been the subject of much discussion, and will be summarized in Chapter 9. The same problem does not arise with photons, because we do not know how big they are.

Heisenberg did not accept the particle nature of electrons:

> I really feel it is better not to say that elementary particles are small bits of matter; it is better to say that they are just representations of symmetries ... the mathematical structures are deeper then the existence of mind or matter. Mind or matter is a consequence of mathematical structure. (Heisenberg quoted Gingerich, 1975, pp. 558–9)

It might be thought that we could determine which slit a particular electron traversed, but this would destroy the interference pattern. To observe the interference pattern the separation of the slits has to be comparable with the wavelength of the electrons, and this is so small that it is not possible to insert a detector.

It is not surprising that the behaviour of electrons seems strange. We form our conceptions of the material world with its particles and waves from our everyday experiences, augmented with what we see through the microscope and the telescope. Why should we expect that the same concepts to apply to the interactions of particles 10^{10} times smaller and of durations 10^{22} times shorter? It is frequently maintained that it is unjustified or even meaningless to apply concepts developed in the macroscopic world in areas of the microscopic world where sufficiently accurate measurements cannot be made. This is an example of the positivistic attitude, a philosophical position now discredited. It is not necessary to deny the possibility of a detailed causal description just because it cannot at present be observed. Such descriptions aid conceptual clarity and often lead to new advances that make it possible to observe what was previously unobservable. What must be avoided is to try to imagine logical contradictories, such as an entity that is a combination of a wave and a particle. We should therefore push the application of our everyday concepts as far as we can while recognizing that there are phenomena that seem to have no picturable mechanism, such as particle production and decay. This does not prevent them from being studied, and even if we cannot find a pictorial explanation, processes such as these can still be described mathematically.

Radioactivity

Many nuclei are radioactive; they emit alpha particles or electrons (beta decay). If we take a sample of a radioactive material, containing a very large number of atoms, we find that the probability that a particular nucleus decays is a constant, independent of time. As a consequence, the radioactivity of the sample decays exponentially with time. The rate of decay is characterized by the half-life, defined as the time it takes for the radioactivity of a large sample to decay to half its initial value. We can measure the time that a particular nucleus decays, but we cannot predict it or influence it in any way. It appears to be a totally random quantity. It is only the half-life that can be measured, using a sample containing a large number of nuclei. Like any statistical quantity, the measurements of the number of nuclei decaying in successive time intervals fluctuate around the value corresponding to the exponential decay curve, so the greater the number of nuclei in the sample, the more accurate is the value found for the half-life.

In the early days of nuclear physics, the half-lives of many radioactive decays were measured, together with the corresponding energies of the emitted particles. It was found empirically by Geiger and Nuttall (1911) that for each series of alpha-particle decays the logarithm of the half-life is linearly related to the logarithm of the energy. Alpha-particle half-lives vary from a very small fraction of a second to times comparable with the age of the universe, so it is a challenge to see how such a huge range can be explained. This was done by Gamow by applying the new quantum mechanics to the nucleus, as will be described in the next chapter.

Beta decay is more complicated because a neutrino is also emitted, and so it will not be further discussed.

Radioactive decay also raises problems about causality. If all nuclei of the same type are identical, then why do they decay at different times? If they are not identical, then how do they differ? All we can measure is the rate at which the number of decays per unit time in a sample decreases; this is a statistical quantity which tells us little about each individual event.

The Stern–Gerlach Experiment

This experiment, and its later elaborations, showed the quantization of spin and so poses many of the most fundamental problems of the quantum world. Stern and Gerlach (1922) passed a beam of neutral silver atoms from a furnace through a strong inhomogeneous magnetic field. Each atom is deflected due to the interaction of its magnetic moment with the field, and so we might expect that, since the atoms are randomly orientated, each atom will be deflected by an amount depending on the component of its magnetic moment in the direction of the field. But they found that the beam did not just fan out, as expected, but was split into two beams. This was the first direct evidence that physical quantities are quantized, that is, they can only take particular values and not a continuous spectrum of values. Descriptions of the Stern–Gerlach experiment can be found in many textbooks (e.g. Bleaney and Bleaney, 1976, p. 590).

The result of the experiment is then explained by saying that the valence electron of the silver atom can exist in two spin states. In the magnetic field, the spin of the electron must align itself either parallel or antiparallel to the field, and since the sign of the force due to the magnetic moment is different in the two cases, the beam is split into two.

This interpretation can be confirmed by additional experiments. Thus if one of these beams is passed through a second magnet with its field in the same direction as the first, it is deflected but not split. If, however, the second magnet is rotated so that its field is at right angles to that of the first, the beam is again split into two.

These observations can be explained by saying that the initial beam contains atoms with randomly oriented spins, and that the magnet separates them into two groups, according to the components of the spin along the direction of the magnetic field. However, we can make another experiment in which the beam is passed successively through three magnets, each with its field at right angles to its neighbour. It is found that the beam is split at each magnet, whereas according to our simple picture we would not expect any further splitting at the third magnet. To understand this result it seems that we have to abandon some of the assumptions of classical physics.

However, it seems from the account of Hughes (1989, p. 5) that this last experiment has not actually been done, although he does say that the result is consistent with all the evidence from actual experiments, some of which are very close in principle. Nevertheless, the result is not an actual observation, but what is predicted by quantum mechanics.

The Stern-Gerlach experiment is often incorrectly described in books on the quantum world; some even describe it as using electrons, a process shown to be impossible by Mott (192) and by Kalckar (1972).

CHAPTER 8

Quantum Mechanics

Introduction

The difficulties of the old quantum theory were largely dispelled by the development of quantum mechanics in the 1920s. First Heisenberg (1925) developed the rather abstract matrix mechanics and soon after Schrödinger (1926; see also Eckart, 1926) developed the physically more appealing wave mechanics. Subsequently he showed them to be mathematically equivalent. The physicists were greatly relieved; now they had once again a mathematical formalism that enabled the results of experiments to be calculated. It was possible to move forward.

It is certainly a very elegant and indeed beautiful formalism, and does enable the results of many physical measurements to be calculated with great accuracy. It is used daily by atomic and nuclear physicists; there is no other way to make calculations. From the earliest days there has been intense debate about the interpretation of quantum mechanics, and it shows no signs of being settled; if anything it is becoming more intense over the years. As Penrose has remarked, no one understands quantum mechanics. Feynman (1967; see also Sykes, 1994) also admitted that 'nobody understands quantum mechanics', and Einstein once remarked: 'I have thought a hundred times as much about the quantum problems as I have about general relativity theory' (Pais, 1994, p. 57). It should therefore be evident that the most that can be done here is to try to show where the real difficulties lie, and how the failure to recognize that quantum mechanics is an essentially statistical theory has led to a series of confusing quantum paradoxes. It is just these paradoxes that have often been used to support theological speculations.

It is useful to ask what 'understanding quantum mechanics' actually means. Certainly it means being able to calculate the results of many measurements. The same applies to Newton's theory of gravitation, which we understand in the sense that we can use it as a basis of calculation, although we do not really understand the gravitational force itself. Very often, especially in modern physics, the mathematical formalism does not give us the sort of intuitive physical feeling for what is going on that we often obtain from classical mechanics. Perhaps we can never achieve more than this for quantum mechanics. In classical mechanics we can assume that a property that is measured objectively exists prior to the interaction of the measuring apparatus with the observed system. Quantum mechanics, however, 'is incompatible with the proposition that measurement discovers some unknown but pre-existing property' (Peres, 1997, p. 14). There is an important distinction between mysteries and absurdities. We may be forced to live with mysteries, but there is no reason why we should put up with absurdities such as the wave–particle duality, tunnelling through potential barriers, acausal events and the collapse of the wave function. These are the quantum paradoxes that will be discussed later on. They arise within the Copenhagen interpretation of quantum mechanics and are solved by other interpretations. These alternative interpretations enable us to make conjectures about what is going on, even though we cannot understand it in detail. This is acceptable and a stimulus to further research. It is certainly difficult enough to understand quantum mechanics, but there is no need to try to visualize logical absurdities in the effort to do so.

Quantum mechanics is a mathematical formalism that makes it possible to calculate the results of some experiments. Anything more than this, such as questions about the interpretation of what is measured and whether it tells us what is actually going on in the system being studied, belongs to philosophy. Thus we are concerned here with what is essentially a philosophical debate; if it were just a matter of physics the debate would have been settled long ago. One of the difficulties is that it invokes the results of experiments and uses the language of quantum mechanics. Inevitably this language uses philosophical terms and then it is easy to give the impression that the philosophical propositions are in some way entailed by the physical results. These in turn can influence theological thinking. In order to be quite clear which arguments are justified and which are not, it is essential to separate the three levels of discourse: physical, philosophical and theological.

Our task is to relate these together, and this immediately raises the traditional problems of the philosophy of science, including the relation of experiment to theory, and of theory to explanation.

We begin by discussing experiments, distinguishing between those that are real and those that are imaginary.

Real and Imaginary Experiments

Experiments are the essential basis of science. Without careful and systematic experiments we would still be at the level of speculation attained by the ancient Greeks. The vital role of experiments in science is often underemphasized or even practically ignored in books on the philosophy of quantum mechanics, possibly because they are usually written either by theoretical physicists who are more at home in the abstract world of symbolism than in messy laboratories, or by philosophers who have never in their whole lives been anywhere near a laboratory. The lack of understanding of how experiments are actually done, and all the laborious cross-checking that is carried out, accounts for the bloodless (and often incorrect) descriptions of experiments often found in books on the philosophy of science. Alan Franklin (1987), a philosopher of science who was previously an experimental elementary-particle physicist, was so incensed by this that he wrote a book called *The Neglect of Experiment*.

Books on the philosophy of science frequently contain descriptions of experiments, complete with drawings of the apparatus and accounts of the results, that omit to inform the reader that the experiment has never actually been done. It is what is called an imaginary (or thought or *Gedanken*) experiment (see Duhem, 1954, ch. 6, s. 6). Such experiments have an important and valued role in the development of science. They serve to clarify our concepts and may suggest actual experiments. Nevertheless, it cannot be too strongly emphasized that, to use the title of a paper by another exasperated physicist, 'Unperformed Experiments have no Results' (Peres, 1984). Willis Lamb (1986, p. 185) expressed the same sentiment when he said 'It is impossible to make a measurement by only talking about a measurement. Doing something is required.'

The danger of confusing real and imaginary experiments is obvious: if the experiment is actually done, it may give a result that confounds our expectations. That is indeed one of the reasons why we do experiments. An example of this is the white spot already mentioned in Chapter 4 that confirmed the wave theory of light. Other examples of unexpected results are the Michelson–Morley experiment, the behaviour of gyroscopes and the tip-top.

If experiments are neglected, all that remains are the writings of the founders of quantum mechanics, and of later commentators. These are frequently studied by philosophers with great erudition as if they were sacred texts. Since the founders were physicists, they were unfamiliar with philosophical terms and often write in a confusing way. It is then all too easy to read into their writings ideas and beliefs that they did not hold. This perhaps accounts for the wide variety of books on the philosophy of Niels Bohr. Whatever one may think of Bohr's ideas, he was really grappling with real problems of physics, and unless one understands that physics one has no hope of understanding what he is trying to say.

Another failure of many of these philosophical writings is lack of understanding of the mathematical basis of quantum mechanics. All physics, and especially quantum physics, is written in the language of mathematics. Quantum mechanics is a formal mathematical theory of great power and beauty, and a knowledge of the mathematical structure is essential for an understanding of the theory. Of course, it can be described in words, and this is done in many popular books, some by the founders themselves. But at most these books can only give some imperfect glimpses of quantum mechanics, like a written description of a great symphony or the translation of a poem into a foreign tongue.

In a valid physical argument it is highly desirable that the physical understanding and the mathematical formalism are held together in a perceived unity. Before beginning a formal calculation one should have some qualitative idea of how the phenomenon under study is likely to behave. Ideally the calculation confirms quantitatively this physical intuition. Occasionally our physical intuition fails us, and such cases require special care. Not only should the physical intuition be controlled by mathematical argument, but also our mathematics should be controlled by our intuition. If it is not, it is fatally easy to make an invalid inference, an unjustified approximation, or simply an error, without realizing it. This union of physical insight and mathematical formalism is not always easy in classical physics; it is much more difficult in quantum mechanics. An example that will be discussed later is von Neumann's argument for the impossibility of hidden variables. Niels Bohr (in French and Kennedy, 1985, p. 136) 'never trusted a purely formal argument or mathematical argument. "No, no", he would say, "You are not thinking; you are just being logical".' Bohr of course valued logic in its proper place, but recognized that all logical reasoning must ultimately be based on propositions or assumptions that cannot be proved logically, and so the real discussion is whether these are true. David Cook (1988) has pointed out that

> the weakness of logic is that it is only logic; a machine for the transformation of statements. There is nothing illogical about the assumption that, since no one has observed them, dinosaurs never existed, or that only recently has the far side of the moon come into existence. These assumptions are not illogical, they are merely preposterous; yet their substance has been made the foundation of a whole interpretation of quantum mechanics.

Physicists understand this very well, but are less sensitive to another danger. It is equally hazardous for them to try to talk about the meaning of quantum mechanics without some grasp of philosophical ideas and their history. Many philosophical positions have been analysed in detail, and may be expressed precisely by a recognized vocabulary. It is essential to realize that there is not a one-to-one correspondence between ideas and words. Our everyday words such as 'real', 'object' and 'substance' have specialized meanings in the contexts of particular philosophies. Physicists frequently use analogies and models, and in their hands, as for the philosophers, words such as 'space', 'time' and 'energy' take on a new and more precise meaning. But although they do this, physicists seldom analyse with precision just what they are doing, and their knowledge is like the knowledge of dynamics possessed by a cyclist, or that of hydrodynamics by a dolphin.

The ineptitude of some philosophers when they write about physics sometimes induces physicists to regard them with a hearty contempt. Thus Rutherford once remarked to Samuel Alexander, 'When you come to think of it, Alexander, all that you have said and all that you have written during the last thirty years – what does it amount to? Hot air! Hot air!' (Eve, 1939, p. 240).

More seriously, in response to the toast to 'Science' by the President of the Royal Academy of Arts on 30 April 1932, Rutherford said:

> Quite recently there has been much interest taken by the cultivated public in the metaphysical aspects of science, especially those of theoretical physics. Some of our publicists have boldly claimed that the old ideas which served science so well in the past must be abandoned for an ideal world where the law of causality fails, and the principle of uncertainty, so valuable in the proper domain of atomic physics, is pushed to extremes. The great army in its march into the unknown discusses with interest, and sometimes amusement, these fine spun disputations of what is reality and what is truth. But it still goes marching on, calling out to the metaphysicians 'there are more things in heaven and earth than are dreamt of in your philosophy'. (Oliphant, 1972, p. 66)

Rutherford's attitude to philosophy is not uncommon among physicists, but it is dangerous even to the progress of physics itself. Rutherford himself was seriously misled on one occasion by a false philosophical argument that he was unable to counter; this story will be told later on.

One problem in particular is of such importance that it should be mentioned now. It has roots far in the past, when there was much discussion about whether the purpose of a physical theory is just to 'save the phenomena', or to give a real explanation (Duhem, 1969). If the former, then the theory is simply a formal mathematical structure that enables one to calculate the results of all experiments. What more can one want? A physicist wants a great deal more. He is convinced that he is finding out about a real world, objectively existing apart from himself, and he wants to understand its inner workings. A calculational recipe, however successful, leaves him unsatisfied, but when he ventures beyond the formal mathematics he inevitably becomes philosophical, with all the hazards this entails.

But suppose, as is arguably the case for quantum mechanics, that a scientist has a theory that is extremely successful as a calculational scheme, but seems not to make sense. He can put up with it, and say that there is nothing more to be done, resigning himself to the resulting paradoxes. This view has been expressed by Peres (1993, p. 18):

> Whether or not there exists an objective 'reality' beyond the intersubjective reality may be an interesting philosophical problem, but this is not the business of quantum theory ... Quantum theory is nothing more than a set of rules whereby physicists compute probabilities for the outcomes of microscopic tests.

If this is unacceptable, he can try to probe deeper, but he then finds that he can achieve conceptual clarity only at the cost of much greater formal complexity. As a practical physicist, interested in calculating the results of experiments, he may feel that there is more loss than gain. But he may remain unsatisfied, for often a deeper physical understanding is essential for successful calculation. He will therefore feel that although at present the lack of understanding can be endured by practical people, in the end it is dangerous to shut the door to future advances.

It is useful to remember that

> since all possible experiments have not yet been done, the choice is going to be based on one's guess of the outcome of these experiments when they are performed in the future and on our philosophical inclination. There is no reason why everyone should agree about what that best choice (of future experiments) is. Divergences of opinion must be expected that cannot be reconciled by logical argument. Tolerance is in order! (Schommers, 1989, p. 86)

The Quantum-mechanical Formalism

The problems that caused physicists so much anguish in the 1920s were resolved by the development of quantum mechanics. The wave mechanics of Schrödinger is much easier to handle mathematically than the matrix mechanics of Heisenberg, and is much more physically appealing, so this is the formalism most generally used. Detailed and mathematically rigorous expositions of the formalism of quantum mechanics are given in many books such as those by Von Neumann (1932), Messiah (1970) and Jammer (1966, 1974).

It is not possible to derive the formalism of quantum mechanics from anything else, though it can be made to appear plausible. It is perhaps better to regard it as a series of postulates that enable observable quantities to be calculated. The essential postulate is that to every observable, that is, something that can be measured, there corresponds a mathematical operator. The state of a physical system is represented by a wave function ψ that is an eigenfunction of the operator, and the possible values of the physical quantity are the eigenvalues of the operator. Thus

$$O\psi = \lambda\psi$$

where O is the operator and λ the eigenvalue. The operators in quantum mechanics involve differentiation. An example of a differential operator is d/dx, meaning differentiation with respect to x. The corresponding equation is

$$d\psi(x)/dx = \lambda\psi(x)$$

which has the solution $\exp(\lambda x)$, where the eigenvalue λ is a constant that can have any value.

To obtain the quantum-mechanical operator corresponding to an observable one replaces the momentum p in the classical expression for the observable by $-i\hbar\nabla$, where ∇ is the differential operator corresponding to spatial differentiation in any direction. Thus the operator corresponding to the total energy

$$E = \frac{1}{2}mv^2 + V = \frac{p^2}{2m} + V$$

is

$$-\frac{\hbar^2}{2m}\nabla^2 + V$$

and so

$$\left(-\frac{\hbar^2}{2m}\nabla^2 + V\right)\psi = E\psi$$

which is equivalent to

$$\nabla^2\psi + \frac{2m}{\hbar^2}(E - V)\psi = 0$$

This is Schrödinger's equation.

If we want to solve a particular problem we then have to solve Schrödinger's equation subject to the boundary conditions which specify how the wave functions behave at large distances. Thus in the case of the hydrogen atom we have to solve the equation

$$\nabla^2\psi + \frac{2m}{\hbar^2}\left(E + \frac{e}{r}\right)\psi = 0$$

subject to the boundary condition that ψ tends to zero at large distances. When this is done we find that acceptable solutions exist only for particular values of the energy, and these are just the energies of the states of the hydrogen atom found by Bohr. The probability of a transition from one state to another is then given by the matrix element

$$\left|\langle\psi_f|V|\psi_i\rangle\right|^2$$

where ψ_i and ψ_f are the wave functions of the initial and final states and V is the transition operator.

A system can usually exist in a number of states represented by wave functions $\psi(i)$ corresponding to the eigenvalues $\lambda(i)$. The general wave function of a system is a superposition of such states: $\Psi = \Sigma_i\ a(i)\psi(i)$. When a measurement is made on the system, the probability of it going to the state i is $|a(i)|^2$. This is called the 'collapse' of the wave function.

Quantum-mechanical calculations give only the probability distribution of the possible outcomes, not a definite result. For example, it is possible to calculate the intensity distribution of the electrons hitting a screen after passing through a slit, but not whether a particular electron will hit a particular spot on the screen. Another example is provided by the quantum-mechanical calculation of alpha decay by the tunnelling process described below. This gives mathematically a wave that spreads in all directions, whereas in fact we know that the alpha particle emerges in a particular direction.

The usual explanation is to say that the system remains in a quantum-mechanical superposition of states until the act of measurement collapses the wave function to give the result that is measured. This is hardly convincing. We can ask how the measurement or observation collapses the wave function. Who or what is qualified to be an observer? How does the collapse occur; does the spread-out wave function somehow concentrate itself on a single point? How exactly does it move through space and time, and what equations of motion describe the process?

The first application of quantum mechanics to the nucleus was made by Gamow (1928, 1930). It was known from the early researches on radioactivity that alpha particles are spontaneously emitted from many nuclei. They are characterized by discrete energies and half-lives that are the times taken for half the nuclei in a given sample to decay. Geiger and Nuttall (1911) found empirically that the higher the energy, the shorter the half-life. What is particularly remarkable is the huge range of half-lives, from nanoseconds to billions of years. Gamow showed that this follows from a simple quantum-mechanical calculation. He first assumed that the alpha particle is kept inside the nucleus by a potential barrier for most of the time and calculated its wave function there. Outside the nucleus the solution of the wave equation is a wave again. The wave function must be continuous over the whole region and when this condition is applied it is found that the amplitude of the wave function outside the nucleus is very small, and that the lower the energy of the alpha particle the smaller the amplitude. Since the region inside the barrier is classically forbidden, the wave function is attenuated exponentially and so the half-life is extremely sensitive to the thickness of the barrier and hence to the alpha-particle energy (Leggett, 1984, p. 95). This immediately explains the enormous range of alpha-particle half-lives. In subsequent years the theory of alpha-particle decay has been developed in detail, so that we can now say that it is well understood (Varga et al., 1992; Hodgson et al., 1997). By this we mean that we can calculate the half-life from a knowledge of the structures of the initial and final nuclei. But do we understand what is really happening? Why does a nucleus decay at a particular instant? How does the alpha particle get through the barrier? It is easy to write down the mathematics, but the physical process is vaguely described as 'tunnelling'. If a student asks about these tunnels in more detail, most lecturers become rather shifty, make some disparaging remarks about useless philosophical speculations and hurry on to the next subject. Soon the student learns not to ask such tiresome questions. Stories that they would treat with ridicule in other circumstances are accepted with lamb-like docility when they come from their physics lecturer.

These two simple examples show how quantum mechanics may be used to solve problems in atomic and nuclear physics. It has now been used for about seventy years with outstanding success. There is no other serious way of tackling atomic and nuclear problems. In most cases the difficulties are the choice of interaction potential and the solution of the Schrödinger equation.

Interpretations of Quantum Mechanics

Quantum mechanics is an outstandingly successful theory, but what does it mean? What is this wave function? Is the electron a wave or a particle? What really happens when an alpha particle 'tunnels' through a potential barrier? Most physicists just can't be bothered with what they regard as sterile philosophical questions. They are far too busy solving real problems to waste their time on fruitless discussion of this type. Quantum mechanics gives good results, so what more can you want? If pressed, they become embarrassed and shifty and produce what they remember of Bohr's ideas, before hastily changing the subject and retreating into their laboratories. Other physicists, perhaps more philosophically inclined but certainly in a minority, may produce fairly well-articulated views. They cannot stand what Popper (1982) has called the great quantum muddle, and have definite views on how it might be resolved.

It must be emphasized that quantum mechanics and the problems of its interpretation are quite distinct from each other. This is evident in books on quantum mechanics. The writers usually feel that they must say something about the problems of interpretation, and so devote a few pages to remarks about the Heisenberg uncertainty principle and the double slit experiment. What they say is usually neither very precise nor consistent with what other writers say. Then, with a sigh of relief, they get down to the more congenial task of describing how to use quantum mechanics to solve practical problems.

Although these problems are distinct, they are nevertheless related. It is not satisfactory to accept confusing concepts, even though it is possible to ignore them in practice. Conceptual clarity is important in physics. Furthermore, if one adopts the wrong interpretation it can have a very deleterious effect on one's physics. Some examples of this will be given later on. So I believe that it is important, especially for physicists, to think hard about the interpretation of quantum mechanics.

There are many interpretations of quantum mechanics (Schilpp, 1949; Korner, 1957; Bunge, 1967), and the most fundamental difference is that between the interpretations of Bohr and Einstein. Their ideas developed over the years, and it is not always clear what they said, but the fundamental difference is in the completeness of the theory. Bohr believed that the wave function contains all that can be known about a physical system. Consequently, it is meaningless to ask any questions about entities that cannot be calculated by the quantum-mechanical formalism. Thus it is meaningless to ask which slit the electron went through in the double slit experiment, or what the alpha particle is doing when it goes through the potential barrier. This view of Bohr is generally known as the Copenhagen interpretation.

The other view, due to Einstein, is that the wave function describes the average properties of a large number (or ensemble) of similar systems. This leaves open the possibility that in the future there will be a more detailed theory which will enable the quantum paradoxes to be resolved. On this view, quantum mechanics is rather like thermodynamics, which describes the properties of a gas in terms of macroscopic quantities like pressure and temperature. We know, however, that these may be expressed as averages over the microscopic motions of a large number of molecules which follow definite laws.

The debate between the supporters of these two views, and many other views, is still very much alive. Bell has remarked that 'I hesitate to think that it [quantum theory] might be wrong, but I know that it is rotten' (Bernstein, 1991, p. 68), and also that 'no formulation of quantum mechanics is free from fatal flaws' (Hahn et al., 1955, p. 13). In the preface to his book giving a detailed philosophical analysis of interpretations of quantum mechanics Hoekzema (1993, p. xiii) remarks, 'In the course of my research I have gradually come to the conclusion that standard quantum mechanics, as it is taught at university, is a conceptual garbage can, where the appearance of coherence rests entirely on some highly debatable analogies with classical theory structure.' The Russian physicist L. I. Mandelstam (in Tamm, 1991, p. 275) believes that 'the scheme of contemporary quantum mechanics, operating with non-visualisable concepts, is fundamentally unsatisfactory and must be revised so that such concepts can be eliminated'. It should be remarked that these critical comments are not inconsistent with previous remarks about the beauty of the quantum-mechanical formalism; the difficulties lie in the connection of the formalism with the real world. This is of course very relevant to any claim that quantum mechanics has theological implications.

The Copenhagen interpretation will now be described, and alternative deterministic interpretations in the next chapter.

The Copenhagen Interpretation

The question of the interpretation of quantum mechanics is a philosophical one, and thus depends on the philosophical views, explicit or implicit, of the physicists who first thought about it. During the early decades of the twentieth century, when quantum mechanics was developed, the philosophy of science was much influenced by the ideas of Ernst Mach, a nineteenth-century physicist who wrote on the foundations of mechanics. Reacting against the excessive mechanism of the Victorian physicists, he believed that the aim of physics is to achieve the most economical description of our observations and measurements, and that any discussion of what is really there is superfluous. He thus opposed the existence of atoms and not surprisingly ended his life as a Buddhist (Blackmore, 1972). Mach's sensationalism developed into the positivism of the Vienna Circle. Positivism is now largely discredited among philosophers, but many physicists are unaware of this. Max Planck (1933) has shown in detail how positivism makes science impossible. His views were supported by Hermann Weyl, Max Born and James Frank, among many others. Bohr himself was also strongly influenced by the philosopher Høffding, a friend of his father who often came to his home when he was a boy. Subsequently, he attended Høffding's lectures at the university of Copenhagen, and in later years frequently discussed with him the problems of the interpretation of quantum mechanics (Faye, 1991).

Following the thought of Mach and Høffding, Bohr and Heisenberg emphasized that what is important in physics is to have a way of calculating the results of experiments; all else is superfluous. According to Bohr (1935), 'physics is not about the world, it is about the way we think about the world'. This was echoed by Heisenberg (1927): 'the laws of nature which we formulate mathematically in quantum theory no longer deal with the particles themselves but with our knowledge of the elementary particles', and by Born ([1949], 1964): 'Quantum mechanics does not describe an objective state in an independent external world, but the aspect of this world gained by considering it from a certain subjective standpoint.' Heisenberg recalled that 'the obvious idea occurred to me that one should postulate that nature allowed only experimental situations to occur which could be described within the framework of quantum mechanics' (Rosenthal, 1967, p. 105). This gives mathematical formalism a higher status than reality. So he went on to say that 'The conception of objective reality ... has thus evaporated into the transparent clarity of a mathematics that represents no longer the behaviour of particles, but rather our knowledge of this behaviour', a claim described by Popper (1982, p. 6) as outrageous. Bohr further maintained that 'quantum mechanics was the last, the final, the never-to-be-surpassed revolution in physics'. Thus 'physics has reached the end of the road; that a further breakthrough is no longer possible, although, of course, much is still to be done by way of elaboration and application of the new quantum mechanics' (Popper, 1982, p. 6). This view was developed into what is now known as the Copenhagen interpretation of quantum mechanics, which is to be found in practically every textbook, and is taught to all students.

The act of measurement and its connection with the reality of the world according to the Copenhagen interpretation has been described by Schommers (1989, p. v):

> Within the standard Copenhagen interpretation the world (or any system) consists of options which are equally unreal. By the act of observation a system is forced to select one of its options and this becomes real, i.e. within the Copenhagen interpretation of quantum theory reality is produced by the act of observation, so that any real system (for example an electron) cannot be thought of as having an independent existence; we know nothing about what it is doing when we are not looking at it. Within the Copenhagen interpretation, nothing is real unless we look at it. As soon as we stop looking at it, it ceases to be real.

This idea of the system deciding was earlier discussed by Jordan (1934). When its position is being measured, 'the electron has to make a decision. We force it to take up a well-defined position: before that it was not in general here or there; it has not yet decided on its position ... it is we who produce the facts we observe.' This seems equivalent to attributing free will to electrons, and indeed to everything else.

Although quantum mechanics provides rules for calculating observables such as the frequencies of spectral lines, it gives little or no physical picture of what is actually happening. The atom can no longer be described in terms of particles moving along orbits. It is then necessary to find a way to link the concepts used to describe the atomic world with the actual observations made in the laboratory. It thus became of prime importance to consider the nature of physical measurements. Concepts such as position and momentum are meaningful only in the context of actual experimental operations.

Heisenberg analysed diffraction and found a relation between the uncertainty Δx in the measurement of position and the uncertainty Δp in the measurement of momentum,

$$\Delta x \, \Delta p \geq h/4\pi$$

where h is Planck's constant. There is a similar uncertainty relation between other pairs of variables such as energy and time.

A particle can be represented by a wave packet consisting of an infinite range of frequencies, with a Gaussian distribution centred around a particular value. The width of the distribution then corresponds to the uncertainty in the momentum. To localize the particle requires a wide range of frequencies, while a narrow range of frequencies corresponds to a widely spread wave packet. A mathematical analysis (Rojansky, 1946, p. 234; Popper, 1967, p. 23) gives $\Delta x \, \Delta p = h$.

To illustrate the uncertainty principle, Heisenberg proposed as a thought experiment the measurement of the position and momentum of an electron. To do this, one could use a gamma-ray microscope of high resolving power, and this requires the use of light of short wavelength and therefore high energy. However, the shorter the wavelength the greater the recoil velocity of the electron and hence the greater the uncertainty in its position. There is thus a reciprocal relation between the precision of the measurements of position and velocity. It should be noted, however, that there is an inconsistency in the argument because the light is assumed to be first a wave and then a particle (Cassidy, 1992, p. 240). Bohr also pointed out that the finite aperture of the microscope is vital to the argument, and also that the analysis requires a wave interpretation of the scattered light quanta. Indeed, the very formulae for the energy and momentum of the light quantum embody the wave–particle duality. To combine these two views, Bohr developed his idea of complementarity – wave and particle are not antithetical; 'they are mutually exclusive and yet jointly essential' (Cassidy, 1992, p. 243). The gamma-ray microscope has been re-analysed by C. F. von Weisacker (ibid., p. 258).

Margenau and Cohen (1967) have listed four difficulties in drawing conclusions about Heisenberg's uncertainty principle from the gamma-ray microscope. First, Δx refers to the position before the measurement, whereas Δp refers to the period after the measurement. To avoid this difficulty one would have to maintain that measurements do not determine what is, but what will be, or both. Second, the argument depends on classical electrodynamics, so the results should be both controllable and predictable. If the interactions are considered mysterious, the argument begs the question. Third, if quantum mechanics is a deeper theory than classical mechanics, so that it reduces to classical mechanics as a limiting case, it is not possible to use classical reasoning to derive a quantum-mechanical result. Finally, the symbol Δ must refer to a large number of interactions, and then some of the disturbances are large but others are small, and it is not clear how this can be so. They conclude that there is no way of removing these four difficulties.

According to Heisenberg, the limit to the precision of measurement has important philosophical implications. The strict formulation of determinism, that if we know the present we can calculate the future, is inadequate because now we cannot know the present accurately. This led Heisenberg (1927) to declare that 'since all experiments are subject to the laws of quantum mechanics and thereby to the uncertainty principle, the invalidity of the law of causality is definitely proved by quantum mechanics'. The implication is that the laws of quantum mechanics are generally statistical. Bohr has also remarked: 'It seems to me important to emphasise that the new quantum mechanics gives up determinism'. This was echoed by Teller (1987, p. 210) when he remarked that 'the laws of cause and effect really hold only for large aggregates of material ... In a microscopic world behaviour is as capricious as that of humans. Yet the average behaviour of many atoms obeys strict statistical laws.' However, in a lecture in 1975 quoted in Gingerich (1975, pp. 226–7), Heisenberg reached a somewhat different view of causality. He stated that the basis of the confidence of the Renaissance pioneers in the new method of science was mainly theological, reporting Kepler as saying that

> God created the world in accordance with his ideas of creation. These ideas are the pure archetypal forms that Plato termed ideas, and they can be understood by man as mathematical constructs. They can be understood by man, because man was created in the spiritual image of God. Physics is reflection on the divine ideas of creation; therefore physics is divine service. We are in our time very far from this theological foundation or justification of physics. We still follow this method, however, because it has been so successful. The essential basis for this success is the possibility of repeating the experiments. We can finally agree about the results because we have learned that experiments carried out under precisely the same experimental conditions do actually lead to the same results. This is not at all obvious. It can only be true if events exactly follow a causal chain, a sequence of cause and effect. On account of its success, in the course of years this kind of causality has been accepted as one of the fundamental principles of science. The philosopher Kant has stressed the point that causality in this sense is an empirical law, but it belongs to our method of science. It is the condition for the kind of science that was inaugurated in the 16th century and which has been elaborated ever since.

Furthermore, Planck (1933, p. 33) remarks that 'Heisenberg would be one of the first to protest against the idea of interpreting his principle of uncertainty as tantamount to a denial of the principle of causation'. More recently, Bethe (1999, p. 10) has said: 'The uncertainty principle has profoundly misled the lay public: they believe that everything in quantum theory is fuzzy and uncertain. Exactly the reverse is true.'

There is also intense discussion about the meaning of the wave function. Schrödinger interpreted it as a matter wave, giving the matter density over all space, while Born considered it as a probability wave, so that $\psi(r)$ gives the probability of finding a particle at the point r. The former allows a continuum interpretation, while the latter allows discrete quantum jumps.

Since we can only calculate probabilities, it is 'fruitless and senseless' to seek further information about the motion of the electron. Bohr explained that we can never know nature as it really is, but only as it appears to be as we become part of the experiment itself. Furthermore, since quantum mechanics is complete, there is no hope of ever improving on this. Another consequence is that all past and all future experimental research is and will be subsumed under quantum mechanics. Future research would never alter the fundamental validity of quantum mechanics, nor would it offer any hope of surmounting the limits imposed by the uncertainty principle. (Cassidy, 1992, p. 234)

An even more radical view seemed to follow from Dirac's formulation of the relation between matrix and wave mechanics. According to this, the world is essentially discontinuous, rendering the notion of velocity strictly meaningless. Heisenberg concluded (Cassidy, 1992, p. 236) that the path only comes into existence through this: 'that we observe it'.

Another characteristic of the Copenhagen interpretation is brought out by Bohr in his reply to the Einstein–Podolsky–Rosen argument, considered later. To respond to Einstein he argued that no two objects that have once interacted can, at a later time, be observed separately. With the great rapidity of interaction, and the time that has elapsed since the big bang, it would therefore seem that everything interacts with everything else, and so no system can be isolated. If these interactions are appreciable, as Bohr requires, this would seem to make science impossible.

The Copenhagen interpretation blurs the distinction between observer and observed, object and subject, physics and nature. Every observation destroys the independence of the observed phenomenon, forces a descriptive scheme on the experiment and introduces uncertainties in measurement through the uncertainty relations (Cassidy, 1992, p. 253).

Over the years the thought of Bohr and Heisenberg was developed in a series of lectures and books, and it has been analysed in many biographies (e.g. Rosenfeld, 1961; Rosenthal, 1967; Folse, 1985; Moore, 1985; Honnor, 1987; Murdoch, 1987; Blaedel, 1988; Faye, 1991; Pais, 1991). Bohr has been variously described as a positivist, a realist, an idealist, a pragmatist and an operationalist, and was influenced by Høffding, Hegel, Kierkegaard and W. James. According to Rosenfeld (1961), he was 'unable to feel any respect for metaphysical problems because they appeared to him utterly barren, so devoid of any utility for the great aim of science, that he deemed it entirely superfluous to take them into consideration'. He defined the 'Copenhagen spirit' as 'complete freedom of judgement and discussion', and emphasized that 'every sentence I utter must be understood not as an assertion, but as a question'. He does not fit easily into any of the philosophical categories and, like that of most physicists, his thought is not expressed with philosophical precision. Some reflections of John Bell on the difficulty of understanding Bohr are shown in Figure 8.1 (see also Bernstein, 1996, pp. 52–3). Bohr had many supporters among the founders of quantum mechanics, including Heisenberg, Pauli, Dirac, Born and Rosenfeld, and naturally they did not always express their ideas in the same way. The spread of the Copenhagen interpretation was rapid, partly because of the missionary fervour of its proponents, most of whom

1989 *July* 18

Dear Peter,

thank you for your letter.

Of the 5 books on Bohrs' philosophy that you have seen, I have seen only three. I do not think I could face any more. Probably I am so completely committed now to the idea that nobody understands Bohr that I do not read in a very positive spirit. One thing that I liked in one of the three books I read (I don't remember which) was the remark "one of the difficulties in understanding Bohr is that there is so little to understand" — or something like that, and from a Bohr sympathiser.

Warm regards

John Bell

Figure 8.1 Letter from John Bell on the difficulty of understanding Bohr.

worked with Bohr at some time, and then returned to their home countries to occupy prestigious chairs.

It is not possible to find in their writings a definitive expression of the Copenhagen interpretation, but a list of its main features has been compiled by Stuart (1991, p. 591):

1   The completeness postulate that the wave function completely specifies what can be known about a particular quantum state.
2   The superposition principle that a quantum state represented by a linear superposition of allowable quantum states is itself an allowable quantum state.
3   The Heisenberg uncertainty principle.
4   The probability interpretation of the wave function.
5   The principle of inseparability: the object under investigation is inseparable from the experimental apparatus used to observe it.
6   The principle of complementarity.
7   The correspondence principle.

He went on to show that there are many inconsistencies between these features.
The Copenhagen interpretation thus leads to a number of paradoxes:

1   The wave–particle duality. An electron behaves like a point particle and leaves a track in a cloud chamber or emulsion, but also can be diffracted and show interference just like light. Is an electron a wave or a particle, or perhaps some unimaginable combination of the two? If it is a particle, then why does the uncertainty principle say that it cannot have a definite position and momentum at the same time? If it is a wave, then why does it not spread out over all space?
2   The quantum-mechanical explanation of alpha decay requires the alpha particle to 'tunnel' through the potential barrier of the emitting nucleus. What does this mean? How can a particle exist in a classically forbidden region?
3   When we observe or measure some quantum event, we say that we thereby 'collapse' the wave function of the system. What does this mean?
4   What determines the time that a radioactive nucleus decays?
5   Does quantum mechanics apply to macroscopic systems? If not, why not, and where is the dividing line? If so, then how can a cat exist in a superposition of states?
6   The Einstein–Podolsky–Rosen Paradox. This is added to the list for completeness, but will be considered later in Chapter 9.

Further insight into the Copenhagen interpretation is provided by the way it deals with these quantum paradoxes. The single slit diffraction pattern shows that the more accurately we try to measure the position of an electron, the less accurately we know its momentum, and vice versa. These are known as conjugate variables. Energy and time are another pair of these variables. According to the Copenhagen interpretation this constitutes a fundamental limitation to our knowledge, so that it is meaningless to speak of the exact position or momentum of an electron.

The problem of the double slit is that neither the wave nor the particle picture seems at first to be satisfactory: if the electrons are waves, then why are they detected like particles, each at a particular point on the screen, whereas if they are particles, then they must go through one slit or the other, and then how does the interference pattern arise? This dilemma may be avoided by concentrating on what is actually observed. Since the Copenhagen interpretation admits only observable quantities, the question about which slit the electron traverses is dismissed as meaningless. We cannot observe which slit it goes through, so that is a non-question.

Bohr developed his idea of complementarity to deal with this situation. We can arrange the experiment in one way or another, and if we ask a particle-like question, then we get a particle-like answer, and similarly for waves. The objects we study are thus sometimes waves, sometimes particles (Bohr, 1935). We can have either one description or the other, but not both together, and each tells us part of what is happening. This also applies to conjugate variables. Thus we measure position with a fixed ruler, but if we want to measure momentum we use a moveable detector that recoils. Our measuring instrument must be either fixed or moveable, so we cannot measure both position and momentum together (Hughes, 1989, p. 229).

Since the wave function refers to only one system, the uncertainties Δx and Δp must be interpreted as intrinsic limits to the precision of measurement. This in turn implies that quantum mechanics is the ultimate theory that is the limit of physical research. The quantum world is thus inherently fuzzy.

There are several other answers to the wave–particle dilemma. Thus De Broglie (1953) thought of the particles as being carried along with the wave, while Bunge (1967) used the concept of 'quantons' that are neither waves nor particles but combine aspects of both. Weisskopf (1991, p. 65) refers to 'the discovery that electrons behave sometimes as waves and sometimes as particles. An electron is neither a wave nor a particle, but it exhibits one or the other set of properties under certain well-defined conditions.'

In a similar way it is maintained that it is meaningless to ask why a particular nucleus decayed at a particular time. Since the wave function completely specifies the nucleus, the decay has no cause.

The explanation of the Stern–Gerlach experiment follows from the principle of superposition: the incident beam contains a quantum-mechanical superposition of states and the act of measurement forces it into one state or the other.

In all these examples the system is initially described by a wave function that is a superposition of all possible eigenstates, and it is the act of measurement that projects this onto a single state. This is called the collapse of the wave function. This is a most curious phenomenon. The word itself is misleading: in ordinary speech collapse implies motion through space from one configuration to another. But no one really supposes that the wave function collapses in this literal way; certainly no one has specified the equations of motion followed by the collapsing wave function. Nevertheless there has been considerable debate about what is meant by the collapse of the wave function. This has been dramatized by the stories of Schrödinger's cat and of Wigner's friend; taken together they show that the Copenhagen interpretation ends in solipsism (see Chapter 9).

The formalism of quantum mechanics enables us to calculate the probability that a system will collapse into a particular eigenstate but not why it collapses into one state rather than another; it is thus an inherently acausal process. This probability refers to a single system, and so must refer to our knowledge of the system, not to the system itself. This in turn implies that physics is not concerned with the world but with our knowledge of the world.

Hidden Variables

The assumption that quantum mechanics is complete implies a rejection of the possibility that there are any hidden variables that describe the underlying process. Thus the quantum paradoxes are resolved by changing the very concept of science. As Santos (1985, p. 369) has remarked, 'In the prequantal era the purpose of science is to describe as closely as possible a real external world which is independent of any theory', so the description of the world can only be complete if there is some element of the theory corresponding to each element of physical reality. 'In contrast, for Bohr and the followers of the Copenhagen interpretation, the purpose of science is to predict (to be able to calculate) the results of experiments or observations. The question of the existence of a real world is rejected as metaphysical. Then, completeness is not the adequacy between the theory and the real world, but the adequacy between what can be predicted and what can be measured' (ibid.).

The Copenhagen interpretation avoids the quantum paradoxes by concentrating on the observables and dismissing any questions about the underlying reality as meaningless. Normally, however, a physicist faced with a phenomenon he does not understand will try to postulate some hidden mechanism to render it intelligible. The Copenhagen interpretation explicitly rejects any such 'hidden variables'. The impossibility of hidden variables was proved mathematically by von Neumann (1932), and this greatly strengthened the Copenhagen interpretation. What he actually proved was that, on the basis of some general assumptions, dispersionless ensembles cannot be incorporated into the formal structure of quantum mechanics. This leaves open the question whether these assumptions are unduly restrictive and also the more fundamental question whether quantum mechanics is a complete account of reality. As Belinfante (1973, ch. 2) has remarked, it should have been obvious that von Neumann's proof is based on incorrect axioms, and it is surprising that this was not realized long ago.

Nevertheless, von Neumann's proof was believed for many decades to exclude the possibility of hidden variables. The situation changed when Bohm (1952) succeeded in constructing a hidden variable theory, and although this was in some respects unappealing and unfruitful, it certainly showed that there is something wrong with von Neumann's proof. Subsequently, Bell (1963, pp. 448–9) identified the key assumption in von Neumann's proof, namely that 'any real linear combination of any two Hermitian operators represents an observable and the same linear combination of expectation values is the expectation value of the combination'. This is true for quantum-mechanical states, and von Neumann very reasonably thought that it is true of the hypothetical dispersion-free states. However, Bell showed, by a single counter-example, namely the measurement of the two spin orientations σ_x and σ_y, that this assumption is false. Jauch and Pirion (1963) proposed a new version of von Neumann's argument, but Bell showed that it is subject to the same objection. Thus Bell and also Kochen and Specker (1967) showed 'that hidden variables could actually be introduced in such a way that statistical averages reproduced the results of quantum mechanics' (Peres, 1993, p. 21).

However, there still remains the possibility of other interpretations of quantum mechanics, and these are the subject of the next chapter.

CHAPTER 9

Deterministic Interpretations of Quantum Mechanics

Introduction

The dominance of the Copenhagen interpretation is the result of a historical accident (Cushing, 1994). At the Solvay conference in 1927, Louis de Broglie put forward the deterministic pilot wave theory, described later. Never slow to criticize, Pauli jumped up and demolished de Broglie's proposal, and de Broglie was so discouraged by this that he did not develop his interpretation any further. The Copenhagen interpretation was then developed by Bohr, Heisenberg, Pauli and many others, as described in the previous chapter. It was strongly supported by von Neumann's proof of the impossibility of hidden variables. Years later, in 1952, Bohm published a deterministic hidden variable theory, showing that there must be something wrong with von Neumann's proof. The error was found by John Bell in 1966, as described in the last chapter, and he also showed how Pauli's objections to de Broglie's original idea can be answered. If this had been done at the conference in 1927, quantum mechanics could have been interpreted deterministically from the beginning.

The essential mistake in the Copenhagen interpretation is to treat it as a complete account of the behaviour of each individual system. It is frequently claimed that it enables us to calculate, at least in principle, everything that can be measured. Thus Hooft (1997, p. 11) said that 'The laws of quantum mechanics have been formulated very accurately. We know exactly how to compute anything we would like to know.' Also Peierls (1997, p. 25) has said that quantum mechanics 'had become a complete and consistent scheme capable of giving a unique answer to any questions relating to actual or possible observations'. Even if this were true, it would not imply that it is the final complete theory, for it is always possible that some new phenomenon might be found that cannot be calculated quantum-mechanically. However, it is not true: there are many phenomena such as the time of decay of a radioactive nucleus, or the direction a particle is scattered by a nucleus, that cannot be calculated, even in principle. Quantum mechanics is therefore an incomplete theory. We can only calculate the statistical properties of these systems, such as the half-life of a radioactive decay or the differential scattering cross-section that gives the probabilities that a particle is scattered through various angles. All measurements of quantum systems are of this statistical character. It might be thought that the possibility of making measurements on a single electron provides an exception to this. However, even in such cases the electron is continually bathed in a fluctuating background radiation from nearby atoms. Since this is variable, that electron is a member of an ensemble of electrons subject to different fluctuations. All these examples clearly demonstrate the statistical character of quantum mechanics. 'I am rather firmly convinced', Einstein (in Schilpp, 1949, pp. 666, 671) remarked, 'that the essentially statistical character of contemporary quantum theory is solely to be ascribed to fact that this theory operates with an incomplete description of physical systems'. As a result, 'the ψ-function is to be understood as the description not of a single system but of an ensemble of systems'. So, 'if the statistical quantum theory does not pretend to describe the individual system completely, it appears unavoidable to look elsewhere for a complete description of the individual systems'. Thus 'the difficulties of theoretical interpretation disappear, if one views the quantum-mechanical description as a description of an ensemble of systems'. If this is achieved, 'the statistical theory would, within the framework of future physics, take an approximately analogous position to statistical mechanics within the framework of classical mechanics'. 'Thus, essentially, nothing has changed since Galileo or Newton or Faraday concerning the status of the "observer" or our "consciousness" or of our "information" in physics' (Popper, 1982, p. 46). Once this is accepted, the quantum paradoxes that plagued the Copenhagen interpretation are easily resolved, as described below.

In any textbook of quantum mechanics problems such as the calculation of the energy levels of the hydrogen atom are solved as if that hydrogen atom is alone in the universe. As Feynman (1972) remarked, 'when we solve a quantum-mechanical problem, what we really do is to divide the universe into two parts – the system in which we are interested and the rest of the universe. We then usually act as if the system in which we are interested comprised the whole universe.' In fact, however, every hydrogen atom on which measurements are made is surrounded by other atoms and exposed to their radiations. Quantum mechanics somehow takes this into account and gives the average behaviour of an ensemble of hydrogen atoms. A more detailed theory takes these influences into account. One attempt to do this is stochastic electrodynamics, described in a later section.

Einstein's Interpretation of Quantum Mechanics

Einstein (1954, p. 266) always refused to accept the Copenhagen interpretation, maintaining that 'the belief in an external world independent of the perceiving subject is the basis of all natural science.' In correspondence with Max Born (quoted in Jammer, 1999, p. 222), he declared: 'Quantum mechanics is very worthy of regard, but an inner voice tells me that it is not the true Jacob. The theory yields much, but it hardly brings us close to the secrets of the Old One. In any case, I am convinced that He does not play dice ... You believe in the God who plays dice, and I in complete law and order in a world that objectively exists and which I, in a wildly speculative way, am trying to discover.' In a letter to Schlick, he wrote, 'In general your presentation fails to correspond to my conceptual style in so far as I find your whole orientation so to speak too positivistic ... I tell you straight out: Physics is the attempt at the conceptual construction of a model of the *real world* and of its lawful structure' (Broda, 1983, p. 153). In a letter to Schrödinger on 22 December 1950 he remarked, 'You are the only contemporary physicist, besides Laue, who really sees that one cannot get around the assumption of reality – if only one is honest. Most of them simply do not see what a risky game they are playing with reality – reality which is something independent of what is experimentally established' (Prizbram, 1967, p. 39). He was convinced that 'deep down it is wrong, even if it is empirically and logically right' (Pauli, 1994, p. 21).

Experimental scientists, who struggle daily in the laboratory to understand the physical and biological world, are instinctively convinced that they are gradually, in spite of many difficulties, obtaining valid and enduring knowledge about a real, objective world. It is a familiar experience to be confronted by an apparently unintelligible phenomenon, to have an idea about what is going on, to base a theory on that idea, and then to show that using it they can explain quantitatively what is already known and also make predictions about new phenomena that are subsequently verified. This is intelligible if we are gradually finding out about the world, but not if we are simply projecting our ideas on the world. Often scientists have struggled for a long time to interpret the world according to their own ideas, only to be forced by the evidence to adopt a different view. Planck's discovery of the quantum is an example of this.

The basic conviction underlying all scientific research is that its purpose is to learn about the structure and interactions of an objectively existing world. This world exists independently of us; it was here before we were born and will be here after we are gone. For scientific research to be possible, the world must be rational and consistent, and at least partly open to the human mind. These beliefs are seldom explicitly formulated, but are implicitly held by all working scientists, especially those engaged on experimental research. This is underlined by the writings of many scientists. Thus John Houghton (1995, p. 203) has recently written:

> An important element in the attitude of scientists is the idea of transcendence, the idea that in science we are dealing with something objective and 'given'. It is basic to scientific enquiry that there is objective reality to be discovered and described – there is something to be found 'out there'. The facts and descriptions resulting from scientific enquiries are not invented by scientists as they pursue their work; rather, they are there to be discovered.

In his Tarner lectures Michael Redhead (1995, p. 9) noted that

> physicists in their unreflective and intuitive attitude to their work, the way they talk and think among themselves, tend to be realists about the entities they deal with, and while being tentative as to what they say about these entities and their exact properties and interrelations, they generally feel that what they are trying to do, and to some degree successfully, is to get a 'handle on reality'.

Richard Feynman (see Dudley and Kwan, 1966, p. 694) expressed himself with his usual inimitable directness when asked about the counter-intuitive nature of the rules of quantum electrodynamics:

... you'll have to accept it. Because it's the way nature works. We looked at
it, carefully. Looking at it, that's the way it looks. You don't like it? Go
somewhere else. To another universe, where the rules are simpler,
philosophically more pleasing, more psychologically easy. I can't help it,
okay? If I'm going to tell you honestly what the world looks like to the
human beings who have struggled as hard as they can to understand it, I
can only tell you what it looks like.

The instinctive belief among working scientists that we are trying to find out
about a real external world comes through very clearly in a series of interviews
conducted by Lewis Wolpert (see Wolpert and Richards, 1988) and broadcast
by the BBC. In them the physicist Michael Berry says:

Physics describes the real world. It isn't a sort of low level mathematics,
which it would become if one lost contact. It's very important always to
realise that there are phenomena, that there is a world outside our heads
that we're trying to explain. Otherwise it's a curious game, a form of self
indulgence which I think is intellectually not very worthwhile. (p. 47)

The biologist Stephen Jay Gould spoke in a similar way, but also showing that
he was aware of the subjective elements in scientific research:

Radicals in the history of science will actually claim something close to
relativism. They may not deny that there's an empirical truth out there
somewhere, but it's in a fog, so distantly behind cultural presuppositions
that you can never find it, so you might as well not talk about it. Therefore,
for them, the history of the field really is the history of changing social
context and psychological predisposition. I don't take that position at all. I
can't – an empirical scientist cannot. If I didn't believe that in working with
these snails I was really finding out something about nature, I couldn't keep
going. I'd like to be honest enough to admit that everything I'm doing is
filtered through my psychological presuppositions, my cultural vices, and I
think that honesty is very important because you have to subject yourself to
continuous scrutiny. If you really believe that you're just seeing the facts of
nature in the raw you'll never be aware of the biasing factors in your own
psyche and in your prevailing culture. But that's quite a separate issue from
whether something is true or not. The truth value of a statement has to do
with the nature of the world, and there I do take the notion that you can
test and you can refute, and so I have fairly conventional views about that.
(p. 146)

Einstein believed that quantum mechanics, successful though it undoubtedly is,
constitutes just one step on the long road of our efforts to understand the
world. The wave function tells us about the average behaviour of an ensemble
of systems, not all that we can know about a single system (Home and
Whitaker, 1992). Quantum mechanics is a logically complete theory of
statistical events, but not of each particular event. Nature is much richer than
we know and there is a microstructure still undiscovered whose average
behaviour is what we measure and calculate by quantum mechanics. Working
physicists have always used concepts that are not directly linked to

measurements. This has been defended by J. J. Thomson (Rayleigh, 1942, p. 265):

> I hold that if the introduction of a quantity promotes clearness of thought, then even if at the moment we have no means of determining it with precision, its introduction is not only legitimate but desirable. The immeasurable of today may be the measurable of tomorrow. It is dangerous to base philosophy on the assumption that what I know not can never be knowledge. One day we may find ways of measuring these 'hidden variables'.

In a letter to Schrödinger on 9 August 1939, Einstein wrote: 'I am as convinced as ever that the wave representation of matter is an incomplete representation of the state of affairs, no matter how practically useful it has proved itself to be.' After discussing Schrödinger's cat, he goes on:

> If one attempts to interpret the psi-function as a complete description of a state, independent of whether or not it is observed, then this means that at the time in question the cat is neither alive nor pulverised. But one or the other situation would be realised by making an observation. If one rejects this interpretation then one must assume that the psi-function does not express the real situation but rather that it expresses the contents of our knowledge of the situation. This is Bohr's interpretation, which most theorists today probably share. But then the laws of nature that one can formulate do not apply to the change with time of something that exists, but rather to the time variation of the content of our legitimate expectations ... I am as convinced as ever that this most remarkable situation has come about because we have not yet achieved a complete description of the actual state of affairs. (Przibram, 1967, p. 35)

As Popper (1967) has emphasized, quantum mechanics is always used to tackle statistical problems. The results of quantum-mechanical calculations, such as the half-lives of radioactive decay or scattering cross-sections, are statistical quantities that can only be found by measuring a large number of similarly prepared systems. The spread of the measured values is a consequence of their statistical nature; it is only if we make the mistake of attaching the properties of an ensemble of similarly prepared systems to a single system that we generate unnecessary paradoxes.

According to Einstein, the Copenhagen interpretation avoids problems rather than solving them. As he wrote to Schrödinger on 31 May 1928, 'The Heisenberg–Bohr tranquillising philosophy – or religion – is so delicately contrived that, for the time being, it provides a gentle pillow for the true believer from which he cannot very easily be aroused. So let him lie there.' (Przibram, 1967, p. 31).

Einstein was not alone in opposing the Copenhagen interpretation. In different ways, Planck, Schrödinger, Landé, Fermi and Dirac all spoke against it. Planck repeatedly called for a revival of determinism and objectivity in atomic physics. Fermi early on expressed doubts about the validity of the Copenhagen interpretation, criticizing its tendency 'to refrain from understanding things' (see Tarozzi and Van der Merwe, 1988, p. vii). In his biography of Fermi, Segré (1970, p. 65) remarks that 'in his last years Fermi seemed less convinced that the current interpretation of quantum mechanics was the final word on the subject'. This was echoed by Santos when he remarked that the Copenhagen interpretation hides rather than solves problems. In his Nobel Prize lecture in 1976, Murray Gell-Mann, referring to the search for an adequate philosophical presentation of quantum mechanics, remarked, 'Niels Bohr has brainwashed a whole generation of theorists into thinking that the job was done fifty years ago' (Huff and Prewett, 1979, p. 29).

Not long before he died, Dirac (in Holton and Elkana, 1979, p. 85) said in a lecture that

> it seems clear that the present quantum mechanics is not in its final form. Some further changes will be needed, just about as drastic as the changes which are made in passing from Bohr's orbits to quantum mechanics ... It might be that the new quantum mechanics will have determinism in the way that Einstein wanted. I think it is very likely, or at any rate quite possible, that in the long run Einstein will turn out to be correct, even though for the time being physicists will have to accept the Bohr probability interpretation – especially if they have examinations in front of them.

In a recent book, 't Hooft (1997, p. 13) has written: 'The history books say that Bohr has proved Einstein wrong. But others, including myself, suspect that, in the long run, the Einsteinian view might return.' In his current research on the unification of quantum mechanics and general relativity 't Hooft (2003, p. 12) aims to 'preserve the powerful notion of determinism'.

Even Bohr and Heisenberg occasionally spoke in a way that recognized the limitations of quantum mechanics. In a letter to Dirac on 29 August 1930 Bohr speculated on the possibility of a minimum fundamental length, about the size of an electron or proton, below which quantum mechanics is no longer applicable: 'I believe firmly that the solution of the present troubles will not be reached without a revision of our general physical ideas still deeper than that contemplated in the present quantum mechanics' (Cassidy, 1992, p. 289). Heisenberg endorsed the same idea in an article in 1938 when he said that the fundamental length, now identified as the critical length of meson theory, marks the lower boundary, the limits of applicability of the present quantum theory (ibid., p. 407). In a subsequent article on cosmic-ray showers, he speculated that the non-linear field interactions due to strong coupling at distances less than the critical length provided 'access to the region in which the present quantum mechanics fails' (ibid., p. 411). Throughout his writings, like other physicists, Heisenberg repeatedly referred to science as 'the quest for reality'.

There is a very considerable body of research on the foundations of quantum theory that regards the Copenhagen interpretation with serious reservation. For example, in the Epilogue to a Conference on 'Open Questions on Quantum Physics' (Tarozzi and Van der Merwe, 1985, p. 391) we read, with reference to the open questions in quantum mechanics, 'such an acknowledgement of unsolved conceptual problems in the foundations of microphysics is by contrast inadmissible within the purview of the stagnant philosophy of the Copenhagen interpretation, which culminated in the absurd myth of the completeness of the quantum formalism'. Thus 'it therefore appears evident that a radical emancipation from the negative philosophy of the Copenhagen school is a necessary precondition if one is to look for a real solution of the main quantum paradoxes'.

Indeed, as Popper has pointed out, emancipation from the Copenhagen interpretation already took place long ago, since 'most physicists who quite honestly believe in it do not pay any attention to it in actual practice' (Bunge, 1967, p. 8). They think about it only when they are asked about the foundations of quantum mechanics; in their everyday work they ignore it completely. As Goldstein (1998, p. 42) remarked,

> the Bohr–Einstein debate has already been resolved, and in favour of Einstein: what Einstein desired and Bohr deemed impossible – an observer-free formulation of quantum mechanics, in which the process of measurement can be analysed in terms of more fundamental concepts – does, in fact, exist.

Following its demise as a component of serious physics, the Copenhagen interpretation has acquired a new life with Bohr's enthusiastic extension of the notion of complementarity to the life sciences, the mind–body problem and parapsychology. It has become invaluable to all who want to pose as gurus of the new mysticism, to promote subjectivism and to reconcile irreconcilables at the expense of facing reality.

It is now necessary to see how the quantum paradoxes are viewed by Einstein.

Einstein's Solution of the Quantum Paradoxes

According to Einstein, quantum mechanics gives only the result of measurements on an ensemble of similarly prepared systems. Indeed, all atomic and nuclear measurements whose results can be calculated by quantum mechanics fall into this category. It is thus possible that the result of each measurement is precisely determined by events that are at present undetectable.

Thus in the case of the single slit, the trajectories of the individual electrons differ slightly, and they impinge on different parts of the region in the slit, so it is not surprising that they reach different parts of the screen. It is not true that measurements of the position and momentum of an electron cannot be made with greater precision than that specified by the Heisenberg uncertainty principle. The width of the slit specifies the uncertainty in position, and the spread of the diffraction pattern gives the uncertainty in the transverse momentum. But if we place a particle detector at the screen, we can determine the point of arrival of each electron, and hence we can measure its

transverse momentum with an accuracy much greater than that corresponding to the distribution as a whole. Thus while it remains true that we cannot
predict the transverse momentum of the electron after it has passed through
the slit, nevertheless a subsequent measurement enables it to be determined to
an accuracy much greater than specified by the uncertainty principle. Physics
therefore gives us no ground for saying that the position and momentum of
an electron are unknowable within the limits of the uncertainty principle, and
still less that it does not have position and momentum (Ballentine, 1970).
Thus 'there can be no question whether, according to quantum theory, an
electron can "have" a precise position and momentum. It can' (Popper, 1956,
p. 63).

The double slit experiment raises a number of questions, such as how can an
interference pattern be formed if the electron is a particle that goes through
only one slit. According to the Copenhagen interpretation this question is
meaningless and so must not even be asked. Bransden and Joachain (1989,
p. 59) conclude that 'the particle is not localised before it is detected, and hence
must be considered as having passed through both slits'. And yet we know that
an electron behaves like a point particle down to a very small distance. The
problem seems to be insuperable, and indeed contrary to the laws of logic. As
Feynman (1965, Vol. III, p. 1) remarked, it is 'impossible, absolutely
impossible, to explain in any classical way, and has in it the heart of quantum
mechanics'. A detailed analysis by Fine (1972, p. 3) led him to the conclusion
that it is necessary to abandon the distributive law of logic. If this were the
case, it would indeed be an example of a philosophical implication of modern
physics.

According to the Einstein interpretation, the electron, being a point-like
particle, goes through only one of the slits, and its trajectory is influenced, as in
the single-slit case, by its incident direction and by where it passes through that
slit. But how can we explain the observed interference? It is necessary that if the
electron passes through one slit, then its motion is affected by whether the
other slit is open or not. It is then possible to give a consistent account of the
observations (Popper, 1982; Brody, 1993, p. 263). One way of doing this is by
stochastic electrodynamics, considered in a later section.

To observe the interference pattern it is necessary for the two slits to be
exceedingly close to each other, a point that is not well brought out in the
diagrams in many textbooks. Since the separation of the slits is so small, it is
not difficult to see that the motion of the electron through one slit can be
affected by the configuration of the other, thus resolving the paradox. Thus
once again we see that a detailed examination of the actual physical situation
removes support for far-reaching philosophical conclusions.

The possibility of determining which slit is traversed by an electron is
suggested by the following thought experiment. Suppose we have a source so
constructed that it emits pairs of electrons in exactly opposite directions, so
that detecting the point of arrival on a screen of one electron tells us the
direction of motion of the other electron. Now let this second electron
encounter a double slit and be diffracted and then detected on a second screen.
If this happens a large number of times an interference pattern is built upon the

second screen and coincidence observations of the electrons reaching the first screen tell us the slit through which each of the electrons has passed.

The wave–particle duality is thus simply a category confusion. On the one hand we have particles moving along definite trajectories with definite momenta, and on the other we recognize that due to their interactions with the slits and with other matter and radiation these trajectories have a certain probability distribution calculable from Schrödinger's equation. The so-called wave nature of these particles is no more an intrinsic property than, for example, actuarial statements are intrinsic properties of a particular individual. Mott (1964, p. 401) says that only particles have real existence, and waves are the collective behaviour of many particles. Peierls (1955, pp. 173, 176) also says that 'both light quanta and electrons must be regarded as particles' whose 'behaviour is described by waves. If electrons were really waves they would spread out to infinity. The waves determine only the probability of finding them and thus the spreading out of a wave packet does not mean that the electron itself has spread out but merely that our knowledge of its whereabouts has become more uncertain.'

In the case of radioactive decay, each decay process is determined by the motions of the nucleons in the nucleus before the decay, or perhaps by some external influence. Thus the nuclei before decay all differ in their internal dynamical structure. We do not yet know how this structure could determine the instant of decay, and still less how we could ever find out enough to calculate this, but these are problems for the future.

In all these experiments the quantum-mechanical calculations are compared with the results of a large number or ensemble of measurements. The half-life of a radioactive decay can only be determined by measuring very many decay events, and the same applies to the interference pattern in the double-slit experiment and the angular distribution in a scattering problem. The time of decay of a particular nucleus, or the point on the screen where one electron arrives, or the direction in which one particle is scattered, is of no scientific interest on its own, at least in the context of the present development of scientific theories. It is thus very natural to say with Einstein that quantum mechanics describes the behaviour of ensembles of similarly prepared systems, and gives only a partial account of the behaviour of each individual system. The very fact that quantum mechanics cannot tell us about the details of each individual system is a strong argument for supposing that it is an incomplete theory.

There are some recent experiments where measurements are made on a single particle, but even in such cases the particle is subject to the fluctuating background radiation and so is a member of a statistical ensemble. Any event in the real world is affected by the surrounding material due, for instance, to the fluctuating electromagnetic radiation caused by nearby moving particles. Thus in the Brownian motion a single particle must be treated statistically due to the effects of the surroundings. It is only in textbooks of quantum mechanics that we encounter a single and totally isolated hydrogen atom. Many who write on quantum mechanics have in mind the abstract mathematical world, not the real world. As Peres (1993, p. 1) has remarked, 'quantum phenomena do not occur in a Hilbert space, they occur in a laboratory'.

Since the wave function simply gives the probability of a system to be in a certain state, the difficulties associated with the collapse of the wave function disappear. Probabilities are not material entities and so the very notion of collapsing is inapplicable.

It will be noticed that all these interpretations of the quantum paradoxes postulate some hidden process that determines the observed outcome, but say little or nothing about the process itself. That is a notable characteristic of Einstein's interpretation: while the Copenhagen interpretation shuts the door to further advances in understanding, Einstein leaves it open, and thus provides the stimulus to further thought and experimentation.

There have been many attempts to probe deeper into the quantum world, and to try to give a more detailed account of what we observe, and some of these are described later.

Einstein and others who thought like him also devised a whole series of thought experiments designed to show the inadequacy of the Copenhagen interpretation. Some of these were attempts to show internal inconsistencies in quantum mechanics, and are described in the remainder of this chapter, along with others, such as the Einstein–Podolsky–Rosen thought experiment, which attempt to show its incompleteness.

Schrödinger's Cat

The role of philosophical presuppositions is shown very clearly in the debate about quantum-mechanical measurements. If we believe that there is no way of describing meaningfully the state of an unobserved system, then we have no alternative but to suppose that such systems are in a quantum-mechanical superposition of all possible states, and that when we observe such a system we find it in just one of those states, and that when we do so, the act of observation has brought about the instantaneous collapse of the wave function.

This is dramatically illustrated by the story of Schrödinger's cat. This is an experiment that could easily be done, but one may hope that this is considered unnecessary. It is indeed one of the most famous of the thought experiments. Schrödinger imagined a cat incarcerated in a sealed opaque box containing a phial of poison that may be broken by a hammer triggered by the decay of a radioactive nucleus. (John Bell, a gentle and compassionate man, never used the story in this form. Instead he spoke of a phial of milk and the cat being thirsty or contented.) Since the time of the decay is unknown, we do not know at any particular instant whether the cat is alive or dead. Before we open the box, the cat is in a quantum-mechanical superposition of states, one corresponding to its being alive and the other to its being dead. When I open the box, according to the Copenhagen interpretation, I collapse the wave function, and at that time the cat becomes definitely either alive or dead. According to Einstein's interpretation, the cat dies at a certain time whether we know about it or not, and when we open the box we find out what had already occurred. There is another consequence of the Copenhagen interpretation that is less well known. Suppose there is an observer, known as Wigner's friend, outside the room that contains the box with the cat inside. If he cannot see into the room he does not know whether I have found the cat to be alive or dead, and so for him the wave function of the interior of the room contains both possibilities. It is only when he opens the door and looks into the box that his wave function collapses. Thus his wave function must be different from mine. I am the only person who can collapse my wave functions, and thus my wave function and hence my science is unique to me. This solipsistic conclusion is radically opposed to the universal belief that scientists are all engaged on a common search to understand the same objective reality.

Feynman (1999, p. 13) has remarked:

> does this then mean that my observations become real only when I observe an observer observing something as it happens? This is a horrible viewpoint. Do you seriously entertain the thought that without the observer there is no reality? Which observer? Any observer? Is a fly an observer? Is a star an observer? Was there no reality in the universe before 10^a BC when life began? Or are you the observer? Then there is no reality in the world after you are dead? I know a number of otherwise respectable physicists who have bought life insurance. By what philosophy will the universe without man be understood?

Redhead (1995, p. 38) has asked

> whether it has to be human consciousness or whether a humble mouse idly looking at the unfortunate cat can resolve it into life and death; or what about the cat's own self-consciousness, could this result in the cat's own demise. I think it would only be reasonable to take such a solution of the measurement problem seriously if there were absolutely no other viable way of proceeding ... Quantum mechanics may be queer, but it is certainly not clear that it is that queer.

Einstein's Box

At the Como Conference in 1932, Einstein proposed a thought experiment designed to circumvent the energy–time uncertainty relation. He imagined an opaque box from which a photon is allowed to escape by a shutter controlled by a clock. The box can be weighed before and after the photon emission, giving the energy of the photon. Since both the time and the energy can thus be measured to arbitrary accuracy, the uncertainty relation is violated.

Bohr was initially very upset by this argument, and retired to discuss it with his friends. By the next morning he emerged with the solution to the problem, which ironically used Einstein's own general relativity theory.

Einstein's Bouncing Particle

Unlike the two previous examples, this one is little known, mainly because it was written in German and published in an article in a book of papers presented to Max Born. Einstein (1953, p. 33) considered a particle of any mass that bounces back and forth in one dimension between perfectly reflecting walls. The solution of the Schrödinger equation for a particle in a box is a sine wave with frequency and phase adjusted to ensure that it goes to zero at the walls. If we calculate the expectation value of the momentum of the particle we find that it is zero, which is indeed correct for a large number of particles hitting the walls at random times. But for just one particle, the momentum is zero only instantaneously when it is being reflected, and the rest of the time it has a definite positive or negative value. There could hardly be a clearer demonstration that quantum mechanics applies to ensembles of systems, and fails to describe the motions of individual systems.

The essays were intended to honour Born, and we can only hope that he appreciated the irony of being presented with such a cogent argument against his own position.

The Einstein–Podolsky–Rosen Thought Experiment[1]

The thought experiment of Einstein, Podolsky and Rosen ([1935], 1977) is often referred to as a paradox, but it is more correctly described as an argument for the incompleteness of quantum mechanics. It is sometimes considered to be a definitive statement of Einstein's mature views, but it is now known that he neither wrote the paper nor much liked the argument it contained, and that he preferred a rather different argument for incompleteness (Howard, 1990).

The argument is set within the context of definite beliefs about the nature of science and of reality. First of all they specify a completeness condition that must be satisfied by any acceptable scientific theory: 'every element of the physical reality must have a counterpart in the physical theory'. This is followed by a sufficient condition for the existence of elements of physical reality: 'If, without in any way disturbing the system, we can predict with certainty the value of a physical quantity, then there exists an element of physical reality corresponding to that physical quantity.' This is referred to as the Einstein reality criterion.

They then describe a thought experiment that shows how both the position and the momentum of a particle can be determined exactly. To do this, they imagine a particle that breaks up into two identical particles which recoil with equal velocities in opposite directions. A measurement of position is made on one of them at a particular time, and a measurement of momentum on the

---

[1] The debate initiated by this paper is still very much alive. See Mann and Revzen (1966) and Lahti and Mittelstaedt (1985).

other at the same time. Since the particles have equal velocities in opposite directions, the measurement of the position of one particle immediately gives the position of the other particle, and similarly for the momentum measurement. Thus both the position and the momentum of each particle may be determined with unlimited accuracy, contrary to the uncertainty principle implied by quantum mechanics. Thus quantum mechanics is incomplete.

Bohr was initially much upset by this argument (Bernstein, 1996) but with the help of colleagues such as Rosenfeld he composed his reply (Bohr, 1935). In it, he maintained that if two particles have interacted, they remain thereafter a single system, so that a measurement on one automatically and instantaneously affects the other. Thus if we measure the position of one particle accurately, the momentum of the other is automatically rendered indeterminate, however far away it may be. This immediately implies a holistic universe in which it is impossible to isolate any system. But if everything is liable immediately to influence everything else, it is difficult to see how any consistent account of the universe is attainable. Such influences of course exist in classical mechanics, through the gravitational and electromagnetic fields, for instance, but such influences are either negligible or cancel out or can be calculated and allowed for, and in addition their effects fall off rapidly with distance. This makes possible measurements on what is to all intents and purposes an isolated system. What Bohr is saying is quite different, namely that the influence of one system on the other is large, immediate and (apparently) is not in any detectable sense transmitted through the intervening space. Such an interaction violates special relativity, although it cannot be used to transmit a signal. This is what is called a non-local interaction (Van Laer, 1953). If one holds with Bohr that quantum mechanics is complete, then non-locality follows. Einstein (1971) 'took locality as an absolutely inevitable requirement for any reasonable physical theory'. Thus, in commenting on the possibility of non-locality in quantum theory, he said: 'Quantum theory cannot be reconciled with the idea that physics should represent reality in time and space, free from spooky action at a distance.' The positions of Einstein and Bohr are thus each logically coherent, but imply very different views of science and indeed of the physical world. They have been compared in detail by Bohm and Hiley (1980, p. 56).

The above account is an attempt to present the arguments as clearly and simply as possible. Whether they indeed reflect accurately the views of Einstein and Bohr is another and rather different question. Partly this is a matter of history, which is not our primary concern, and partly it is a matter of finding out what Einstein and Bohr really thought. The difficulty concerning Einstein and EPR has already been mentioned; that concerning Bohr is due to the notorious obscurity of his writings. Our concern is thus with the arguments themselves, not with whether or not they were really held by Einstein or Bohr or indeed by anyone else.

To take up again the story of the EPR argument, when it was first published, and for many years afterwards, it remained a thought experiment. However, Bohm (1951, p. 614) reformulated the experiment in a way that was experimentally practicable, at least in principle. He considered two identical particles, A and B, each of spin one-half that are emitted by the break-up or decay of a particle in a single state with total spin zero, such as the decay of a neutral pion into two electrons. When they separate and fly apart in opposite directions it is possible to make spin measurements on each of them along two different directions.

The total spin wave function of the system is therefore

$$\psi(A \cdot B) = 1/\sqrt{2}(X^{(+)}(A)X^{(-)}(B) - X^{(-)}(A)X^{(+)}(B))$$

where $X^+(A)$ means that the spin wave function of particle A has projection $+1/2$ in a specified direction and so on.

We now measure the joint probability of finding particle A with spin component along the direction specified by the vector α and particle B with spin component along the direction b specified by the vector β; this is

$$|\rho_{ab}| = \langle\psi|(\sigma_A \cdot \alpha)(\sigma_B \cdot \beta)|\psi\rangle = -\cos(\alpha - \beta)$$

These measurements are repeated for other directions a' and b', and Bell (1995, p. 70) was able to show that these quantities satisfy the inequality

$$|\rho_{ab} - \rho_{a'b}| + |\rho_{ab'} + \rho_{a'b'}| \leq 2$$

It is, however, easy to choose the directions a, a', b, and b' so that this inequality is violated. Furthermore, a series of experiments has shown that the quantum-mechanical correlation ρ_{ab} is confirmed to high accuracy (Aspect et al., 1981, 1982). It is concluded that at least one of the assumptions made in the derivation of Bell's inequality is false. These assumptions have been listed by D'Espagnat as realism, induction and locality and, preferring to retain realism and induction, he concluded that locality must be violated.

The consequences of the violation of the Bell inequality may also be shown by the following argument. The derivation of the inequality makes two assumptions:

1   It is possible to go beyond quantum mechanics by a hidden variable theory.
2   Two systems that have one been in contact can move so far apart that all interactions between them become negligible. This is the locality assumption.

Since the inequality is violated, one or other of these assumptions must be false. If it is the first assumption, then there is no hope of improving on quantum mechanics. If, however, the second is false, then science itself becomes impossible, for everything influences everything else, as there is no possibility of isolating a single system for study.

However, it is desirable before choosing between these alternatives to see if there are other possibilities. It will be seen that the above argument requires two other assumptions:

3   No other assumption is required to prove the inequality.
4   There is no other way of proving the inequality.

These two assumptions are both false. Examination of several alternative proofs shows that many of them do not mention locality, which is therefore irrelevant. All of them, however, require the joint measurability assumption (Brody and de la Pena, 1979); this is the assumption that has been expressed by Dirac (1947, p. 36): 'from physical continuity if we make a second measurement of the same dynamical variable immediately after the first, the result of the second measurement must be the same as that of the first'. This is not correct, as Peres (1993, p. 28) shows by the example of the measurement of the energy of a neutron by observing the recoiling proton, which changes the momentum of the neutron. More generally, a particular measurement with definite settings of the two detectors can give say *Pab*, but then it is not possible to measure any other correlation coefficient because the system has been disturbed by the first measurement. Thus all we can conclude from the violation of the Bell inequality is that joint measurability is false (Brody, 1993, p. 215). This is, however, just what is required by quantum mechanics, so the violation of the inequalities is to be expected, and implies nothing new about locality or the possibility of hidden variables (Brody, 1985). As Marshall (1985) has remarked, 'it is not at all difficult to construct a local realist explanation of the results of photon-correlation experiments of the Aspect type'.

    Another proof of the presence of non-local interaction was proposed by Greenberger et al. (1989, 1990). In a version of their argument due to Mermin (1990), a source that breaks up into three photons A, B and C is prepared in a particular entangled state. After the break-up the polarization of each photon is then analysed by detectors at 0 and 45 degrees. Let $A(\theta,\lambda)$ be the result of measuring the spin of A along the axis making an angle of θ degrees to the vertical. The result will be $+1$, as determined by the hidden variable λ. With a similar notation for the other photons, the following relations hold

$$A(0,\lambda)B(0,\lambda)C(0,\lambda) = +1$$
$$A(0,\lambda)B(45,\lambda)C(45,\lambda) = -1$$
$$A(45,\lambda)B(0,\lambda)C(45,\lambda) = -1$$
$$A(45,\lambda)B(45,\lambda)C(0,\lambda) = -1$$

If these four equations are multiplied together, the product of the right-hand sides is -1, but that of the left-hand sides is $+1$, since each quantity appears twice and is equal to $+1$ or -1. Thus the equations cannot all be true, and the assumption of hidden variables must be false. If non-local interactions occur, any one of these quantities could depend on the results of the other two measurements, and the contradiction would disappear (Hardy, 1998). This argument for non-local interaction is, however, invalid because it assumes joint measurability, i.e. that $A(0,\lambda)$ and $A(45,\lambda)$ can both be measured on the same system. This is a counterfactual conditional: it is not logically possible for Dr Jekyll to converse with Mr Hyde.

More recently, Hess and Philipp (2000, 2001) have pointed out that if the 'hidden variables are time-dependent and time correlated, Bell's theorem breaks down. Bell assumed that the joint conditional probability density of a set of experimental outcomes are equal to the product of the individual conditional densities. With time-correlated variables this is not the case.'

A possible argument supporting the conclusion of non-locality is that even if two quantities are not jointly measurable, it is still legitimate to discuss them because either could have been measured. Thus I know that if I release my pen it will fall, even though I decide to hold on to it. This can be admitted, but it is different from the situation when we are considering two measurements on the same system and one of them actually prevents the making of the other. If, for example, we want to know the life of a particular light bulb for a particular voltage we can make the measurement once only. We cannot also ask what would be its life if subjected to a different voltage. It makes no sense to talk about the result of a measurement that we could have made but were prevented from making because we chose to make another measurement that excluded the possibility of making the first. Physics is concerned with actual results, but not with actually impossible results. Peres (1993, p. 15) has shown that counterfactual arguments may appear quite reasonable but they lead to inadmissible consequences. He considers a Stern–Gerlach experiment in which the measurement of the magnetic moment μ along a particular direction e gives $\pm \mu$. Now choose three directions e_1, e_2 and e_3 making 120 degrees with each other so that $e_1 + e_2 + e_3 = 0$. Assume that $\mu.e_1$, $\mu.e_2$ and $\mu.e_3$ are all measured, and add the results: $\mu.e_1 + \mu.e_2 + \mu.e_3 = \mu.(e_1 + e_2 + e_3) = 0$. This is impossible, since each of the three terms is $\pm \mu$. This is no problem, since is impossible to make these three measurements without the first measurement interfering with the second and so on. It is therefore illegitimate to combine the results of these three counterfactual measurements. Another example is given by Peres (1993, p. 207).

This raises the question of the relation between joint measurability and reality, and whether a system can be said to possess certain properties before a measurement is made. For example, do physical properties such as momentum or spin have definite values before we measure them, or do they come into being as a result of a measurement? A realist will be inclined to say that there are possessed values before measurement, whereas an instrumentalist, or a supporter of the Copenhagen interpretation, will be inclined to say that it is meaningless to speak of possessed values before the measurement takes place. If variables cannot be measured together, are they real? If we consider, for example, the x and y projections of the spin operator, they satisfy Einstein's reality condition but cannot be measured together. Does the system, a particle of spin one-half, possess these two spin projections? What is meant by 'possess'? My pen? My age? My idea? My reaction to a message that does not arrive?

It may be useful to distinguish between classical and quantum mechanics. A physicist is familiar with variables such as position and momentum, and finds it repugnant to think of them as only coming into existence as a result of measurement. Particles have a position and a momentum whether we are looking at them or not.

It is rather different for quantum variables like spin. The word 'spin' is used in a highly metaphorical sense, and we should not be lulled by familiarity with the word to forget the profoundly mysterious nature of spin. We can of course manipulate the spin operators and establish a formalism that enables us to calculate the results of measurements, but we really have no clear idea of what spin actually is. It would therefore seem quite possible that the result of a measurement of spin does come into being only during the measurement process, as a result of the interaction of the system with the measuring apparatus, and is not necessarily present before the measurement. It is thus quite consistent to take a robustly realist view of position and momentum and to be much more reserved about quantum variables such as spin.

It is possible that in future a conclusive argument for the existence of non-local interactions will be found, but at present the evidence is not convincing.

The Denial of Reality

Many physicists are inclined to dismiss all discussions of the interpretations of quantum mechanics as so much inconclusive philosophical waffle that may amuse people with a taste for such things but is totally irrelevant to the serious day-to-day work of the practical scientist.

This is not so. Our philosophical beliefs, whether they are implicit or explicit, are vitally important and whether we recognize them or not they inevitably affect our actions. This is particularly so in quantum mechanics. Does it imply a denial of reality, is it to be identified with reality, or does it tell us something about reality, in a limited and probabilistic way? The remorseless inner logic of the consequences of our philosophical presuppositions may be illustrated by many examples from the history of atomic and nuclear physics.

According to the Copenhagen interpretation, only statistical statements are permitted, and all reference to an underlying reality are excluded. Within this perspective, it was quite natural that Bohr et al. (1924) were willing to envisage that atomic processes are essentially statistical, so that the principles of the conservation of energy and momentum are not valid for each individual event. This radical proposal was soon found to be incompatible with the measurements of Bothe and Geiger (1924), which showed that the conservation laws do indeed hold for each individual event.

Another example is provided by the widespread scepticism in the early years of the present century concerning the reality of atoms, expressed for example by Mach and Ostwald. As Einstein remarked, 'the antipathy of these scholars towards atomic theory can indubitably be traced back to their philosophical attitudes. This is an interesting example of the fact that even scholars of audacious spirit and fine instinct can be obstructed in the interpretation of facts by philosophical prejudices' (Schilpp, 1949, p. 49).

A particularly striking example of this is provided by the fate of Rutherford's early speculations on the shell structure of nuclei (Wilson, 1984, pp. 440, 579). Years before, Rutherford had shown that atoms have a structure and it was recognized that the electrons in the atom are arranged in a series of shells. Naturally he thought about the structure of nuclei, and devised experiments to investigate it. Bohr, however, thought of the interior of the nucleus as an undifferentiated soup that occasionally presents a particle to the outside world. From such events, he maintained, it is not possible to deduce anything about the pre-existence of the particle in the nucleus. Rutherford and Bohr frequently discussed this problem, and ultimately Rutherford was convinced that Bohr was correct, and abandoned his attempts. Ten years after Rutherford's death, experimental evidence for the shell structure of nuclei began to accumulate and now it is accepted as a basic and essential feature of nuclei and the foundation of nuclear spectroscopy. While it is true that the apparatus available to Rutherford was probably not sufficiently sensitive to detect the shell structure, Bohr's views certainly hindered the development of nuclear structure physics. If Rutherford had recognized the importance of philosophical presuppositions he would have been better equipped to resist Bohr's arguments.

Another example of the debilitating effect of philosophical beliefs is provided by Heisenberg's refusal, in his capacity as a senior scientific adviser, to allocate funds for the construction of a new accelerator to look for quarks on the grounds that this was the wrong approach. On being questioned about this decision, he replied that the world is made up of mathematical resonances. At a meeting in 1973, Heisenberg remarked:

> I really feel that it is better not to say that the elementary particles are small bits of matter; it is better to say that they are just representations of symmetries. The further we go down to smaller particles, the more we get into a mathematical world, rather than into a mechanical world. (Heisenberg, 1975)

This story lends additional weight to a comment of Popper (1972, p. 248):

> The metaphysical belief in causality seems more fertile in its various manifestations than any indeterminist metaphysics of the kind advocated by Heisenberg. Indeed we can see that Heisenberg's comments have had a crippling effects on research. Connections which are not far to seek may easily be overlooked if it is continually repeated that the search for any such connections is 'meaningless'.

The overwhelming majority of physicists, particularly those who struggle daily in the laboratory, instinctively reject these debilitating beliefs, and continue to believe, in the words of Einstein (in Schilpp, 1949, p. 9), that 'something deeply hidden had to be behind things'. To pursue scientific research within the framework of the opposing belief that all we are doing is trying to correlate our sense-impressions is to cut oneself off from the source of scientific creativity.

Realist Theories of Quantum Mechanics

Once it is admitted, following Einstein, that the quantum-mechanical wave function represents the behaviour of an ensemble of similar systems, the way is open to investigate the detailed structure of the underlying determinist reality. Can this be described in terms of hidden variables, in much the same way that the velocities of the molecules provide the deterministic substructure to thermodynamics, and to the apparently erratic fluctuations of the Brownian motion? Some of the answers to this question have been sketched in the section on hidden variables, and in this chapter two of these theories are described in more detail.

The ensemble theory can be used to resolve at a certain level the quantum paradoxes created by the Copenhagen interpretation, without having any specific idea about the nature of the hidden variables. One can indeed hold the ensemble interpretation without having any such ideas, and this leaves the way open to further advances. It is then important to try to develop such theories, because this will not only give much greater insight into quantum mechanics, but could also lead to predictions at variance with quantum-mechanical calculations. If such predictions were confirmed by experiment, this would open up a whole new realm of physics.

The Pilot Wave Theory

It has already been remarked in the section on hidden variables that von Neumann's proof of the impossibility of hidden variables received a severe setback when Bohm (1952) succeeded in developing such a theory, known as the pilot wave theory. Apparently unknown to him, a similar formalism was published by Madelung (1926).

Bohm began with the time-dependent Schrödinger equation

$$\hbar \partial \psi / \partial t = -(h^2/2m)\nabla^2 \psi + V\psi \tag{9.1}$$

and wrote ψ in the form

$$\psi = R(r,t)\exp(iS(r,t)/t) \tag{9.2}$$

where $R(r,t)$ and $S(r,t)$ are real functions of r and t.

Substituting (9.2) into (9.1) and separating into real and imaginary parts gives

$$\partial s/\partial t + (\nabla s)^2/2m + V + Q = 0 \tag{9.3}$$

where $Q = h^2/2m \ \nabla^2 R/R$ is called the quantum potential and

$$1/R \ \partial R/\partial t + \nabla R.\nabla S/mR + \nabla^2 S/2m = 0 \tag{9.4}$$

Defining $\rho = |\psi|^2 = R^2$, (9.4) becomes

$$\partial\rho/\partial t + \nabla(\rho \, \nabla S/m)m = 0 \tag{9.5}$$

Equation (9.4) can be interpreted as the Hamilton–Jacobi equation with particle momentum $mv = \nabla s$ and an additional quantum potential Q. Equation (9.5) is the continuity or conservation equation for ρ.

We can now say that every particle is accompanied by a ψ wave that acts on the particle through the quantum potential. If we specify the initial position of the particle and the form of the wave function, the numerical solution of (9.3) and (9.5) then gives $R(r, t)$ and $S(r, t)$ for all subsequent positions and times. It is notable that the quantum potential Q depends on the wave function. This is quite different from most physical theories, which start with a potential and then calculate the motions of particles in that potential.

Many calculations using this formalism have been made, including the case of a Gaussian wave packet incident on a square potential barrier, alpha decay and also two Gaussian wave packets on each side of a square potential barrier which corresponds to the situation in a neutron interferometer. The trajectories have kinks that most physicists would reject as unphysical.

This formalism may be extended to include particles with spin, and can then account for all the fundamental features of non-relativistic quantum mechanics, including the correlations between separated particles in the Einstein–Podolsky–Rosen experiment.

The pilot wave theory shows how it is possible to construct a fully deterministic theory that gives some insight into the processes that are treated by quantum-mechanical calculations. It is, however, a purely formal theory that fails to give any physical insight into why the particles behave as they do, and the origin of the quantum potential and how it acts on the particle. For this we must look to physical theories, and one of these, stochastic electrodynamics, is the subject of the next subsection.

Stochastic Electrodynamics

Every physical system is subject to the influence of its surroundings through the medium of gravitational and electromagnetic forces, and bombardment by photons, electrons and neutrinos, to mention just a few. In classical physics we argue that most of these influences are irrelevant to the variables of interest, or average out, or can be calculated, and this allows us to consider a system in isolation and to set up its equations of motion. Another possibility is to include some of the outside influences explicitly and to average over them subsequently; this is what we do in statistical physics. If neither of these methods were practicable, science would be impossible.

Quantum mechanics is an attempt to formulate the physics of closed systems in a way that assumes that all external influences are negligible in a situation where the external influences are in fact not negligible. It provides a way 'that allows us to take the average interaction between the system under consideration and the rest of the universe into account, without it being necessary to introduce this interaction in the equation in an explicit manner' (Julg, 1998, p. x). This is the root of the difficulties with quantum mechanics, and to obtain an insight into them it is necessary to identify these external influences and to formulate them explicitly. This is done in stochastic electrodynamics (De la Pena and Cetto, 1996).

Thus when considering the structure of the atom, to consider a single isolated atom and then a purely classical treatment encounters the difficulty that the orbiting electrons must rapidly spiral into the nucleus, since any electron subject to an accelerating force continually radiates energy. Bohr overcame this difficulty in an *ad hoc* way by imposing quantization rules, and in the framework of quantum mechanics these come automatically from the solution of the wave equation. In stochastic electrodynamics it is recognized that each atom is bathed in radiations coming from all directions from the rest of the universe, and these are taken into account by quantum mechanics.

There have been many attempts to do this, both formally and by physical models. The formal stochastic theory is conceptually clear and mathematically simple, and has many useful applications. However, it provides only mathematical models without any reference to the underlying physical processes. They provide a mathematical illustration of the ensemble interpretation, but no deeper physical understanding. The physical models are thus more satisfactory, and we concentrate our attention on one of them, stochastic electrodynamics.

This theory identifies the external influence on quantum systems as the fluctuating background electromagnetic field. Any charged particle experiences this field due to the motions of all other accelerated charged particles. This field must account for the stability of atomic structures, since they would rapidly collapse if electrons were classical particles moving in the absence of any external background. The statistical nature of quantum mechanics becomes clear in the context of stochastic electrodynamics. This theory averages over the many influences from the surrounding media as it is impossible to treat each one individually. The theory is thus statistical, but also deterministic, since each of the individual processes is itself determined.

If we consider the motion of an electron, taking into account the possibilities of emission and absorption, its equation of motion is the Newtonian one with the addition of emission and absorption terms

$$m\ddot{r}(t) = f(r, t) + m\tau\,\dddot{r}(t) + eE(t)$$

This is the Braffort–Marshall equation. This form of the equation requires several approximations before a solution is practicable, and even then it is difficult. The important question is of course to see if it can give the same eigenvalues and eigenfunctions as the Schrödinger equation. The calculations that have been made so far have encountered insuperable mathematical difficulties.

The statistical nature of quantum mechanics becomes clear in the context of stochastic electrodynamics. The theory averages over the many influences from the surrounding media because it is impossible to treat them individually. As each of these processes is completely deterministic, the theory is both deterministic and statistical, like the kinetic theory of gases.

Further insight can be obtained by studying the harmonic oscillator problem. In this case the equilibrium distribution has the same form as the Wigner distribution and from it all the quantum results are obtained, including the analysis into states of energy $(n + \frac{1}{2})$hw. However, these are not equilibrium states but average values of the instantaneous energy. This energy fluctuates around the mean values and the fluctuations are highly correlated, so that the widths of the absorption and emission lines have the quantum-mechanical values. Agreement with the quantum-mechanical results is also found when a magnetic field is applied to the harmonic oscillator. It is also possible to incorporate spin.

In cases where a Markov approximation to the stochastic electrodynamical process can be made, the Schrödinger equation can be derived and hence all the quantum-mechanical results follow. In other cases, where non-Markovian aspects are important, there are extra terms in the Schrödinger equation; these could lead to differences from the quantum-mechanical result that could be experimentally tested.

The character of the background field depends on the surrounding medium. In the case of the double-slit problem, the configuration of the background field is influenced by which of the slits is open. If the particle goes through one slit, it is the field that 'knows' whether the other slit is open, and thus determines the motion of the particle. How exactly this happens is not yet known.

The stochastic theory thus provides a conceptually simple way of tackling problems that, like quantum mechanics, have only one undetermined constant, that of Planck. It is unfortunately, and perhaps not surprisingly, complicated, so that only a few simple cases can be worked out. In this respect it is opposite to quantum mechanics, which is conceptually difficult but computationally elegant, allowing a large range of problems to be solved. Furthermore, stochastic electrodynamics is an open theory, in that further developments are very likely that will allow it to be extended to solve a range of problems. Several tests have been proposed (Chaturvedi and Drummond, 1997) and different outcomes are predicted compared with quantum mechanics (Pope et al., 2000), but the requisite experiments have not yet been made.

The pilot wave theory and stochastic electrodynamics provide just two of many possible realist theories of quantum mechanics. There are several others, including decoherent histories and spontaneous localization. Thus

the Bohr–Einstein debate has already been resolved, and in favour of Einstein: what Einstein desired and Bohr deemed impossible – an observer-free formulation of quantum mechanics, in which the process of measurement can be analysed in terms of more fundamental concepts – does, in fact, exist. (Goldstein, 1998, p. 42)

Theology and Quantum Mechanics

There have been many discussions of the possible connections between theology and quantum mechanics, principally in the context of the Copenhagen interpretation. These connections come not from the results of physical experiments, but from the philosophical premises inherent in the various formulations. The Copenhagen interpretation is based on a positivistic view of the world, and physics is reduced to the correlation of sense-impressions. Since we cannot measure everything, and since what cannot be measured is considered meaningless, we are left with a fitful, undetermined quantum world, governed only by chance. Thus 'the clear and determinate character of physical processes, as Sir Isaac understood it, has dissolved at its constituent roots into the cloudy and fitful quantum world' (Polkinghorne, 1988, p. 333). This appears to open the way to theological speculations about free will and about God's action on the world. Perhaps the mind can act on matter within the uncertainties of measurement, allowing free will without violation of physical laws. Similar considerations apply to God's action on the world.

In all these discussions it is vital to distinguish between the quantum world and the real world. Most of the attempts to obtain theological conclusions from considerations of the characteristics of the quantum world fail to acknowledge this difference. Quantum mechanics is an incomplete theory: it does not and cannot describe many measurable physical phenomena, and so does not give a complete account of the physical world.

To the extent that it is based on a positivistic view of the world and denies its objective reality, the Copenhagen interpretation is contrary to the Christian belief in a real world created by God. Thus according to Heisenberg the concept of objective reality has evaporated. However, Bohr (1935) said that 'physics is not about the world, it is about the way we think about the world'. This could be taken as implying acceptance of a real world coupled with a denial that we can know anything about it. One wonders whether Bohr really believed this when he was making experiments in his younger days. Positivism has been on the wane among philosophers in recent years. In a radio interview in 1978 Brian Magee asked Professor A. J. Ayer (1978, p. 131) what he considered were the main defects of positivism. Ayer replied: 'Well, I suppose that the most important of the defects was that nearly all of it was false.' After that verdict by one of the leading exponents of positivism it is unnecessary to say more.

Following Heisenberg's remarks, it is widely believed that the Copenhagen interpretation implies a denial of causality. Thus if one believes that the Heisenberg uncertainty principle limits the accuracy of measurements and if determinism means that from a knowledge of the present we can calculate the future, then, since we cannot know the present exactly, we cannot know the future. Thus Heisenberg (1927) said that 'in a certain sense the law of causality becomes invalid'. Furthermore, according to the Copenhagen interpretation radioactive decay provides an example of an uncaused event. If causality is denied, then it might be thought to affect Aquinas's second way to the affirmation of God's existence, in which God is identified as the first cause.

Aquinas's argument does not, however, depend on the belief that every material event is efficiently caused by prior temporal events that make it what it is. Aquinas was not concerned to argue for God as a being who by His past actions is responsible for the present. In his view, God is outside time, so that, even if one has a causal sequence infinitely extended in time, the whole sequence still requires the sustaining power of God to keep it in existence. There is indeed no evidence that there are uncaused events, nor could there be. But even if there were events without temporal antecedents they would still require God's causality to account for their being. Max Planck (1933, pp. 100, 147) has affirmed: 'I have not been able to find the slightest reason which would force us to give up the assumption of a law-governed universe, whether it is a matter of trying to discover the nature of the physical, or the spiritual forces around us' and 'physical science is based on the strict and universal validity of the law of causality'. Von Laue (1980, p. 94) believed that physics as a science can only exist on the foundations of determinism.

It has been suggested that quantum mechanics can provide an answer to the problem of God's action in the world. It is a basic Christian belief that we are all totally dependent on God, who cares for us and guides our lives. And yet, according to classical mechanics, the world is like a vast machine behaving in a deterministic manner following mathematical equations. If we believe that God gave matter its properties and started its motion on the day of creation, this implies that it continues to act strictly in accord with these laws. How then can we believe that God acts upon the world? Are we not forced to give up either the providence of God or the laws of classical physics?

Quantum mechanics, it has been argued, provides a way out of this dilemma. It has shown that the microworld is fuzzy and indeterministic, and that this provides the means whereby God, by acting within the limits of quantum uncertainty, can affect the world without violating the laws of physics. In this way we can retain the rule of scientific law and also allow God to act freely in the world (Pollard, 1958, p. 139; Polkinghorne, 1988; Russell, 1988; Tracey, 1995; Murphy, 1995; Ellis, 1995; Clayton, 1997).

An early study of the problem of understanding the providential action of God in a world governed by deterministic physical laws is due to Pollard (1958, p. 139). He accepts that physics has become statistical in its innermost core, so that 'no forces, external or internal, known or unknown, can eliminate chance from the picture'. Thus 'at every moment the countless myriad of diverse elements which go to make up and define the state of the universe at that instant have each their separate choices to make among the alternative paths open to them'.

Within the perspective of the Christian revelation, this is not meaningless chaos but God's providence:

> The Christian sees the chances and accidents of history as the very warp and woof of the fabric of providence which God is ever weaving. Seen in this way, they can be gladly and joyously acknowledged and accepted. But apart from this revelation, chance and accident mean anarchy, sheer

meaningless, random incoherence, and utter chaos from which the soul recoils in horror. (Ibid.)

This interpretation implies that God shapes the course of history by continually guiding atomic events within the limits of the Heisenberg uncertainty relations and subject to the overall probability distributions required by quantum mechanics. Whether this conception of God's activity is satisfactory is for the theologians to consider, but there is an alternative possibility that the universe is a fully determined system evolving along a unique path in which each event is completely determined by its antecedents.

This proposal raises a number of questions. First, are the minute interventions constrained within the limits of the uncertainty principle sufficient to produce the required macroscopic effects? We can imagine God making billions of such minute interventions without any measurable violation of physical laws so that they eventually produce macroscopic effects (Clayton, 1997, p. 194), though whether this is consistent with the omnipotence and dignity of God is another question. This may, however, be unnecessary in view of the effects studied in chaos theory (see Chapter 11). It is well known that even in classical systems very small changes in the system often lead to very different subsequent behaviour. For example, a minute change in the trajectory of a gas molecule greatly affects what happens at its next collision, and this is magnified in subsequent collisions so that the state of the system is completely different after a very short time. If we assume that God can foresee the ultimate effects of His intervention at the quantum level, then a minute intervention could indeed produce a macroscopic effect. Furthermore, in certain circumstances a single quantum event can produce a drastic change in a system, as in the case of Schrödinger's cat. This is unacceptable even within the framework of the Copenhagen interpretation because if the wave function contains all possible information about the system there is no room for any information that might be inserted by God, quite apart from the problem of how this may actually be achieved. These remarks apply to cases where God simply causes a change in a system by altering its state. They do not help to explain cases of divine intervention where matter is created, as in the case of Christ's feeding of the five thousand and certain contemporary miracles of healing.

Similar arguments apply to human free will. It is possible to argue that human beings are such large systems from the atomic point of view that even if quantum events are undetermined there are so many of them involved in our actions that the indeterminacy is averaged out to give complete uniformity at the atomic level. This argument is not convincing because the body may be, and in some cases demonstrably is, sensitive to quite small numbers of events at the atomic level. As Planck (1933, p. 191) has remarked, 'our own consciousness tells us that our wills are free'.

In view of this it has been argued that the indeterminacy associated with the Heisenberg uncertainty principle provides a loophole for the action of free will, in just the same way as it provides a way for God to act on the world. This may be answered in the same way. This is not to say that human freedom is an illusion. We can certainly seek determining causes for physical events, but we cannot be sure that all determining physical causes are themselves totally explicable in terms of purely physical causes. This raises questions beyond physical science concerned with the nature of the human person.

All these explanations assume that the world is indeed fuzzy and indeterminate, as implied by the Copenhagen interpretation. However, this is not necessarily the case. As Willis Lamb (1995, p. 203) has remarked, quantum mechanics can be considered a straightforward generalization of classical mechanics:

> Among the advantages gained thereby are that one can forget many of the fuzzy ideas that cluttered the path from classical mechanics to quantum mechanics. These include Bohr's correspondence principle, Heisenberg's uncertainty principle, Bohr's principles of complementarity and wave–particle duality, Dirac's and von Neumann's absurd notions of the collapse of wave packets. We might have been spared much of the agony needlessly suffered with two-slit diffraction paradoxes, the Einstein–Podolsky–Rosen paradoxes, the Schrödinger cat paradoxes, hidden variable theories and Bell's inequalities.

If, however, one adopts a realist position, one can believe that physical reality is a strictly determined system that we only partly understand. The root error in so many contemporary discussions is to suppose that, because it is so outstandingly successful, quantum mechanics gives a complete account of the physical world. We know, however, that there are many questions that cannot be answered, even in principle, by the formalism of quantum mechanics. It is thus an incomplete theory, and we may hope that in the fullness of time a new theory will be developed that will indeed give the same results as quantum mechanics when averaged over a large number of systems, but will also give a detailed account of the behaviour of each individual system. If this is so, we will once again have a fully determined physical theory. The world of quantum mechanics is a fuzzy world, but it is not the real world. Thus quantum mechanics gives no support to the philosophical propositions that have been associated with it nor, *a fortiori*, to any additional theological speculations. In particular, it provides no new insight into free will or God's action in the world. These problems remain, and quantum mechanics provides no help with their solution.

Furthermore, it is surely an impoverished conception of God to suppose that He is bound by His own laws. God is the supreme lord of nature, and can make and unmake its laws, and bring it into being, modify or extinguish it at will. The God who designed the universe and brought it into existence and caused it to follow definite laws can also cause it to act in different ways should He choose to do so. As Aquinas noted, 'The divine will is not limited to this particular order of causes and effects in such a manner that it is unable to produce immediately an effect in things here below without using any other causes.' It is unnecessary to think that He has to confine His interventions into our lives by keeping with the limits of quantum indeterminacy.

There is, however, one area where there could conceivably be useful applications of quantum mechanics to theology, namely by providing analogies that assist the understanding of spiritual truths. An example is provided by the argument that when we try to understand how Christ can be both God and man, we may be helped by recalling that an electron is both a particle and a wave: we cannot understand the latter, so we may more readily accept the former. As has already been explained, it is incorrect to describe an electron as a wave: the characteristics of its behaviour that are described by the same equation as wave motion only appear when we consider an ensemble of trajectories that are independent of each other. Since in this case the physics is incorrect, the analogy is worthless.

Inspired by what they see as the mysteries of the quantum world, many writers have applied quantum ideas to the realms of mysticism, parapsychology and spiritualism. Particularly influential are those of Capra and Zukav, who have compared modern physics with Hinduism, Buddhism and Taoism. Their views on the natural world are characterized by vague statements and a complete absence of mathematics and are discussed in more detail in Chapter 12. Here it is sufficient to remark that modern science did not arise in the East, but in the West, as described in Chapter 2. Furthermore, if there is a real congruence between Eastern mysticism and modern science, we might expect the mystics to be able to give some useful information to scientists. As John Bell (1987, p. 310) once remarked, 'We'll all go and sit at the feet of the Maharishi if he tells us where the Higgs boson is to be found!' (see Crease and Mann, 1990, p. 302; see also Stenger, 1995, ch. 9; Khalatnikov, 1989, p. 283).

CHAPTER 10

Cosmology

Introduction

From the earliest times men have contemplated the starry skies and wondered what it all means. They noticed that most of the stars are in a fixed pattern relative to each other, and they grouped them into constellations. Other bodies, called the planets, move relative to the starry background, and they wondered if they had some influence on our lives, a belief still widespread today.

There is evidence of systematic observations of the skies by early man. At a palaeolithic site at Ishango in the mountains of central equatorial Africa there was found a bone tool with engraved marks along the edges. The marks were in groups that suggested that they were not just decoration but had a definite numerical purpose. These marks were studied in detail by Alexander Marschak[1] and he concluded that they refer to the days in the lunar cycle, and the groups to the phases of the moon. It did not seem likely that these markings were unique to that particular part of Africa, so he read widely in the literature and looked through collections of artifacts in museums. He found a large number of bones, antlers and stones inscribed with a variety of marks that could be connected in similar ways to the lunar cycle. Such markings are thus a ubiquitous feature of the artifacts of early man.

For the Israelites, the regularity of the movements of the stars and of the seasons provided an impressive witness to the power and reliability of the Creator. This power is emphasized in the words of Yahweh to Job:

> Can you fasten the harness of the Pleiades
>   Or untie Orion's bands?
> Can you guide the morning star season by season
>   and show the Bear and its cubs which way to go?
> Have you grasped the celestial laws?
>   Could you make their writ run on the earth?
> Can your voice carry as far as the clouds
>   and make the pent-up waters do your bidding?
> Will lightning flashes come at your command
>   And answer 'Here we are'?
>
> (Job 38:31–35)

The doctrine of creation is the most basic of all Judeo-Christian beliefs. It affirms that God made the world out of nothing, that He is absolutely distinct from His creation, and that all creation depends completely on Him.

---

[1] Marschak (1972). See also Cunliffe (2001), p. 71.

This revelation was first given to the Israelites, and their acceptance set them apart from the surrounding idolatrous and pantheistic tribes. The Bible is saturated with the belief in creation from the powerful words addressed to Job to the confident, matter-of-fact acceptance by the mother of the seven martyred brothers in Maccabees.

We cannot understand the creation of the universe. It is difficult enough to understand creation when it is applied to our own activities. How does a painter create a picture? He has an idea, but to realize that idea he reorders existing matter. But God created the universe out of nothing. When the painter has finished his work, the picture remains, even if he forgets about it. But the universe depends utterly on God not only for its initial creation but also for its continuance in being.

The belief that the universe had a beginning is strikingly different from the beliefs held by most of the nations of antiquity. Almost without exception they believed in an eternal cyclic universe (Dawson, 1929; Jaki, 1974). The Hindus believed in a Great Year, after which everything was to be repeated again and again. Such a belief is intensely debilitating, and played no small part in preventing the rise of genuine science: why should we strive to improve our understanding if everything that happens has already happened many times before and will happen many times again?

As Jaki (1986, p. 113) has remarked, religions fall into two categories: in one there is the Judeo-Christian religion with its belief in a linear cosmic story running from 'in the beginning' to 'a new heaven and earth'. In the other are all pagan religions, primitive and sophisticated, old and modern, which invariably posit the cyclic and eternal recurrence of all, or rather the confining of all into an eternal treadmill, the most effective generator of the feeling of unhappiness and haplessness. Concerning that treadmill, Chesterton (1932, p. 150) has remarked: 'I am exceedingly proud to observe that it was before the coming of Christianity that it flourished and after the neglect of Christianity that it returned.'

The medieval philosophers actively discussed the nature of the universe. They made full use of Greek philosophy, but did not hesitate to depart from it if it was contrary to their Christian faith. Along with other Greek philosophers, Aristotle believed in an eternal, cyclic universe, and this was rejected because it was contrary not only to the Christian belief that the world has a beginning and an end, but also to the belief in the unique Incarnation of Christ.

Aristotle's speculations, particularly his belief in the eternity of the world and on the difference between unchanging celestial matter and corruptible terrestrial matter, prevented the rise of science in ancient times. They were broken by the Judeo-Christian beliefs in the creation of the universe by an all-powerful God, totally distinct from his creation. The creation of the universe out of nothing transformed a circular view of time to a linear one, and implied that celestial and terrestrial matter, being both created by God, obey the same laws.

Christian theology emphasized the belief in the orderliness of nature that is the essential basis of all science. Our philosophy of the material world is absolutely crucial for the development of science, and it has its roots in theology. We believe that God created the world out of nothing by the free exercise of the creative power that belongs to Him alone. It is sustained in being by God, and without His sustaining power it would immediately lapse into nothingness.

The created world has its own intrinsic nature, given to it by God. Normally it continues to exist, sustained always by God, and to behave in the way determined by its nature. The material world, the universe, defined as the totality of consistently interacting things, is thus a totally determined system. If we knew exactly its initial state, and the laws of its nature, we could calculate exactly how it would subsequently behave. This is not of course possible in practice because we cannot know the present exactly, we do not know the laws well enough and we cannot do the calculations. This determined development is not, however, a logically necessary development, in the sense that it could not be otherwise. God always has the power to intervene, to override the development otherwise determined by the intrinsic nature of the material world.

Throughout the preceding paragraph we are speaking only of the material world, not of man. Man is made in the image of God and has freedom of action and so is not wholly part of the universe as defined above.

This account of the material world specifically excludes other possibilities that are widely held and are inimical to the development of science.

First, it excludes the concept of the world as immediately dependent on the will of God, who determines its behaviour from instant to instant. On this view the world is like a cinema picture, a series of disconnected flashes that appear to have continuity but in fact have none, a world that is re-created continually from one instant to the next. It denies the idea that things have their own intrinsic natures that normally determine their behaviour. This view of the world stresses the freedom of God at the expense of His rationality.

Second, it excludes the concept of the world held by deists. This is the idea that God created the world like a clock, wound it up and then let it go so that thereafter it inevitably develops according to its intrinsic design. This idea stems from the concept of God that stresses His rationality at the expense of His freedom.

Third, it excludes the idea that God was obliged to create the world or to do it in a particular way, so that it is a necessary world. Such a belief also stresses the rationality of God at the expense of His freedom. It denies that the world is contingent and so destroys science by removing the need for experiment. If the world is a necessary world we might hope to find out about it by pure thought.

Fourth, it excludes pantheism, the idea that the universe is an emanation from God or a part of God, because Christ is the only-begotten Son of God. The universe was made, not begotten.

Fifth, it excludes any form of dualism, the idea that different parts of the world were created or are controlled by different spirits or gods. All creation takes place through Christ and is therefore wholly good and wholly dependent on God.

Sixth, it implies that the world, though contingent, is completely orderly. This again is necessary for science, for if the world was not orderly science would be impossible. God could not create a chaotic world.

Seventh, it denies that there is any intrinsic indeterminism in the world, and thus excludes the misuse of the word 'chance' as if it were a causative agent. Chance is simply a word that indicates that we do not know the determining causes.

The science made possible by Christian theology has repaid the debt by revealing God's creation in ever more detail.

The Discovery and Exploration of the Universe

It is one of the most astonishing achievements of man that he is able to probe the extremes of the very small and the very large, the recesses of the atomic nucleus and the vastness of cosmic space and time.

In the centuries following the birth of science much was learned about the motions of the planets, the constitution of the stars and the structure of the galaxies. This was made possible by the development of ever more powerful telescopes, by spectroscopic analysis and by Einstein's general theory of relativity. For the first time the entire universe, spread out in space and time, has become the subject of scientific investigation.

Before describing these discoveries it is necessary to recall a qualification that applies to all science, but especially to cosmology. By experiments in the laboratory we attain some knowledge of the laws of nature, and then we extend them to the realms of the very small and the very large, and to the distant past. Sometimes they break down, as they did for the atom and at very high velocities, and this led to quantum mechanics and special relativity. How then can we be sure that our present understanding is adequate to discuss what happened billions of years ago? Very small changes in the laws, quite undetectable by us, could have large effects when applied to the whole universe. Yet in spite of this difficulty, we must extrapolate the laws of nature, because we have no alternative, but it is important to remember the provisional character of all our knowledge of the distant past, as this sets severe limits on, or even excludes, any possibility of drawing theological conclusions.

The observations of the nineteenth-century astronomers showed that our sun is a rather ordinary star in one of the spiral arms of a galaxy of about two hundred thousand million stars that we see in faint outline as the Milky Way. Billions of similar galaxies are visible in all directions, and Hubble found that the frequency of the light from them is shifted in a way that shows that they are all moving rapidly away from us. Furthermore, the greater the distance from us, the faster they are receding. In other words, all the galaxies are moving in just the way we would expect if they had all come from a mighty explosion at a time that we now know to be about fifteen thousand million years ago (Lemaître, 1972). This figure is subject to considerable uncertainty, not only due to inevitable difficulties of measurement, but also because it assumes that the expansion is uniform. It has also been suggested that in the early stages there was a period of more rapid expansion.

A deeper understanding of this expansion of the universe was provided by Einstein's general theory of relativity. His cosmological model was shown to lead to the observed expansion, and Lemaître derived from it the measured velocity of recession of the galaxies. For the first time the universe as a whole became an object of scientific study. Thus theory and experiment combine to support the idea that what we now see is an ageing universe, the scattered ashes and sparks remaining from the compressed incandescence of its fiery beginning.

Although we see the galaxies flying away from us with velocities proportional to their distance, this does not mean that we are in a specially privileged position. Every galaxy is receding from every other galaxy, so that a being on any of the other galaxies would see just the same recession. More subtly, we must not think of the galaxies as flying apart into an already-existing infinite space, but rather that the space itself is expanding. We cannot imagine this, but the analogy of particles on an expanding balloon may be helpful.

Several other lines of evidence, such as the motions of clusters of galaxies and the relative proportions of various types of nuclei, also give about the same result for the time when all the matter of the universe was concentrated in a small volume. We can apply the laws of physics to understand many of the processes occurring during the expansion of the universe from this initial compressed state, but at present there seems no possibility of finding out by scientific means what happened before the expansion began. It seems to be the ultimate limit of science, a limit that some have ventured to call the Creation.

It must however be emphasized again that this is not a scientific inference. It is not possible to show scientifically of any state that there can be no antecedent state. We cannot exclude the possibility that there was a previous state, perhaps one of contraction. It has been suggested that the universe is eternal, either remaining always more or less the same on a sufficiently large scale, or perhaps alternately expanding or contracting. These theories will now be discussed in more detail.

Theories of the Universe

The Big Bang Theory

As already mentioned, several lines of evidence indicate that the universe has expanded from a compressed state about fifteen billion years ago. This suggests that the development of the universe is a continuous progression from an explosive beginning to a silent end. The processes occurring in the first few instants of the expansion have been reconstructed in considerable detail, making use of the latest knowledge of nuclear and elementary-particle physics. The details are highly technical and still somewhat speculative for the very earliest times, namely the first fraction of a second. The evolution of the universe from about one hundredth of a second from the beginning of the expansion is better understood (Weinberg, 1977).

At that time the temperature of the universe was about one hundred thousand million degrees and consisted of matter and radiation in very close interaction. It was expanding rapidly, but the interaction was so strong that it remained essentially in a state of thermal equilibrium. The most abundant particles were electrons and neutrinos and their anti-particles, and also photons. There were also some nucleons in the proportion of one neutron or proton for every thousand million photons, electrons or neutrinos. These protons and neutrons were in constant interaction with the electrons and neutrinos so that the numbers of protons and neutrons remained the same. There was no possibility of forming more complex particles as the temperature was so high that they would be broken up as soon as they were formed.

As the expansion continued the temperature fell and soon it became slightly easier for a neutron to interact to form a proton than conversely. By the time a tenth of a second had elapsed there were about twice as many protons as neutrons. The density and temperature continued to fall, and after one second the temperature was about ten thousand million degrees. At this stage the neutrinos no longer interacted appreciably with the other particles, and so play no further part in the story, except in so far as their energy contributes to the gravitational field of the universe.

After about fourteen seconds the temperature had fallen to three thousand million degrees, and now the electrons and their anti-particles the positrons annihilated to produce more photons. This rapidly removed most of the electrons and positrons, and also momentarily slowed down the rate of cooling because of the energy released in the annihilation process. Neutrons were still being converted into protons, though much more slowly, and now there were about four protons to every neutron. At this stage it was cool enough for helium nuclei to form, but this could not happen yet because it can only come about through the formation of deuterons consisting of a proton and a neutron, and then tritons (a proton and two neutrons) and helions (a neutron and two protons). These intermediate particles on the way to helium formation are much less stable, and so were broken apart as soon as they were formed. However, as soon as the temperature fell low enough for the deuterons to survive, the reactions leading to the formation of helium took place very rapidly and nearly all the neutrons combined with protons to form helium.

After about half an hour the temperature had fallen to three hundred million degrees. All the electrons and positrons had been annihilated apart from the small number of electrons needed to provide one for each proton, so that the universe as a whole is uncharged. Most of the nuclear particles were either free protons or helium nuclei (about 25 per cent in weight), with very small proportions of deuterons and helions and an even smaller amount of lithium. The period of intense activity was now over, but the universe continued to expand, cooling all the time, and after about one million years the temperature had fallen to approximately three thousand degrees, sufficient to allow the electrons and the nuclei to combine to form atoms. The disappearance of the free electrons then made the universe transparent to radiation.

This cloud of hydrogen and helium was slightly non-uniform, which allowed gravitational forces to enhance areas of higher density to form galaxies and then individual stars. As the stars contracted still further due to the intense gravitational pressure they became hotter, and when the central temperature reached about ten million degrees the hydrogen burned to form helium. When most of the hydrogen had been converted to helium the star expanded to become a red giant. The central core continued to contract and the helium burned to form carbon. Further reactions produced oxygen and then heavier elements up to iron. Since iron is the most stable nucleus no more energy can be gained by burning, so the core collapsed and the star exploded, to be seen as a supernova. The cloud of nuclei formed in this way again condensed to form a new generation of stars, and still heavier nuclei were formed. This process proceeded through several generations of stars until all stable nuclei were produced. The nuclear reactions taking place in these processes have been studied in laboratories (see Rowan Robinson, [1977], 1981), and so we can calculate the proportions of the different chemical elements in the universe. This is very similar to what is observed, showing that we have a detailed and quantitative understanding of the processes that took place so long ago.

About five thousand million years later the evolution of living beings took place, among them men and women who are able to understand and reconstruct the details of the processes that made their existence possible.

What is the evidence supporting this theory? Some parts of it are of course better understood than others, and research is continually providing more details of the various stages, even of the processes occurring in the first hundredth of a second. As already mentioned, the formation of the nuclei is quite well understood, and the results of calculations agree with the measured abundances of the various chemical elements in the universe.

Additional confirmation came from the observation of what is called the cosmic microwave background radiation (Ferreira, 2003). At the stage of the formation of the atoms about four hundred thousand years after the Big Bang all the electrons were captured by light nuclei and thereafter the photons no longer interacted strongly with the rest of the universe and so could propagate freely through space. These photons were in statistical equilibrium with each other and their energy distribution related to their temperature. This energy distribution is well known from the early days of quantum theory, and is given by Planck's formula. As the universe expanded the temperature fell, and with it the average energy of the photons. Since we know the temperature at the time when matter and radiation were decoupled, the initial energy distribution of these photons can be calculated, and also the way that temperature falls as the universe expands. These photons are still present in the universe, and their temperature was estimated by Alpher et al. (1948) to be about five degrees above the absolute zero of temperature. Photons of this temperature are in the microwave region.

At the same time as these calculations were being made in Princeton, this microwave radiation was actually observed by Penzias and Wilson (1965). These two radio astronomers were hoping to measure the radio waves emitted by our galaxy, but first they had to make sure that there was no spurious noise in their detecting antenna that could mask the signals they were looking for. They found that however they turned their antenna they always detected some radiation, and furthermore it came with equal intensity from all directions and so could not come from our own galaxy. It must come from the universe as a whole. It was then realized that this was probably the radiation left over from an early stage in the evolution of the universe.

It might be asked why the scientists did not actually look for this radiation, since it was predicted long before it was observed. Partly this may be the difficulty of the measurements, but it seems that even theoretical physicists sometimes find it hard to appreciate that their abstract mathematical calculations refer directly to physical reality, that they reach across the vastness of space and time to predict the presence of hitherto unknown radiation, and that if we turn a radio aerial to the sky we find that it is there.

Since that time the background microwave radiation has been studied in detail, and in particular it has been shown to have a spectral distribution closely agreeing with Planck's formula at a temperature of 2.735 degrees, and coming almost equally to one part in 10^5 from all directions. It is just what would be expected for the theory of the evolution of the universe, and provides a compelling verification of its truth. The very slight departures from isotropy, found by the COBE satellite in 1992, are just what are needed to allow the formation of galaxies. The Wilkinson Microwave Anisotropy Probe launched in 2001 can now measure the temperature of the microwave background with a precision of one millionth of a degree.

Another prediction of the theory that can be verified experimentally is the proportion of helium in the universe. The helium is formed at an earlier stage than the heavy elements, and so its proportion is a sensitive indication of the relative numbers of the nuclear particles and of photons. This ratio in turn fixes the temperature of the microwave background radiation. Thus from the measured temperature of three degrees it can be estimated that the proportion of helium in the matter from which the stars were formed must be about 25 per cent by mass. This is just the same as the value for the hydrogen–helium ratio obtained from theories of stellar evolution.

It is worth noting at this stage the extreme specificity of the whole process, a feature that will be returned to later on. In particular the ratio of nuclear particles to photons, electrons and neutrinos must be about one to one thousand million. If there are more photons the number of neutrons and protons will remain about the same, so that as soon as the temperature falls low enough for helium to be formed, they will all combine in this way. Nearly all the nuclear particles will become helium, and then it is not possible to build up any of the heavier nuclei. On the other hand, if there are fewer photons the interaction that keeps the number of neutrons and protons the same will cease too soon, and before the helium formation can begin most of the neutrons will have decayed to protons. Nearly all the nuclear particles will then be protons, and so not enough helium can be formed to lead to the production of heavier nuclei. Thus the ratio is exceedingly critical: if it is too large or too small there can be no nuclei heavier than helium, and so no possibility of life.

One of the first detailed applications of nuclear physics to cosmology was Bethe's explanation of the origin of the sun's heat. As mentioned in Chapter 5, this could not be accounted for by any classical processes such as chemical reactions or by gravitational energy. In an early lecture Rutherford suggested that the necessary energy could come from some radioactive processes, and Eddington (1920) identified the main process as the conversion of hydrogen to helium. Bethe (1937) identified a series of reactions called the proton cycle that achieves this:

$$p + p \rightarrow d + e + \upsilon$$
$$d + p \rightarrow {}^3He + \gamma$$
$${}^3He + {}^3He \rightarrow {}^4He + 2p$$

The net result of these three reactions is:

$$4p \rightarrow {}^4He + 2e + 2\upsilon + 24.7\,MeV$$

The cross-sections of these three reactions have been measured in the laboratory, and hence the rate of energy generation can be calculated. This process continues until the hydrogen is exhausted, and then the star collapses gravitationally. The temperature then rises to about $10^8\,°K$ and this is sufficient to allow reactions to take place that build up the heavier elements. Eventually carbon is formed, and this makes possible another chain of reactions called the carbon–nitrogen–oxygen (CNO) cycle that also converts protons into helium.

The reactions that are responsible for the formation of carbon show several remarkable features. Carbon is essential to life and, like other heavier elements, it has been made inside stars by a series of reactions starting from hydrogen and helium. The chain of reactions starts from the alpha particle, and two of them combine to form beryllium 8. Then another alpha particle is added to give carbon 12, and another to give oxygen 16 and so on. For this to produce carbon 12 several conditions have to be satisfied. If beryllium 8 were stable, the process would proceed so explosively that the star would be blown apart and the synthesis of heavier elements would be impossible. Beryllium 8 is, however, just unstable, so this does not happen. It is then difficult to see how carbon 12 can be formed. Beryllium 8 has an extremely short lifetime, and so if carbon 12 is to be formed, another alpha particle must collide with it before it decays. The collision of three particles is a very rare event and so the reaction rate is so slow that any carbon formed in this way would soon be transformed into oxygen. The only way the carbon-forming reaction could occur more rapidly is if there is a state in carbon 12 just about the threshold at 7.65 MeV that would make possible a resonance reaction. No such state was known, so Hoyle (1953, 1997) suggested to some experimentalists that they should look for it. Within a few days it was found, at just the predicted energy (Dunbar et al., 1953). The formation of carbon 12 also requires that it is not all transformed into oxygen 16 by the addition of a alpha particle, and this would happen if there were a state in oxygen 16 around the threshold energy. There is indeed such a state, but its energy is 7.12 MeV, far enough below the threshold at 7.19 MeV. for the reaction not to take place. Thus the possibility of the formation of carbon 12 depends on the energies of three states in beryllium 8, carbon 12 and oxygen 16.

Is this just a coincidence, or was it planned? This discovery astounded Hoyle, and led him to consider profound questions such as whether the laws of physics are deliberately designed to permit the existence of life, or whether the existence of life is the result of 'a set of freakish coincidences in nuclear physics'. This is connected with arguments about what is called the anthropic principle, to be discussed later on.

The Inflationary Universe

A serious difficulty of the big bang theory concerns the mass density of the universe, which determines whether the universe will go on forever expanding, or eventually slow down, stop and then begin to contract. The density corresponding to the behaviour at the dividing line between these two possibilities is called the critical density. Calculations show that what happens depends extremely sensitively on the mass density near the beginning of time. Indeed, at one second after the big bang the mass density must have equalled the critical density to an accuracy of one part in one thousand million million. If the mass density were outside these limits the universe would either collapse or expand so rapidly that there would be no time for the development of life. Does this have a rational explanation?

Then it was found that the calculations of the density of magnetic monopoles using the well-supported Grand Unified Theory showed that they should be as numerous as protons and neutrons. Since the monopoles are very massive, they would exert such a strong gravitational attraction that the universe would rapidly collapse.

A further difficulty was posed by the extreme uniformity (to one part in one hundred thousand) of the temperature of the cosmic microwave background radiation. Such uniformity could only come about by strong energy-sharing interactions, and yet the parts of the background radiation are too far apart for this to happen.

The solution of all these problems finally came from the concept of the inflationary universe developed from 1979 onwards by Alan Guth (1998). In the very early stages of the big bang (around 10^{-35} seconds from the beginning) the universe is driven into a stage of very rapid expansion by the repulsive gravitational field due to what is called the false vacuum. This increases the diameter of the universe by a factor of about 10^{52} compared with what was previously thought. Before this expansion begins, thermal equilibrium is established and this is retained during the expansion, thus solving the uniformity problem. The production of magnetic monopoles is reduced by the supercooling of a delayed phase transition. The process also automatically drives the mass density to the same value as the critical density. The very small perturbations that remain are just what are required to lead to the formation of stars, galaxies and clusters of galaxies. Thus what appeared at first to be astonishing coincidences or serious problems all received a rational explanation within the inflationary model, although it must be added that this requires the initial parameters to be assigned values in a narrow range.

In the years since Guth's proposal, many varieties of inflationary theories have been developed, and these are still the subject of intense debate. The general idea is very probably correct, but the details have still to be established. One of the difficulties of cosmology is that there are many imaginative and speculative theories but rather few experimental observations that enable them to be tested. The situation in this respect is now greatly improving. New satellites should provide even more accurate data, and correspondingly sharp tests of cosmological models.

The whole story shows in ever more detail the extraordinary way the universe has developed from the initial singularity to its present state. It is the ongoing task of the scientists to explore this in every way possible. It is also clear that it is always unwise to ascribe any cosmological event, however improbable it may seem, to the direct action of the deity. So often it is later found to be entirely explicable by a new theory.

The Steady State Theory

As an alternative to the big bang theory, Bondi and Gold (1948) and also Hoyle (1948) proposed the steady state theory. This was based on what they called the perfect cosmological principle, which says that on a sufficiently large scale the universe is always the same, both in space and time. In particular, the number of galaxies in any large volume of space is constant. Since, however, we know that the galaxies are receding from each other, this can only be ensured if new galaxies are coming into being to replace those that are moving away. They therefore postulated that hydrogen atoms continually appear out of nothing and ultimately condense and coalesce to form new galaxies at a rate just sufficient to replace those lost by recession. The rate of appearance of the hydrogen atoms came out to be so small that there is no possibility of ever observing it, just one hydrogen atom per year in every cubic mile of space.

The motivation behind this theory was avowedly to provide a rival to the big bang theory which, although it does not prove that creation in time has occurred yet, seems to be more consonant with it. To do this, they were obliged to postulate what they called continuous creation, and yet they resolutely refused to consider how this creation occurred, or to attribute it to a creator. It thus seemed to many to be a somewhat gratuitous hypothesis, and yet they were correct to maintain that it is a legitimate scientific theory that stands or falls when its consequences are compared with observational data. In response to criticisms the theory was continually developed by its originators during the 1950s (Kragh, 1996).

The most direct test of the theory is to see if indeed the galaxies are uniformly spread throughout all space. At first this seemed to be the case: the number of galaxies increased as the cube of the distance, as it should. Then it was found by the techniques of radio astronomy that at very large distances the galaxies start thinning out; there are not enough of them for the steady state theory to be correct.

The observation of the 3 degrees background radiation by Penzias and Wilson provided further evidence against the steady state theory since it shows that the present expansion of the universe started some fifteen thousand million years ago. On the steady state theory we would not expect this background radiation to be there. The red shifts of quasi-stellar objects are also inconsistent with the theory. For these reasons the steady state theory has now been abandoned and scientists reluctant to envisage the possibility of a creation turned their attention to the possibility of an oscillating universe.

The Oscillating Universe

At present the universe is expanding, but the question is whether it will go on expanding for ever, the galaxies and the stars getting colder and colder, or whether at some epoch the expansion will slow down and go into reverse, leading eventually to the collapse of the universe into a very small volume. If the universe is ultimately destined to collapse we can then see the present expansion and collapse as possibly just one of a whole series of expansions and contractions going on for ever, a spectacle that banishes the possibility of a creation at a particular instant but not, it must be added, the need for a continuing sustainer of the whole oscillating process.

This question is physically the same as asking whether a rocket fired upwards will escape from the earth's gravitational field or eventually fall back to the ground. We can answer it in two ways: by examining the way the velocity of the rocket is changing after the motors have been switched off, or by comparing the velocity at that moment with the velocity that we can calculate to be sufficient to take the rocket out of the earth's gravitational field. When we apply this test to the receding galaxies we find that we cannot yet measure the velocities of recession at great enough distances to determine whether they are on the road of eternal expansion or the road of eventual contraction. We therefore have to fall back on the second method, which requires a knowledge of the total mass of the universe. We can also calculate the mass that the universe must have if its gravitational attraction is to be sufficient to slow down and ultimately reverse the recessional motion of the galaxies. If this mass is greater than the actual mass, then the expansion will go on for ever, but if it is less, then the expansion will ultimately turn into a contraction.

Present estimates of the mass of the universe show that it is between ten and one hundred times too small to reverse the motion of the galaxies. This has led to a hunt for the missing mass, particularly among those with a vested interest in an oscillating universe. It is possible that there is a halo of unseen mass around the galaxies, and the neutrinos may account for some more, but even then the best estimate is that only about one tenth of the required mass can be found. This is of course open to revision in the light of further research. It is worth noting in passing that it is remarkable that the masses are so nearly the same, and this may well have a deeper significance. The relative abundance of the light elements also supports continual expansion.

There are other difficulties with the idea of an oscillating universe, in particular those connected with the second law of thermodynamics, which requires the total entropy of any system to increase continually. As Tolman (1934) showed, when this is applied to an oscillating universe the result is that the amplitude of oscillation increases from one cycle to the next, so that any particular cycle can have only a finite number of preceeding ones (Sakharov, 1992). Thus the second law of thermodynamics appears to exclude the possibility of an oscillating universe.

More recently, Penrose (in Ellis, 2002) has shown that gravitational effects prevent light rays being traced back forever. This requires the gravitational force to be always attractive. This argument has been extended by Hawking, Geroch and Ellis, and renders unacceptable the idea of an oscillating universe. Thus at the present time there are considerable difficulties with the theory of an oscillating universe, but it cannot yet be entirely ruled out. It is always possible that further developments will weaken the arguments mentioned above. Scientifically it remains an open question.

Philosophically, an eternal universe is open to the objection that if we are in such a universe then everything would already have happened an infinite time ago. The only way to avoid this conclusion is to say that the whole of history is indeed repeated in all its details an infinite number of times. The periodicity of this repetition need not be the same as that of the universe as a whole, providing it is equal or greater. Such a belief in an oscillating universe has indeed often occurred in human history, but in our civilization this idea was rejected because the incarnation of Christ is a unique event that cannot be repeated. God's plan in history is a linear one, from the beginning to the end, and is incompatible with eternally recurring cycles. That is why the Church has always believed in creation in time, and conversely it is notable that belief in an oscillating universe is always one of the hallmarks of atheism.

Necessary or Singular?

With the abandonment of the steady state theory and the uncertain future of the oscillating universe theory, those who are unable to accept the idea of a creator have turned their attention to developing the concept of a necessary universe, that is, a universe that must be the way that it is. If the universe is necessary, then there is no need to enquire why it is the way it is; it could not be otherwise and so there is no need to look for an explanation, in particular no need for a creator.

The idea of a necessary universe has a long history, going back to Aristotle. As a scientific hypothesis it encourages the idea that it is possible to obtain the whole of science, including even the values of the fundamental constants, by pure deductive reasoning. There is no need to make experiments: physics, like mathematics, may be carried out by thought alone. Strenuous efforts were made along these lines by Eddington, but in spite of instructive insights, he did not succeed in his endeavours. The structure of the universe is far richer and more sophisticated than could ever be imagined by the mind of man.

But even if it is not possible to discover the structure of the world by thought alone, it remains possible that it is a necessary world. Due to the limitations of our minds we need the help of experiments to understand the order of the universe, and then we might realize that it is in fact a necessary order. The experiments serve as intellectual scaffolding that can be discarded when we have reached our goal.

There are indeed many features of the universe that might seem at first to be given, but which turn out on further examination to be necessary. For example, the number of spatial dimensions must be three, for otherwise the solar system would not be stable. As science advances, more and more features of the world seem to be linked together and not at all arbitrary. Indeed, the aim of theoretical physics is the unification of our knowledge of the world expressed inevitably in mathematical terms. Already the unification that has been achieved is remarkable, and areas of experience that seem to be quite distinct are seen to be but different manifestations of the same underlying order, as for example electricity, magnetism, optics and radio are all governed by Maxwell's equations. Great efforts are being made to unify the four fundamental forces of nature, and important progress has already been made.

It is quite possible that scientists will eventually succeed in developing a comprehensive theory that explains all phenomena and enables the results of all conceivable experiments to be calculated. Even this, however, will fall short of proving that the universe is a necessary one, as a consequence of a theorem of Gödel (1930; see Nagel and Newman, 1958), who showed that no set of non-trivial mathematical propositions can have its proof of consistency within itself, and that there are always meaningful propositions that cannot either be proved or disproved within the system. Thus any scientific cosmology that is necessarily expressed in mathematical terms must fall short of being a theory that shows that the world must necessarily be what it is. There is always the possibility of the surprising, the unexpected, that points beyond this world for those who have eyes to see.

The Singularity of the Universe

The more closely scientists study the evolution of the universe the more evidence they find of its extreme singularity. A striking example of this has already been quoted: if the proportion of nuclear particles and photons had been slightly different there would have been nearly all hydrogen or nearly all helium, and in each case no heavier nuclei and so no possibility of life. Again, it has been noted that the universe is remarkably homogeneous on a large scale, and this is the result of the initial conditions. It is very difficult to understand why these inhomogeneities should be so small, and yet if they were any larger the matter of the universe would have collapsed into black holes long ago, while if they had been any smaller, there would have been no galaxies.

The evolution of the solar system is also highly specific. There is still no satisfactory theory of how the system of planets was formed, and in particular how they came to be rotating around the sun in nearly circular orbits, and nearly in the same plane. Yet it is only on a planet of a certain size moving on a nearly circular orbit that life could have evolved. The more this evolution is studied, the more we realize that it is immensely improbable that we should be here at all. We have come to where we are on an exceedingly narrow track.

Man in the Universe

We always tend to think that we are at the centre of all things. The ancient Hebrew cosmology, the cosmology of the Greeks, and the cosmology of the Hindus all put man in the centre of the universe. In Genesis man appears as God's supreme handiwork on the sixth day, and all creation is his to dominate. This anthropocentric picture received a crushing blow when Copernicus showed that the motions of the planets can be much better understood if they rotate about the sun, so now the sun is the centre, with the earth a rather small planet revolving around it. Man's centrality received further blows when it was shown that the sun, so impressive to us, is a rather undistinguished star near the end of one of the spiral arms of a vast galaxy of billions of such stars, and that this galaxy is but one of many billions of similar galaxies scattered through an unimaginably large universe.

What remains of the centrality of man, and of the world made for him by God? Compared with the vastness of space, we are totally insignificant. We can be filled with awe and reverence, and with the Psalmist we can rejoice that the heavens show forth the glory of the Lord. Or, with Pascal ([1995], 1999, pp. 72–3), we can be terrified by the vastness of space, realizing that 'man is but a reed, the most feeble thing in nature. The entire universe need not arm itself to crush him; a vapour, a drop of water, suffices to kill him.' As the Psalmist said: 'Look up at those heavens of thine, the work of thy hands, at the moon and the stars, which thou hast set in their places; what is man that thou shoudst remember him?' (Psalms 8:5).

It is true that we can reply, again with Pascal, that man 'is a thinking reed. If the universe were to crush him, man would still be nobler than that which killed him, because he knows that he dies, and the advantages the universe has over him; of this the universe knows nothing.' But how can we be sure even of this? Is it not very likely that around some other stars in far-away galaxies there are sentient beings in civilizations immeasurable superior to our own, who know what we are doing and regard our activities in much the same way as we regard those of ants and bees. There are indeed few grounds for pride when we consider our position in the universe. And if there is no other life in the universe, this raises another question, posed by Margaret Knight, a well-known humanist: 'If life is the purpose of creation, what conceivably can be the point of countless millions of lifeless worlds? Or of the aeons of astronomical time before life existed? The Church has glanced uneasily at these questions but it has never answered them.' In saying this she was but echoing Maimonides (1956):

> Consider then how immense is the size of these bodies, and how numerous they are. And if the earth is thus no bigger than a point relative to the sphere of the fixed stars, what must be the ratio of the human species to the created Universe as a whole? And how then can any of us think that these things exist for his sake, and that they are meant to serve his uses?

Now, when we know far more about the universe, when we begin to understand in a detailed way the evolution of the very matter of which it is composed, we begin at the same time to glimpse a new truth, that it looks more and more as if the universe was indeed made just for man. At each stage in its development there seem to be many possibilities, and every time the one is chosen, that alone leads to a universe that can produce man. Within this perspective the insignificance of man takes on a completely different aspect. We wonder at the vastness of the universe in space and time compared with the smallness and frailty of man. Why this apparent prodigality? Now we see the answer: all this stupendous evolution was necessary in order that the earth should be made as a habitation for man. The process of nucleosynthesis, by which the elements constituting man's body are built up in the interiors of stars, takes billions of years. And in this time the galaxies containing these stars will inevitably move vast distances from their point of formation. So the universe must be as large and as old as it is, in order that it can be prepared as a home for man.

This is why we can say that it is our universe. Freeman Dyson (1971) has summed this up in the words: 'As we look out into the universe and identify the many accidents of physics and astronomy that have worked together for our benefit, it almost seems as if the universe must in some sense have known that we were coming.'

The idea that the universe has taken just that path in its evolution that leads to man is called the anthropic principle. It must be noted that this principle does not explain why the universe evolved in this particular way, unless we already believe in a creator who intended this result. Since we are indeed here, then of course the universe must be such as to allow our emergence. If the universe had so to speak taken the wrong turning, then we would not be here to talk about it. Or perhaps there have been millions of different universes in non-interacting spaces, and this is just the one that happened to be such as to allow for the evolution of man. We may or may not think that these arguments are plausible, but they are certainly tenable.

It has sometimes been objected that the anthropic principle is not scientific because it is not testable and leads to no new discoveries. However, the prediction of a resonance level in carbon at 7.65 MeV by Hoyle and its subsequent discovery provides an example of a scientific result deduced from the anthropic principle.

There is an even stronger form of the anthropic principle that deserves mention. We are accustomed to think of the constants of nature like the velocity of light or the mass of an electron as fixed and unalterable. Now the strong form of the anthropic principle says that the values of these constants are in fact fixed by the requirement that the universe will allow man to evolve. Some rather detailed arguments have been made to support this idea. This raises the possibility that there are many universes with different values of the fundamental constants, and only those with the values we know can produce man. There is, however, a difficulty with this argument. The number of fundamental constants is about ten, whereas the number of conditions they must satisfy is substantially greater. This implies that it is not possible, even in principle, to fix the parameters so as to ensure the evolution of man; there are not enough of them. The values of the constants cannot be the result of a random process; the universe is our universe, at the deepest level.

It should also be remarked in connection with the anthropic principle that it is possible that when science advances further we shall see that what appear to be arbitrary choices in the evolutionary process are in fact necessary – that, for example, we might find that the ratio of nuclear particles to photons must be as it is, and similarly for the other apparently very singular parameters. The inflationary theory has already shown how several apparently extraordinary coincidences can have a physical explanation. At an even deeper level, the very values of the fundamental constants as we know them might be necessary values, as indeed Eddington (1946) tried to show. This would make it even more surprising that we are here. It is also possible that the constants of nature vary with time. It is possible to set limits on such variations, and these are exceedingly small (Webb, 2003).

Random or Ordered?

There are two contemporary lines of argument that appear to support the idea of a purely random world, one derived from quantum mechanics and the other from the recent work on chaotic motion.

Quantum mechanics was developed in the 1920s and has been extremely successful in accounting for a wide range of atomic and nuclear phenomena. It is an indispensable part of modern physics. There is, however, still much dispute about its interpretation, and this is essentially a continuation of the dispute between Bohr and Einstein discussed in Chapters 8 and 9.

According to Bohr the world is radically indeterministic, so there is no reason to seek the cause of the universe. Furthermore, if physics is concerned only with what we can say about nature, our grasp of objective reality is weakened. It is not surprising that another fruit of the Copenhagen interpretation is the misuse of the Heisenberg uncertainty principle to explain the production of matter out of nothing. Even more bizarre is the claim that the universe can exist only because of the presence of an observer, necessary to collapse its wave function.

The other line of thought that has strengthened the general belief in the randomness of the world is that connected with what is called chaotic motion, as discussed in Chapter 11. It is found that in many systems the motion is exceedingly sensitive to the initial conditions so that a very slight change soon leads to completely different behaviour. The effect of this is that it is impossible to predict the future behaviour of such systems. All measurements are limited in precision, and the imprecision of our measurement is always such that our calculations of the future behaviour of a system very soon become quite unreliable. Once again it is an ontological matter. Because we cannot predict the behaviour of a system, it does not mean that the system is undetermined or random.

Thus whenever we hear talk about a process that is described as chance or random, this refers to the way it is described mathematically, not to its intrinsic nature, which is strictly determined. We cannot prove that this is so by the methods of science; we know it from the Christian doctrine of creation, on which all science is ultimately based.

Creation from Nothing

There have recently been many speculations about the possibility of providing a scientific explanation of creation itself. The first difficulty is to know whether the laws of physics still apply. It is always possible to invoke the power of God, but it is the duty of the physicist to try to solve problems by the methods of physics alone. Thus it might well be thought that creation requires violation of the conservation laws, but it seems that this is not necessarily the case. There is no difficulty about the total electric charge and angular momentum, since these have values consistent with zero, and the total linear momentum is not definable. The main problem concerns the principle of conservation of energy, and it was realized that the negative potential energy of the universe could exactly balance its positive kinetic energy, so that the total energy of the universe is just zero. So there is no need for God to override the conservation laws during the creation of the universe. Thus 'we cannot prove the creation of the universe from nothing, but the creation of the universe from nothing is not prohibited by any basic physical law' (Starobinsky and Zeldovich, 1992).

Vilenkin (1983) has suggested that the universe could have come into being by quantum tunnelling from nothing; this assumes that quantum mechanics can be applied to the whole universe, an assumption that rests on a discredited interpretation of quantum mechanics. Hawking (1998, p. 136) has suggested that time, like space, has no boundary. There is thus no initial singularity, no moment of creation. Thus 'the boundary condition of the universe is that it has no boundary. The universe would be completely self-contained and not affected by anything outside itself. It would be neither created nor destroyed. It would just BE.' This proposal has the merit that it does not require an initial singularity where the laws of physics break down. However, Hawking also supposes that if there is no beginning there is no need for a creator. This is a misunderstanding of the nature of creation, which is the causing of existence, an activity that is continuous. The continuation in existence requires God's causal agency just as much as an initial beginning, so even if there is no initial singularity, the creative act of God is still necessary.

It should be remembered that the physicist's concept of the vacuum is quite different from that of the theologian. For a physicist, a vacuum is rich in potentialities, but even then it requires an external agency to cause anything to happen. The theologian's vacuum is absolutely nothing at all, no matter, no space, no time and no potentialities of any kind. From that nothing, nothing can come. The physicist's vacuum, however, needs to be created.

Cosmology and Theology

From the times of the Psalmist to the present, contemplation of the heavens has been linked to our belief in God. If we read about these discoveries in scientific articles and books we seldom find any references to theology. And yet, as Chesterton (1912, p. 262) once remarked, 'religion means something that commits man to some doctrine about the universe.' Since everyone has some religious beliefs, explicit or implicit, it is not surprising that, just as theology was of vital importance for the birth of modern science, so it continues to influence, in many subtle ways, the continuing development of our knowledge of the universe. Much more obvious is the popularity of books on cosmology containing accounts of the latest discoveries, frequently linked with speculations about creation and the big bang, and how it all leads us to religion and a knowledge of the mind of God, or to atheism, depending on the inclinations of the author.

Science and Creation

The traditional philosophical arguments for the existence of a creator do not, of course, depend on particular scientific theories of the universe. They are based on simple everyday experiences of order in the world, and of the dependent nature of material things. Nevertheless the desire to integrate our scientific and our theological knowledge into a coherent whole often provides an extra-scientific criterion for preferring some theories of the universe over others. Thus if we believe from Revelation that the universe was created at a particular instant of time, we must notice that this is more plausibly brought into coherence with scientific theories that describe the development of the universe from a unique beginning than with those that maintain that the universe has always existed. Thus Christians might be expected to favour such theories, while those who wish to do away with the need for a creator might prefer the alternative steady state or oscillating universe theories.

Such preferences run as hidden, and sometimes not so hidden, threads through all the scientific discussions of the origin of the universe. When they do surface they are mentioned as feelings rather than as argued conclusions. Eddington (1928, p. 85) once said: 'I simply do not believe that the present order of things started off with a bang'. He repeated this later: 'Philosophically, the notion of a beginning of the present order is repugnant to me' (Eddington, 1931, p. 497). Hoyle similarly remarked: 'In the older theories all the matter in the Universe is supposed to have appeared at one instant of time, the whole creation process taking the form of one big bang. For myself I find this idea very much queerer than continuous creation.' He also found the big bang theory unacceptable on scientific grounds because it postulates an irrational process that cannot be described in scientific terms, and on philosophical grounds because it lies in principle beyond the realm of observation, irrespective of its success: 'it simply cannot be a good scientific theory. Under no circumstances ought anything that sounds like a cosmic beginning be acquiesced in by the scientist.' Another cosmologist, Harrison, recoiled from the evidence that the universe will keep expanding forever as a 'horrible thought' that 'would make the whole universe meaningless'. Marxist-Leninist writers naturally reject the notion of an absolute beginning as fundamentally incompatible with the principles of dialectical materialism. Thus Sivderskii rejected the big bang theory as an 'unscientific popish conclusion'.

This does not imply that it is legitimate to argue from a scientific theory to a theological conclusion. Although some Christians have indeed used the big bang theory as evidence for creation, others have been more cautious, notably the originator of the theory, the Belgian Abbé Lemaître, a Catholic priest. Modern Christian writers on cosmology recognize that it is quite unwarranted to argue from a scientific theory, however successful, to a theological belief. It is always hazardous to make links of this character, as has been found very often in the development of science. Science is concerned with the relation between one state of the world and another; it can never provide evidence for an absolute beginning.

The real connection is rather different: it is that the basic beliefs of the time tend to encourage or discourage different types of scientific theories, and these may or may not raise different theological questions. Thus the big bang theory inevitably raises the question about what happened before, whereas the continuous creation theory does not.

Now that Christians have realized that it is unwise to argue from the success of the big bang theory to the fact of creation, and agnostics have seen the steady state and oscillating theories subjected to severe criticism on scientific grounds, the arena of argument has shifted. Some theists point to the specificity of the universe as suggesting that it was created purposefully, while agnostics tend to emphasize either its necessary or its random character, and therefore its lack of need for a creator.

All these scientific developments show in ever-increasing detail the awesome extent and wonderful complexity of our universe. Beneath this complexity we are finding a unified structure, so that the discoveries of nuclear and particle physics can enable us to calculate in detail the processes that took place billions of years ago and eventually spread out over unimaginable distances. Thinking about this can increase our reverence for the power of the Creator. However, as many examples have shown, it is always unwise to base any arguments for the existence of God on particular scientific results. Very often what has seemed at first to have been a remarkable coincidence suggesting a supernatural cause has been shown by further work to be entirely explicable by the laws of physics.

Some attempts have been made to give a scientific account of creation out of nothing by a chance process. Chance is referred to as if it is a causative agent, not as indicating unknown causes. There is a more general difficulty: all a scientific theory can do is to say that if there exists matter with such-and-such properties that obeys certain equations, then if it is started off in a particular configuration it will behave subsequently in a way calculable from those equations. What it cannot say is whether there indeed exists matter with such-and-such properties, and how it is put into a particular configuration and no other. As Hawking (1988, pp. 136, 174) asked, 'what is it that breathes fire into the equations and makes a universe for them to describe?' And who sets the initial conditions? Furthermore, a scientific theory is only reliable in the regions where it has been thoroughly tested; when it is extrapolated to other regions its predictions must be less certain. And what is more unpredictable or more singular than the moment of creation?

Another point worth noticing is the way creation is associated with the very simplest structures. Thus Atkins (1981, p. 113) has remarked, 'The creation can generate only the most primitive structures, structures of such simplicity that they can drop out from absolutely nothing.' But it must be said that, simple or complicated, small or large, the passage from non-existence to existence is the most radical of all steps. It cannot be glossed over, and no one with any sense of ontological reality could accept this for an instant. However large or small the object may be, the passage from non-being to being is the greatest possible transition. We are talking about creation itself, and that is an activity that belongs to God alone.

The transition from not-being to being is beyond the power of science to detect. It is impossible to show by scientific methods that there is nothing in a specified volume, because it is always possible that there is something there that cannot be detected by our present instruments. *A fortiori*, it is impossible by scientific methods to detect the creation of everything, for before the creation there were no scientists and no scientific instruments.

Once these fundamental truths are understood, it is easy to assess the casual and flippant statements made by some popularizers of modern cosmology. Thus to say that the universe stumbled into being by accident through a chance fluctuation in a vacuum, or that space-time formed itself out of its own dust is not just an unwarranted speculation, but simply nonsense. Even if it is granted that a fluctuation in a vacuum could produce material objects, then such a 'vacuum' is rich in potentialities, and so cannot properly be described as nothing.

There is another form of the argument that is worth mentioning. It has been remarked that the total energy of the universe is zero, so creation could take place without violating the principle of the conservation of energy. The uncertainty relation between energy and time says that we can violate energy conservation by a small amount, but only for a correspondingly small time. Thus the universe could come into being by a fluctuation, even if its total energy is not exactly zero.

This speculation conflates two errors: first the absolute distinction between being and not-being, and second the application to a single system of the uncertainty principle which, like all quantum-mechanical statements, applies only to an ensemble of similar systems.

Cosmology remains highly speculative, with many new theories but insufficient data to test them thoroughly. One of the most recent is the instanton theory proposed by Hawking and Turek. An instanton is a 'sort of lump which couples gravity, space, time and matter together', 'a twist in matter and spacetime'. It forms the rounded top of the space-time cone at the initial singularity of the big bang. In this region the distinction between space and time is blurred. The authors of this theory have been asked what are the implications for the existence of a creator, and have replied that there are none.

However, they add, with remarkable confidence, that 'if a divine being wanted to create a univese, the simplest way to do it would be to use our instanton'.

Following the COBE satellite in 1992, the Wilkinson Microwave-Anisotropy Probe was launched in 2001, and that of the Planck Explorer is planned for 2005. These can provide extensive data to test the wide range of current cosmological speculations. Turek comments that 'cosmology is on the threshold of turning into a science', and is confident 'that an understanding of the beginning of our universe is within sight'.

The Search for Extra-Terrestrial Intelligence (SETI)

Over the years there have been many speculations about the possibility that the planets are inhabited. Immanuel Kant (1981, p. 186) in his *Universal Natural History and Theory of the Heavens* declared that 'most planets are certainly inhabited, and those that are not, will be some day'. He went on to describe these inhabitants and their interrelationships. Even more detailed were the accounts given by Swedenborg of his communications with the inhabitants of the moon and five other planets, together with details of their anatomy and behaviour. Among other writers, Anatole France declared that 'it is infinitely probable that it [Mars] is inhabited' (Kant, 1981, p. 294). However, despite all these writings, and many more, astronomical research has now shown that the physical conditions on the other planets are such that people similar to ourselves could not survive. It remains possible that primitive forms of life exist on some of the planets, and much research is devoted to looking for evidence of such life in meteorites and by using space probes.

Speculations about extra-terrestrial intelligent life have now shifted to the possibility that other stars have planets that are inhabited, perhaps with civilizations more highly developed than our own. Attention is concentrated on stars in our own galaxy, as those in other galaxies are much too far away.

At present it is impossible to verify such speculations by direct observation. If, however, a star has a planet it will appear to wobble slightly because the star and its planet rotate about their common centre of mass. Such wobbles have recently been detected in a few stars. This is evidence for the existence of planets, but there is at present no means of knowing whether they are suitable for living organisms, and if so whether they have indeed evolved there.

If there are intelligent beings on such planets, they might send us signals or respond to signals we send to them. There is now a substantial research effort devoted to the search for extra-terrestrial intelligences. Ingenious messages have been devised and sent, but no answer has been received. Estimates have been made, particularly by Drake (1992), of the probability that there are intelligent beings on other planets in our galaxy. He began with the number of stars in the galaxy, about one hundred billion, and then reduced it by a series of factors: the probability of a star having planets; the probability that life will develop; the probability that this life will evolve into intelligent beings to form a civilization and finally a factor to account for the limited lifetime of such a civilization. He made reasonable guesses for these factors, and found that there should be about 10,000 planets with civilizations capable of sending messages to us. This estimate, however, leaves out several important factors, the most critical being the presence of a moon. It is generally accepted that life first began in tidal basins, and these depend on the moon. The formation of the moon is generally attributed to a glancing collision between an asteroid and the earth. For the moon to be formed from this collision, its dynamics have to satisfy several very strict conditions. It is difficult to estimate the factors involved, but it is likely that this reduces Drake's estimate by a factor between one million and ten thousand million, so that it becomes very unlikely that there are any extra-terrestrial civilizations. In addition, there are many other factors concerning human history that should be taken into account, including the lives of the physicists who made radio communication possible. The net result is that extra-terrestrial intelligence is so improbable that it is not worth taking seriously. One of the most prominent Darwinists, Ernst Mayr, considers SETI to be a deplorable waste of money. It is just as well that we are unlikely to be invaded by extra-terrestrials, as they are likely to have a superior technology, and would simply eliminate us or make us their slaves.

It is interesting to ask why this has not happened. If there are planets in our galaxy where intelligent life has developed, then it would be very unlikely that ours is the first. If it is not the first, then the civilizations that developed long ago on other planets would be very likely to have developed space travel and colonized the whole galaxy. So why have they not shown up? Perhaps civilizations destroy themselves by nuclear war or by pollution long before they reach the stage of making spaceships.

The possibility of life on other planets and of intelligent beings on the planets of other stars is the subject of considerable theological debate (Dick, 2000). If there is life, however rudimentary, on other planets, it strengthens the argument that life emerges by natural evolutionary processes whenever the conditions are suitable, and so is not the result of a special creation by God. If there are intelligent beings on other planets, we must ask whether they are always perfect or whether they could sin and fall like Adam and therefore need redemption. If so, does the incarnation, suffering and death of Christ on earth suffice to redeem them as well? If not, then could God redeem them in any other way? These and similar speculations may serve as interesting theological exercises, but until the little green men visit us it is difficult to see how they could be tested.

Conclusion

These scientific studies of the universe show in ever-increasing detail the awesome extent and wonderful complexity of our universe. Beneath this complexity is revealed a unified structure, so that the discoveries of nuclear and particle physics enable us to calculate in detail the processes that took place billions of years ago and subsequently spread out over unimaginable distances. Thinking about this can increase our reverence for the power of the creator but, as many arguments have shown, it is always unwise to base any arguments for the existence of God on particular scientific results. Very often what has seemed at first to be a remarkable coincidence suggesting a supernatural cause has been shown by further work to be entirely explicable by the laws of physics.

The story of our attempts to understand the world thus shows a complex interaction of theological beliefs, scientific observations and theoretical speculations. It is notable that Christian theology greatly contributed to the development of modern science, and with it all the vast development that has led to our modern understanding of the universe.

CHAPTER 11

Chaos and Symmetry

Introduction

The world around us contains elements of order and disorder. Crystals are regular, clouds are not. Sometimes regular behaviour becomes irregular: water pours steadily from a tap at low velocities, but if we turn it on full the steady flow becomes turbulent. Similarly, smoke from a cigarette first rises smoothly and then becomes turbulent. Physicists select for study just those phenomena that behave in a simple and regular way, such as the free fall of a particle or the motions of the planets, where any disturbing influences such as air resistance or the attractions of the other planets are either negligible or can be allowed for if high accuracy is needed. The astonishing success of these simple laws in accounting for many phenomena to great accuracy is deeply impressive, and inspired Laplace to declare that from a knowledge of the present a being with great mathematical ability could predict the future as well as the past. Nature seemed to be a rigidly determined system.

It was then found that the time evolution of many systems of at least three particles shows such a sensitive dependence on the initial conditions that prediction of future behaviour soon becomes impossible. If we add the belief associated with certain interpretations of quantum mechanics that the world is fundamentally fuzzy, then we conclude that the behaviour of the universe is in principle unpredictable. Even without considering quantum effects, the solar system apparently becomes chaotic on a timescale of a few million years. All this is a consequence of laws that prescribe exact behaviour. The world is thus ruled by deterministic chaos.

Chaotic behaviour is found more frequently than the simple phenomena of classical physics. Even in apparently simple systems we find chaotic behaviour that seems to be impossible to describe, and yet its average behaviour can often be described in a simple way. This applies also to the scale-invariant structures of Mandelbrot. Even in the midst of chaos, there is hidden order.

The properties of the elementary particles show characteristic symmetries. Sometimes a symmetry appears to have exceptions, the symmetry is broken, but is always found to be subsumed in a higher symmetry.

Chaos

The success of Newtonian dynamics strongly reinforced the idea that the natural world is a rigidly deterministic system governed by relatively simple equations, and that in principle they enable the future development of physical systems to be calculated from a knowledge of the initial conditions. It is now becoming increasingly clear that this is only possible in rather special cases, and that it was the great achievement of the pioneers to choose for study just those systems for which this is possible. Thus Galileo chose to study the motion of freely falling bodies, and established a simple relation between the distance fallen and the time taken. This was indeed an idealized case, because in the real world there are various additional effects, such as those due to air resistance and the motion of the earth. Such effects were smaller than the inevitable uncertainties in his measurements and so did not affect the validity of his conclusions. In a similar way Newton first studied the motion of the moon around the earth, neglecting the perturbing effects due to the sun and the other planets. Once the validity of his dynamics was established, these perturbing effects could be included to give results of ever higher accuracy. It was believed that, at least in principle, this process could be continued indefinitely to give results of any desired accuracy. During the years after Newton's work, more and more refined calculations were indeed found to agree to high accuracy with the latest measurements, thus further supporting this belief.

Recent work has shown that this belief is false. This became apparent through the efforts of many mathematicians to calculate the behaviour of the moon. Newton was never satisfied with the results of his efforts, and during the eighteenth and nineteenth centuries strenuous efforts were made by Laplace, Euler, Clairaut and D'Alembert. It was possible, of course, to make satisfactory predictions that were accurate for a few years, but eventually unacceptable discrepancies always appeared. Finally Poincaré discovered the reason for this behaviour. The motion of the moon is principally governed by the attractions of the earth and the sun, together with those of the planets. It is justified to neglect the effects of the planets, but that leaves what is called a three-body problem. This was studied in detail by Poincaré, and he found that the solution of the three differential equations describing the motion has remarkable features. He found that, even when the masses of the three bodies are markedly different, so that perturbation theory may be used, the solutions are divergent. It had always been assumed that if the initial conditions were very slightly changed, the resulting orbits will remain similarly close. This apparently very reasonable expectation is in fact false. A very slight change in the initial conditions can, after several thousand years, give quite different orbits. Such motions are called chaotic.[1] After much longer times, say one million years, the orbits show chaotic behaviour with structures having a regular period.

The situation is a little more complicated than this. It is found that the motion is chaotic only for some regions of parameter space, while adjacent regions show regular behaviour. The difference between regular and chaotic behaviour can be stated more precisely: in the case of regular behaviour a small change in the parameters will produce orbits that diverge linearly, whereas for chaotic behaviour they diverge exponentially. There are two types of chaotic behaviour: in one the orbits, though chaotic, remain within a bounded region, whereas in the other the orbits can diverge to infinity. The bounded orbits can

---

[1] See Bai-Lin (1984); Gleick (1989); Peterson (1993); Ruelle (1991).

move irregularly but periodically around particular regions called strange attractors, and then flip to another set of orbits around another strange attractor. Such calculations have been made possible by modern high-speed computers.

An example of such behaviour was found by Lorenz (1963) when he was studying models of thermal convection in liquids. He established a set of three simple differential equations and found that the solutions depended very sensitively on the initial conditions. When applied to the weather it is called the butterfly effect and shows why it is impossible to predict the weather for more than a short time ahead, even if the atmosphere is governed by strictly deterministic equations.

The possibility of chaotic behaviour has important consequence for our understanding of the solar system. The chaotic solutions of the equations of motion could imply that it is possible for a planet to be ejected. This leads us to ask for a physical explanation. A clue is provided by examination of the belt of asteroids between Mars and Jupiter. If the orbital periods of hundreds of asteroids are examined, it is found that they are not more or less uniformly spaced but are bunched at some values and are rarely found at others. The reason for this behaviour is the presence of resonances when the orbital period of the asteroid is in a simple ratio to that of Jupiter. These resonances are formed by the accumulation of a large number of small effects occurring in phase over a long time that is eventually significant enough to lead to ejection from the solar system. This can only happen if the chaotic behaviour is unbounded. It is possible that this provides an explanation for the formation of the solar system out of a dense cloud of asteroids surrounding the sun.

It must be emphasized that both regular and chaotic motions are strictly deterministic and that both types of motion follow from Newton's simple equations. Chaotic motion provides a useful way to define chance. Thus Poincaré (1903, p. 67) suggested that if 'a very small cause that escapes our notice determines a considerable effect that we cannot fail to see, then we say that the effect is due to chance'. It is vital to notice that this does not imply that the world is somehow intrinsically fuzzy or undetermined. A strictly determined world can contain chance phenomena in the sense described. Since its initial formulation, chaos theory has found a wide range of applications such as the theory of turbulent motion, population dynamics, medical epidemics and economic systems.

At first sight it is very surprising that the solutions of very simple equations can show extremely complex behaviour. This is strikingly illustrated by the simple non-linear difference equation that gives, for example, the population at time $(t + 1)$ in terms of the value at time t, where the variable t labels equal time intervals:

$$F(t + 1) = aF(t)(1 - F(t))$$

where a is a constant.

The solutions of this equation show quite different behaviour for different values of the constant a: for some ranges the behaviour is regular and in others chaotic in very complicated ways. Such equations have been applied to study the variations of populations of insects and animals over the years (May, 1976).

The discovery of chaotic behaviour, with its extreme sensitivity to the initial conditions together with the belief in the fundamental uncertainty of the world, has led to the conclusion that knowledge of the future is impossible even in principle. It has even been suggested that this provides a way to reconcile our knowledge of physics with our personal experience of human free will.

Although the world shows many causal features, it is not possible to establish by scientific methods that it is either fully determined or radically undetermined. We may never succeed in attaining a fully deterministic account of the quantum world, but we certainly do not know that it is undetermined. Einstein tried hard to find a deterministic theory but failed, but the problem is still open. As described in Chapter 9, some promising possibilities are being explored, in particular the pilot wave theory of de Broglie and the more physical theory of stochastic electrodynamics.

It is much the same with chaos theory. It has been known for centuries that the time evolution of dynamical systems is often extremely sensitive to the initial conditions but, as in the case of quantum mechanics, this does not imply that the trajectory is not completely determined by the initial conditions.

There is thus no reason to believe that the material world is not a fully determined system that behaves exactly according to God's laws. We may rightly marvel at the beauty and intricacy of God's creation, but the theological conclusions that have been drawn from quantum mechanics are thus without foundation. Quantum mechanics has nothing whatever to do with free will, which is an attribute of our immortal souls and therefore above the laws of the natural world.

Symmetry

We are all familiar with the symmetries of the natural world, in seashells and crystals, in sunflowers and cacti, and we have looked at the photographs of snowflakes, all different and yet all symmetrical. This shows us that the laws of nature automatically produce things that we recognize as beautiful. It is thus not surprising that the fundamental laws of nature are themselves beautiful, but it has taken many centuries to show how profoundly this is true, and to express that beauty in mathematical form. Beauty is in the eye of the beholder, but symmetry is an objective mathematical concept, so the search for beauty is the search for symmetry.

The greatest scientists, who seek the most fundamental laws, are convinced that these laws must be beautiful. Einstein thought of the most beautiful way to design matter, expressed this mathematically and then looked for experimental verification. He took a God's-eye view of nature, and asked himself how God would have made the world. Relativity is often considered to be difficult and complicated, but properly understood it is simpler and more elegant than Newtonian dynamics. Thus the Lorentz transformation is simply a rotation in four-dimensional space-time. Similarly Dirac said that he considered it more important that his equations were beautiful than that they agreed with experiment. This of course implies that eventually more careful experiments will agree with his equations; otherwise, however beautiful they are, they must be rejected. When he examined his relativistic wave equation he was surprised to find that it has two solutions. Initially he was not bold enough, and interpreted the additional solution as that of a proton, but afterwards he realized that he had predicted the existence of positively charged electrons, and these were indeed found experimentally soon afterwards.

A remarkable connection between invariance under symmetry transformations and conservation laws was found by Emmy Nother. She showed that translational invariance implies the conservation of linear momentum, rotational invariance the conservation of angular momentum, and time invariance the conservation of energy.

This may be shown by considering a system, not subject to external forces, whose motions are described by generalized coordinates $q_i(t)$ and $\dot{q}_i(t)$. Then the Lagrangian $\mathscr{L}(q_i, q_i)$ of the system satisfies the equations

$$\frac{\partial \mathscr{L}}{\partial q_i} - \frac{d}{dt}\left(\frac{\partial \mathscr{L}}{\partial \dot{q}_i}\right) = 0$$

Now suppose that the Lagrangian $\mathscr{L}$ is independent of a particular coordinate q_j; such coordinates are called cyclic. Then $(\partial \mathscr{L})/(\partial q_i) = 0$, so that the conjugate momentum $p_j \equiv (\partial \mathscr{L})/(\partial \dot{q}_j)$ is a constant of the motion. For example, if the system is unaffected by spatial translation in the x-direction, then $\mathscr{L}$ does not depend on x and so the conjugate momentum

$$p_x = \frac{\partial}{\partial \dot{x}}\left(\frac{1}{2}m\dot{x}^2\right) = m\dot{x}$$

is conserved. Thus spatial symmetry, that is the homogeneity of space, implies the conservation of linear momentum. If the system is unaffected by rotation through an angle θ, then $p_\theta = (\partial \mathscr{L})/(\partial \theta)$ is a constant. Since the rotational kinetic energy is $(1/2)mr^2\dot{\theta}^2$, $p_\theta = mr\dot{\theta}^2$, which is the angular momentum. This rotational symmetry, that is the isotropy of space, implies the conservation of angular momentum about the axis of symmetry.

If the system is unaffected by time, then energy is conserved. This is shown by considering the total time derivative of $\mathscr{L}$ when $\mathscr{L}$ is not an explicit function of time:

$$\frac{d\mathscr{L}}{dt} = \sum_i \frac{\partial \mathscr{L}}{\partial q_i}\frac{dq_i}{dt} + \sum_i \frac{\partial \mathscr{L}}{\partial \dot{q}_i}\frac{d\dot{q}_i}{dt}$$

$$= \sum_i \frac{d}{dt}\left(\frac{\partial \mathscr{L}}{\partial \dot{q}_i}\right)\dot{q}_i + \sum_i \frac{\partial \mathscr{L}}{\partial \dot{q}_i}\frac{d\dot{q}_i}{dt} = \sum_i \frac{d}{dt}\left(\dot{q}_i\frac{\partial \mathscr{L}}{\partial \dot{q}_i}\right)$$

Thus

$$\left(\sum_i \dot{q}_i \frac{\partial \mathscr{L}}{\partial \dot{q}_i} - \mathscr{L} \right)$$

is constant.

Now we consider only conservative systems for which the potential energy V is independent of the velocities $\dot{q}_i$, so that

$$\frac{\partial \mathscr{L}}{\partial \dot{q}_i} = \frac{\partial T}{\partial \dot{q}_i}$$

Since T is a homogeneous quadratic function of the $\dot{q}_i$, then, by Euler's theorem,

$$\sum_i \dot{q}_i \frac{\partial T}{\partial \dot{q}_i} = 2T$$

Thus $2T - \mathscr{L} = 2T(T + V) = T + V$ is constant, and this is the total energy of the system. Thus symmetry under temporal transition, that is the homogeneity of time, implies the conservation of energy (Lucas and Hodgson, 1990).

The development of quantum mechanics made it possible to calculate atomic and nuclear structure, and provided an explanation of the observed energy levels and transition probabilities. It was found that these could be more elegantly expressed using the language of group theory, which classifies the types of symmetry. Later on, this provided the key to the classification of the elementary particles.

After Chadwick discovered the neutron, Heisenberg suggested that the proton and the neutron can usefully be considered as the two possible states of the nucleon, and thus introduced the concept of isospin. This proved extremely fruitful in classifying nuclear states and also provided a new selection rule for nuclear reactions. However, since the proton and the neutron have slightly different masses, which Heisenberg attributed to the charge on the proton, the symmetry is not perfect.[2]

In the following years, many different types of elementary particles were discovered, first in cosmic radiation and then using the new giant accelerators. It was found that the strongly interacting particles, called hadrons, can be grouped into two classes, called baryons and mesons. The lightest baryons can be subdivided into a doublet consisting of the proton and the neutron, a triplet of sigma hyperons and a doublet of xi hyperons. In addition, there is the lambda (λ) particle forming a singlet on its own. The mesons can be similarly divided into two kaon doublets with masses around 500 MeV, a triplet of pions with masses around 140 MeV and the singlet eta (η) and eta' (η') mesons. How can one make sense of this? Can symmetry help? Sakata tried the

---

[2] The following account is based on a review of *Fearful Symmetry*, by A. Zee (Zee, 1999).

three-dimensional representation of the symmetry group SU_3, but it did not fit. Then Gell-Mann and Ne'eman independently tried the eight-dimensional representation of the same group and found that it gives a triplet, two doublets and a singlet, exactly as required. This is called the eightfold way.

In addition to these hadrons and mesons, there are nine very short-lived baryons called resonances, but unfortunately the group SU_3 has no nine-dimensional representation. Gell-Mann therefore used the ten-dimensional representation and this implies the existence of a tenth particle, called the omega minus, that had not been found. Symmetry considerations give the properties of this particle, and it was subsequently found experimentally with just the predicted properties. This was a convincing demonstration of the deep symmetries in nature and the power of group theory to reveal them.

This success left unresolved the puzzle why there are no particles described by the three-dimensional representation of SU_3. Perhaps there are such particles, but somehow they have not been detected. They are called quarks. Group theory tells us that this gives representations of one, eight, eight and ten particles, corresponding to hadrons and resonances. Consideration of the transformation properties shows that we can think of the barons and resonances as each made up of three quarks and the mesons of quark–antiquark pairs. This proved to be a very useful way to think about baryons and mesons and helped to understand the selection rules governing interactions and processes like pion and kaon production in energetic nucleon–nucleon collisions.

Experimentalists naturally tried to isolate quarks, but so far they have failed. It seems that the quark–quark interaction becomes stronger as the separation increases, unlike all other forces, so that if they are pulled far enough apart the bond breaks, producing a quark–antiquark pair. So instead of pulling out a quark one has produced a meson. However, the scattering of high-energy electrons from nucleons is just what would be expected if the nucleon consists of three quarks, so indirect evidence for their existence has been obtained.

There are two types of symmetry. First there are those known to Einstein: rotation and Lorentz invariance that are absolute and exact. Second, there is Heisenberg's approximate isospin symmetry, parity in weak interactions and the even less exact symmetries of the eightfold way. These approximate symmetries horrified Einstein's devotees, and it was a long time before perfect symmetry returned. This return began when Yang and Mills invented a new and beautifully exact symmetry called non-Abelian gauge symmetry that completely determines a quantity called the action. Unfortunately this theory did not fit the real world.

Noether's proof of the connection between conservation and symmetry prompted a search for the symmetry responsible for charge conservation. Einstein in his work on gravity used the idea of a local transformation that differs from point to point. Weyl, following Einstein, decided that the symmetry responsible for charge conservation must be local, and was astonished to find that this requires the inclusion of the electromagnetic field in the action. In other words, local symmetries imply the existence of light. Just as local coordinate invariance forced the graviton on Einstein, so local symmetry forced the photon on Weyl. He called it gauge symmetry. Yang and Mills put all this together, making Heisenberg's symmetry exact and local. Then, just as Weyl's theory demanded the photon, the Yang–Mills theory demands several fields, each associated with a massless particle called a gauge boson.

The next step came with an attempt to calculate the lifetime of the neutral pion. This disagreed with experiment by a factor of three, which could be put right if each quark came in three types, labelled colours, and these have the exact symmetry required by the Yang–Mills theory. Thus the strong interaction is fundamentally controlled by the exact symmetries of Yang and Mills, and Einstein is vindicated again. The different colours are transformed into each other by the symmetry group SU_3, implying the existence of eight gauge bosons. These are called gluons, as it is believed that they mediate the force between quarks, just as the photon mediates the electromagnetic force.

Does perfect symmetry characterize nature's design? If the universe were perfectly symmetrical, there could only be one interaction, and all the fundamental particles would be identical. The universe would be very dull: no atoms, no stars, no planets, no flowers and no physicists. To ask for both unity and diversity seems like asking for the impossible.

How can the four fundamental interactions, gravitational, electromagnetic, strong and weak, be unified? Their strengths are so different that this seems impossible. The electromagnetic and the strong interactions are mediated by particles, the electromagnetic by the photon and the strong by the pion, and the range of the interaction is related to the mass of the particle: the heavier the particle, the shorter the range. The strong interaction is short-ranged because the pion is relatively massive. Conversely the weak interaction is weak because its range is even smaller, so it is mediated by a very massive particle. Knowing the strength of the weak interaction, it is then possible to calculate the mass of the mediating particle, called the W boson. The symmetry of the weak and the electromagnetic interactions then determines the group, and this was found to imply the existence of another gauge boson, called the Z boson. These ideas were confirmed when the W and Z bosons were found experimentally.

It remained unclear why the W and Z bosons, together with the photon, have very different masses, although they are all gauge bosons and transform into each other by the same symmetry group, and also why the strengths of the fundamental forces are so different. Then it was realized that these strengths vary very slowly with energy, and at some very high energy they could become the same. Such high energies, around 10^{18} MeV, are far beyond anything realizable experimentally, but they did occur in the first instant of the big bang at around 10^{-35} seconds. At these high temperatures all four forces were identical and perfectly symmetrical, and then as the universe cooled they separated out due to a process called spontaneous symmetry breaking. Their strengths and the masses of the mediating particles changed in different ways as the universe evolved, ultimately settling down to the values we find today.

It is still not clear exactly how this happened. One suggestion due to Kaluza and Klein is that space is really five-dimensional, the two extra dimensions being curled up into tiny circles. The radii of the circles are approximately

10^{-18} of that of the proton, and so they appear to be points. Astonishingly, in such a world there must be two types of force that can be interpreted as the gravitational force and the electromagnetic force, and this is now understood as a consequence of local symmetry. Thus Einstein's gravitational theory implies Maxwell's theory. In order to account for the variety of particles the number of dimensions has to be increased to ten, and this is called superstring theory. The development and application of superstring theory are highly controversial and the subject of much current research. Thus the search for symmetry in nature began with Plato's musical strings and may end with superstrings.

Many of the symmetries of nature appear obvious. Thus it was confidently believed that the laws of nature are invariant under a parity transformation. This means that if we make two experiments, one being the mirror image of the other, the results will be the same. Parity invariance was widely used in the construction of theories. However, Lee and Yang realized that this had never been tested and they proposed some experiments to test it. It was a great surprise when it was found that parity is not conserved in some nuclear decays. It was later discovered that there is a higher symmetry that is conserved, namely the product of parity and charge conjugation, the transformation of a particle into its anti-particle. The second surprise was the discovery that even this higher symmetry is broken, and indeed this is necessary if the universe is to contain matter. It then appears that this is a consequence of a yet higher symmetry; if time reversal is added, the product of the three is conserved, as far as we know at present. At each stage in this process of discovery the symmetry seems at first to be broken, and is then restored at a deeper level. This threefold symmetry is one of the deepest truths known, and we do not really understand it.

We can well ask, with Einstein, whether in creating the universe God was driven by implacable mathematical symmetries to create it in the way He did, or whether, as implied by the Christian doctrine of creation, that denies necessity to God's actions, there were alternatives that allowed Him some freedom to choose. In any case, we know that the world is far from being fuzzy or chaotic, but is locked together by the steely framework of layer upon layer of symmetries so related that even if one symmetry is inexact or broken, this is restored by other symmetries at a deeper level.

CHAPTER 12

Science and Non-Christian Religions

Introduction

If Christian beliefs about the natural world form the essential presuppositions of modern science, it is interesting to see what happens to that science when these Christian beliefs are either absent, repudiated or ignored. In the first category come primitive societies and ancient civilizations, together with the religions of the East, Buddhism, Hinduism and Taoism, which have existed for thousands of years. In the second category come the totalitarian regimes of Nazi Germany and Soviet communism that repudiated Christianity. In the third category comes our own materialistic, hedonistic and capitalist society. These will now be considered, except for the ancient civilizations that have already been considered in Chapter 2, and the Muslim civilization that has been considered in Chapter 3. In each case it is found that when science is deprived of its Christian roots, it eventually withers and dies. An apparent counter-example is provided by Japan, and this is discussed in a later section of this chapter. As this chapter deals with wider social problems, references are made to other sciences as well as to physics.

Primitive Societies

The psychology of primitive peoples, both ancient and contemporary, is shaped by their continuing struggle to survive. They are surrounded by forces that they can neither understand nor control. A recent book on the history of South Africa summed up the outlook of the Bushmen:

> If the future is both uncertain and uncontrollable, it does not do to think or worry too much about it. Better to live for the moment, to eat heartily when there is plenty and to starve stoically when there is nothing. There is no spirit of acquisitiveness in a subsistence economy, no deep-seated sense of work being intrinsically good apart from what it can produce, or of idleness being shameful; nor any great pressure to save for the future when there is no snowbound winter. Time is of little consequence when it is related only to the rising and the setting of the sun, when there is nowhere to go and no deadlines to keep. (Sparks, 1990, p. 20)

The absence of a sense of causality, namely the belief that events can be strictly correlated with previous events, and of a sense of time, makes it very difficult for Bushmen to cope with modern civilization or to understand science. Our beliefs about the world that are essential for science are embedded so deep in our subconscious that we seldom if ever advert to them explicitly. They are not taught in schools or universities. We simply take them for granted, like the air we breathe. Even if people in other cultures master the rules and are able to carry out some scientific work, it remains in some sense an alien graft. It is never for them a natural activity, and it is very difficult for them to perform really original research.

This is shown by the situation in some of the developing countries. Although science is held in high esteem and its products are widely used, the standard of scientific research remains low. It is proving unexpectedly difficult to train indigenous scientists, and the few who are trained in the more developed countries frequently remain there. Thus in spite of its popularity, science fails to strike deep roots, and it remains dependent on the science in more developed countries.

A teacher from Glasgow who worked for eight years in a West African university, Mr R. J. Riggs, has commented on the same problem. He pointed out that

> western science was built on certain convictions that the world makes sense, that events have causes that can be found out in a systematic way, that ideas can be tested by experiment and so I found in teaching physics that I was often trying to build without these foundations. The students slowly came to accept them but it was uphill work and that is partly why so many of them take refuge in memory work rather than understanding.

Eastern Religions

In recent years there have been several books (e.g. Capra, 1975; Zukav, 1979) on the similarities between Eastern religions and modern physics. This is not an easy subject to study because of the difficulties in trying to understand systems of belief so different from our own. Inevitably we have to rely on translations of their canonical texts, and it may be that there are in many cases no really satisfactory words to convey key ideas in our own language. Here, we are, as in the case of Islam, concerned mainly with their beliefs about the natural world and its accessibility to the human mind.

Before examining these beliefs, it may be remarked that it is a matter of historical fact that modern science developed in Western Europe and not in the East. The religions of the East with which we are concerned, namely Buddhism, Hinduism and Taoism, have existed for thousands of years, but in none of the countries where they flourished has science in its modern form developed from their indigenous culture. All the modern science that is now to be found in these countries has been learned from the West. This by itself is a strong argument against the belief that there is some fundamental congruence between Eastern religions and modern science.

The Eastern view of the world is organic, in contrast to the Western, which is mechanistic: 'For the Eastern mystic, all things and events perceived by the senses are interrelated, connected' (Capra, 1975, p. 23). 'Our tendency to divide the world into individual and separate things and to experience ourselves as isolated egos in this world is seen as an illusion which comes from our measuring and categorising mentality. It is called ignorance in Buddhist philosophy, and is seen as the state of a disturbed mind which has to be overcome' (ibid.). The various schools of Eastern mysticism 'all emphasise the basic unity of the universe' (ibid.). 'In the Eastern view, the division of nature into separate objects is not fundamental and any such objects have a fluid and ever-changing character' (ibid.).

A recurring theme is the unity of space and time: 'Throughout Eastern mysticism, there seems to be a strong intuition of the space-time characteristic of reality. The fact that space and time are inseparably linked, which is so characteristic of relativity physics, is stressed again and again' (ibid.). Space and time are seen as interpenetrating, but it is not clear what this means. The Galilean and Lorentz transformations both relate the space-time vector in one frame to that in another frame, so why is the Lorentz transformation linked to the strong intuition of Eastern mysticism whereas the Galilean transformation is not? These transformations were first written down in the West, not in the East. If the Eastern sages had intuited the Lorentz transformation or the constancy of the velocity of light, that would have been some achievement, but they did not (Bernstein, 1982).

An observer can only experience phenomena as a series of space-time actions, whereas the mystics claim that they can experience 'the full span of space-time where time does not flow any longer' (ibid., p. 196). 'Vision is bound up with a space of higher dimension, and therefore timeless' (ibid.) (Govinda). This is compared with the space-time diagrams used in modern physics: 'Eastern mystics assert that in transcending time, they also transcend the world of cause and effect. Time, space and causation are like the glass through which the Absolute is seen ... In the Absolute there is neither time, space nor causation' (ibid.) (Swami Vivekananda). However, the utility of space-time diagrams does not imply the absence of causation in the real world. The concept of a timeless being is also present in Western religions: for the Christian God, all eternity is one ever-present now. The insights of the mystics of the East did not lead them to propose the space-time diagrams of modern physics.

Capra (ibid., p. 221) stresses the importance of unity: 'The conception of things and phenomena as transient manifestations of an underlying funda-mental unity is not only a basic element of quantum theory, but also a basic element of the Eastern world view.' Physicists are indeed trying to unify the various types of fields into a single field incorporating all physical phenomena: 'The Brahman of the Hindus, like the Dharmakaya of the Buddhists and the Tao of the Taoists, can be seen, perhaps, as the ultimate field theory from which spring not only the phenomena studied in physics, but all other phenomena as well' (ibid., p. 222). Perhaps indeed. We look forward to a paper on this appearing in the pages of the *Physical Review*.

The Indian philosopher Rabindranath Tagore discussed the relation between truth and beauty with Einstein. Tagore maintained that truth and beauty depend on man. Einstein agreed concerning beauty, but not truth, and affirmed his belief that scientific truth is objective and independent of man (Pais, 1994).

The idea, found in the Copenhagen interpretation of quantum mechanics, that it is the action of the observer that brings events into existence, has supported the belief that things and events are creations of the mind. As Capra (ibid., p. 294) remarks, 'if the S-matrix theory proves successful, this would mean that the basic structures of the physical world are determined, ultimately, by the way we look at the world':

> Such a theory of subatomic particles reflects the impossibility of separating the scientific observer from the observed phenomena ... It implies, ultimately, that the structure and phenomena we observe in nature are nothing but creations of our observing and categorising mind. That this is so is one of the fundamental tenets of Eastern philosophy. The Eastern mystics tell us again and again that all things and events we perceive are creations of the mind, arising from a particular state of consciousness and dissolving again if this state is transcended. (Ibid., p. 292)

Thus, 'all phenomena in the world are nothing but an illusory manifestation of the mind and have no reality on their own' (ibid., p. 293) (Ashvaghosha).

As it happens, S-matrix theory has not proved successful. The idea that our scientific theories and what we see as reality can be derived from an examination of our measuring apparatus was studied in detail by Eddington (1939), and found to be a blind alley. If it were true, it would remove the necessity of experiments, and reduce us all to solipsists creating our own realities. It is hardly necessary to emphasize that scientists know that we are studying an objective world in a systematic and communicable way. Solipsism makes nonsense of science.

'In Buddhist thought, all things are seen as dynamic, impermanent and illusory' (ibid., p. 198). 'Both the modern physicist and the Eastern mystic have realised that all phenomena in this world of change and transformation are dynamically interrelated. Hindus and Buddhists see this interrelation as a cosmic law, the law of Karma, but they are generally not concerned with any specific patterns in the universal network of events' (ibid., p. 205). Once again we see the contrast between the vagueness of Eastern thought and the specificity of modern science. Scientists reject the dream-world picture of science from the East.

A recurring theme, connected with quantum phenomena that have been interpreted as providing evidence for non-local interactions, is the interconnectedness of everything. In the Eastern view, as in the view of modern physics, everything in the universe is connected to everything else and no part of it is fundamental. The Eastern mystics, therefore, are generally not interested in explaining things, but rather in obtaining as direct non-intellectual experience the unity of all things. This was the attitude of the Buddha, who answered all questions about life's meaning, the origin of the world or the nature of Nirvana, with a noble silence.

It would hardly be possible to find a better illustration of the emptiness of Eastern thought and of its radical incompatibility with the scientific method. Physicists are satisfied with an approximate understanding of nature only if they fall captive to the Copenhagen interpretation of quantum mechanics.

Capra (ibid., p. 307) remarks that 'To free the human mind from words and explanations is one of the main aims of Eastern mysticism.' This is indeed true: Aquinas at the end of his life remarked that all he had written was as straw, but this state was attained only at the end of a lifetime of reasoning, that is by logical thought, not by denying logic. Such insights are attained by Western as well as by Eastern mystics, and have nothing to do with science.

This brief consideration of the writings of some Eastern mystics, illustrated by quotations from Capra, show that their insights and intuitions are either banal and trivial, so vague as to be useless, or just wrong, particularly in the sense that if they are held they are inimical to the development of modern science. Whatever they say that is of value is found also in the Western mystics, themselves firmly rooted in an objective and rational way of knowing that did indeed lead to the development of modern science.

Science in Japan

There is no doubt that the standard of science in Japan is very high, certainly comparable in quality and quantity with that in the best European countries. There are numerous well-staffed universities and research institutes producing research of high quality. This has all been achieved since the beginning of the Meiji era in 1868, when Japan was opened up after centuries of isolation. The Japanese have high moral standards, but do not appear to be particularly religious. The main religions are Buddhism and Shintoism, but religious observance among the Japanese seems to be mainly at the social level: they visit the Shinto temple at the beginning of the New Year, and when they want to ensure success in examinations. Despite heroic missionary efforts over many years, the proportion of Christians among the Japanese remains very low. Does this not provide a counter-example to the thesis of this chapter?

It is not easy to answer this question, but a few preliminary remarks may be made. The Japanese have an extraordinary ability to absorb ideas from other cultures. Their religions and their script come from the mainland. The Spanish and Portuguese Jesuit missionaries, including St Francis Xavier, were very active in the sixteenth century, particularly in the island of Kyushu. A group of Japanese noblemen visited Rome, where they were warmly received. The Jesuits established schools and printing presses and at the peak there were around 200,000 Catholics in Japan. Then came the persecution in the Tokagawa era. The Jesuits were expelled and Japanese Catholics were savagely persecuted. Many were martyred when they refused to renounce their faith. Many remained secret Christians, while outwardly conforming to Buddhism. These secret Christians were particularly numerous in the Amakawa islands off Kyushu. The descendants of these secret Christians held on to their faith for centuries, and were still numerous, especially in Kyushu, when the missionaries returned in the nineteenth century. As soon as they had identified the Catholic Church they revealed themselves to the astonished missionaries. They built their cathedral at Urukami, a suburb of Nagasaki; it was destroyed by the atomic bomb.

The people who led the intellectual revolution in the Meiji era were mainly from Kyushu. They had thought that Japan was the most powerful country, but the arrival of the black ships in Tokyo Bay told them differently. They reacted with a strong determination to restore Japanese supremacy, set about it in a very systematic way, and succeeded in about fifty years. Perhaps this determination and ability was partly due to the Catholic beliefs so deeply embedded in their collective minds three hundred years previously. This is no more than a speculation, and further research is desirable.

I once discussed this problem with an eminent Japanese physicist, a member of the same family that was represented in the delegation that had visited Rome in the sixteenth century. He remarked that he often felt that he was doing physics from the neck up; in other words the beliefs on which his physics was based were not deep-rooted in his own culture, but came from outside.

Science in Nazi Germany

Over the centuries, the German contributions to science have been of the highest order, and German science was flourishing when Hitler came to power in the 1930s. Nazi ideology was based on the superiority of the Ayran race that was destined to rule the world, and from this followed the inferiority of other races, particularly the Jews, who were expelled from their university posts and forced to flee overseas (Bullock, 1964; Gratzer, 2000, ch. 10).

In spite of their political skill, the Nazis had no understanding of the importance of science not only for itself but also as the foundation of Germany's immensely strong chemical industry. Carl Bosch warned Hitler that the expulsion of Jewish scientists was ruining German science, only to be told: 'Then we will do without chemistry and physics for the next hundred years.' In their speeches, the Nazis promised to rid German academic life of all traces of Jewishness. This even extended to scientific theories due to Jewish scientists, and a particular object of their venom was Einstein's theory of relativity. The universities were soon controlled by the Nazis, and each faculty had a *Dozentenführer* responsible for Nazification who ensured that only Party members were promoted. About three thousand academics were dismissed for being Jewish or politically unreliable (Mendelssohn, 1973).

The case of Einstein is a reminder that the highest eminence was no protection. He was briefly in Oxford before going on, like so many others, to the United States. Born and Franck were two other eminent physicists who had to leave, as well as a large number of younger scientists. They were welcomed in Britain and in the United States, and made great contributions to the scientific life of those countries (Peierls, 1997, p. 348). Einstein went to the Institute of Advanced Study in Princeton, Born was appointed to the Chair of Natural Philosophy in Edinburgh and Franck went to a high position in the

United States. Rutherford led a public appeal for funds to support the refugee scientists when they arrived in England, often having left all their possessions behind. Cambridge even welcomed the ailing Haber (see Perutz, 2000), who had made immense contributions to the German chemical industry, not only the Haber process for fixing nitrogen, so important for manufacturing explosives, but also the process for manufacturing poison gas.

It has been suggested that the welcome extended to these refugees was simply 'a shrewd move on the part of those countries to secure for themselves first-rate scientists at low cost'. Kurt Mendelssohn (1973), himself a refugee who made great contributions to science in Oxford, said that 'nothing could be further from the true facts and it is the duty of those who benefited by this manifestation of academic solidarity to repudiate this explanation emphatically. It was done for humanitarian motives and academic solidarity, and as a protest against Nazi barbarism with its ruthless contempt for learning and scholarship' (p. 14). Furthermore, the most eminent of the refugee scientists were beyond the age of their greatest achievements and most of the remainder were relatively young and unknown.

The German physicists reacted in different ways to the Nazi policies. A few, like the Nobel Laureates Lenard and Stark, supported the Nazi regime, and rose to positions of great power. Lenard became President of the Physicalisch-Technische Reichsanstalt after the previous director Paschen, a Jew, was dismissed. Many lesser men, seizing their opportunity, used their Party membership to gain positions that they would never have reached on their scientific merits alone. Thus Wilhelm Muller wrote a book on the international Jewish conspiracy to pervert science and destroy humanity; he was appointed to succeed Arnold Sommerfeld in Munich. On the occasion of Muller's inauguration, Stark castigated 'white Jews' (Aryans who taught in 'the Jewish spirit'), such as Planck and Heisenberg, who continued to accept Jewish science such as the theory of relativity. Others, such as Max von Laue, spoke out with great courage against the Nazis and endangered their very lives. The majority, while disliking what was going on, decided that the best thing was to keep their heads down and preserve what they could of German science so that it could flourish again in better times.

The doyen of German physicists, Max Planck, (see Heilbron, 1986; also Peierls, 1997) an honourable man of the old school, was appalled at what was happening. Already in his seventies when the Nazis came to power, and president of the Kaiser Wilhelm Gesellschaft, he could well have retired. He went to see Hitler personally in 1933, in his capacity as Secretary of the Prussian Academy of Sciences, and asked him to reconsider the anti-Jewish policies. Predictably, he failed to make any impression on Hitler, and was treated to a characteristic anti-Jewish tirade. Planck decided that it was his duty to stay at his post and do what he could to protect German science, without compromising his principles. There was very little resistance to the Nazis from the academic community. As Mendelssohn remarks,

> The spirit of resignation was aptly put into words by Otto Hahn who, in 1966, said in his biography: 'as acting Director I tried to soften especially

harsh orders from the people in power, but of course I could not do anything about the general situation'.

Einstein has recalled:

'When the revolution came to Germany, I looked to the newspaper editors who in times past had proclaimed their love of freedom, but they were silent. Then I looked to the universities, but they too were soon silenced. Only the Church stood squarely in the path of Hitler's aggression. I am thus forced to declare that what I once despised I now unreservedly praise.' (Ibid.)

Werner Heisenberg, the brilliant young theoretician who gained the Nobel Prize at the age of thirty-two, was torn in two. An ardent nationalist, he longed to see the triumph of Germany, but he was also disturbed by what was happening in German universities. He was urged by friends in the United States to emigrate while he still had the chance, but considered it his duty to remain in Germany.

The early history of the atomic bomb illustrates both the failure of the Nazis to understand the importance of science and the dramatic deterioration of German science that resulted from their policies. In 1939 the German chemists Hahn and Strassmann found barium among the products of the irradiation of uranium by neutrons. Otto Frisch, an Austrian who emigrated to England, and his aunt Lise Meitner, who worked with Hahn, realized that this could be explained if the uranium nucleus had split into two pieces, a process they called fission. Frisch came to England and joined Rudolph Peierls, a German refugee who was working in Birmingham. Together they made the vital calculation of the amount of fissile material needed to make a practicable atomic bomb. They found it to be a few tens of kilograms, small enough to be carried by a plane, and immediately realized that the future of humanity was changed for ever. They alerted the British government in a short memorandum that outlined the future possibilities with great prescience. If Hitler had encouraged and supported science, all these scientists might have remained in Germany, and the course of history might have been somewhat different (see Hodgson, 1961).

After the outbreak of war, when it became known that it might be possible to make an atomic bomb, Heisenberg was asked to lead the research programme. He accepted this appointment and gathered together a team of scientists. They tried to build a reactor, but thought that it would be impossible to build a bomb. Even the much larger effort in the United States did not complete the task until the war in Europe was over. It has recently been maintained that Heisenberg deliberately held back for moral reasons, in contrast to the Allied scientists at Los Alamos who actually made the bombs that were dropped on Japan. This is completely incorrect. Heisenberg would have made the bomb if he could, but the scale of his effort was quite inadequate, and his knowledge of the requisite nuclear physics was not nearly detailed enough. This has been confirmed recently by the release of the Farm Hall transcripts (Bernstein,

1995), giving the conversations of the captured German scientists when they heard about the use of the atomic bombs on Japan.

Science in Soviet Russia

The duration of Nazi power in Germany was relatively brief, whereas that of Marxism in Russia was much longer. It therefore provides a better opportunity to assess the effects of an alien ideology on the status of scientific research.

For many decades Soviet science enjoyed high prestige. The Soviets sent up the first artificial satellite, the sputnik, and before the collapse of the Soviet Union we used frequently to read about Soviet triumphs in almost every branch of science. There have, however, been few serious attempts to analyse objectively the standing of Soviet science. There were perhaps good reasons for this: the higher the prestige of Soviet science, the more likely were Western governments to make available funds for research and development, in order to ensure that we kept pace with and if possible surpass the Soviet achievements. The launch of sputnik was a bombshell that galvanized the government of the United States into providing massive support for science. It was thus to everyone's benefit to maintain the high prestige of Soviet science.

From the time of Peter the Great, founder in 1725 of the Imperial Academy of Science, science in Russia has been part of the mainstream of European science. Originally it was brought to Russia by Western scientists, including the mathematician Euler and the brothers Nicholas and Daniel Bernoulli. Science remained strictly controlled by the state, and so tended to wax and wane with the political situation. Russian scientists travelled freely around Europe and the United States, and often studied abroad as part of their training. Michael Lomonosov travelled extensively in Europe and on his return worked on the kinetic theory of gases and on atomic theory. In 1755 he founded the university of Moscow. Throughout the nineteenth century science in Russia continued to grow and produced many outstanding scientists. These included Mendeleef the chemist who proposed the periodic table of the elements, Pavlov the physiologist and the mathematicians Lobachevsky and Bolyai who independently discovered non-Euclidean geometry.

Marx was not a scientist in any sense of the word, but he shared the enthusiasm for science typical of the nineteenth century. It is the proud claim of Marxist-Leninism that it embodies an essentially scientific view of the world, and if this is so we would expect science to flourish after the Bolshevik revolution (Johnson, 1998, ch. 3; Jaki, 1966, esp. ch. 11; Gratzer, 2000).

In the pages of his *Das Kapital*, Marx compared his method to that used by physicists, and 'claimed to have discovered a basic set of rules unconditionally valid in both the natural and the political sciences' (Jaki, 1966, p. 481). This is a large claim, with momentous consequences. If it is true, then science under Marxism is set on its right course. But if it is false, and if that same Marxism has complete political power, then the stage is set for the enslavement of science.

Marx himself had little scientific knowledge and relied on Engels to develop the theory of the application of dialectical materialism to the sciences. He maintained that in future science must be ruled by philosophy. He laid down a series of rules that physics must obey, rules that are invariably erroneous. The roots of this may be traced back to Hegel, well known for his ability to legislate about the material world. It is thus not surprising that Engels castigated a whole galaxy of physicists including Newton, Maxwell, Helmholtz, Clausius, Thomson and Tait. It is therefore necessary for physicists to study dialectical materialism because it is the source of scientific truth (Jaki, 1966).

In the midst of his revolutionary activity, Lenin was aware of the revolutionary changes in physics in the early years of the twentieth century, and he saw the connection between the two revolutions: 'Modern physics is in travail; it is giving birth to dialectical materialism' (Jaki, 1966, p. 484). He greeted the discoveries of the new physics with enthusiasm, while realizing that they implied the end of crude mechanical materialism. Thus he believed that in some sense the dialectic responds to the advance of science. There is an apparent inconsistency between the subservience of science to the dialectic as taught by Engels and the effects of science on dialectical materialism described by Lenin. These views may be reconciled by saying that science and dialectical materialism are joined in a symbiotic resonance that shows both aspects at different times.

In the early years after the revolution, the Soviet scientists carried on their work much as before, in accord with the inner logic of scientific growth, paying whatever lip-service to Party dogma that was required of them. The political pressures existed from the very beginning, but Soviet scientists learned to insulate themselves as best they could.

During the 1920s the revolutionaries were preoccupied with the crumbling economy and by internal struggles, and generally left the scientists alone. Soviet physicists were free to travel and many worked for years in Göttingen, Cambridge and in American universities. Most of them were uninterested in Marxism, and avoided ideological discussions.

By 1929 the situation was somewhat easier for the Party, and Stalin turned his attention to science. The economists and statisticians, whose surveys of the economic situation did not support the Party line, were the first to be purged. By April 1931 Bukharin was threatening scientists with 'moral and physical guillotine', meaning the systematic imposition of Marxism. Throughout the 1930s, scientists were forced to subscribe to Marxist doctrine, and many who resisted were purged from the Academy.

Among the scientists who came to England at that time was Peter Kapitza, who worked with Rutherford in the Cavendish Laboratory in Cambridge. He made important researches on magnetism, and in the mid-1930s the Soviet authorities recognized his value and he was told, during a visit home, that henceforth he would work in the Soviet Union. Protests were of no avail. Rutherford commented in a letter to Bohr on 28 January 1935: 'Governments as a whole are pretty bad, but I think the USSR can give them all points on mendacity' (Peierls, 1997, p. 43). Accepting the inevitable, Rutherford arranged for Kapitza's experimental equipment to be sent to Russia so that he could continue his work there. When he learned that he could not return to Cambridge he wrote poignantly to Rutherford: 'After all, we are only small particles of floating matter in a stream which we call fate. All that we can manage is to deflect our tracks slightly and keep afloat – the stream governs us' (ibid., p. 353). These sad and resigned words may be set beside those of one of the greatest Russian scientists, Mendeleev, who lived in tsarist times: 'Knowing how contented, joyous and free is the life in the realms of science, one fervently wishes that one may enter its portals' (Posin, 1948).

In the 1920s and 1930s the USSR, together with the USA, led the world in genetics, but from about 1935 genetics was attacked by Lysenko. The Michurin doctrine, supported by Lysenko, was everywhere enforced and no other views were permitted. The most famous Russian geneticist, Vavilov, and several other leading geneticists were arrested in 1940 and were never heard of again. Platonov, one of Lysenko's disciples, wrote:

> The main and decisive force that has brought about the victory of of Michurin's doctrine has been the Communist party ... The classics of Marx-Leninism, Marx, Engels and Stalin have not only created the philosophy of dialectical materialism, on the abiding principles of which the Michurinist biology is developing, but have given a series of clear instructions about the direction in which Darwin, and which aspects of this theory should be discarded in building the truly materialist biology.

Lysenko underlined this, writing, 'We owe it to the genius of mankind, to Comrade Stalin, that in our great country biological science has entered a new and advanced stage of development' (quoted by Dobzhansky, 1952). In spite of this, neither Lysenko nor his followers produced a single original idea (Kohn, 1986, p. 63; Gratzer, 2000, ch. 9). Michurinist biology is simply a relapse towards views that were current in the nineteenth century and were discarded mainly due to the advances in genetics.

The views of Lysenko underwent several changes through the years. At first he supported Darwin, but subsequently he preferred the views of Lamarck, who was considered a predecessor of Michurin. It is difficult to understand why the rulers of the USSR supported Lysenko, whose views seriously harmed Soviet agriculture. This could only happen in a country governed by autocrats.

During the war years the struggle for survival left little time for scientific work, but as soon as the war was over the battle between science and Maxism was resumed. In a speech in 1947 Zhadanov called for a fight against 'countless philosophical weeds', against the 'whole arsenal of the philosophical lackeys of imperialism' and even against 'smuggling God into science'. Einstein's theory of relativity was condemned (see Chapter 6), together with the theory of molecular bonding (Müller-Markus, 1960).

Soviet science in the post-war years was characterized by extreme nationalism. References were made to Soviet research, but not to Western. Much effort was devoted to establishing Soviet priority in discoveries, and overseas travel by Soviet scientists was severely restricted. The result was to isolate Soviet scientists from their colleagues in other countries.

Mathematics in Russia has been of the highest standard from the time of Euler onwards. Up to the 1920s and early 1930s, Russian mathematicians travelled abroad freely. Later in the 1930s this changed and in 1936 they were prevented from attending the international congress of mathematics in Oslo. The same happened after the war at the Harvard conference in 1950 (Kline, 1952).

At various times historians, geneticists, physiologists, philologists and physicists were purged to ensure that they followed the Party line and to put Russian science into the straitjacket of Marx–Lenin–Stalinism. This was emphasized by the Secretary of the Academy of Sciences, Topchiev, in 1949:

> The Soviet scientist must remember that he labours not simply to develop spiritual culture in general – such culture does not exist – but to develop the socialist, Communist culture. This means that in his creative activity he proceeds from the principles of the Marx–Leninist world outlook and fights implacably all manifestations and survivals of the corrupt bourgeois ideology. This means that the Soviet scientist sees clearly the irreconcilable opposition between socialist and bourgeois culture and relies on the Bolshevik party approach in science, thrusting aside the reactionary tendencies of the professional lackeys of imperialism. (Volin quoted in Christman, 1952, p. 85)

Stalin was treated as the final authority in scientific matters. According to an editorial in *Pravda* on 4 July 1950: 'The great leader of science, Comrade Stalin, is creatively developing Marx–Leninism. There is not a single branch of science or culture which does not reflect the guiding thought, the creative genius of the great Stalin.' In 1948 the Presidium of the Russian Academy of Medicine wrote to Stalin:

> The Academy of Medical Sciences, USSR, with all its scientific collectives, is faced with the urgent task of eradicating the reactionary doctrines of Weissmann–Morganism from medical science ... We promise you, our dear leader, to rectify in the shortest possible time the mistakes we have permitted to occur, and to reconstruct our scientific work in the spirit of the directives issued by the great Party of Lenin and Stalin. We will fight for the Bolshevik party spirit in medicine and public health and will eradicate bourgeois ideology and servility before foreign isms in our midst. (Zircle quoted in Christman, 1952, p. 100).

Volin summarizes the situation in the following words:

> Russian science, then, is forced to pay for its existence a heavy tribute to the Kremlin of general subservience to the State: renunciation of all attempt at objectivity; of hostility to the West; of adoption of the meaningless mumbo-jumbo of Marx–Leninism and of a chauvinistic style of writing; readiness to fall in with the Kremlin's latest propaganda line and programmes, however unsound they may appear; and of submission to a shackling and humiliating party control. One cannot help but draw a comparison to the late nazi regime. For Hitler, too, is reported to have said: 'The idea of a free

and unfettered science ... is absurd.' (Volin quoted in Christman, 1952, p. 97).

In 1952, I. V. Kuznetzov, a Party theoretician, claimed that 'Soviet science is the standard-bearer for the most modern and progressive ideas of contemporary natural science'. Concerning relativity, he declared that the development of science can only be secured by 'total renunciation of Einstein's conception, without compromise or half-measure'. Physicists of the stature of Landau, who had hitherto kept out of ideological disputes, rebelled against this nonsense. They could argue from a secure position of strength. Whatever the Marxist theoreticians may say, the real world goes on behaving according to its intrinsic nature. You may re-write history to your heart's content, and if you control the media and the educational system, no one will stop you. But if you insist on designing a nuclear accelerator without using Einstein's equations, then on the great day when you switch it on for the first time, nothing will happen. The physicists had no difficulty in tearing to shreds the diatribes of the Party theoreticians. Experiences such as these convinced that Party that science, especially physics because of its relation to industry, must be accorded some measure of autonomy.

Soviet science then moved into a new phase. The scientists were allowed to carry on their work according to scientific criteria, but the aims of their research must be governed by the needs of society. The deleterious effects of applying this criterion of 'social relevance' have already been discussed in Chapter 1.

The main strength of state direction of science appears when there is a well-defined technological objective, such as to make an atomic bomb or to launch an artificial satellite. Even these achievements, it may be noted, relied greatly on Western science, the one on the work at Los Alamos and the other on the German research at Pennemunde, which was taken over by the Red Army at the end of the war.

So great is the intrinsic vitality of science, and the natural abilities of the Russian people, that excellent work continued to be done, even under the most severe disadvantages. The names of Landau, Tamm, Migdal, Cerenkov, Kurchatov, Fock, Bogliubov, Kapitza, Markov and Sakharov will always be remembered by physicists. Yet even these experienced difficulties in the Stalin regime. A single remark in the biography of Landau by Anna Livanova (1980, p. 73; see also Khalatnikov, 1989) hints at his incarceration: 'In one burdensome year, Landau reconstructed for himself the theory of shock waves. He made all the calculations mentally, without paper and pencil.'

More recently, the treatment of Sakharov (1990) has received much publicity. A distinguished scientist with many contributions to cosmology and to elementary particle physics, and the designer of the Soviet hydrogen bomb, he became an outstanding spokesman for human rights and disarmament. As a result he was banished without trial to Gorky and almost totally isolated. The KGB removed his notebooks and manuscripts in an attempt to stop his intellectual activity.

An objective analysis of the standing of Soviet science in the period between the two great wars was made by John Baker (1945), an Oxford biologist. Without giving any reason for his request, he asked seven of his colleagues in various scientific departments to list the two dozen most important discoveries made in that period. The results showed that the work was mostly in the USA, Germany and Britain; the Soviet Union was not mentioned.

In an editorial in *Physics Today* (January 1984, p. 192) Robert Marshak, the President of the American Physical Society, discussed the perils of curbing the freedom of science. He asked:

> Why has the Soviet Union found it necessary to rely so heavily on Soviet technology? Science education in the Soviet Union is a source of envy to those of us who are concerned with the crisis in our own schools. Individually, Soviet scientists are as dedicated and creative as any in the world. The Soviet government is generous in its support of basic and applied science. And yet experimental science in the Soviet Union is scandalously bad. Much of the explanation, I believe, is in the fact that the Soviets have created barriers to free communication for their own scientists not unlike those that some would like to impose here.

These are the objective measures of the state of science in what was once one of the great superpowers, a country that exalts science, that has numerous great universities where scientific studies have high priority, that honours its scientific academicians with lavish favours, that founded science cities, that poured out ceaseless propaganda praising the excellence of its scientific achievements, that poured scorn on the decadent science of the West, that claimed to found its ideology on scientific principles and to be the one nation able to lead mankind to a glorious and scientific heaven on earth.

The failure of Soviet science was indeed one of the principal factors that led to its collapse. It was simply not able to keep up with the technology of the West. This disparity was particularly notable in the field of modern electronics, especially the fast computers that are now so essential in many areas of our lives. Unable to make their own, they made great efforts to smuggle computers and microchips into the Soviet Union from the West, but this proved to be quite inadequate. The final verdict on Marxist science is: by their fruits you will know them.

Western Materialism

The Western world, by which is meant Europe, North America, Japan and some other developed countries, is increasingly dominated by a materialist capitalist mentality. The poorer countries, many of which can hardly be called developing, are eager to reach the standard of living enjoyed by the Western world. Television and a flood of manufactured goods show them the lives they would like to enjoy. All this is made possible by modern technology, and this in turn is based on scientific research.

As already mentioned, technology is easy to export, and many factories are built in developing countries. It is far more difficult to establish flourishing schools of research, and so the technologies of the developing countries remain dependent on the research carried out in the Western world. Few of the young people in the poorer countries have the opportunity to become effective scientists, and the few who do frequently emigrate to the Western world, where they can develop their potentialities to the full.

The situation in the Western world also gives rise to concern. The prevailing materialism lays stress on enjoying the good life, and young men and women in all countries know that a career in science requires years of hard study, and that even if they are successful the material rewards are small. In this climate, it is no wonder that the percentage of young people who choose a career in science is steadily falling in most Western countries. What is lacking is the will to devote their lives to seeking the truth about the material world. They would not understand the mentality of the medieval woodcarver who devoted as much care to carving the parts of the pulpit that no one would see as to those in public view. He was doing his work primarily for the glory of God, who sees everything.

While there are many causes for the decline of science, the decline of Christian belief must be among them. The prevailing ethos is the theological liberalism that says in effect that it does not matter what you believe so long as you are sincere and mean well. This soon degenerates into no belief at all. Christianity teaches us that matter is holy, an expression of God's creative energy. The right use of matter is holy, and its abuse crucifies again the body of Christ. The exploitation of men or matter for commercial gain, the debasement of the arts and the perversions of the intellect are evil. It is an inversion of the right order to subordinate man to economics, so that profitability is the criterion of worth. The aim of work should not be primarily to make money, but to work as well as possible for the glory of God. 'Work is not primarily a thing we do to live, but a thing we live to do' (Sayers, 1947). There is at the present time a shift from the attitude that we must always give of our best as part of our responsibility to God and the community to the attitude that we must seek only our own material gain. When this happens, it is then no longer possible to trust anyone to do their work properly and so an army of inspectors is needed to oversee what everyone is doing. Teachers and doctors are deluged with instructions and forms, and scientists are subjected to absurd and time-wasting research assessment exercises. This erodes the commitment to personal responsibility, devastates morale and decimates efficiency. It encourages the mentality that resolves to do no more than is specified in our contract of employment instead of concentrating on our primary duties and looking out for new ways in which we can serve our fellow men.

The decline of science in the Western world will not be sudden. Scientific research is strongly supported by governments and industries for their own purposes, and this support is likely to increase. Furthermore, in my own limited experience, there are substantial numbers of Christian and Jewish scientists in universities and in industry, together with others who take their work seriously, and this is not without its effects on the ethos of the community.

The ruling politicians, conscious of the social benefits of science and ignorant of the nature of scientific research, frequently support scientific research only if it promises tangible returns, and apply the criterion of 'social relevance'. When applying for support, scientists often now have to say what useful applications may be expected from their work. This is a repellent attempt to force scientists to behave in a way that goes counter to our very vocation as scientists. Our vocation, our first duty, is to devote our efforts towards becoming the best scientists our abilities and circumstances allow, and to do our work as well as we can. The advancement of scientific knowledge is our first duty as scientists, and no consideration of possible applications should deflect us from this aim. No one should ever work in a scientific laboratory with the intention of 'doing good' to humanity. Anyone who utters such sentiments should be expelled, for their work will certainly be mediocre. We know, of course, that research undertaken simply to understand the natural world frequently leads to important practical applications that were never envisaged when it was started (see Chapter 1), but this cannot be the motive for starting the research: 'Seek ye first the kingdom of God and righteousness, and all these things shall be added to you.' When possible applications of the results of scientific research become apparent, other scientists, called technologists or applied scientists, can work to develop these applications and ensure that their benefits are made generally available.

A notable failure of politicians is that they often allow their decisions to be governed by political expediency rather than by scientific objectivity, as shown for example by the attitude of the British government to the problems associated with energy generation (Hodgson, 1999). When dealing with such problems, it is essential first of all to establish the facts as carefully and accurately as possible, and then to take the decisions most likely to lead to the desired end, irrespective of other considerations such as public misconceptions and emotional propaganda.

In all these respects, the decline of Christian belief and the decline in recognition of the value of science go together.

CHAPTER 13

Epilogue

Modern physics has been established only after a long struggle down the centuries from the time of the ancient Greeks to the present. It is the result of sustained efforts to understand the world around us. These efforts were and are influenced, inspired and sustained by many beliefs about the world. Some of these beliefs were false, and they prevented the birth of modern science; others were partially true and enabled some progress to be made, and finally there came the system of beliefs that made possible the birth of modern physics and ultimately the whole scientific and technological enterprise that has made our civilization possible.

Many ancient civilizations such as those in Babylon, Egypt, China and India achieved a high level of culture and with it an extensive empirical knowledge of the natural world from the properties of materials to the motions of the heavenly bodies. Their achievements were surpassed by those of ancient Greece, which was the scene of one of the most astonishing outpourings of genius in the history of mankind. In literature, architecture, theatre, philosophy and history their achievements were unparalleled, and the first steps were taken towards an understanding of the natural world. Some thought that the obvious complexity of the world could be understood in terms of the interactions of smaller and simpler entities, and Democritus formulated his atomic theory. This vision that all could be attributed to the motions of atoms in the void horrified Aristotle. If this is so, how can we account for our free actions, and with them our duties and responsibilities? So he postulated a world of purpose, and attributed the motions of even inanimate bodies to their purposeful striving to reach their natural place. He developed an all-encompassing cosmology that accounted in a qualitative way for the whole natural world from inanimate matter, plants and animals to the sun, the moon the planets and the stars. In doing so he rescued purpose, but in the process put physics into a form that hindered its further development for two thousand years.

The ancient Greeks also developed mathematics to a high degree, and many centuries later this provided the language that is essential for modern physics. In addition, they had all the material necessities for the birth of science: a well-developed social structure, language, writing and mathematics, but they lacked many of the essential beliefs about the natural world that form the basis of modern science. Some were certainly present: Aristotle believed in an orderly world that could be understood by the human mind, although he was over-optimistic about how easy it is to intuit fundamental principles and undervalued both mathematics and the need for experiments. Other Greeks, such as Archimedes and Aristarchus, were embarked on studies of nature in a way that showed a true scientific spirit and could conceivably have initiated a continuing development leading to modern science. However, they lacked the support of a society permeated with the set of beliefs underlying science and so this never took place.

These beliefs were held by the Israelites, a small nomadic tribe surrounded by the mighty empires of Babylon, Assyria and Egypt. These empires bowed down to a multitude of gods, but the Israelites worshipped the one true God who created heaven and earth, gave matter its properties and keeps it in being. The essential presuppositions of science, that matter is good, orderly, rational, contingent and open to the human mind, are all to be found in the Old Testament. In the absence of these beliefs modern science never developed in primitive societies or in any of the ancient civilizations. They certainly gained extensive empirical knowledge of the properties of materials and the movements of the heavenly bodies, but that knowledge was never locked into an all-embracing structure governed by differential equations.

The birth of Christ further ennobled matter and replaced the debilitating cyclic time of previous civilizations by a linear time of purpose and progress. The Christological debates of the early centuries reinforced and extended our beliefs concerning the relations between God, man and the natural world. The early Christians were preoccupied with their survival in the hostile Roman Empire and subsequently in the chaos after its fall, so science did not develop in Europe in the first millennium.

Meanwhile in the East the Muslim civilization arose, and inherited the work of the ancient Greeks. The Qur'an provided many of the beliefs essential for science and important work was done in physics, astronomy and medicine. Islamic mathematicians also carried further the work of the Greeks. From the eighth to the fourteenth century Islamic science led the world, but in the following centuries it gradually declined. The basic reason was the dominance of the fundamentalist Asharite theologians who denied secondary causality and thus had a weakened sense of the inherent rationality of the natural world. This follows from their stress on the freedom of Allah, who decides what happens from event to event. A contributory cause is the emphasis of some Muslim theologians on the duty to seek only useful knowledge. So ultimately the Muslim civilization also failed to give birth to modern science.

The birth of modern science finally took place in Europe in the High Middle Ages when for the first time in history there was a civilization permeated by Christian beliefs. The new universities made possible wide-ranging and critical discussions of philosophical and scientific questions in the light of Christian theology. The writings of the Greeks became available, mainly through translations from Arabic to Latin made in Spain. Aristotle was held in high esteem, and his philosophical concepts were used by theologians to formulate Christian beliefs with ever-increasing precision. Nevertheless, they did not hesitate to reject any of Aristotle's views that conflicted with Christian revelation, and this facilitated the development of modern physics. Science eventually came to maturity in the Renaissance and thereafter it became a self-sustaining enterprise.

This is not to say that modern science could never have developed in the absence of the Christian revelation, but in actual historical fact it did not. Science does not easily take root in non-Christian counties and it languishes wherever Christianity is persecuted or ignored. The historical connection between modern science and Christian revelation does not, by itself, prove the truth of Christianity but, at the very least, it shows that they are in essential harmony.

The great success of modern science, particularly of Newtonian dynamics, once again led to the idea that the natural world is a giant mechanism that moves according to inexorable laws. As in Greek atomism there seems to be no place for the higher things that make life worth living, for duty and responsibility, praise and blame, hope and despair. Science, a most purposeful enterprise, seems to have abolished purpose. What was initially a methodological limitation was mistaken for an ontological conclusion, and the great medieval synthesis of theology, philosophy and science was forgotten.

Once again there was a reaction, and this took many forms. Some pointed to a range of phenomena that seem scientifically inexplicable as evidence of an unseen, spiritual world. Some sought a new set of beliefs in science itself while others denied objective truth and declared science to be just a matter of subjective opinion. Others again revolted against reason itself.

There are many instances of events that seem to contradict the inexorable laws of nature, such as those associated with spiritualism, psychokinesis, spoon-bending, thought transference and miracles. Scientists instinctively brush all these aside as so much nonsense, and indeed many of the reported events have been exposed as bogus or fraudulent. However, to believe absolutely in the uniformity of nature is just as credulous as to deny it. We just do not know. It is arrogant to deny that such things can happen, and the true scientific attitude is to subject them to meticulous investigation before reaching a conclusion.

It is not easy to establish the truth about the natural world. Our observations may be biased or untypical; our experiments may fail due to some unknown effect. Understanding of any phenomenon is only attained after a long series of false starts, blind alleys, blunders and misunderstandings. Scientific papers make no mention of this, but instead trace out a clear road from the beginning to the conclusion. Popular writers sometimes embellish the stories about scientific research, and it is hardly surprising that myths abound. The same experimental results can usually be interpreted in several ways, strongly influenced by various philosophical beliefs that are in no way required by the science itself. All that we can really rely on are the equations that give an approximate account of a limited range of phenomena. The accompanying stories may be true or partly true, but are often false and misleading. There are numerous examples of this, such as the denial of absolute space and time, the variation of mass with velocity, spooky action at a distance, the fuzzy quantum world and the world as an organism or as a machine. This certainly sensitizes us to the trickiness of arguments. We are often surprised when we compare our intuitions with experimental results. Sometimes this surprise is fully explained by a deeper mathematical analysis, but sometimes the results are an indication that a new theory is needed. The incomplete and uncertain knowledge provided by scientific research gives no ground for theological conclusions, and it is still less justifiable to see it as a new way to God. Thus to interpret the big bang theory of the origin of the universe as evidence of creation, and hence of a creator, is to overstep the limits of science in an unacceptable way. At the very most, the discoveries of modern science can suggest questions about the meaning of it all, but the answers must be sought elsewhere.

Another instructive example is provided by quantum mechanics, which is widely used to support a whole range of beliefs going far beyond the actual formalism and the physics on which it is based. These include the activity of the mind of the observer when he collapses a wave function, the denial of causality, wave–particle duality and the belief in a fuzzy indeterminate world. All these are the result of a very simple error, namely to consider quantum mechanics as the final theory so that the wave function provides all that we can know about each individual system. Quantum mechanics is an incomplete theory: it does not and cannot provide the means to calculate many measurable physical phenomena. As soon as we recognize that quantum mechanics is essentially a statistical theory that applies to ensembles of similar systems, all the beliefs alleged to be implied by quantum mechanics are deprived of their foundations. It is vitally important to distinguish between the quantum world as described by quantum mechanics and the real world. Thus to conclude from the Heisenberg uncertainty principle that the world is fuzzy or to deny causality on the basis of radioactive decay is to mistake an inability to measure for an objective conclusion. Electrons are particles, and quantum mechanics enables us to calculate the probability distribution of their trajectories, which happens to follow a wave equation. The wave–particle duality is thus a category confusion.

Quantum mechanics is but one step along a long road, an incomplete theory that gives us some knowledge of an objectively existing world. The universe, which may be defined as the totality of consistently interacting things, is thus a completely determined system evolving through time following exact deterministic laws originally given to it by God. This does not deny our humanity, because we are more than just things; we have immortal souls.

Modern science can certainly bring home to us more forcefully the incredibly intricate structure of God's creation. It may also suggest ideas and analogies that have some use in theology. But to suppose that it can supplant traditional theology or provide new theological understanding is a chimera.

Modern science has certainly enlarged our vision of the world. Instead of the cosy, man-centred world of Aristotle, we now have a vast number of huge galaxies flying away from a primeval explosion several billion years ago. In the spiral arm of one of these galaxies is the rather undistinguished star which we call the sun. This change of perspective inevitably changes the way we think of ourselves and may cause us to speak in a different way about our Christian beliefs, but it does not change in any way our fundamental convictions concerning the creation of everything by God, and the birth, death and resurrection of Christ.

Acknowledgements

I thank the editors and publishers who have kindly permitted me to use extracts from articles and reviews: An earlier version of Chapter 2 was published in *Logos* 4(2) Spring 2001 and of Chapter 10 in *Teologiczny w Tarnowie*, Tom XIV.47.1995-6. Parts of Chapters 6 and 11 were previously published in *Contemporary Physics*. I also acknowledge permission to reproduce the figure.

Bibliography

General References

The Jerusalem Bible (1966), London: Darton, Longmans and Todd.
The Knox Bible (1949), London: Burns, Oates and Washbourne.

History and Philosophy of Physics

Applebaum, W. (2000), *Encyclopedia of the Scientific Revolution from Copernicus to Newton*. New York and London: Garland Publishing.
Boorstein, D. J. (1983), *The Discoverers: A History of Man's Search to Know His Work and Himself*. New York: Vintage Books.
Brush, S. G. (1988), *The History of Modern Science: A Guide to the Second Scientific Revolution 1800–1950*. Ames, IA: Iowa State University Press.
Burtt, E. A. (1932), *The Metaphysical Foundations of Modern Physical Science*. London: Routledge and Kegan Paul.
Butterfield, H. (1958), *The Origins of Modern Science*. London: Bell.
Bynum, W. F., Browne, E. J. and Porter, Roy (eds) (1981), *Dictionary of the History of Science*. London and Basingstoke: Macmillan.
Copelston, F. (1950), *A History of Philosophy*. 10 vols. London: Burns, Oates and Washbourne.
Crombie, A. C. (1952), *Augustine to Galileo: The History of Science 400–1650*. London: Falcon Press.
Crombie, A. C. (1994) *Styles of Scientific Thinking in the European Tradition*. 3 vols. London: Duckworth.
Curd, M. and Cover, J. A. (1998), *Philosophy of Science: The Central Issues*. New York and London: W.W. Norton and Co.
Duhem, P. (1913–59), *Système du Monde*. 10 vols. Paris: A. Hermann et Fils.
——— (1954), *The Aim and Structure of Physical Theory*. Princeton, NJ: Princeton University Press.
Ferngren, G. B. (2000), *The History of Science and Religion in the Western Tradition: An Encyclopedia*. New York and London: Garland Publishing.
——— (ed.) (2002), *Science and Religion: A Historical Introduction*. Baltimore, MA and London: The Johns Hopkins University Press.
Ferris, T. (ed.) (1991), *The World Treasury of Physics, Astronomy and Mathematics*. Boston, MA, Toronto and London: Little Brown and Co.
Holton, G. (1954), *Thematic Origins of Scientific Thought: Kepler to Einstein*. Cambridge, MA: Harvard University Press.
Jaki, S. L. (1966), *The Relevance of Physics*. Chicago, IL and London: University of Chicago Press.
——— (1978), *The Road of Science and the Ways to God*. Chicago, IL and London: University of Chicago Press.

Lindberg, D. C. (1992), *The Beginnings of Western Science: The European Scientific Tradition in Philosophical, Religious and Institutional Context. 600 BC to AD 1450*. Chicago, IL and London: University of Chicago Press.

Newton-Smith, W. H. (ed.) (2000), *A Companion to the Philosophy of Science*. Oxford: Blackwells.

Olby, R. C., Cantor, G. N., Christie, J. R. R. and Hodge, M. J. S. (eds) (1990), *Companion to the History of Modern Science*. London and New York: Routledge.

Peierls, R. E. (1955), *The Laws of Nature*. London: George Allen and Unwin.

Ronan, C. A. (1983), *The Cambridge Illustrated History of the World's Science*. Cambridge: Cambridge University Press.

Serres, Michael (ed.) (1995), *A History of Scientific Thought*. Oxford: Blackwell.

Singer, C. (1959), *A Short History of Scientific Ideas to 1900*. Oxford: Oxford University Press.

Westaway, F. W. (1934), *The Endless Quest: Three Thousand Years of Science*. London: Blackie and Son.

Whewell, W. (1837), *Philosophy of the Inductive Sciences*. 2 vols. London: John W. Parker.

——— (1847), *History of the Inductive Sciences*. 3 vols. London: John W. Parker.

Wightman, W. P. D. (1965), *The Growth of Scientific Ideas*. London: Oliver and Boyd.

Windle, Sir Bertram C. A. (1917), *The Catholic Church and Science*. London: The Catholic Truth Society.

Physics and Theology

Barbour, Ian G. (1997) *Religion and Science: Historical and Contemporary Issues*. San Francisco, CA: Harper.

Bavink, B. (1933), *Science and God*. London: G. Bell and Sons.

Butterfield, H. (1958), *The Origins of Modern Science*. London: Bell.

Clayton, P. (1997), *God and Contemporary Science*. Grand Rapids, MI: W. M. B. Eerdmans Publishing.

Ferngren, G. B. (ed.) (2000), *The History of Science and Religion in the Western Tradition: An Encyclopedia*. New York and London: Garland Publishing.

Jaki, S. L. (1978), *The Road of Science and the Ways to God*. Chicago, IL: Chicago University Press.

——— (1986) *Science and Creation*. Edinburgh: Scottish Academic Press.

Mascall, E. A. (1956), *Christian Theology and Natural Science*. London: Longmans Green.

Mooney, C. E. (1995), *Theology and Scientific Knowledge*. Notre Dame, IN: Notre Dame Press.

Smethurst, A. F. (1955), *Modern Science and Christian Belief*.

Southgate, C., et al. (1999), *God, Humanity and the Cosmos*. Edinburgh: T. and T. Clark.

Preface

Angel, R. B. (1980), *Relativity: The Theory and its Philosophy*. Oxford: Pergamon Press.

Bacon, R. (1897), *Opus Maius IV.1.1* (ed. J. H. Bridges). Oxford.

Bradwardine, T. *Tractatus de Coninuo*. MS Erfurt Amplon, Q.385, fol. 31v.

Burtt, E. A. (1932), *The Metaphysical Foundations of Modern Physical Science*. London: Routledge and Kegan Paul.

Davis, P. J. and Hersh, R. (1983), *The Mathematical Experience*. London: Pergamon Press.

Dirac, P. A. M. (1982), 'Early Years of Relativity', in G. Holton and Y. Elkana (eds), *Albert Einstein: Historical and Cultural Perspectives*. Princeton, NJ: Princeton University Press.

Drake, S. (tr.) (1957), *Discoveries and Opinions of Galileo*. New York: Doubleday, Anchor Books.

Einstein, A. (1976), *Ideas and Opinions*. New York: Bonanza Books.

Feynman, R. (1992), *The Character of Physical Law*. Cambridge, MA: MIT Press.

Franklin, A. (1986), *The Neglect of Experiment*. Cambridge: Cambridge University Press.

Hull, L. W. H. (1959), *History and Philosophy of Science: An Introduction*. London: Longmans.

Jaki, S. L. (1984), *Uneasy Genius: The Life and Work of Pierre Duhem*. The Hague: Martinus Nijhoff.

Kragh, H. (1996), *Cosmology and Controversy*. Princeton, NJ: Princeton University Press.

Macaulay, T. B. (1840), Review of Leopold von Ranke's History of the Popes. In: *Lord Macaulay's Essays and Lays of Ancient Rome*. London: Longmans Green and Co.

Sykes, C. (ed.) (1994), *No Ordinary Genius. The Illustrated Richard Feynman*. New York: Norton.

Wigner, E. P. (1960), Communications in *Pure and Applied Mathematics*, **13**.

Woodhouse, N. M. J. (2003), *Special Relativity*. London: Springer.

Zycinski, J. M. (2003), 'Between Mathematics and Transcendence: The Search for the Spiritual Dimension of Scientific Discovery', *Logos*, **6**(2).

Chapter 1.   Theology, Philosophy and Physics

Baker, J. R. (1942), *The Scientific Life*. London: George Allen and Unwin.

────── (1945), *Science and the Planned State*. London: George Allen and Unwin.

Barbour, I. G. (1997), *Religion and Science: Historical and Contemporary Issues*. San Francisco, CA: Harper.

Basalla, G. (1968), *The Rise of Modern Science: External or Internal Factors?* Lexington, MA: D. C. Heath and Co.

Baum, R. and Sheehan, W. (1997), *In Search of Planet Vulcan*. Cambridge, MA: Basic Books.

Bavink, B. (1933), *Science and God*. London: G. Bell and Sons.

Bernal, J. D. (1946), *The Social Function of Science*. London: Routledge.

Brody, T. A. (1993), *The Philosophy Behind Physics*. Eds L. de la Pena and P. E. Hodgson. Berlin: Springer-Verlag.

Carrell, A. (1961), *Man, the Unknown*. New York: Macfadden Publishers.

Chase, C. T. (1930), 'The Scattering of Fast Electrons by Metals II. Polarisation by Back Scattering at Right Angles', *Physical Review*, **36**, 1060.

Cox, R. T., McIlwraith, C. G. and Kurrelmeyer, B. (1928), 'Apparent Evidence of Polarisation in a Beam of Beta-rays', *Proceedings of the National Academy of Sciences* (USA), **14**, 544.

Cushing, J. T. (1998), *Philosophical Concepts in Physics*. Cambridge: Cambridge University Press.

Davies, B. (1992), *The Thought of Thomas Aquinas*. Oxford: Clarendon Press.

Davies, P. (1983), *God and the New Physics*. London: Dent.

Duhem, P. (1954), *The Aim and Structure of Physical Theory*. Princeton, NJ: Princeton University Press.

Finocchiaro, M. A. (1989), *The Galileo Affair: A Documentary History*. Berkeley, CA: University of California Press.

———— (2001), 'Science, Religion and the Historiography of the Galileo Affair', *Osiris*, **16**, 114.

Franklin, A. (1986), *The Neglect of Experiment*. Cambridge: Cambridge University Press.

Gill, H. V. (1944), *Fact and Fiction in Modern Science*. Dublin: Gill.

Gilson, E. (1955), *History of Christian Philosophy in the Middle Ages*. London: Sheed and Ward.

Gratzer, W. (2000), *The Undergrowth of Science*. Oxford: Oxford University Press.

Hall, A. R. (1983), *The Revolution in Science 1500–1700*. London: Longmans.

Hessen, B. (1931), 'The Social and Economic Roots of Newton's Principia', in *Science at the Cross Roads*. London: Kinga (England) Ltd.

Holton, G. (1978), *The Scientific Imagination*. New York: Cambridge University Press.

———— (1996), *Einstein, History and Other Passions*. Reading, MA: Addison-Wesley.

Jaki, S. L. (1984), *Uneasy Genius: The Life and Work of Pierre Duhem*. The Hague: Martinus Nijhoff.

———— (1990), *The Purpose of it All*. Washington, DC: Regency Gateway.

———— (1992), *Genesis I Through the Ages*. London: Thomas More Press.

———— (1996), *The Bible and Science*. Front Royal: Christendom Press.

———— (1999a), *The Creator's Sabbath Rest: A Clue to Genesis I*. Royal Oak, MI: Real View Books.

———— (1999b), *Means to Message: A Treatise on Truth*. Grand Rapids, MI: W. B. Eerdmans.

Kitcher, P. (1983), *Abusing Science: The Case Against Creationism*. Milton Keynes: Open University Press.

Klotz, I. M. (1986), *Diamond Dealers and Feather Merchants*. Boston, MA, Basel and Stuttgart: Birkhauser.

Kneller, K. A. (1995), *Christianity and the Leaders of Modern Science*. Fraser, MI: Real View Books.

Kohn, A. (1986), *False Prophets: Fraud and Error in Science and Medicine*. Oxford, Blackwell.

Lee, T. D. and Yang, C. N. (1956), 'Question of Parity Non-Conservation in Weak Interactions', *Physical Review*, **104**, 254.

Lucas, J. R. (1979), 'Wilberforce and Huxley: A Legendary Encounter', *The Historical Journal*, **22**(2), 313.

McMullin, E. (1998), 'Galileo in Science and Scripture', in Machamer, P. (ed.), *The Cambridge Companion to Galileo*. Cambridge: Cambridge University Press.

Mascall, E. A. (1956), *Christian Theology and Natural Science*. London: Longmans Green.

Millikan, R. A. (1911), 'The Isolation of an Ion: A Precision Measurement of its Charge and the Correction of Stokes' Law', *Physical Review*, **32**, 349.

——— (1913), 'On the Elementary Electrical Charge and the Avogadro Constant', *Physical Review*, **2**, 109.

Newman, J. H. (1947), *Essay in Aid of a Grammar of Assent*. London: Longmans Green.

——— (1960), *An Essay on the Development of Christian Doctrine*. London: Sheed and Ward.

Oppenheimer, J. R. (1954), *Science and the Common Understanding*. London: Oxford University Press.

Peterson, I. (1993), *Newton's Clock: Chaos in the Solar System*. New York: H. Freeman and Co.

Planck, M. (1933), *Where is Science Going?* London: George Allen and Unwin.

Poincaré, H. (n.d.), *Science and Method*. London: Thomas Nelson and Sons.

Polanyi, M. (1958), *Personal Knowledge*. London: Routledge and Kegan Paul.

Pope John Paul II (1979), Discourse to the Pontifical Academy of Sciences, 10 November; (1992), Origins. **22**(2).

Sharratt, M. (1994), *Galileo: Decisive Innovator*. Oxford: Blackwell.

Smethurst, A. F. (1955), *Modern Science and Christian Belief*. London: James Nisbet and Co.

Southgate, C. et al. (1999), *God, Humanity and the Cosmos*. Edinburgh: T. and T. Clark.

Weisskopf, V. F. (1991), *The Joy of Insight*. New York: Basic Books.

Wu, C. S., Ambler, E., Hayward, R. W., Hoppes, D. D. and Hudson, R. P. (1957), 'Experimental Test of Parity Non-Conservation in Beta Decay', *Physical Review*, **105**, 1413.

Chapter 2. The Judeo-Christian Contribution to the Development of Modern Science

Baldner, S. (1989), 'St Bonaventure on the Temporal Beginning of the World', *The New Scholasticism*, **63**, 206.

——— and Carroll, W. E. (trs) (1997), *Aquinas on Creation*. Toronto: Pontifical Institute of Medieval Studies.

Barbour, J. (1989), *Absolute or Relative Motion? Vol. 1 The Discovery of Dynamics*. Cambridge: Cambridge University Press.

Caldin, E. F. (1949), *The Power and Limits of Science*. London: Chapman and Hall.

Chandrasekhar, S. (1979a), *Truth and Beauty*. Chicago, IL: Chicago University Press.

——— (1979b), 'Beauty and the Quest of Beauty in Science', *Physics Today*, July

Clagett, M. (1959), *The Science of Mechanics in the Middle Ages*. Madison, WI: University of Wisconsin Press.

Craig, W. L. and Smith, Q. (1993), *Theism, Atheism and Big Bang Cosmology*. Oxford: Clarendon Press.

Crombie, A. C. (1952), *Augustine to Galileo. The History of Science 400–1650*. London: Falcon Press.

——— (1953), *Robert Grosseteste and the Origins of Experimental Science 1100–1700*. Oxford: Oxford University Press.

——— (1994). *Styles of Scientific Thinking in the European Tradition*. 3 vols. London: Duckworth.

Duhem, P. (1956), *The Aim and Structure of Physical Theory*. Princeton, NJ: Princeton University Press.

——— (1985), *Modern Cosmology. Theories of Infinity, Place, Time, Void, and the Plurality of Worlds. Extracts from Systeme du Monde*. Ed. and tr. R. Arieu. Chicago: Chicago University Press.

Emery, K., and Speer, A. (2001), In: *Nach der Verurteilung von 1277*. Berlin and New York: Walter de Gruyer.

Foster, M. B. (1934), 'The Christian Doctrine and the Rise of Modern Science', *Mind*, 43, 446; Christian Theology and Modern Science of Nature I Mind. 44.439; Mind. Ibid II 45.1.

Geanakopolos, D. J. (1966). *Byzantine East and Latin West*. London: Harper Torchbooks.

Gilson, E. (1936), *The Spirit of Medieval Philosophy*. London: Sheed and Ward.

——— (1955), *The History of Christian Philosophy in the Middle Ages*. London: Sheed and Ward.

Grant, E. (1977), *Physical Science in the Middle Ages*. Cambridge: Cambridge University Press.

——— (1981a), *The Condemnation of 1277, God's Absolute Power, and Physical Thought in the Middle Ages*. Studies in Medieval Science and Natural Philosophy. London: Varriorum Reprints XIII.

——— (1981b), *Jean Buridan: A Fourteenth Century Philosopher. Studies in Medieval Science and Natural Philosophy*. London: Varriorum Reprints, IV.

——— (1981c), *Scientific Thought in Fourteenth Century Paris: Jean Buridan and Nicholas Oresme*. London: Varriorum Reprints, XV.

Gruner, R. (1975), *Science, Nature and Christianity. Journal of Theological Studies*. XXVI. Part 1.55.

Hesse, M. B. (1954), *Science and the Human Imagination*. London: SCM Press.

Hooykaas, R. (1972), *Religion and the Rise of Modern Science*. Edinburgh and London: Scottish Academic Press.

Huff, T. E. (1993), *The Rise of Early Modern Science: Islam, China and the West*. Cambridge: Cambridge University Press.

Jaki, S. L. (1980), 'Cosmic Beauty', in *Cosmos and Creator*. Edinburgh: Scottish Academic Press.

———— (1986), 'The Greeks of Old and the Novelty of Science', in *Chance or Reality and Other Essays*. Intercollegiate Studies Institute, Lanham, MD and London: University Press of America.

———— (1991), *Scientist and Catholic: Pierre Duhem*. Front Royal: Christendom Press.

———— (1974), *Science and Creation*. Edinburgh: Scottish Academic Press.

———— (1978), *The Road of Science and the Ways to God*. Chicago, IL: Chicago University Press.

———— (1984), *Uneasy Genius: The Life and Work of Pierre Duhem*. The Hague: Martinus Nijhoff.

———— (1988), *The Saviour of Science*. Washington, DC: Regency Gateway.

———— (1992), *Reluctant Heroine: The Life and Work of Hélène Duhem*. Edinburgh: Scottish Academic Press.

Kaiser, C. (1991), *Creation and the History of Science*. London: Marshall Pickering; Grand Rapids, MI: William B. Eerdmans.

Klaaren, E. M. (1977), *Religious Origins of Modern Science*. Grand Rapids, MI: Willian B. Eerdmans.

Lindberg, D. C. (1978), *Science in the Middle Ages*. Chicago, IL: Chicago University Press.

———— (1992), *The Beginnings of Western Science*. Chicago, IL and London: University of Chicago Press.

———— (2000), *Medieval Science and Religion in the Western Tradition: An Encyclopaedia*, ed. G. B. Ferngren. New York and London: Garland Publishing.

———— (2002), 'Early Christian Attitudes to Nature', in Gary B. Ferngren (ed.), *Science and Religion*. Baltimore, MD and London: The Johns Hopkins University Press, ch. 4.

Murdoch, J. E. (1991), 'Pierre Duhem and the History of Late Medieval Science and Philosophy in the Latin West', in Ruedi Imbach and Alfonso Maieru (eds), *Gli Studi de Philosophis Medievale fra Otto e Novocento*. Storia e Litteratura 179. Roma: Edizioni do Storia e Litteratura.

———— (2000), 'Pierre Duhem', in H. Damico (ed.), *Medieval Scholarship*, Vol. 3: *Philosophy and the Arts*. New York and London: Garland Publishing.

Nesteruk, A. V. (2003), *Light from the East: Theology, Science and the Eastern Orthodox Tradition*. Minneapolis, MN: Fortress Press.

Neubegauer, O. (1952), *The Exact Sciences in Antiquity*. Princeton, NJ: Princeton University Press.

O'Connor, D. and Oakley, F. (1969), *Creation: The Impact of an Idea*. New York: Charles Scribner's Sons.

Pais, A. (2000), *The Genius of Science*. Oxford: Oxford University Press.

Sherrard, P. (1991), *The Rape of Man and Nature: An Enquiry into the Origin and Consequences of Modern Science*. Suffolk: Golgonooza Press.

Smethurst, A. F. (1955), *Modern Science and Christian Belief*. London: James Nisbet and Co.

Sorabji, R. (ed.) (1987), *Philoponus and the Rejection of Aristotelian Science*. London: Duckworth.

St Augustine (1982), *The Literal Meaning of Genesis*. Tr. John Hammond Taylor, SJ, in Johannes Questan, W. J. Burghardt and T. C. Lamb (eds), *Ancient Christian Writers: The Works of the Fathers in Translation*. New York: Newman.

―――― (1991), *Confessions*. Tr. H. Chadwick. Oxford: Clarendon Press.

Templeton, J. M. and Herman, R. L. (1989), *The God Who Would Be Known*. Philadelphia, PA and London: Templeton Foundation Press.

Truesdell, C. (1968), *Essays in the History of Mechanics*. Berlin: Springer-Verlag.

―――― (1984), *An Idiot's Fugitive Essays on Science: Methods, Criticism, Training, Circumstances*. New York: Springer-Verlag.

Walsh, J. J. (1924), *The Thirteenth: Greatest of Centuries*. New York: Catholic Summer School Press.

Weil, S. (1968), *On Science, Necessity and the Love of God*. Oxford: Oxford University Press.

Weisheipl, J. A. (1959), *The Development of Physical Theory in the Middle Ages*. London: Sheed and Ward.

Whitehead, A. N. (1926), *Science and the Modern World*. Cambridge: Cambridge University Press.

Whitrow, G. J. (1988), *Time in History*. Oxford: Oxford University Press.

Wilson, C. (1956), *William Heytesbury: Medieval Logic and the Rise of Mathematical Physics*. Madison, WI: University of Wisconsin Press.

Zernov, N. (1961), *Eastern Christendom*. London: Weidenfeld and Nicolson.

Chapter 3. The Muslim Centuries

Arnold, Sir Thomas and Guillaume, A. (1931), *The Legacy of Islam*. London: Oxford University Press.

Dhanani, A. (2002), 'Islam', in G. Ferngren (ed.), *Science and Religion*. Baltimore, MD and London: The Johns Hopkins University Press, ch. 6.

Feynman, R. (1998), *The Meaning of it All*. London: Allen Lane, The Penguin Press.

Golshani, M. (1997), *The Holy Qur'an and the Sciences of Nature*. Binghamton, NY: Institute of Global Cultural Studies, Binghamton University.

Hoodbhoy. P. (1991), *Islam and Science: Religious Orthodoxy and the Battle for Rationality*. London: Zed Books.

Huff, Toby E. (1993), *The Rise of Early Modern Science: Islam, China and the West*. Cambridge: Cambridge University Press.

Iqbal, M. (2002), *Islam and Science*. Aldershot: Ashgate.

Jaki, S. L. (1974), *Science and Creation*, Edinburgh: Scottish Academic Press,

——— (1988), 'The Physics of Impetus and the Impetus of the Koran', in *The Absolute Beneath the Relative and Other Essays*. The Intercollegiate Studies Institute Inc. Lanham, MD; University Press of America, ch. 9.

Kinross, Lord (2003), *The Ottoman Empire*. London: The Folio Society.

Lewis, B. (1995), *Cultures in Conflict: Christians, Muslims and Jews in the Age of Discovery*. Oxford: Oxford University Press.

——— (2002), *What Went Wrong? The Clash between Islam and Modernity in the Middle East*. London: Weidenfeld and Nicolson.

——— (2003), *The Crisis of Islam*. London: Wiedenfeld and Nicolson.

Nasr, S. H. (1976), *Islamic Science: An Illustrated Study*. Westerham: World of Islam Festival Publishing Company Ltd/Westerham Press Ltd.

——— (1987), *Science and Civilisation in Islam*. Cambridge: The Islamic Texts Society.

O'Leary, De Lacy (1949), *How Greek Science Passed to the Arabs*. London: Routledge and Kegan Paul.

Palin, M. (2002), *Sahara*. London: Weidenfeld and Nicolson.

Qadir, C. A. (1988), *Philosophy and Science in the Islamic World*. London: Routledge.

Rashed, R. (ed.) (1996), *Encyclopaedia of the History of Arab Science*. 3 vols. London: Routledge.

Sabra, A. (1976), 'The Scientific Enterprise', in Bernard Lewis (ed.), *The World of Islam*. London: Thames and Hudson, ch. 7.

Sabra, A. I. (1987), 'Greek Science in Islam', *History of Science*, **XXV**, 223.

Salam, A. (1987), *Ideals and Realities: Selected Essays of Abdus Salam*, ed. C. H. Lai. Singapore: World Scientific.

Sardar, Z. (1979), 'A Revival for Islam, a Boost for Science?', *Nature*, **282**, 354.

——— (1989), *Explorations in Islamic Science*. London and New York: Mansell.

Singer, C. (1959), *A Short History of Scientific Ideas to 1900*. Oxford: Oxford University Press.

Thurston, H. (1996), *Early Astronomy*. Berlin: The Folio Society.

Winder, R. B. et al. (1976), *The Genius of Arab Civilisation: Source of Renaissance*. Oxford: Phaidon.

Zaidat, A. A. (1986), *Western Science in the Arab World: The Input of Darwinism 1860–1930*. London: Macmillan.

Chapter 4. The Renaissance

Applebaum, W. (ed.) (2000), *Encyclopedia of the Scientific Revolution from Copernicus to Newton*. New York and London: Garland.

Barbour, J. B. (1989), *Absolute or Relative Motion?* Vol. 1. *The Discovery of Dynamics*. Cambridge: Cambridge University Press.

Barker, P. and Goldstein, B. R. (2001), 'Theological Foundations of Kepler's Astronomy', *Osiris*, **16**, 88.

Basalla, G. (1948), *The Rise of Modern Science: External or Internal Factors*. Lexington, MA: D. C. Heath and Co.

Bennett, J., Cooper, M., Hunter, M. and Jardine, L. (2003), *London's Leonardo: The Life and Work of Robert Hooke*. Oxford: Oxford University Press.

Blackwell, R. J. (1991), *Galileo, Bellarmine and the Bible*. Notre Dame, IN: Notre Dame University Press.

Brewster, Sir David (1855), *Memoirs of the Life, Writings and Discourses of Sir Isaac Newton*. 2 vols. Edinburgh: Thomas Constable and Co.

Carrell, A. (1975), *Man, The Unknown*. London: Hamish Hamilton.

―――― ([1935], 1994), *The Voyage to Lourdes*. Fraser, MI: Real View Books.

Carroll, W. E. and Hodgson, P. E. (1998), *Galileo*. Lectures on audiotape and videotape, International Catholic University, Notre Dame, IL.

Caspar, M. ([1962], 1993), *Kepler*. New York: Collier, Dover.

Chandrasekhar, S. (1993), *Newton's Principia for the Common Reader*. Oxford: Oxford University Press.

Christianson, G. E. (1984), *In the Presence of the Creator: Isaac Newton and His Times*. London: Macmillan.

Christianson, J. R. ([2000], 2003), *On Tycho's Island*. Cambridge: Cambridge University Press.

Cohen, I. B. ([1958], 1978), *Isaac Newton's Papers and Letters on Natural Philosophy*. Cambridge, MA: Harvard University Press.

Cook, A. (1998), *Edmund Halley*. Oxford: Clarendon Press.

Coyne, G. V., Heller, M. and Zycinski, J. (eds) (1985), *The Galileo Affair: A Meeting of Faith and Science*. Proceedings of the Cracow Conference, May 1984. Vatican City State: Specola Vaticana.

De Santillana, G. (1976), *The Crime of Galileo*. Chicago, IL: University of Chicago Press.

Dobbs, B. J. T. (1975), *The Foundations of Newton's Alchemy*. Cambridge: Cambridge University Press.

Drake, S. (1957), *Discoveries and Opinions of Galileo*. New York: Doubleday Anchor Books.

―――― (1967), 'Mathematics, Astronomy and Physics in the Work of Galileo', in Charles S. Singleton (ed.), *Art, Science and History in the Renaissance*. Baltimore, MD: The Johns Hopkins University Press.

―――― (1978), *Galileo at Work: His Scientific Biography*. Chicago, IL: University of Chicago Press.

―――― (1980), *Galileo*. Oxford: Oxford University Press.

Dreyer, J. L. E. (1965), *Tycho Brahe*. New York: Dover.

Eiseley, L. (1961), *The Man who saw through Time*. New York: Charles Scribner's Sons.

Farrington, B. (1951), *Francis Bacon: Philosopher of Industrial Science*. London: Lawrence and Wishart.

Feldhay, R. (1995), *Galileo: for Copernicanism and for the Church*. Vatican City State: Vatican Observatory Publications.

Finocchiaro, Maurice A. (ed. and tr.) (1989), *The Galileo Affair: A Documentary History*. Berkeley, Los Angeles and London: University of California Press.

―――― (ed.) (1997), *The Galileo Affair*. Chicago, IL: University of Chicago Press.

Geymonat, L. (1957), *Galileo Galilei: A Biography and Inquiry into his Philosophy of Science*. New York: McGraw-Hill.

Gingerich, O. (ed.) (1975), *The Nature of Scientific Discovery*. Washington, DC: Smithsonian Institution Press.

Grisez, G. (1975), *Beyond the New Theism*. Notre Dame, IN: University of Notre Dame Press.

Hall, A. R. ([1954], 1962). *The Scientific Revolution*. London: Longmans.

—— (1983). *The Revolution in Science 1500–1750*. London: Longmans.

—— (1992), *Isaac Newton: Adventurer in Thought*. Cambridge: Cambridge University Press.

Hill, C. (1965). *Intellectual Origins of the English Revolution*. Oxford: Clarendon Press.

Hoffmann, B. (1983), *Relativity and its Roots*. New York: Doubleday.

Inwood, S. (2002), *Robert Hooke (1635–1703). The Man Who Knew too Much*. London: Macmillan.

Jaki, S. L. (1969), *The Paradox of Olbers' Paradox*. New York: Herder and Herder.

—— (1978), *The Road of Science and the Ways to God*. Chicago, IL: Chicago University Press.

—— (1999), *God and the Sun at Fatima*. Royal Oak, MI: Real View Books.

—— (1999), *Miracles and Physics*. Front Royal: Christendom Press.

Jammer, M. (1954), *Concepts of Space*. Cambridge, MA: Harvard University Press.

Jardine, L. (2004), *The Curious Life of Robert Hooke: The Man Who Measured London*. London: HarperCollins.

Kearney, H. (1964), *Origins of the Scientific Revolution*. London: Longmans.

Kesten, H. (1956), *Copernicus and his World*. London: Secker and Warburg.

Kneller, Karl A. (1999), *Christianity and the Leaders of Modern Science*. Fraser, MI: Real View Books.

Koestler, A. (1959), *The Sleepwalkers*. London, Hutchinson.

—— (1961), *The Watershed: A Biography of Johannes Kepler*. London, Melbourne and Toronto: Heinemann.

Koyré, A. (1978), *Galileo Studies*. Sussex: Harvester Press.

Kozhamthadam, J. (1994), *The Discovery of Kepler's Laws*. Notre Dame, IN: University of Notre Dame Press.

Langford, J. J. ([1971], 1995), *Galileo, Science and the Church*. Ann Arbor, MI: University of Michigan Press.

Lindberg, D. C. and Westman, R. S. (eds) (1990), *Reappraisals of the Scientific Revolution*. Cambridge: Cambridge University Press.

McMullin, E. (ed.) (1967), *Galileo: Man of Science*. New York and London: Basic Books.

—— (1986), *Newton on Matter and Activity*. Notre Dame, IN: University of Notre Dame Press.

Mach, E. (1907), *The Science of Mechanics*. Chicago, IL: Open Court.

Manuel, F. E. (1968), *A Portrait of Isaac Newton*. Cambridge, MA: Harvard University Press.

More, L. T. (1934), *Isaac Newton: A Biography*. New York: Dover.

Newton, I. (1686), *The Principia*, Tr. I. B. Cohen and A. Whitman (1999).
   Berkeley: University of California Press.
——— (1952), *Opticks*. New York: Dover.
Peterson, I. (1993), *Newton's Clock: Chaos in the Solar System*. New York: W.
   H. Freeman and Co.
Quinton, A. (1988), *Francis Bacon*. Oxford: Oxford University Press.
Redondi, P. (1998), *Galileo: Heretic*. London: Penguin.
Reston, J. (1994), *Galileo: A Life*. London: Cassell.
Robertson, John M. (1905), *The Philosophical Works of Francis Bacon*.
   London: George Routledge and Sons.
Russell, J. L. (1975), 'Kepler and Scientific Method', in Arthur and Peter Beer
   (eds), *Four Hundred Years. Proceedings of a Conference in Honour of
   Johannes Kepler*. Oxford: Pergamon Press.
Seeger, R. J. (1996), *Galileo Galilei: His Life and his Works*. Oxford: Pergamon
   Press.
Settle, T. B. (1961), 'An Experiment in the History of Science', *Science*, **133**, 19.
Sharratt, M. (1994), *Galileo: Decisive Innovator*. Oxford: Blackwell.
Shea, W. R. (1970), 'Galileo's Claim to Fame: The Proof that the Earth Moves
   from the Evidence of the Senses', *History of Science*, **5**(18), p. 112.
——— (1977), *Galileo's Intellectual Revolution: Middle Period, 1610–1632*.
   New York: Science History Publications.
Smith, A. G. R. (1972), *Science and Society in the 16th and 17th Centuries*. New
   York: Science History Publications.
Smith, G. (1995), *Galileo: A Dramatised Life*. Janus Publishing.
Stace, W. T. (1952), *Religion and the Modern Mind*. Westport, CT: Greenwood
   Press.
Thayer, H. S. (ed.) (1953), Newton's Philosophy of Nature: Selections from His
   Writings. New York: Hafner.
Thoren, V. E. (1990), *The Lord of Uraniborg: A Biography of Tycho Brahe*.
   Cambridge: Cambridge University Press.
Wallace, W. A. (1981), *Prelude to Galileo*. Dordrecht: Reidel.
——— (1984), *Galileo and His Sources*. Princeton, NJ: Princeton University
   Press.
——— (ed.) (1986), *Reinterpreting Galileo*. London and Lanham, MD:
   Catholic University of America Press.
——— (1995), 'Galileo's Trial and the Proof of the Earth's Motion', *Catholic
   Dossier*, **1**(2), 7.
Webster, C. (1975), *The Great Instauration*. London: Duckworth.
Westfall, R. S. (1980), *Never at Rest: A Biography of Isaac Newton*. Cambridge:
   Cambridge University Press.
——— (1989), *Essays on the Trial of Galileo*. Vatican City State: Vatican
   Observatory Publications.
Whewell, William (1847), *History of the Inductive Sciences from the Earliest to
   the Present Time*, 3 vols. London: Parker.
White, M. (1997), *Isaac Newton: The Last Sorcerer*. London: Fourth Estate.
Wightman, W. P. D. (1997), *The Growth of Scientific Ideas*. London: Oliver
   and Boyd.

Zycinski, J. M. (1988), *The Idea of Unification in Galileo's Epistemology*. Vatican City State: Vatican Observatory Publications: Studi Galileiani Vol. 1, No. 4. Specola Vaticana.

Chapter 5. Classical Physics

Basalla, G., Coleman, W. and Kargan, R. H. (1970), *Victorian Science*. New York: Doubleday.

Berkson, W. (1974), *Fields of Force: The Development of a World View from Faraday to Einstein*. London: Routledge and Kegan Paul.

Burchfield, J. D. (1980), 'Kelvin and the Age of the Earth', in Colin Chant and John Fauvel (eds), *Darwin to Einstein*. London: Open University.

Cereignani, C. (1998), *Ludwig Boltzmann*, ch. 5. Oxford: Oxford University Press.

Einstein, A. and Infeld, L. (n.d.), *The Evolution of Physics*. London: The Scientific Book Club.

Elkana, Y. (1974), *The Discovery of the Conservation of Energy*. London: Hutchinson.

Hiebert, E. (1967), 'Thermodynamics and Religion', in Frederick J. Crosson (ed.), *Science and Contemporary Society*. Notre Dame, IN: University of Notre Dame Press, ch. 3.

Jaki, S. L. (1984), *Uneasy Genius: The Life and Work of Pierre Duhem*. The Hague: Martinus Nijhoff.

Knight, D. (1986), *The Age of Science: The Scientific World View in the Nineteenth Century*. Oxford: Blackwell.

Maxwell, J. C. (1870), 'Ether', in *Encyclopedia Britannica*, 9th edn., vol. VIII, p. 568.

May, C. P. (1964), *James Clerk Maxwell and Electromagnetism*. London: Chatto and Windus.

Michelson, A. A. and Morley, E. W. (1887), *American Journal of Science*, **34**, 333.

Nye, M. J. (1972), *Molecular Reality: A Perspective on the Work of Jean Perrin*. London: MacDonald and Janes; New York: American Elsevier.

Steffens, H. J. (1979), *James Prescott Joule and the Concept of Energy*. New York: Science History Publications.

Stewart, B. and Tait, P. G. ([1875], 1889), *The Unseen Universe*. London: Macmillan.

Stranathan, J. D. (1946), *The Particles of Modern Physics*. Philadelphia, PA and London: Blakiston.

Thomson, J. J. (1906), *Conduction of Electrons through Gases*. Cambridge: Cambridge University Press.

Windle, B. C. A. (1926), *The Church and Science*. London: Catholic Truth Society.

Chapter 6. Space, Time and Relativity

A useful test of the value of books on the theory of relativity is to see if they satisfy the following criteria: 1. Use of matrices and the four-vector notation. 2. Definition of velocity and acceleration in terms of differentiation with respect to the proper time, not the Newtonian time. 3. Mass independent of velocity.

Anderson, J. L. (1967), *Principles of Relativity Physics*. New York: Academic Press.

Angel, R. B. (1980), *Relativity: The Theory and its Philosophy*. Oxford: Pergamon Press.

Aspect, Alain, Dalibard, J. and Roger, G. (1982), 'Experimental Test of Bell's Inequalities Using Time-Varying-Analyser', *Physical Review Letters*, **49**, 1804.

Barbour, J. (1989), *Absolute or Relative Motion? 1. The Discovery of Dynamics*. Cambridge: Cambridge University Press.

Bell, G. K. A. (1935), *Randall Davidson*. Oxford: Oxford University Press.

Bernstein, J. (1996), *A Theory for Everything*. New York: Springer-Verlag.

Born, M. (1956), *Physics and Relativity*. London: Pergamon Press.

—— (1965), *Einstein's Theory of Relativity*. New York: Dover.

Clark, R. W. (1979), *Einstein: The Life and Times*. London: Hodder and Stoughton.

Conklin, E. K. (1972), 'Velocity of the Earth with Respect to the Cosmic Background Radiation', *Nature*, **222**, 971.

Craig, W. L. (2000), Private communication.

Dicke, R. H. (1965–68), *The Theoretical Significance of Experimental Relativity*. New York: Gordon and Breach.

Earman, J. (1970), 'Who's Afraid of Absolute Space?', *Australasian Journal of Philosophy*, **48**, 288, 371.

Einstein, A. (1905), 'Zur Electrodynamik bewegter Körper', *Annalen der Physik*, **17**, 891.

Elkana, Y. (1974), *The Interaction between Science and Philosophy*. Atlantic Highlands, NJ: Humanities Press.

Galison, P. (2003), *Einstein's Clocks, Poincaré's Maps: Empires of Time*. London: Sceptre, Hodder and Stoughton.

Ginzburg, V. I. (2001), 'Who Created the Theory of Relativity and How was it Developed?', in *The Physics of a Lifetime*. Berlin: Springer.

Goldberg, S. (1984), *Understanding Relativity: Origin and Impact of a Scientific Revolution*. Oxford: Clarendon Press.

Graham, L. R. (1981), *Between Science and Values*. New York: Columbia University Press.

Hardy, L. (1992), 'Quantum Mechanics, Local Realistic Theories and Lorentz-Invariant Theories', *Physical Review Letters*, **68**, 2981.

—— (1998), 'Spooky Action at a Distance in Quantum Mechanics'. *Contemporary Physics*, **39**, 419.

Harrod, R. F. (1971), *The Prof: A Personal Memoir of Lord Cherwell*. London: Macmillan.

Hawking, S. W. and Israel, W. (eds) (1987), *Three Hundred Years of Gravitation*. Cambridge: Cambridge University Press.

Heisenberg, W. (1971), *Physics and Beyond: Encounters and Conversations*. London: George Allen and Unwin; New York: Harper and Row.

Hodgson, P. E. (2000), 'God's Action in the World: The Relevance of Quantum Mechanics', *Zygon*, **35**, 505.

———— (2003), 'Relativity and Religion: The Abuse of Einstein's Theory', *Zygon*, **38**, 393.

Hoffmann, B. (1983), *Relativity and its Roots*. New York: Dover Publications.

Holton, G. (1973), *Thematic Origins of Scientific Thought: Kepler to Einstein*. Cambridge, MA: Harvard University Press.

———— (1974), 'Finding Favour with the Angel of the Lord: Notes towards the Psychobiographical Study of Scientific Genius', in Y. Elkana (ed.), *The Interaction between Science and Philosophy*. Atlantic Highlands, NJ: Humanities Press.

Jaki, S. L. (1978), *The Road of Science and the Ways to God*. Chicago, IL: Chicago University Press.

———— (1988), *The Absolute beneath the Relative*. London: University Press of America.

Jammer, M. (1954), *Concepts of Space*. Cambridge, MA: Harvard University Press.

———— (1999), *Einstein and Religion*. Princeton, NJ: Princeton University Press.

Kaufmann, W. (1906), 'Über die Konstitution des Electrons', *Annalen der Physik*, **19**, 487.

Kennedy, R. J. and Thorndike, E. W. (1932), *Physical Review*, **42**, 400.

Klotz, I. M. (1986), *Diamond Dealers and Feather Merchants: Tales from the Sciences*. Boston, MA, Basel and Stuttgart: Birkhauser.

Leighton, R. B. (1959), *Principles of Modern Physics*. New York: McGraw-Hill.

Lucas, J. R. and Hodgson, P. E. (1990), *Spacetime and Electromagnetism*. Oxford: Clarendon Press.

Mach, E. (1907), *The Science of Mechanics*. Chicago, IL: Open Court; London: Kegan Paul, Trench, Trübner and Co.

Miller, A. I. (1981), *Albert Einstein's Special Theory of Relativity: Emergence (1905) and Early Interpretation (1905–1911)*. Reading, MA: Addison-Wesley.

Minkowski, H. (1923), 'Space and Time', in A. Einstein et al., *The Principles of Relativity*, with notes by A. Sommerfeld. Tr. W. Perrett and G. B. Jeffery. New York: Dover Publications.

Ne'eman, Y. (1974), 'Concrete versus Abstract Theoretical Models', in Y. Elkana (ed.), *The Interaction between Science and Philosophy*. Atlantic Highlands, NJ: Humanities Press, p. 1.

Pais, A. (1982), *Subtle is the Lord. The Science and Life of Albert Einstein*. Oxford: Oxford University Press.

———— (1994), *Einstein Lived Here*. Oxford: Oxford University Press.

Planck, M. (1933), *Where is Science Going?* London: George Allen and Unwin.

——— (1960), *A Survey of Physical Theory*. New York: Dover Publications.

Popper, K. (1956), *Quantum Theory and the Schism in Physics*. Ed. W. W. Barclay III. London: Hutchinson.

Powers, D. C. (1982). *Philosophy and the New Physics*. London: Methuen.

Prokhovnik, S. J. (1992), 'A Cosmological Basis for Bell's Views on Quantum and Relativistic Physics', in A. Van Der Merwe, F. Selleri and G. Tarozzi (eds), *Bell's Theorem and the Foundations of Modern Physics*, Cesena Conference, Italy, 7–10 October. Singapore: World Scientific.

Reiser, A. (1930), *Albert Einstein*. New York: A. and C. Boni.

Rindler, W. (1960), *Special Relativity*. Edinburgh and London: Oliver and Boyd.

Robertson, D. S. and Carter, W. E. (1984), 'Relativistic Deflection of Radio Signals in the Solar Gravitational Field Measured with VLBI (Very Long Baseline Interferometry)', *Nature*, **310**, 572.

Rosen, N. (1968), *Inertial Systems in an Expanding Universe. Proceedings of the Israel Academy of Science and Humanities* (Section of Science), **12**.

Rosenthal-Schneider, I. (1980), *Reality and Scientific Truth: Discussions with Einstein, Von Laue and Planck*. Detroit, MI: Wayne State University Press.

Sakharov, A. (1990), *Memoirs*. London: Hutchinson.

Sandin, T. R. (1989), *Essentials of Modern Physics*. New York: Addison-Wesley.

Sartori, L. (1996), *Understanding Relativity*. Chicago, IL: University of Chicago Press.

Schilpp, P. A. (ed.) (1949), *Albert Einstein: Philosopher–Scientist*. Evanston, IL: Library of Living Philosophers.

Seelig, C. (1956), *Albert Einstein: A Documentary Biography*. London: Staples Press.

Stachel, J. (1990), 'The Theory of Relativity', in R. C. Olby, J. R. R. Christie and M. J. S. Hodge (eds), *Companion to the History of Modern Science*. London and New York: Routledge, p. 442.

Stanley, M. (2003), 'An Expedition to Heal the Wounds of War. The 1919 Eclipse and Eddington as Quaker Adventurer', *Isis*, **94**, 57.

Synge, J. L. (1964), *Relativity: The General Theory*. Amsterdam: North-Holland.

Taylor, E. F. and Wheeler, J. A. (1966), *Spacetime Physics*. San Francisco, CA and London: W. H. Freeman and Company.

Truesdell, C. (1984), *An Idiot's Fugitive Essays on Science*. Berlin: Springer-Verlag.

Whittaker, E. (1948), *From Euclid to Eddington*. Cambridge: Cambridge University Press.

Whittaker, E. T. (1951), *History of the Theories of Aether and Electricity*. 2 vols. London: Thomas Nelson and Sons.

Wien, W. (1909), *Über Electronen*. 2nd edn. Leipzig: B. G. Teubner.

Will, C. M. (1987), 'Experimental Gravitation from Newton's Principia to Einstein's General Relativity', in Hawking and Israel (1987).

Woodhouse, N. M. T. (2003), *Special Relativity*. London: Springer.

Chapter 7. Quantum Theory

Beck, G. and Nussenzweig, M. (1959), 'Uncertainty Relation and Diffraction by a Slit', *Il Nuovo Cimento*, **9**, 1068.

Bender, D. et al. (1984), 'Test of QED at 29 GeV. Centre-of-Mass Energy', *Physical Review*, **D30**, 515.

Bleaney, B. and Bleaney, B. J. (1976), *Electricity and Magnetism*. Oxford: Oxford University Press.

Brush, S. G. (1983), *Statistical Physics and the Atomic Theory of Matter, from Boyle and Newton to Landau and Onsager*. Princeton, NJ: Princeton University Press.

Fierz, M. and Weisskopf, V. F. (eds) (1960), *Theoretical Physics in the Twentieth Century*. New York: Interscience Publishers.

Fraunfelder, H. and Henley, E. M. (1974), *Subatomic Physics*. Englewood Cliffs, NJ: Prentice-Hall.

Geiger, H., and Nuttall, J. M. (1911), 'The ranges of the alpha-particles from various radioactive substances and a relation between Range and Period of Transformation.' *Philosophical Magazine*, 22.613.

Gerlach, W. and Stern, O. (1922), 'Der Experimentelle Nachweis des Magnetischen Moments des Silberatoms', *Zeitschrift für Physik*, **8**, 110; **9**, 349.

Gingerich, O. (ed.) (1975), *The Nature of Scientific Discovery*. Washington, DC: Smithsonian Institution Press.

Heilbron, J. L. (1986), *The Dilemmas of an Upright Man: Max Planck as the Spokesman of German Science*. Berkeley, CA: University of California Press.

Hestenes, D. and Weingartshofer, A. (1991), *The Electron: New Theory and Experiment*. Dordrecht: Kluwer.

Hughes, R. I. G. (1989), *The Structure and Interpretation of Quantum Mechanics*. Cambridge, MA: Princeton University Press.

Jackson, J. D. (1975), *Classical Electrodynamics*. New York: Wiley.

Jonsson, C. (1961), 'Electron Diffraction at Multiple Slits', *Zeitschrift für Physik*, **161**, 454.

——— (1974) 'Electron Diffraction at Multiple Slits', *American Journal of Physics*, **42**, 4.

Kalckar, J. (1972), 'On the Measurement Ability of the Spin and Magnetic Moment of the Free Electron', *Il Nuovo Cimento*, **8A**, 759.

Kuhn, T. S. (1978), *Black-Body Radiation and the Quantum Discontinuity. 1894–1912*. Oxford: Clarendon Press.

Merli, P. G., Missiroli, G. F., and Pozzi, G. (1976), 'On the Statistical Aspect of Electron Interference Phenomena'. *American Journal of Physics*, 44.306.

Pais, A. (1994), *Einstein Lived Here*. Oxford: Clarendon Press.

Peierls, R. E. (1997), *Atomic Histories*. New York: American Institute of Physics.

Penrose, R. and Isham, C. J. (eds) (1986), *Quantum Concepts in Space and Time*. Oxford: Oxford University Press.

Powell, C. F., Fowler, P. H. and Perkins, D. H. (1959), *The Study of Elementary Particles by the Photographic Method*. Oxford: Pergamon Press.

Putnam, H. (1965), 'A Philosopher Looks at Quantum Mechanics', in R. G. Colodny (ed.), *Beyond the Edge of Certainty*. Englewood Cliffs, NJ: Prentice-Hall.

Richtmyer, F. K. and Kennard, E. H. (1942), *Introduction to Modern Physics*. New York: McGraw-Hill.

Ruark, A. E. and Urey, H. C. (1930), *Atoms, Molecules and Quanta*. New York: McGraw-Hill.

Ter Haar, D. (1967), *The Old Quantum Theory*. Oxford: Pergamon Press.

Tonamura, A. (1989), 'Demonstration of Single-Electron Buildup of an Interference Pattern', *American Journal of Physics*, 57.117.

——— (1994), 'Electron Holography shows its Resolve', *Physics World*, March.

Troup, G. (1968), *Understanding Quantum Mechanics*. London: Methuen.

Whittaker, E. T. (1942), *The Beginning and End of the World*. Oxford: Oxford University Press.

Wein, W. (1909), *Über Electronen*. 2nd edn. Leipzig: B. G. Traubner.

Zee, A. (1999), *Fearful Symmetry*. Princeton, NJ: Princeton University Press.

Zeilinger, A. (1986), 'Testing Quantum Superposition with Cold Neutrons', in Penrose and Isham (1986), p. 16.

Zeilinger, A., Gahler, R., Shull, C. G., Treimer, W., and Mampe, W. (1988), Review of 'Single and Double-Slit Diffraction of Neutrons', *Review Modern Physics*, 60.1067.

Chapters 8 and 9.   Quantum Mechanics

A. Philosophy

Albertson, J. (1961), 'Von Neumann's Hidden Parameter Proof', *American Journal of Physics*, **29**, 478.

Auletta, G. (2000), *Foundations and Interpretation of Quantum Mechanics*. Singapore and London: World Scientific.

Ayer, A. J. (1978), 'Logical Positivism and its Legacy'. In B. McGee (ed.). *Men of Ideas*. London. BBC Publications.

Baggott, J. (2004), *Beyond Measure: Philosophy and the Meaning of Quantum Theory*. Oxford: Oxford University Press.

Ballentine, Leslie E. (1970), 'The Statistical Interpretation of Quantum Mechanics', *Review of Modern Physics*, **42**, 358.

Beauregard, O. Costa de (1987), *Time, the Physical Magnitude*. Dordrecht: Reidel.

Belinfante, F. J. (1973), *A Survey of Hidden Variable Theories*. London and New York: Pergamon.

——— (1975), *Measurement and Time Reversal in Objective Quantum Theory*. London and New York: Pergamon.

Bell, J. (1964), 'On the Einstein-Podolsky-Rosen Paradox', *Physics*, **1**, 195.

——— (1966), 'On the Problem of Hidden Variables in Quantum Mechanics', *Reviews of Modern Physics*, 38.447.

Bell, J. S. (1987), *Speakable and Unspeakable in Quantum Mechanics*. Cambridge: Cambridge University Press; Interview on 20 February in Geneva, quoted by Crease and Mann (1990), loc. cit.

—— (1995), *Selected Papers on Quantum Mechanics, High Energy Physics and Accelerators*. Singapore: World Scientific.

Beller, M. (1999), *Quantum Dialogue*. Chicago, IL: University of Chicago Press.

Bernstein, J. (1991), *Quantum Profiles*. Princeton, NJ: Princeton University Press.

—— (1996), *A Theory for Everything*. New York: Springer-Verlag.

Blackmore, J. T. (1972), *Ernst Mach*. Berkeley: University of California Press.

Blokhintsev, D. I. (1968) *The Philosophy of Quantum Mechanics*. Dordrecht: Reidel.

Bohm, D. (1951), *Quantum Theory*. Englewood Cliffs, NJ: Prentice-Hall.

—— (1952), 'A Suggested Interpretation of Quantum Mechanics in Terms of "Hidden" Variables', *Physical Review*, **85**, 166, 186.

—— (1957), *Causality and Chance in Modern Physics*. London: Routledge and Kegan Paul.

—— (1980), *Wholeness and the Implicate Order*. London: Routledge and Kegan Paul.

—— (1985), *Unfolding Meaning*. London: Ark Paperbacks.

—— and Hiley, B. J. (1980) 'Einstein and Non-Locality in the Quantum Theory', In *Einstein: The First Hundred Years*. Ed. M. Goldsmith, A. Mackay and J. Woudhuysen. Oxford: Pergamon Press.

—— (1995), *The Undivided Universe*. London: Routledge.

Bohr, N. (1931, 1934), *Atomic Theory and the Description of Nature*. Cambridge: Cambridge University Press.

—— (1935), 'Can Quantum Mechanical Description of Physical Reality be Considered Complete?', *Physical Review*, **48**, 696.

—— (1958), *Atomic Physics and Human Knowledge*. New York: Wiley.

—— (1934, 1987), *The Philosophical Writings of Niels Bohr*. 4 vols. Woodbridge, CT: Ox Bow Press.

——, Kramers, H. A., and Slater, J. C. (1924), 'The Quantum Theory of Radiation'. *Philosophical Magazine*, 47.785.

Born, M. (1964), *Natural Philosophy of Cause and Chance*. New York: Dover.

—— (1969), *Physics in My Generation*. London: Longmans.

—— (1971), *The Born–Einstein Letters*. London: Macmillan.

Bothe, W., and Geiger, H. (1924), 'Ein Wegzur Experimentellen Nachtprüfung der Theorie von Bohr, Kramers und Slater'. *Zeitscrift für Physik*, 26.44.

Briggs, J. P. and Peat, F. D. (1985), *Looking-Glass Universe*. London: Fontana.

Brody, T. A., and de la Pena, L. (1979), *Nutvo Cimento*, 58B.455.

Brody, T. A. (1985), 'The Irrelevance of the Bell Inequality'. In: *Determinism in Physics*. Ed. E. I. Bisakis and N. Tambakis. Athens: Gutenberg Publishing Company.

Brody, T. A. (1993), *The Philosophy Behind Physics*, eds Luis de la Pena and P. E. Hodgson. Berlin: Springer-Verlag.

Bub, J. (1974), *The Interpretation of Quantum Mechanics*. Dordrecht: Reidel.

Cassidy, D. C. (1992), *Uncertainty: The Life and Science of Werner Heisenberg*. New York: W. H. Freeman and Co.

Chandrankunnel, M. (1993), *Holistic Interpretation of Reality*. Louvain: Katholicke Universiteit.

——— (1997), *In Search of a Causal Quantum Mechanics*. Louvain: Katholicke Universiteit.

——— (2000), *Philosophy of Physics*. New Delhi: Anol Publications.

Clayton, P. (1997), *God and Contemporary Science*. Grand Rapids, Michigan: Eerdmans.

Cook, D. B. (1988), *Schrodinger's Mechanics*. Singapore: World Scientific.

Crease, R. B. and Mann, C. C. (1990), 'The Yogi and the Quantum'. In: *Philosophy of Science and the Occult*. Ed. P. Grin. Second Edition. State University of New York.

Cropper, W. H. (1970), *The Quantum Physicists*. Oxford: Oxford University Press.

Cushing, J. T., (1994), *Quantum Mechanics and the Copenhagen Hegemony*. Chicago, IL: University of Chicago Press.

——— Fine, A. and Goldstein, S. (eds) (1996), *Bohmian Mechanics and Quantum Theory: An Appraisal*. Boston Studies No. 184. Dordrecht: Kluwer.

Darrigol, O. (1992), *From C-Numbers to q-Numbers*. Berkeley, CA: University of California Press.

Davies, E. B. (1976), *Quantum Theory of Open Systems*. New York: Academic Press.

Davies, P. (1984), *Superforce*. London: Heinemann.

De Broglie, L. (1939), *La Méchanique Ondulatoire des Systèmes de Corpuscules*. Paris: Gauthier-Villars.

——— (1954), *The Revolution in Physics*. London: Routledge and Kegan Paul.

——— (1960), *Non-Linear Wave Mechanics: A Causal Interpretation*. Amsterdam: Elsevier.

——— (1969), *The Current Interpretation of Quantum Mechanics*. Amsterdam: Elsevier.

——— (1941), *La Réinterpretation de la Méchanique Ondulatoire*. Paris: Gauthier-Villars.

——— (1982), *Les Incertitudes d'Heisenberg et L'Interpretation Probabiliste de la Méchanique Ondulaire*. Paris: Gauthier-Villars.

——— (1990), *Heisenberg's Uncertainties and the Probabilistic Interpretation of Wave Mechanics*. Dordrecht: Kluwer.

De la Pena, L. and Cetto, A. M. (1996), *The Quantum Dice: An Introduction to Stochastic Electrodynamics*. Dordrecht: Kluwer.

D'Espagnat, B. (1979), *Conceptual Foundations of Quantum Mechanics*. Benjamin.

——— (1983), *In Search of Reality*. Berlin: Springer-Verlag.

——— (1985), *Reality and the Physicist: Knowledge, Duration and the Quantum World*. Cambridge: Cambridge University Press.

Dirac, P. A. M. (1971), *The Development of Quantum Theory*. London: Gordon and Breach.

——— (1978), *Directions in Physics*. New York: Wiley.

Dudley, J. M. and Kwan, A. M. (1966), 'Richard Feynman's Lectures on Quantum Electrodynamics', *American Journal of Physics*, **64**, 694.

Duhem, P. (1954), *The Aim and Structure of Physical Theory*. Princeton, NJ: Princeton University Press.

——— (1969), *To Save the Phenomena*. Chicago, IL: University of Chicago Press.

Einstein, A. (1953), 'Elementare Uberlegungen sur Interpretation der Grundlagen der Quanten-Mechanik', in *Scientific Papers Presented to Max Born*. Edinburgh and London: Oliver and Boyd.

——— (1954), 'Maxwell's Influence on the Evolution of the Idea of Physical Reality'. In: *Ideas and Opinions*. London: Souvenir Press.

———, Podolsky, B. and Rosen, N. (1977), 'Can Quantum Mechanical Description of Reality be Considered Complete?', *Physical Review*, **42**, 777.

——— (1971), *The Bohr-Einstein Letters*. London: Macmillan.

Eisenbud, L. (1971), *The Conceptual Foundations of Quantum Mechanics*. Van Nostrand Reinhold.

Ellis, G. F. R. (1995), 'Ordinary and Extraordinary Divine Action'. In R. J. Russell et al. (eds) (1995) loc. cit.

Eve, A. S. (1939), *Rutherford*. Cambridge: Cambridge University Press.

Faye, J. (1991), *Niels Bohr: His Heritage and Legacy. An Anti-Realist View of Quantum Mechanics*. Dordrecht: Kluwer.

Feynman, R. (1967), *The Character of Physical Law*. Boston, MA: MIT Press.

Feynman, R. P. (1972), *Statistical Mechanics*. Reading, MA: Benjamin-Cumming; (1990), *QED: The Strange Theory of Light and Matter*. London: Penguin Books.

——— (1999), *Lectures on Gravitation*. London: Penguin. See also R. P. Feynman, F. B. Morinigo and W. G. Wagner (1995). *Feynman Lectures on Gravity*. Addison-Wesley, p. 13.

———, Leighton, R. B. and Sands, M. (1965), *The Feynman Lectures in Physics*. Reading, MA: Addison-Wesley.

Fine, A. (1972), 'Some Conceptual Problems of Quantum Theory', in R. Colodney (ed.), *Paradigms and Paradoxes*. Pittsburgh, PA: University of Pittsburgh Press.

——— (1986), *The Shaky Game: Einstein, Realism and the Quantum Theory*. Chicago, IL: University of Chicago Press.

Folse, H. J. (1985), *The Philosophy of Niels Bohr: The Framework of Complementarity*. Amsterdam: North-Holland.

Forrest, P. (1988), *Quantum Metaphysics*. Oxford: Blackwell.

Franklin, A. (1987), *The Neglect of Experiment*. Cambridge: Cambridge University Press.

Garden, R. W. (1984), *Modern Logic and Quantum Mechanics*. Bristol and Boston, MA: Hilger.

Gibbins, P. (1987), *Particles and Paradoxes*. Cambridge: Cambridge University Press.

Gingerich, O. (ed.) (1975), *The Nature of Scientific Discovery*. Washington, DC: Smithsonian Institution Press.

Goldstein, S. (1995), 'Quantum Theory without Observers', *Physics Today*, March, p. 42; April p. 38. American Institute of Physics.

Greenberger, D. (ed.) (1986), *New Techniques and Ideas in Quantum Measurement Theory*. New York: Academy of Sciences.

Greenstein, G. and Zajonc, A. G. (1997), *The Quantum Challenge*. Boston, MA, London and Singapore: Jones and Bartlett.

Gribbin, J. (1984), *In Search of Schrödinger's Cat: Quantum Physics and Reality*. Toronto: Bantam Books.

———— (1995), *Schrödinger's Kittens and the Search for Reality*. London: Weidenfeld and Nicolson.

Gudder, S. P. (1979) *Stochastic Methods in Quantum Mechanics*. Amsterdam: North-Holland.

———— (1988), *Quantum Probability*. New York: Academic Press.

Hahn, Z., Cegla, W. and Jakobczyk, (eds) (1995), 'Stochastic and Quantum Chaos', *Proceedings of the Third Max Born Symposium*. Dordrecht: Kluwer.

Hardy, L. (1998), Contemporary Physics, 39.419.

Healy, R. (1989), *The Philosophy of Quantum Mechanics*. Cambridge: Cambridge University Press.

Heelan, P. J., SJ (1965), *Quantum Mechanics and Objectivity. A Study of the Physical Philosophy of Werner Heisenberg*. The Hague: Martinus Nijhoff.

Heisenberg, W. (1938), 'Die Grenzen der Anwendbarkeit der bisherigen quanten theorie'. *Zeitschrift für Physik*, 110.251.

———— (1927), 'Über die Grundprinzipien der Quantum Mechanik'. *Forschungen und Forschritte*, 3.83.

———— (1958), 'The Representation of Nature in Contemporary Physics'. *Daedalus* 87.95. Summer.

———— (1927), 'Über den anschaulichten Inhalt der quantentheoritischen Kinematik und Mechanik'. *Zeitscrift für Physik*, 43.172. Translated by S. L. Jaki: in Philosophia, 10–11.85. 1980–1981.

———— (1949), *The Physical Principles of the Quantum Theory*. Chicago, IL; (1930), New York: Dover.

————. (1958), *Physics and Philosophy*. London: Allen and Unwin.

———— (1958), *The Physicist's Conception of Nature*. London: Hutchinson.

———— (1971), *Physics and Beyond*. London: Allen and Unwin.

Hendry, J. (1984), *The Creation of Quantum Mechanics and the Bohr–Einstein Dialogue*. Dordrecht: Reidel.

Herbert, N. (1987) *Quantum Reality: Beyond the New Physics*. London: Rider.

Hess, K., and Philipp, W. (2000), 'Bell's Theorem and the Problem of Decidability between the views of Einstein and Bohr'. *Proceedings of the National Academy of Science*, 98 No. 5.14228; (2001), 'A Possible Loophole in the Theorem of Bell.' *Proceedings of the National Academy of Science* No. 5.14224.

Hodgson, P. E., Gadioli, E. and Gadioli, Erba, E. (1997), *Introductory Nuclear Physics*. Oxford: Clarendon Press.

Hoekzema, D. J. (1993), *The Quantum Labyrinth*. Dordrecht: Kluwer.

Hoffmann, B. (1947), *The Strange Story of the Quantum*. London: Pelican.

Holton, G. and Elkana, Y. (eds) (1979), *Albert Einstein: Historical and Cultural Perspectives. The Centennial Symposium in Jerusalem*. Princeton, NJ: Princeton University Press.

Home, D. and Whitaker, M. A. B. (1992), 'Ensemble Interpretations of Quantum Mechanics. A Modern Perspective', *Physics Reports*, **210**, 223.

Honnor, J. (1987), *The Description of Nature: Niels Bohr and the Philosophy of Quantum Physics*. Oxford: Oxford University Press.

't Hooft, G. (1997), *In Search of the Ultimate Building Blocks*. Cambridge: Cambridge University Press; (2003), Theorist Charts a Determinist Future. Physics Today. November.

Houghton, J. (1995), *The Search for God*. Oxford: Lion Publishing.

Howard, D. (1990), '"Nicht sein Kann nicht sein derf", or the Prehistory of EPR, 1909–1935', *Erice Einstein's Early Worries about the Quantum Mechanics of Composite Systems. In: Sixty-Two Years of Uncertainty: Historical, Philosophical and Physical Enquiries into the Foundations of Quantum Mechanics*, Ed. Arthur I. Miller. NATO ASI Series. Erico 1989. Plenum Press.

Huff, Douglas, and Prewett, Omer (1979), *The Nature of the Physical Universe: 1976 Nobel Conference*. New York.

Hughes, R. I. G. (1989), *The Structure and Interpretation of Quantum Mechanics*. Cambridge, MA: Harvard University Press.

Jammer, M. (1966), *The Conceptual Development of Quantum Mechanics*. New York: McGraw-Hill. (1989). New York: American Institute of Physics.

——— (1974), *The Philosophy of Quantum Mechanics*. New York: Wiley.

——— (1999), *Einstein's Religion*. Princeton, NJ: Princeton University Press.

Jauch, J. M. (1968), *Foundations of Quantum Mechanics*. New York: Addison-Wesley.

——— (1971), *Are Quanta Real? A Galilean Dialogue*. Bloomington, IN: Indiana University Press.

Jauch, J. M., and Pirion, C. (1963), 'Can Hidden Variables be Excluded in Quantum Mechanics?' *Helvetica Physica Acta.*, 26.827.

Julg, A. (1998), *From Atoms and Molecules to Cosmos: A Quasi-Ergodic Interpretation of Quantum Mechanics. Lecture Notes in Chemistry*. Berlin: Springer-Verlag.

Kochen, S., and Specker, E. P. (1967), *Journal of Mathematics and Mechanics* 17.59.

Krips, H. (1987), *The Metaphysics of Quantum Theory*. Oxford: Oxford University Press.

Lahti, Pekka and Mittelstaedt, Peter (1985), *Symposium on the Foundations of Modern Physics – 50 Years of the Einstein-Podolsky-Rosen Gedanken Experiment*. Singapore: World Scientific.

Lamb, Willis (1986), 'Theory of Quantum-Mechanical Measurement.' *Proceedings of the Second International Symposium on the Foundations of Quantum Mechanics in the Light of New Technology*, eds M. Namiki, Y. Ohnuki, Y. Murayama and S. Nomura. Tokyo: The Physical Society of Japan.

Lamb, W. (1995), 'From Newton to Schrodinger and Beyond.' In: *Fundamental Problems in Quantum Physics*. Ed. Miguel Ferrero and Alwyn van der Merwe. Dordrecht: Kluwer.

Landé, A. (1951), *Quantum Mechanics*. London: Pitman.

———— (1960), *From Dualism to Unity in Quantum Theory*. Cambridge: Cambridge University Press.

———— (1965), *New Foundations of Quantum Mechanics*. Cambridge: Cambridge University Press.

Leggett, A. J. (1984), 'Microscopic Quantum Tunnelling and All That', W. E. Parry (ed.), in *Essays in Theoretical Physics in Honour of Ter Haar*, Oxford: Pergamon Press.

Ludwig, G. (1985), *An Axiomatic Basis for Quantum Mechanics*. Berlin: Springer-Verlag.

Macrae, N. ([1992], 2000), *John von Neumann*. New York: Pantheon Books.

Madelung, E. (1927), 'Quantentheorie in Hydrodynamischer Form'. *Zeitscrift für Physik*, 43.354.

Mann, A. and Revzen, M. (1966), 'The Dilemma of Einstein, Podolsky and Rosen – 60 Years Later', *Annals of the Israel Physical Society*, **12**.

Marshall, T. W. (1985), 'In Search of Physical Reality.' *Nature*, 313.438.

Mehra, J. and Rechenberg, H. (1982–87), *The Historical Development of Quantum Theory*. 6 vols. Berlin: Springer.

Messiah, A. (1970), *Quantum Mechanics*. Vols 1 and 2. Amsterdam: North-Holland.

Mittelstaedt, P. (1978), *Quantum Logic*. Dordrecht: Reidel.

Miller, A. (1974), *Quantum Mechanics: A Physical World Picture*. Oxford: Pergamon.

Mott, N. F. (1964), 'On Teaching Quantum Phenomena', *Contemporary Physics*, **5**, 401.

Murdoch, D. (1987), *Niels Bohr's Philosophy of Physics*. Cambridge: Cambridge University Press.

Murphy, N. (1995), 'Divine Action in the Natural Order.' In Russell, R. J. (1995), loc. cit.

Nelson, E. (1985), *Quantum Fluctuations*. Princeton, NJ: Princeton University Press.

Oliphant, M. (1972), *Rutherford*. Cambridge: Cambridge University Press.

Omnes, R. (1994), *The Interpretation of Quantum Mechanics*. Princeton, NJ: Princeton University Press.

———— (1999), *Understanding Quantum Mechanics*. Princeton, NJ: Princeton University Press.

———— (1999), *Quantum Philosophy*. Princeton, NJ: Princeton University Press.

Pais, A. (1994), *Einstein Lived Here*. Oxford: Clarendon Press.

———— (2000), *The Genius of Science*. Oxford: Oxford University Press.

Pauli, W. (1994), *Writings on Physics and Philosophy*. Eds C. P. Enz and K. Von Meyenn. Berlin: Springer-Verlag.

Peat, F. D. (1990), *Einstein's Moon: Bell's Theorem and the Curious Quest for Quantum Reality*. Chicago, IL: Contemporary Books.

Peierls, R. E. (1955), *The Laws of Nature*. London: George Allen and Unwin.

―――― (1997), *Atomic Histories*. New York: American Institute of Physics.

Penrose, R. and Isham, C. J. (1961), *Quantum Concepts in Space and Time*. Oxford: Oxford University Press.

Peres, A. (1984), The Classical Paradoxes of Quantum Theory. *Foundations of Physics*, 14.1131.

―――― (1993), *Quantum Theory: Concepts and Methods*. Dordrecht: Kluwer.

―――― (1997), *Quantum Theory*. Dordrecht: Kluwer.

Peterson, Aage (1968), *Quantum Physics and the Philosophical Tradition*. Cambridge, MA: MIT Press.

Petruceili, S. (1993), *Atoms, Metaphysics and Paradoxes*. Cambridge: Cambridge University Press.

Planck, Max (1933), *Where is Science Going?* London: George Allen and Unwin.

Polkinghorne, J. C. (1984), *The Quantum World*. London and New York: Longmans. (1988), The Quantum World. In: Physics, Philosophy and Theology: A Common Quest for Understanding. Ed. R. J. Russell, W. R. Stroeger and G. V. Coyne. Vatican City State; Vatican Observatory.

Pollard, W. G. (1958), Chance and Providence: God's Action in a World Governed by Scientific Thought. New York. Charles Scribner's Sons.

Popper, K. R. (1982), *Quantum Theory and the Schism in Physics*. London: Hutchinson.

Powers, J. (1982), *Philosophy and Physics*. London: Methuen.

Przibram, K. (ed.) (1967), *Albert Einstein, Max Planck and H. A. Lorentz. Letters on Wave Mechanics*. Tr. and int. by Martin J. Klein. London: Vision Press.

Rae, A. (1986), *Quantum Physics: Illusion or Reality?* Cambridge: Cambridge University Press.

Rayleigh, Lord (1942), *The Life of Sir J. J. Thomson*. Cambridge: Cambridge University Press.

Redhead, M. (1955), *From Physics to Metaphysics*. Cambridge: Cambridge University Press.

―――― (1987), *Incompleteness, Non-Locality and Realism*. Oxford: Oxford University Press.

―――― (1995), *From Physics to Metaphysics*. Cambridge: Cambridge University Press.

Reichenbach, H. (1994, 1998), *Philosophic Foundations of Quantum Mechanics*. Mineola, NJ: Dover.

Russell, R. J. (1988), 'Quantum Physics in Philosophical and Theological Perspective'. In Russell, R. J. et al. (1988) loc. cit.

Russell, R. J., Stroeger, W. R., and Coyne, G. V. (eds). Physics, Philosophy and Theology. A Common Quest for Understanding. Vatican City State. Vatican Observatory.

Russell, R. J., Murphy, N., and Peacocke, A. R. (eds) (1995), Chaos and Complexity: Scientific Perspectives on Divine Action. Vatican City State: Vatican Observatory and Berkeley; Center for Theology and Natural Science.

Sachs, M. (1988), *Einstein versus Bohr: The Continuing Controversies in Physics*. La Salle, IL: Open Court.

Santos, E. (1985), 'The Search for Hidden Variables in Quantum Mechanics', in Selleri (1985).

Scheibe, E. (1973), *The Logical Analysis of Quantum Mechanics*. Oxford: Pergamon.

Schrödinger, E. (1956), *What is Life and Other Essays*. New York: Doubleday.

——— (1995), *The Interpretation of Quantum Mechanics*. Woodbridge, CT: Ox Bow Press.

Schulman, L. S. (1997), *Time's Arrow and Quantum Measurements*. Cambridge: Cambridge University Press.

Segré, E. (1970), *Enrico Fermi: Physicist*. Chicago, IL: University of Chicago Press.

Selleri, F. (1990), *Quantum Paradoxes and Physical Reality*. Ed. Alwyn van der Merwe. Dordrecht: Kluwer.

Sharpe, K. J. (1993), *David Bohm's World. New Physics and New Religion*. Lewisburg, PA: Bucknell University Press.

Shimony, A. (1993), *Search for a Naturalistic World View*. Vol. 2. Cambridge: Cambridge University Press.

Smith, W. (1995), *The Quantum Enigma*. Peru, IL: Sherwood Sugden.

Squires, E. (1986), *The Mystery of the Quantum World*. Bristol and Boston, MA: Hilger.

——— (1990), *Conscious Mind in the Physical World*. Bristol and Boston, MA: Hilger.

Stenger, V. J. (1995), The Unconscious Quantum: Metaphysics in Modern Physics and Cosmology. New York: Prometheus Books. ch. 9.

Stuart, C. I. J. M. (1991), 'Inconsistency of the Copenhagen Interpretation', *Foundations of Physics*, **21**, 591.

Sudbury, A. (1986), *Quantum Mechanics and the Particles of Nature*. Cambridge: Cambridge University Press.

Sykes, C. (1994), *No Ordinary Genius: The Illustrated Richard Feynman*. New York: Norton.

Talbot, M. (1987), *Beyond the Quantum*. Toronto: Bantam Books.

Tamm, I. E. (1991), *Selected Papers*, eds B. M. Bolotovskii and V. Ya Frenkel. Berlin: Springer-Verlag.

Teller, E. (1987), *Better a Shield than a Sword: Perspectives on Defense and Technology*. New York and London: Macmillan.

Tracey, T. F. (1995), Particular Providence and the God of the Gaps. In: Chaos and Complexity: Scientific Perspectives on Divine Action. Ed. R. J. Russell, N. Murphy and A. R. Peacocke. Vatican City State: Vatican Observatory, and Berkeley: Centre for Theology and the Natural Sciences.

Van Fraasen, C. Bas (1991), *Quantum Mechanics*. Oxford: Clarendon Press.

Van Laer, P. H. (1953), Philosophico-Scientific Problems. Pittsburgh Pa: Duquesne University Press.

Varga, K., Lovas, R. G. and Liotta, R. J. (1992), 'Cluster-Configuration Model for Alpha Decay', *Nuclear Physics*, **A550**, 423.

Von Neumann, J. (1932), *Mathematical Foundations of Quantum Mechanics.* Berlin: Springer-Verlag; (1935) Princeton: Princeton University Press.
Weisskopf, V. F. (1991), *The Joy of Insight.* New York: Basic Books.
Whitaker, M. A. B. (1996), *Einstein, Bohr and the Quantum Dilemma.* Cambridge: Cambridge University Press.
Wigner, E. (1983), *Quantum Theory and Measurement.* Princeton, NJ: Princeton University Press.
Wolpert, L. and Richards, A. (1988), *A Passion for Science.* Oxford: Oxford University Press.
Zeh, H. D. (1992), *The Physical Basis of the Direction of Time.* 2nd edn. Berlin: Springer-Verlag.

B. Conferences and Symposia

Barut, A. O., van der Merwe, A. and Vigier, J.-P. (eds) (1984), *Quantum, Space and Time – The Quest Continues.* Cambridge: Cambridge University Press.
Bilbol, M. and Darrigol, O. (eds) (1992), *Erwin Schrödinger – Philosophy and the Birth of Quantum Mechanics* Paris: Editions Frontières.
Born, M. (1953), *Scientific Papers Presented to Max Born.* Edinburgh and London: Oliver and Boyd.
Bunge, M. (ed.) (1967), *Quantum Theory and Reality.* Berlin: Springer-Verlag.
Cini, M. and Levy-Leblond, J.-M. (1990), *Quantum Theory without Reduction.* Bristol and Boston, MA: Hilger.
Colodney, R. G. (ed.) (1972), *Paradigms and Paradoxes: The Philosophical Challenge of the Quantum Domain.* Pittsburgh, PA: Pittsburgh University Press.
Cushing, J. T. and McMullin, E. (eds) (1989), *Philosophical Consequences of Quantum Theory: Reflections on Bell's Theorem.* Notre Dame, IN: University of Notre Dame Press.
De Boer, J., Dal, E. and Ufbek, O. (eds) (1986), *The Lesson of Quantum Theory. Niels Bohr Centenary Symposium, 1985.* Amsterdam: North-Holland.
De Witt, B. and Graham, N. (eds) (1973), *The Many-Worlds Interpretation of Quantum Theory.* Princeton, NJ: Princeton University Press.
Edge, D. (ed.) (1962), *Quanta and Reality.* London: Hutchinson.
Feshbach, H., Matsui, T. and Oleson, A. (eds) (1988), *Physics and the World: Niels Bohr Centennial Symposium.* Chur: Harwood.
Fierz, M. and Weisskopf, V. F. (eds) (1960), *Theoretical Physics in the Twentieth Century.* New York: Interscience Publishers.
Flato, M., Maric, Z., Milojevic, A., Sternheimer, D. and Vigier, J.-P. (1976), *Quantum Mechanics, Determinism, Causality and Particles.* Dordrecht: Reidel.
French, A. P. and Kennedy, P. J. (eds) (1985), *Niels Bohr: A Centenary Volume.* Chur: Harwood.
Garda, C. and Rossi, A. (eds) (1993), *The Foundations of Quantum Mechanics – Historical Analysis and Open Questions.* Lecce, Singapore: World Scientific.

Gorini, V. and Frigerio, A. (1986), *Fundamental Aspects of Quantum Theory*. NATO ASI Series. Como Meeting, 1985. New York: Plenum Press.

Hiley, B. J. and Peat, F. D. (1987), *Quantum Implications. Essays in Honour of David Bohm*. London: Routledge and Kegan Paul.

Hooker, C. A. (ed.) (1975), *The Logico-Algebraic Approach to Quantum Mechanics. Vol. I. Historical Evolution*, (1979), Vol. II. *Contemporary Consolidation*. Dordrecht: Reidel.

────── (ed.) (1973), *Contemporary Research in the Foundations and Philosophy of Quantum Theory*. Dordrecht: Reidel.

────── (ed.) (1979), *Physical Theory as Logico-Operational Structure*. Dordrecht: Reidel.

Kafatos, M. (ed.) (1989), *Bell's Theorem, Quantum Theory and Conceptions of the Universe*. Dordrecht: Kluwer.

Kilmister, C. W. (ed.) (1987), *Schrödinger: Centenary Celebrations of a Polymath*. Cambridge: Cambridge University Press.

Körner, S. (ed.) (1957), *Observation and Interpretation in the Philosophy of Physics with Special Reference to Quantum Mechanics*. New York: Dover.

Lahti, P. and Mittelstaedt, P. (eds) (1985), *Symposium on the Foundations of Modern Physics – 50 Years of the Einstein–Podolsky–Rosen Gedankenexperiment. Joensuu, Finland, 1985*. Singapore: World Scientific.

Lahti, P. and Mittelstaedt, P. (eds) (1990), *Symposium on the Foundations of Modern Physics, 1990. Quantum Theory of Measurement and Related Problems. Joensuu 1990*. Singapore: World Scientific.

Leite Lopes, J. and Paty, M. (eds) (1974), *Quantum Mechanics, a Half-Century Later. Papers of a Colloquium on Fifty Years of Quantum Mechanics*. University Louis Pasteur, Strasbourg. Dordrecht: Reidel.

Mehra, L. (ed.) (1973), *The Physicists' Conception of Nature*. Dordrecht: Reidel.

Miller, A. I. (ed.) (1990), *Sixty-Two Years of Uncertainty*. NATO ASI Series. Erice Meeting, 1989. New York: Plenum.

Mizerski, J. (ed.) (1990), *Conference on Problems in Quantum Physics II; Gdansk 1989*. Singapore: World Scientific.

Namiki, M., Ohnuki, Y., Murayama, Y. and Nomura, S. (eds) (1987), *Proceedings of the Second International Symposium on the Foundations of Quantum Mechanics*. Physical Society of Japan.

Nelkowski, H., Herman, A., Poser, H., Schrader, R. and Seiler, R. (eds) (1979), *Einstein Symposium. Lecture Notes in Physics*. Berlin: Springer-Verlag.

Noz, M. E. and Kim, Y. S. (1988), *Special Relativity and Quantum Theory. A Collection of Papers on the Poincaré Group*. Dordrecht: Kluwer.

Plendl, H. S. (ed.) (1982), *Philosophical Problems of Modern Physics*. Dordrecht: Reidel.

Roth, L. M. and Inomata, A. (eds), *Fundamental Questions in Quantum Physics. Albany Conference, 1984*. London: Gordon and Breach.

Salam, A. and Wigner, E. P. (eds) (1972), *Aspects of Quantum Theory*. Cambridge: Cambridge University Press.

Schommers, W. (ed.) (1989), *Quantum Theory and Pictures of Reality*. Berlin: Springer-Verlag.

Selleri, F. (ed.) (1985), *Quantum Mechanics Versus Local Realism: The Einstein–Podolsky–Rosen Paradox*. New York: Plenum.

—— (ed.) (1992), *Wave–Particle Duality*. New York: Plenum.

Suppes, P. (ed.) (1976), *Logic and Probability in Quantum Mechanics*. Vol. 78. Syntax Library. Dordrecht: Reidel.

Swinburne, R. (ed.) (1983), *Space, Time and Causality*. Dordrecht: Reidel.

Tarozzi, G. and Van der Merwe, A. (1985), *Open Questions in Quantum Physics. Bari Workshop, 1983*. Dordrecht: Kluwer.

Tarozzi, G. and Van der Merwe, A. (1988), *The Nature of Quantum Paradoxes. Cesana Conference, 1985*. Dordrecht: Kluwer.

Van der Merwe, A., Selleri, F. and Tarozzi, G. (eds) (1988), *Microphysical Reality and Quantum Formalism*. 2 vols. Dordrecht: Kluwer.

Wheeler, J. A. and Zurek, W. H. (eds) (1983), *Quantum Theory and Measurement*. Princeton, NJ: Princeton University Press.

Wick, D. (1995), *The Infamous Boundary*. Berlin: Springer-Verlag.

Wilbur, K. (ed.) (1984), *Quantum Questions*. Boulder, CO: Shambhala, and London: New Science Library.

Zurek, W. H., Van de Merwe, A. and Miller, W. A. (eds) (1988), *Between Quantum and Cosmos*. Princeton, NJ: Princeton University Press.

C. Biographies

Aserud, F. (1990), *Redirecting Science: Niels Bohr*. Cambridge: Cambridge University Press.

Bernstein, J. (1991), *Quantum Profiles*. Princeton, NJ: Princeton University Press.

Blaedel, N. (1988), *Harmony and Unity: The Life of Niels Bohr*. Berlin: Science Technical Publications, Springer-Verlag.

Broda, E. (1983), *Ludwig Boltzmann*. Woodbridge, CT: Ox Bow Press.

Cassidy, D. C. (1992), *Uncertainty: The Life and Science of Werner Heisenberg*. New York: W. H. Freeman and Co.

Dresden, M. (1987), *H. A. Kramers: Between Tradition and Revolution*. Berlin: Springer-Verlag.

Diner, S. et al. (eds) (1984), *The Wave–Particle Dualism. A Tribute to Louis de Broglie on his 90th Birthday*. Dordrecht: Reidel.

Gotschl, J. (1992), *Erwin Schrödinger's World View*. Dordrecht: Kluwer.

Gibbin, J., and Gibbin, M. (1998), *Richard Feynman – A Life in Science*. London: Penguin Books.

Khalatnikov, I. M. (1989), *Lev. Landau, The Physicist and the Man*. Oxford: Pergamon Press.

Kragh, H. (1990), *Dirac: A Scientific Biography*. Cambridge: Cambridge University Press.

Kursunoglu, B. N. and Wigner, E. P. (1987), *Paul Adrien Maurice Dirac*. Cambridge: Cambridge University Press.

Laurikainen, K. V. (1988), *Beyond the Atom: The Philosophical Thought of Wolfgang Pauli*. Berlin: Springer-Verlag.

Moore, R. (1985), *Niels Bohr*. Cambridge, MA: MIT Press.

Moore, W. (1989), *Schrödinger's Life and Thought*. Cambridge: Cambridge University Press.

Pais, A. (1991), *Niels Bohr's Times: In Physics, Philosophy and Polity*. Oxford : Oxford University Press.

Peat, D. (1997), *Infinite Potential: The Life and Times of David Bohm*. New York: Addison-Wesley.

Rosenfeld, L. (1961), *Niels Bohr: An Essay*. Amsterdam: North-Holland.

Rosenthal, S. (ed.) (1967), *Niels Bohr: His Life and Work as seen by his Friends and Colleagues*. Amsterdam: North-Holland.

Schilpp, P. A. (ed.) (1949), *Albert Einstein: Philosopher–Scientist*. Evanston, IL: Library of Living Philosophers.

Thomson, J. J. (1936), *Recollections and Reflections*. London: Bell.

Wilson, D. (1984), *Rutherford, Simple Genius*. London: Hodder and Stoughton.

D. Quantum Mechanics

Aspect, A., Grangier, P., and Roger, G. (1981), Experimental Realisation of Einstein-Podolsky Rosen Gedanken Experiment: A New Violation of Bell's Inequalities. Journal de Physique (Paris), 42.C263.

Aspect, A., Dalibard, J., and Roger, G. (1982), Experimental Test of Bell's Inequalities Using Time-Varying Analyser. Physical Review Letters, 49.1804.

Ballentine, L. E. (1990), *Quantum Mechanics*. Englewood Cliffs, NJ: Prentice-Hall.

Birtwistle, G. (1929), *The Quantum Theory of the Atom*. Cambridge: Cambridge University Press.

—— (1929), *The New Quantum Mechanics*. Cambridge: Cambridge University Press.

Blokhintsev, D. I. (1964), *Principles of Quantum Mechanics*. Ed. Sven Bjorklund. Allen and Brown.

Bohm, D. (1981), *Quantum Theory*. New York: Dover.

Bransden, B. H. and Joachain, C. J. (1989), *Introduction to Quantum Mechanics*. London: Longmans.

Chaturvedi, S., and Drummond, P. D. (1997), Macroscopic Test of Quantum Mechanics versus Stochastic Electrodynamics. Physical Review, 55.912.

Dirac, P. A. M. (1958), *The Principles of Quantum Mechanics*. 4th edn. Oxford: Oxford University Press.

Eckart, C. (1926), Operator Calculus and the Solutions of the Equations of Quantum Dynamics. Physical Review, 25.711.

Feynman, R. P. and Hibbs, A. R. (1965), *Quantum Mechanics and Path Integrals*. New York: McGraw-Hill.

Fock, V. A. (1978), *Fundamentals of Quantum Mechanics*. Mir

Frenkel, J. (1934), *Wave Mechanics: Advanced General Theory*. Cambridge: Cambridge University Press.

Gamow, G. (1928), Zur Quantentheorie des Atomkerns. Zeitscrift für Physik, 51.204; (1930), Proceedings of the Royal Society, A213.386.

Goldman, I. I. (1960), *Problems in Quantum Mechanics*. Infosearch.

Gottfried, K. (1966), *Quantum Mechanics*. New York: Benjamin.

Gurney, R. W. (1940), *Elementary Quantum Mechanics*. Cambridge: Cambridge University Press.

Heisenberg, W. (1925), Über quantentheorische umdentung Kinematischer und Mechanischer Bezichung. Zeitscrift für Physik, 33.879; Ibid (1938), 110.251.

Holland, P. R. (1995), *The Quantum Theory of Motion*. Cambridge: Cambridge University Press.

Howard, D. (1990), ' "Nicht sein kann was nicht sein darf", or the Prehistory of EPR, 1909–1935: Einstein's Early Worries about the Quantum Mechanics of Composite Systems' in *Sixty-Two Years of Uncertainty: Historical, Philosophical and Physical Enquiries into the Foundations of Quantum Mechanics*, ed. Arthur I. Miller. New York: Plenum Press.

Jordan, P. (1934), Quantenphysikalische Bermerkungen zur Biologie und Psychologie. Erkenntnis, 4.215.

Landau, L. and Lifshitz, E. M. (1965), *Quantum Mechanics*. Oxford: Pergamon Press.

Landshoff, P. and Meherall, A. (1979), *Simple Quantum Physics*. Oxford: Oxford University Press.

Lawden, D. F. (1967), *The Mathematical Principles of Quantum Mechanics*. London: Methuen.

Levy-Leblond, J.-M. and Balibar, F. (1990), *Quantics: Rudiments of Quantum Physics*. Amsterdam: North-Holland.

Lindemann, F. A. (1952), *The Physical Significance of Quantum Theory*. Oxford: Clarendon Press.

Mackay, G. W. (1963), *Mathematical Foundations of Quantum Mechanics*. New York: Benjamin.

Mavromatis, H. A. (1987), *Exercises in Quantum Mechanics*. Dordrecht: Reidel.

Messiah, A. (1970), *Quantum Mechanics. Vols 1 and 2*. Amsterdam: North-Holland.

Mott, N. F. (1952), *Elements of Wave Mechanics*. Cambridge: Cambridge University Press.

―――― and Sneddon, I. N. (1948), *Wave Mechanics and its Applications*. Cambridge: Cambridge University Press.

Pope, D. T., Drummond, D., and Munro, W. J. (2000), Disagreement between Correlations of Quantum Mechanics and Stochastic Electrodynamics in a Damped Parametric Oscillator. Physical Review, A62.042108.

Rojansky, V. (1955), *Introductory Quantum Mechanics*. New York: McGraw-Hill.

Schiff, L. I. (1955), *Quantum Mechanics*. New York: McGraw-Hill.

Schrödinger, E. (1926), Quantisierung als Eigenwertproblem Annalen der Physik, 79,361; 89,734.

Sudbury, A. (1986), *Quantum Mechanics and the Particles of Nature*. Cambridge: Cambridge University Press.

Thouless, D. J. (1961), *The Quantum Mechanics of Many-Body Systems*. New York: Academic Press.

Van Frassen, B. C. (1991), *Quantum Mechanics*. Oxford: Clarendon Press.

Chapter 10. Cosmology

Alpher, R. A., Herman, R. C., and Gamow, G. (1948), Thermonuclear Reactions in the Expanding Universe. Physical Review, 74.1198.

Atkins, P. W. (1981), *The Creation*. Oxford and San Francisco, CA: W. H. Freeman and Co.

Baldner, S. E. and Carroll, W. E. (1997), *Aquinas on Creation*. Toronto: Pontifical Institute of Medieval Studies.

Barrow, J. D. and Silk, J. (1984), *The Left Hand of Creation*, London, Heinemann.

Barrow, John D. (1994), *The Origin of the Universe*. London: Weidenfeld and Nicolson.

Bethe, H. A. (1939), Energy Production in Stars. Physical Review, 55.434.

Bondi, H., and Gold, T. (1948), The Steady State Theory of the Expanding Universe. Monthly Notices of the Royal Astronomical Society, 108.252.

Brody, T. A. (1993), *The Philosophy Behind Physics*. Berlin: Springer-Verlag.

Burrell, D. B. and McGinn, B. (eds) (1990), *God and Creation*. Notre Dame, IN: University of Notre Dame Press.

Carroll, W. E. (1988), 'Big Bang Cosmology, Quantum Tunnelling from Nothing, and Creation', *Laval Théologique et Philosophique*, **44**, 59.

────── (1997), *Thomas Aquinas and Big Bang Cosmology*, Thomistic Institute, University of Notre Dame.

Chesterton, G. K. (1912), A Miscellany of Men. London: Methuen.

Chesterton, G. K. (1932), *All is Grist*. New York: Dodd, Mead.

Contopoulos, G. and Kotsakis, D. (1987), *Cosmology: The Structure and Evolution of the Universe*. Berlin: Springer-Verlag.

Craig, W. L. and Smith, Q. (1993), *Theism, Atheism and Big Bang Cosmology*. Oxford: Oxford University Press.

Cunliffe, B. (ed.) (2001), *The Oxford Illustrated History of Prehistoric Europe*. Oxford: Oxford University Press.

Dawson, C. (1929), *Progress and Religion*. London: Sheed and Ward.

Dick, S. (ed.) (2000), *Many Worlds: The New Universe, Extraterrestrial Life and the Theological Implications*. Philadelphia, PA and London: Templeton Foundation Press.

Drake, F., and Sobel, Dava (1992), Is Anyone out There? The Scientific Search for Extraterrestrial Intelligence. New York: Delacorte Press.

Drees, W. B. (1990), *Beyond the Big Bang*. La Salle, IL: Open Court.

Dunbar, D. N. F., Pixley, R. E., Wensel, W. A., and Whaling, W. (1953), The 7.68 Met. State in ^{12}C. Physical Review, 92.649.

Dyson, F. (1971), Energy in the Universe *Scientific American*, **225**, 59 September.

Eddington, A. S. (1920), The Internal Constitution of Stars. Nature, 106.14.

Eddington, A. S. (1946), Fundamental Theory. Cambridge: Cambridge University Press.

Eddington, A. S. (1928), The Nature of the Physical World. Cambridge: Cambridge University Press.

Eddington, A. S. (1931), The End of the World from the Standpoint of Mathematical Physics. Nature, 127.497.

Evans, J. (1998), *The History and Practice of Ancient Astronomy*. Oxford: Oxford University Press.

Ferriera, P. G. (2003), 'The Cosmic Microwave Background', *Physics World*.

Gleiser, M. (1997), *The Dancing Universe: From Creation Myths to the Big Bang*. London: Dutton/Penguin Press.

Godel, Kurt, See Nagel, E., and Newman, J. R. (1958), Godel's Proof. New York.

Guth, A. H. (1998), *The Inflationary Universe*. Vintage Press.

Hawking, S. (1988), *A Brief History of Time*. Bantam Press.

Helm, P. (ed.) (1999), *Faith and Reason*. Oxford: Oxford University Press.

Hodgson, P. E. (1995), 'Cosmology and Theology'. Second Coyne Lecture, Cracow.

Hoyle, F. (1948), A New Model for the Expanding Universe. Monthly Notices of the Royal Astronomical Society, 108.372.

Hoyle, F., Dunbar, D. N. F., Wentzel, W. A., and Whaling, W. (1953). Physical Review, 92.1095.

Hoyle, F. (1997), *Home is Where the Wind Blows*. Chapters from a Cosmologist's Life. Oxford: Oxford University Press.

Jaki, S. L. (1974), *Science and Creation*, Edinburgh: Scottish Academic Press.

––––––– (1974), *Cosmos and Creator*, Edinburgh: Scottish Academic Press.

––––––– (1986), *Chesterton, A Seer of Science*. Urbana and Chicago, IL: University of Illinois Press.

––––––– (1989), *God and the Cosmologists*. Edinburgh: Scottish Academic Press.

––––––– (1990), *The Only Chaos and other Essays*. Intercollegiate Studies Institute Inc., Lanham, MD: University Press of America.

––––––– (1993), *Is There a Universe?* Liverpool: Liverpool University Press.

Kant, Immanuel, (1981), Universal Natural History and Theory of the Heavens. Tr. S. L. Jaki. Edinburgh: Scottish Academic Press.

Kragh, H. (1996), *Cosmology and Controversy: The Historical Development of Two Theories of the Universe*. Princeton, NJ: Princeton University Press.

Lemaître, G. (1972), Papers published by the Pontifical Academy of Sciences on the 50th Anniversary of his Death. Pontificiae Academiae Scientiarum Scripta Varia No. 36.

Maimonides, Moses (1956), A Guide for the Perplexed. New York: Dover.

Marschak, A. (2001), *The Roots of Civilisation*. London: Weidenfeld and Nicolson.

Nilsson, J. S., Gustafsson, B. and Skagerstam, B. S. (eds) (1991), *The Birth and Early Evolution of the Universe*. Nobel Symposium, Singapore: World Scientific.

Pascal, B. (1995, 1999), Pensées. Tr. Honor Levi. Oxford: Oxford University Press.

Penrose, R. See Ellis, G. F. R. (ed.) (2002), The Far-Future Universe. Philadelphia and London: Templeton Foundation Press.

Penzias, A. A., and Wilson, R. W. (1965). A Measurement of Excess Antennae Temperature at 4080 Mc/s. Astrophysical Journal, 142.419.

Rowan-Robinson, M. (1981), *Cosmology*. Oxford: Clarendon Press.

Sakharov, A. (1992), Memoirs. New York: Vintage Books.

Sciama, D. W. (1971) *Modern Cosmology*. Cambridge: Cambridge University Press.

Smolin, Lee (1997), *The Life of the Cosmos*. Oxford: Oxford University Press.

Smoot, G. and Davidson, K. (1993), *Wrinkles in Time: The Imprint of Creation*. London: Little, Brown and Company.

Starobinsky, A. A., and Zeldovich, Y. B. (1992), The Spontaneous Creation of the Universe. Ch. 5 in 'My Universe: Selected Reviews'. By Y. B. Zeldovich. Chur: Harwood Academic Publishers.

Templeton, J. M. (ed.) (1997), *How Large is God? The Voices of Scientists and Theologians*. London and Philadelphia, PA: Templeton Foundation Press.

Thurston, H. (1996), *Early Astronomy*. Berlin: Springer-Verlag.

Tolman, R. C. (1934), *Relativity, Thermodynamics and Cosmology*. Oxford: Oxford University Press.

Vilenkin, A. (1983), Birth of Inflationary Universes. Physical Review D27.12.

Webb, J. (2003), Are the Laws of Nature Changing with Time. Physics World. April.

Weinberg, S. (1977), *The First Three Minutes*. New York: Basic Books.

Whitehead, A. N. (1925), *Science and the Modern World*. London: Macmillan.

Wilders, N. M. (1982), *The Theologian and his Universe*. New York: The Seabury Press.

Chapter 11.   Chaos and Symmetry

Bai-lin, Hao (1984), *Chaos*. Singapore: World Scientific.

Doncel, M. G., Herman, A., Michel, L. and Pais, A. (1987), *Symmetries in Physics 1600–1980*. Proceedings of the 1st International Meeting on the History of Scientific Ideas. Universidad Autonoma de Barcelona.

Gleick, J. (1987), *Chaos: Making a New Science*. London: Heinemann.

Hargittai, I. and M. (2000), *In Our Own Image: Personal Symmetry in Discovery*. Dordrecht: Kluwer.

Lorenz, E. N. (1963), 'Deterministic Non-Periodic Flow', *Journal of Atmospheric Science*, **20**, 130.

Lucas, J. R. and Hodgson, P. E. (1990), *Spacetime and Electromagnetism*. Oxford: Clarendon Press.

May, Robert M. (1976), 'Simple Mathematical Models with very Complicated Dynamics', *Nature*, **261**, 459.

Peterson, I. (1993), *Newton's Clock: Chaos in the Solar System*. New York: W. H. Freeman and Co.

Poincaré, H. (1903), *Science and Method*. London: Thomas Nelson and Sons.

Ruelle, D. (1991), *Chance and Chaos*. Princeton, NJ: Princeton University Press.

Weyl, H. (1952), *Symmetry*. Princeton, NJ: Princeton University Press.

Zee, A. (1999), *Fearful Symmetry*. Princeton, NJ: Princeton University Press.

Chapter 12.   Science and Non-Christian Religions

Baker, John R. (1945), *Science and the Planned State*. London: Allen and Unwin.

Bernal, J. D. (1939), *The Social Function of Science*. London: Routledge.

Bernstein, J. (1982), A Cosmic Flow. In : Science Observed. New York: Basic Books. Ch. 16.

Bernstein, J. (1995), *Hitler's Uranium Club: The Secret Recordings at Farm Hall*. New York: American Institute of Physics.

Bloom, A. (1988), *The Closing of the American Mind*. London: Penguin Books.

Bullock, A. (1964), *Hitler: A Study in Tyranny*. London: Pelican.

Capra, F. (1975), *The Tao of Physics*. Wildwood House, Suffolk: Fontana-Collins.

Cassidy, D. C. (1992), *Uncertainty: The Life and Science of Werner Heisenberg*. New York: W. H. Freeman and Co.

Christman, R. C. (1952), *Soviet Science*. Washington, DC: American Association for the Advancement of Science.

Eddington, Sir Arthur (1939), *The Philosophy of Physical Science*. Cambridge: Cambridge University Press.

Goudsmidt, S. A. (1995), *Alsos*. New York: American Institute of Physics.

Graham, L. (1982), 'The Reception of Einstein's Ideas; Two Examples from Contrasting Political Cultures', in, Gerald Holton and Yehuda Elkana (eds) *Albert Einstein: Historical and Cultural Perspectives*. Princeton, NJ: Princeton University Press, p. 107.

Gratzer, W. (2000), *The Undergrowth of Science*. Oxford: Oxford University Press.

Heilbron, J. L. (1986), *The Dilemmas of an Upright Man: Max Planck as Spokesman for German Science*. Berkeley: University of California Press.

Hentschel, K. (1996), *Physics and National Socialism: An Anthology of Primary Sources*. Basel, Boston, MA and Berlin: Birkhauser

Hodgson, P. E. (1961), *Nuclear Physics in Peace and War*. London: Burns and Oates.

———— (1999), *Nuclear Power, Energy and the Environment*. London: Imperial College Press.

Huxley, J. (1949), *Soviet Genetics and World Science: Lysenko and the Meaning of Heredity*. London: Chatto and Windus.

Jaki, S. L. (1966), The Relevance of Physics. Chicago: Chicago University Press.

Johnson, P. (1988), *Intellectuals*. London: Weidenfeld and Nicolson.

Khalatnikov, I. M. (ed.) (1989), *Landau: The Physicist and the Man. Recollections of L. D. Landau*. Oxford: Pergamon Press.

Kline, J. R. (1952), See Christman, R. C. loc. cit. p. 80.

Kohn, A. (1986), *False Prophets*. Oxford: Basil Blackwell.

Livanova, A. (1980), *Landau: A Great Physicist and Teacher*. Oxford: Pergamon Press.

Medvedev, Z. A. (1971), *The Medvedev Papers*. London: Macmillan.

Mendelssohn, K. (1973), *The World of Walter Nernst: The Rise and Fall of German Science*. London: Macmillan.

Muller, H. J. (1964), *The Destruction of Soviet Genetics. Readings in Russian Civilisation*. Chicago, IL: University of Chicago Press.

Müller and Markus (1960), Einstein und die Sovietphilosophie: Krisis einer Lehre. Dordrecht: D. Reidel. Pp. 43–63.

Pais, A. (1994), *Einstein Lived Here*. Oxford: Oxford University Press.

Peierls, R. E. (1997), *Atomic Histories*. New York: American Institute of Physics.

Perutz, M. F. (2000), *I Wish You'd Made Me Angry Earlier*. Oxford: Oxford University Press.

Polanyi, M. (1958), *Personal Knowledge*. London: Routledge and Kegan Paul.

Posin, D. Q. (1948), *Mendeleyev*. New York: Whittlesey House.

Powers, T. (1993), *Heisenberg's War: The Secret History of the German Bomb*. London: Penguin.

Riggs, R. J. (1978), Science in Developing Countries. Physics Bulletin 29.295. p. 246. Vienna.

Rookmaker, H. R. (1970), *Modern Art and the Death of a Culture*. London: Inter-Varsity Press.

Sakharov, A. (1990), *Memoirs*. London: Hutchinson.

Sayers, D. L. (1947), *Creed or Chaos?* London: Methuen.

Solzhenitsyn, A. (1974), *The Gulag Archipelago 1918–1956*. London: Book Club Associates.

Sparks, A. (1990), The Mind of South Africa. London: Heinemann.

Volin, L. (1952), See Christman, R. C. loc. cit. p. 85.

Zircle, C. (1952) see Christman, R. C. loc. cit. p. 100.

Zukav, G. (1979), *The Dancing Wu Li Masters*. London: Fontana Paperbacks.

Name Index

Subject Index